HISTORICAL DICTIONARIES
OF WAR, REVOLUTION, AND CIVIL UNREST
Edited by Jon Woronoff

1. *Afghan Wars, Revolutions, and Insurgencies*, by Ludwig W. Adamec. 1996.
2. *The United States–Mexican War*, by Edward H. Moseley and Paul C. Clark, Jr. 1997.
3. *World War I*, by Ian V. Hogg. 1998.
4. *The United States Navy*, by James M. Morris and Patricia M. Kearns. 1998.
5. *The United States Marine Corps*, by Harry A. Gailey. 1998.
6. *The Wars of the French Revolution*, by Steven T. Ross. 1998.
7. *The American Revolution*, by Terry M. Mays. 1999.
8. *The Spanish–American War*, by Brad K. Berner. 1998.
9. *The Persian Gulf War*, by Clayton R. Newell. 1998.
10. *The Holocaust*, by Jack R. Fischel. 1999.
11. *The United States Air Force and Its Antecedents*, by Michael Robert Terry. 1999.
12. *Civil Wars in Africa*, by Guy Arnold. 1999.
13. *World War II: The War against Japan*, by Anne Sharp Wells. 1999.
14. *British and Irish Civil Wars*, by Martyn Bennett. 2000.
15. *The Cold War*, by Joseph Smith and Simon Davis. 2000.
16. *Ancient Greek Warfare*, by Iain Spence. 2002.
17. *The Vietnam War*, by Edwin E. Moïse. 2001.
18. *The Civil War*, by Terry L. Jones. 2002.
19. *The Crimean War*, by Guy Arnold. 2002.
20. *The United States Army, a Historical Dictionary*, by Clayton R. Newell. 2002.
21. *Terrorism, Second Edition*, by Sean K. Anderson and Stephen Sloan. 2002.
22. *Chinese Civil War*, by Edwin Pak-wah Leung. 2002.
23. *The Korean War: A Historical Dictionary*, by Paul M. Edwards. 2002.
24. *The "Dirty Wars,"* by David Kohut, Olga Vilella, and Beatrice Julian. 2003.
25. *The Crusades*, by Corliss K. Slack. 2003.
26. *Ancient Egyptian Warfare*, by Robert G. Morkot. 2003.
27. *The French Revolution*, by Paul R. Hanson, 2004.
28. *Arms Control and Disarmament* by Jeffrey A. Larsen and James M. Smith, 2005.

Historical Dictionary of Arms Control and Disarmament

Jeffrey A. Larsen
James M. Smith

Historical Dictionaries of War, Revolution, and Civil Unrest, No. 28

The Scarecrow Press, Inc.
Lanham, Maryland • Toronto • Oxford
2005

SCARECROW PRESS, INC.

Published in the United States of America
by Scarecrow Press, Inc.
A wholly owned subsidary of
The Rowman & Littlefield Publishing Group, Inc.
4501 Forbes Boulevard, Suite 200, Lanham, Maryland 20706
www.scarecrowpress.com

PO Box 317
Oxford
OX2 9RU, UK

British Library Cataloguing in Publication Information Available

Library of Congress Cataloging-in-Publication Data

Larsen, Jeffrey Arthur, 1954–
  Historical dictionary of arms control and disarmament / Jeffrey A. Larsen, James
M. Smith.
       p. cm. — (Historical dictionaries of war, revolution, and civil unrest ; no. 28)
  Includes bibliographical references.
  ISBN 0-8108-5060-5 (hardcover : alk. paper)
   1. Arms control—History—Dictionaries. 2. Disarmament—History—
Dictionaries. 3. Arms control—Dictionaries. 4. Disarmament—Dictionaries. I.
Smith, James M., Dr. II. Title. III. Series.

JZ5645.L38 2005
327.1'74'03—dc22
                                                                        2004025199

Contents

v

Editor's Foreword

What a relief it is to read about arms control and disarmament from the relative safety of the post-Cold War era. We—humanity, that is—have seen it all. Small local wars, larger regional wars, world wars, rivalry between two superpowers leading to two political and ideological blocs commanding nearly the full military capacity of the time, and this capacity increasing all the time until it was possible for one, let alone both, to destroy the earth not only once but many times over. Nobody misses the excitement of mutual assured destruction and brinksmanship, and everybody feels more comfortable with the relatively smaller, contained wars of today. So we can be proud of what has been achieved in this field, and continues to be achieved as even some rogue states reform (although terrorists have since emerged as a threat) and the world becomes a more peaceful place.

This *Historical Dictionary of Arms Control and Disarmament* is certainly a welcome addition to the series on War, Revolution, and Civil Unrest, a series that by the way is still growing since war has not quite gone out of fashion. This volume takes a very good look at the situation, from olden times to the present day, and the dictionary part is full of entries on conferences, treaties, and other initiatives, some of them abortive, others amazingly successful. It also includes significant figures who contributed to advances, or pushed the clock back on occasion, as well as the innumerable organizations, governmental and nongovernmental, which militate against armaments or actually control them. The introduction provides a double overview, one of the evolution of thought and action, the other of the more scholarly study of the subject. The long, although still selective, bibliography provides advice on further sources of reading. But in some ways, it is the list of acronyms and abbreviations that is most helpful, since in this field you really cannot tell the players unless you know the initials they go by.

The team of authors is intriguing, since both of them were initially pilots with the U.S. Air Force. Having flown some of the weapons they now write about shows that their understanding of the situation has a reality that may be lacking among pure academics. But they eventually did become academics, teaching at the Air Force Academy and teaching the sort of people for whom this is a very real thing. They have also lectured and taught more broadly, and they have written extensively on security and deterrence, space power and arms control. Between them, Dr. Jeffrey A. Larsen and Dr. James M. Smith have a depth of experience and a broad enough pool of knowledge to produce a reference work that is very informative and also accessible to general readers.

Jon Woronoff
Series Editor

Preface

This book summarizes the rich and proud traditions of arms control and disarmament, their critical role in ensuring a noncatastrophic course throughout history (especially the dangerous period of the Cold War), and their continuing relevance and role in the emerging post-Cold War world. It also seeks to reinforce a broad perspective of key terms in order to capture the scope and range of their application yesterday, today, and tomorrow.

Given this combined tradition and focus, the dictionary seeks to serve two purposes. As a historical dictionary, it chronicles key terms, personalities, events, and agreements as a ready reference from which to launch a more extensive investigation. But it also seeks to capture the breadth of current and future applications by presenting the vocabulary of traditional and nontraditional approaches.

In addressing both sets of imperatives, there is the danger that perhaps it is less than complete on either one. That was the challenge faced in compilation—finding the balance point between the completeness of coverage of past history and the adequacy of coverage of a dynamic history that is still being written. The balancing force was provided by constant reminders of the intended audience.

First, we wanted a useful desk reference for the policy practitioner. The pace and intensity of the practice of arms control often eliminates the luxury of conventional study of past or related arms control efforts. The dictionary seeks to provide a relevant sampling of treaty and agreement details and of the specific terms of reference of arms control to allow productive progress in a policy work environment until the practitioner can arrange time for more detailed study.

Second, we sought to create a useful reference tool for the researcher and student. Much of the formal literature in the field, such as agreement texts and policy pronouncements, is written in technical language without elaboration. Also, many references to agreements are posed in shorthand intended only for the policy practitioner. The dicx Preface

tionary seeks to provide both translation assistance and departure points and directions for more detailed discovery. The "snapshots" provided here also assist in establishing a context for the broader range of international relations at a given point in time, extending the utility of the dictionary beyond just a narrow examination of "arms control."

Finally, in this emerging era we recognize that even government policy makers and senior implementers come to those positions with little foundation knowledge or experience in strategic issues such as arms control and disarmament. Accordingly, the dictionary also serves as a primer in this technical dimension of foreign and national security policy.

The authors would like to thank Abraham Denmark of the Graduate School of International Studies, University of Denver, for his research help while preparing the final stages of this manuscript, and Eric Croddy of United States Pacific Command for providing materials for the entries on biological and chemical warfare.

The cover photo depicts a statue in the courtyard of the United Nations in New York. Created by Yevgeny Vuchetich, it was presented to the UN as a gift from the Soviet Union in 1959. The statue represents mankind beating their swords into plowshares, an allegory for peace from the Old Testament book of Isaiah. Given the often duplicitous nature of Soviet actions during the Cold War, its purpose was most likely for propaganda, while the world witnessed massive increases in Soviet military capabilities during that period. Nonetheless, the concept represents the ultimate goal of disarmament enthusiasts, and has been adopted by many in the arms control community, as well. Our thanks to the United Nations photo library for permission to use this image.

The opinions and analysis offered here do not necessarily reflect the official perspectives of the United States Air Force, the U.S. Air Force Academy, or Science Applications International Corporation.

We dedicate this work to our children, with the hope that they may someday live in a world where arms truly are controlled, and disarmament is more than a dream.

Acronyms and Abbreviations

AAAS	American Academy of Arts and Sciences
ABACC	Brazilian-Argentine Agency for Accounting and Control of Nuclear Materials
ABM	Antiballistic missile
ACA	Arms Control Association
ACDA	Arms Control and Disarmament Agency
ACM	Advanced cruise missile
AEC	Atomic Energy Commission
AECA	Arms Export Control Act
AEI	American Enterprise Institute
ALASAT	Air-launched antisatellite weapon
ALBM	Air-launched ballistic missile
ALCM	Air-launched cruise missile
ALPS	Accidental launch protection system
AMSA	Advanced manned strategic aircraft
ANZUS	Australia, New Zealand, United States Treaty
APS	American Physical Society
ARM	Antiradiation missile
ASAT	Antisatellite weapon
ASBM	Air-to-surface ballistic missile
ASROC	Antisubmarine rocket
ASW	Antisubmarine warfare
ATBM	Antitactical ballistic missile
ATTU	Atlantic to the Urals
AWACS	Airborne warning and control system
BM	Ballistic missile
BMD	Ballistic missile defense
BMDO	Ballistic Missile Defense Organization
BMEWS	Ballistic Missile Early Warning System
BMLNA	Ballistic Missile Launch Notification Agreement
BTW	Biological and toxin weapons

BTWC	Biological and Toxin Weapons Convention
BW	Biological warfare/weapons
BWC	Biological and Toxin Weapons Convention
C2	C-squared; command and control
C3	C-cubed; command, control, and communication
C3I	C-cubed-I; command, control, communications, and intelligence
C4I	C-four-I; command, control, communications, computers, and intelligence
C4ISR	Command, control, communications, computers, intelligence, surveillance, and reconnaissance
CAT	Conventional Arms Transfer Talks
CBM	Confidence-building measures
CBRNE	Chemical, biological, radiological, nuclear, enhanced explosive
CBW	Chemical and biological warfare
C-CBRNE	Counter chemical, biological, radiological, nuclear, enhanced explosive
CCD	Conference of the Committee on Disarmament
CCW	Certain Conventional Weapons Convention
CD	Conference on Disarmament
CDC	Centers for Disease Control (and Prevention)
CDE	Conference on Disarmament in Europe
CENTO	Central Treaty Organization
CEP	Circular error probable
CFE	Conventional Forces in Europe (Treaty)
CFE 1A	Conventional Forces in Europe Treaty 1A
CIA	Central Intelligence Agency
CIS	Commonwealth of Independent States
CJCS	Chairman of the Joint Chiefs of Staff
CMC	Cooperative Monitoring Center (Sandia National Laboratories)
CND	Campaign for nuclear disarmament
CNS	Central nervous system
CNSS	Center for National Security Studies
COCOM	Coordinating Committee for Multilateral Export Controls
CPC	Vienna Center for Conflict Prevention
CPI	Counterproliferation Initiative
CRG	Compliance Review Froup
CSBM	Confidence- and security-building measures
CSCE	Conference on Security and Cooperation in Europe
CSIS	Center for Strategic and International Studies

CTBT	Comprehensive Nuclear Test Ban Treaty
CTBTO	Comprehensive Nuclear Test Ban Treaty Organization
CTRP	Cooperative Threat Reduction Program
CW	Chemical warfare/weapons
CWC	Chemical Weapons Convention
DF	Declared facility
DGP	Senior Defense Group on Proliferation
DHS	Department of Homeland Security
DIA	Defense Intelligence Agency
DNA	Defense Nuclear Agency
DNA	Deoxyribonucleic Acid
DOC	Department of Commerce
DoD	Department of Defense
DOE	Department of Energy
DOS	Department of State
DPSS	Designated permanent storage sites
DSP	Defense satellite program
DSP	Defense support program
DSWA	Defense Special Weapons Agency
DTRA	Defense Threat Reduction Agency
EAA	Export Administration Act
EAR	Export Administration Regulations
EC	European Community
EFTA	European Free Trade Association
EIF	Entry into force
ELF	Extremely low frequency
EMP	Electromagnetic pulse
EMT	Equivalent Megatonnage
ENDC	Eighteen-Nation Disarmament Conference (UN)
EPA	Environmental Protection Agency
EU	European Union
EURATOM	European Atomic Energy Community
FBS	Forward-based systems
FEMA	Federal Emergency Management Agency
FMCT	Fissile Material Cutoff Treaty
FOBS	Fractional orbital bombardment system
FSC	Forum for Security Cooperation
FSU	Former Soviet Union
GCD	General and complete disarmament
GLBM	Ground-launched ballistic missile
GLCM	Ground-launched cruise missile
GPS	Global Positioning System

GPALS	Global protection against limited strikes
GRIT	Gradual and reciprocal initiatives in tension reduction
G-7/G-8	Group of Seven/Group of Eight (Group of Seven plus One)
HAND	High altitude nuclear detonation
HASC	House Armed Services Committee
HEU	Highly enriched uranium
HLD	Homeland defense
HLG	High Level Group
HLS	Homeland security
HML	Hard mobile launcher
HNSC	House National Security Committee
IAEA	International Atomic Energy Agency
ICBM	Intercontinental ballistic missile
IDC	International Data Center
IDDS	Institute of Defense and Disarmament Studies
IGO	Intergovernmental organization
IISS	Institute for International Strategic Studies
IMS	International Monitoring System
INF	Intermediate-Range Nuclear Forces
INSS	Institute for National Security Studies
INSS	Institute for National Strategic Studies
IOI	Item of inspection
IRBM	Intermediate-range ballistic missile
JCIC	Joint Compliance and Inspection Commission
JCS	Joint Chiefs of Staff
JSTPS	Joint Strategic Target Planning Staff
KT	Kiloton
LEU	Low enriched uranium
LOW	Launch on warning
LPAR	Large phased-array radar
LRNA	Long-range nuclear air-launched cruise missile
LRTNF	Long-range theater nuclear forces
LTBT	Limited Test Ban Treaty
LUA	Launch under attack
MAD	Mutual assured destruction
MARV	Maneuvering reentry vehicle
MAS	Mutual assured security
MBFR	Mutual and balanced force reductions
MCTL	Militarily Critical Technologies List
MDA	Missile Defense Agency
MINATOM	Ministry of Atomic Energy (Russia)
MIRV	Multiple independently targetable reentry vehicle

MOA	Memorandum of agreement
MOU	Memorandum of understanding
MRBM	Medium-range ballistic missile
MRI	Mutual reciprocal inspection
MRTNF	Medium-range theater nuclear forces
MRV	Multiple reentry vehicle
MT	Megaton
MTCR	Missile Technology Control Regime
MUF	Materials unaccounted for
MX	Missile experimental
NACC	North Atlantic Cooperation Council
NAOC	National airborne operations center
NATO	North Atlantic Treaty Organization
NBC	Nuclear, biological, and chemical weapons
NBCR	Nuclear, biological, chemical, and radiological weapons
NCA	National Command Authorities
NDP	National Defense Panel
NEACP	National Emergency Airborne Command Post
NFX	Nuclear-free zone
NGO	Nongovernmental organization
NIE	National intelligence estimate
NIPP	National Institute for Public Policy
NMD	National missile defense
NNPA	Nuclear Nonproliferation Act
NNSA	National Nuclear Security Agency
NNWS	Non-nuclear weapons state
NORAD	North American Aerospace Defense Command
NORTHCOM	United States Northern Command
NPG	Nuclear Planning Group
NPR	Nuclear Posture Review
NPT	Nuclear Nonproliferation Treaty
NRC	Nuclear Regulatory Commission
NRDC	Nuclear Reaction Data Centers Network
NRO	National Reconnaissance Office
NRRC	Nuclear Risk Reduction Centers
NSA	National Security Agency
NSC	National Security Council
NSD	National Security Directive
NSDD	National Security Decision Directive
NSDM	National Security Decision Memorandum
NSG	Nuclear Suppliers Group
NSNW	Nonstrategic nuclear weapons

NST	Nuclear and Space Arms Talks
NSTL	National strategic target list
NTI	Nuclear Threat Initiative
NTM	National technical means
NUWEP	Nuclear weapons employment policy
NWFZ	Nuclear-weapon free zone
NWS	Nuclear-weapon state
NWSS	Nuclear weapon storage site
OPANAL	Agency for the Prohibition of Nuclear Weapons in Latin America
OPCW	Organization for the Prohibition of Chemical Weapons
OS	Open skies
OSCC	Open Skies Consultative Commission
OSCE	Organization for Security and Cooperation in Europe
OSD	Office of the Secretary of Defense
OSI	On-site inspections
OSIA	On-Site Inspection Agency
OTA	Office of Technology Assessment
PAL	Permissive action link
PD	Presidential Decision
PGM	Precision-guided munition
PIV	Physical inventory verification
PNE	Peaceful nuclear explosives
PNET	Peaceful Nuclear Explosions Treaty
PNI	Presidential nuclear initiative
PPRA	Plutonium Production Reactor Agreement
PRC	Peoples' Republic of China
PSI	Pounds per square inch
PSI	Proliferation Security Initiative
PTBT	Partial Test Ban Treaty
Pu	Plutonium
QDR	Quadrennial Defense Review
RCA	Riot control agent
RV	Reentry vehicle
SAARC	South Asian Association for Regional Cooperation
SAC	Strategic Air Command
SALT	Strategic Arms Limitation Talks
SALT I	Strategic Arms Limitation Treaty I
SALT II	Strategic Arms Limitation Treaty II
SAM	Surface-to-air-missile
SAMOS	Satellite and missile observation system
SAR	Synthetic aperture radar

SASC	Senate Armed Services Committee
SCC	Standing Consultative Commission
SCCC	Joint System for Accounting and Control of Nuclear Materials
SDI	Strategic Defense Initiative
SDIO	Strategic Defense Initiative Office
SEATO	Southeast Asia Treaty Organization
SICBM	Small intercontinental ballistic missile
SIOP	Single Integrated Operations Plan
SIPRI	Stockholm International Peace Research Institute
SLBM	Submarine-launched ballistic missile
SLCM	Sea- or ship- or submarine-launched cruise missile
SLV	Space launch vehicle
SNDV	Strategic nuclear delivery vehicle
SNM	Special nuclear material
SORT	Strategic Offensive Reductions Treaty
SPOT	*Satellite pour l'Observation de la Terre*
SRAM	Short-range attack missile
SRBM	Short-range ballistic missile
SRF	Strategic Rocket Forces
SSBN	Nuclear-powered ballistic missile submarine
SSI	Strategic Studies Institute
SSM	Surface-to-surface missile
SSP	Stockpile stewardship program
START	Strategic Arms Reduction Talks
START I	Strategic Arms Reduction Treaty I
START II	Strategic Arms Reduction Treaty II
START III	Strategic Arms Reduction Treaty III
STI	Safeguards, transparency, and irreversibility
SUBROC	Submarine rocket
SVC	Special Verification Commission
TASM	Tactical air-to-surface missile
TEL	Transporter erector launcher
THAAD	Theater high-altitude air defense
TMD	Theater missile defense
TNF	Theater nuclear forces
TTBT	Threshold Test Ban Treaty
UK	United Kingdom
UN	United Nations
UNGA	United Nations General Assembly
UNMOVIC	United Nations Monitoring, Verification, and Inspection Commission
UNSC	United Nations Security Council

UNSCOM	United Nations Special Commission (on Iraq)
U.S.	United States
USA	United States Army
USAF	United States Air Force
USG	United States Government
USN	United States Navy
USNORTHCOM	United States Northern Command
USSPACECOM	United States Space Command
USSR	Union of Soviet Socialist Republics
USSTRATCOM	United States Strategic Command
UXO	Unexploded ordnance
VCC	Verification Coordinating Committee
VD	Vienna Document
WEU	Western European Union
WHG	Western Group of Forces (Soviet)
WHO	World Health Organization
WMD	Weapons of mass destruction
WTO	Warsaw Treaty Organization
XON	HQ USAF Nuclear and Counterproliferation Directorate

Chronology

1100 B.C.	Israelite-Philistine Term of Peace (limited Israel's use of iron).
448 B.C.	Athens-Persia Accord (Peace of Callias) (demilitarized the Aegean Sea).
202 B.C.	Rome-Carthage Treaty (Treaty of Zama) (limited Carthage's military capabilities, including the use of war elephants).
188 B.C.	Peace of Apamea (Rome imposed military restrictions on defeated Antioch).
989 C.E.	Peace and Truce of God proclaimed in the Synod of Charroux, France (established noncombatant status for civilians). (Similar truces repeated by multiple synods and dioceses in Europe over the next 150 years.)
1139	Second Lateran Council Decrees, Canon 29 (outlawed the use of crossbows).
1179	Third Lateran Council (Eleventh Ecumenical Council), Canon 24 (excommunicated supporters of Saracen).
1675	Treaty of Strassbury (French and German agreement to outlaw poison weapons).
24 October 1688	Peace of Westphalia (ended Hundred Years' War and defortified the Rhine).
12 April 1713	Treaty of Utrecht between France and Great Britain (included defortification of Dunkirk).
15 November 1715	Treaty between Spain, Great Britain, and the Netherlands to defortify Liège.
1785	United States-Prussia Treaty of Amity and Commerce (included protections for civilians and prisoners of war).

4 August 1787	Anglo-French Naval Pact (limited size of both navies to peacetime levels, with advance notification of increases).
1805	Turkish Straits Pacts (stabilized Eastern Mediterranean).
8 September 1808	Franco-Prussian Treaty (whereby Napoleon limited the size of Prussia's army).
28 August 1814	Treaty between Great Britain and Spain restricting trade with rebels in Spain's American colonies.
20 November 1815	Declaration of Swiss Neutrality.
28-29 April 1817	Rush-Bagot Agreement (United States and Great Britain agree to demilitarize the Great Lakes).
1824	Convention as to the Pacific Ocean and Northwest Coast of America (Russia and the United States).
1833	Convention of Amity and Commerce (United States and Siam).
1833	Treaty of Amity and Commerce (United States and Muscat [Zanzibar]).
19 April 1839	Neutralization of Belgium.
1 June 1841	Limitation of Egyptian Arms (by Ottoman Turks).
19 April 1850	Panama Canal Treaty (also called the Clayton-Bulwer Treaty) regulating transportation and use of any future canal (superseded by Hay-Pauncefote Treaty, 1901).
30 March 1856	Black Sea Naval Convention in the Treaty of Paris (Russia and Turkey agreed to neutralize the Black Sea).
24 April 1863	The Lieber Code ("Instructions for the Government of Armies of the United States in the Field;" established a set of rules governing behavior by Union forces).
11 May 1867	Neutralization of Luxemburg.
11 December 1868	St. Petersburg Declaration (international commission meeting in Russia agreed to prohibit explosive projectiles, e.g., dum-dum bullets).
27 August 1874	Declaration of Brussels (limited conduct of warfare, including prohibiting the use of poison; never ratified).
23 July 1881	Straits of Magellan Treaty signed by Argentina and Chile (neutralized the straits).

1890	Brussels Convention (outlawed the African slave trade).
29 July 1899	Hague Convention (II) with Respect to the Laws and Customs of War on Land signed in The Hague, Netherlands (codified laws of war and outlawed chemical, bacteriological, and biological weapons, and expanding bullets).
28 May 1902	Argentine-Chilean Naval Pact (reduced and limited size of both sides' fleets).
1907	Convention Relative to the Laying of Automatic Submarine Contact Mines (prohibiting such acts of war).
18 October 1907	Hague Convention IV prohibited aerial bombardment from balloons and prescribed the rules of war.
1915-1918	Both sides of World War I use chemical weapons in offensive attacks.

1919

18 January-28 June	Versailles Peace Conference, Paris, leading to the Versailles Treaty (World War I peace treaties and German disarmament, including prohibition on poisonous gases, and demilitarization of the left bank of the Rhine).
May	Embargo of China begins (through April 1929).
5 May	Agreement Restraining Sale of Armaments in China signed by United States, Great Britain, Spain, Portugal, Russia, Brazil, and Japan in Peking.
29 June	League of Nations International Convention for the Supervision of the International Trade in Arms and Ammunition and Implements of War begins (through 1936).
10 September	Convention for the Control of the Trade in Arms and Ammunition (Treaty of St. Germain-en-Laye) signed by 23 states in Paris.

1920

9 February	Spitzbergen Convention (gave full sovereignty of the peninsula to Norway).

5-16 July	Spa Conference, Spa, Belgium (on German reparations and disarmament, first of a series of conferences on these topics held through 1935 in Brussels, Paris, London, Cannes, The Hague, Lausanne, and Stresa).

1921

10-20 October	Neutralization of the Aaland Islands Conference, Geneva (awarded Finland sovereignty over the islands).
12 November	Washington Naval Conference begins.
23-26 November	German-Polish Conference on Upper Silesia held in Geneva.

1922

6 February	Washington Naval Treaty (also known as the Five Power Naval Limitation Treaty) signed by United States, United Kingdom, Italy, France, and Japan (limited size of signatory fleets, particularly battleships, and defortified Pacific Islands). Treaty in force through 1936.
6 February	Washington Treaty on Use of Submarines and Gases in Wartime signed (prohibited submarine attack and gas warfare without warning).
10 April-19 May	Genoa Conference on East European borders and world economic issues.
20 November	Lausanne Conference begins (peace negotiations on Turko-Greek War; treaty signed 24 July 1923).

1923

March-May	Santiago Naval Conference (part of the Fourth Pan-American Conference on Latin American affairs and the pacific resolution of disputes), Santiago, Chile.
24 July	Treaty of Lausanne (demilitarized straits from Black Sea to Mediterranean).
February	Rules of Air War drafted by Hague Commission of Jurists (never ratified).

7 February Central American Arms Limitation Treaty signed (limited size of armies in Guatemala, El Salvador, Costa Rica, Honduras, Nicaragua).

1925

17 June Convention for the supervision of the International Trade in Arms and Ammunition and in Implements of War signed in Geneva (never ratified).

17 June Geneva Protocol signed (also called Geneva Convention) (outlawed use of asphyxiating and poisonous gases and biological warfare).

16 October Locarno Treaties signed by France and Poland (dealing with aerial bombardment, German demilitarization, Rhineland demilitarization, and security guarantees to Eastern Europe).

17 December Treaty between Greece and Turkey.

1927

20 June-4 August Geneva Naval Conference (also called the Three Power Naval Conference).

1928

15 February Soviet Draft Convention to the League of Nations on Immediate, Complete and General Disarmament.

27 August Kellogg-Briand Pact for the Renunciation of War signed by 11 states.

1929

27 July Red Cross Convention (Convention for the Amelioration of the Condition of the Wounded and Sick of Armies in the Field) signed in Geneva.

27 July Convention on Treatment of Prisoners of War signed in Geneva.

29 August League of Nations passes Draft Convention with Regard to the Supervision of the Private Manufacture and Publicity of the Manufacture of Arms and Ammunition and of Implements of War.

1930

22 April	London Naval Treaty signed (United States, United Kingdom, France, Italy, and Japan agreed to naval reductions and rules of submarine warfare).
30 October	Turko-Greek Naval Protocol to 1925 treaty (both sides agreed to notify the other of any naval increases).

1931

7 March	Turko-Soviet Naval Protocol to 1925 treaty; expanded in 1930 protocol.
29 September	League of Nations proposes one-year armament truce.

1932

2 February	League of Nations World Disarmament Conference begins (through summer 1933)
8 June	Report of Air Commission, World Disarmament Conference.

1933

2 February-14 Oct	World Disarmament Conference held in Geneva.
10 October	Argentina Antiwar Treaty of Nonaggression and Conciliation signed in Rio de Janiero, Brazil.

1934

10 April	Conference for the Reduction and Limitation of Armaments held in Geneva.
29 May-11 June	Geneva International Disarmament Conference.
23 October-19 Dec	London Naval Conference.

1935

15 April	Roerich Pact (Protection of Artistic and Scientific Institutions and Historic Monuments, Inter-American Agreement) signed by 21 states in Washington.

18 June Anglo-German Naval Agreement (limited size of German fleet relative to British fleet).

2 December London Naval Conference resumes (through 25 March 1935).

1936

25 March London Naval Limitation Treaty (bilateral treaties between Great Britain, Germany, and the Soviet Union, reducing and limiting fleet sizes).

20 July Montreux Convention (ensured security of the Straits of Bosporus and Dardanelles).

1938

29 September Munich Conference (settled the Sudetenland Crisis on terms favorable to Germany).

1941

9-12 August Atlantic Conference (United States and United Kingdom), leads to Atlantic Charter.

22-28 December Washington Conference (first of a series of conferences between Allied leaders to determine war strategy and discuss a future United Nations, including meetings in Washington and Moscow in 1942, Casablanca, Quebec, and Cairo in 1943, and Quebec and Cairo in 1944).

1942

1 January United States, USSR, Great Britain, China, and 22 other nations sign United Nations Declaration, creating an anti-Axis coalition.

1943

28 November-1 Dec Teheran Conference (United States, United Kingdom, and USSR on a second front and postwar occupation of Germany).

1944

1-22 July
Bretton Woods Conference, Bretton Woods, New Hampshire (also known as United Nations Monetary and Financial Conference); 44 nations agreed to create International Monetary Fund and World Bank for postwar era.

21 August-9 Oct
Dumbarton Oaks Conference, Washington, D.C., negotiates draft of United Nations Charter.

1945

4-11 February
Yalta Conference between United States, USSR, and United Kingdom (on postwar German disarmament and division of country).

3-22 March
Arab League Conference, Cairo (creating a pact of Arab states).

25 April-26 June
United Nations Conference on International Organization (also called the San Francisco Conference).

26 June
United Nations Charter signed in San Francisco following two-month conference (entry into force 24 October 1945).

16 July
United States tests world's first atomic bomb in New Mexico.

17 July-2 August
Potsdam Conference, Berlin, leading to Potsdam Protocol signed by the United States, United Kingdom, France, and USSR (dealing with Germany's disarmament and division into occupied zones).

1946

10 January
First session of United Nations General Assembly.

4 April
Atomic Energy Act (also known as the McMahon Act) passes, creates U.S. Atomic Energy Commission (through 1952, when it was absorbed into the UN Disarmament Commission).

14 June
Baruch Plan (also known as Dumbarton Oaks Plan) presented by the United States to UN Atomic Energy Commission to place all global

	atomic material, weapons, and energy under UN control (vetoed by USSR in December 1946).
3 November	Japanese Constitution drafted (enacted by Japan's parliament 1947) (included renunciation of war and demilitarization of Japan).

1947

10 February	Italian Peace Treaty signed in Paris (limited Italy's military and removed fortifications along borders); also treaties for Bulgaria, Finland, Hungary, and Romania signed.
11 June	Soviet proposals to United Nations for International Control of Atomic Energy.
8 July	Commission on Conventional Armaments established (through 1952, when absorbed into the UN Disarmament Commission).
26 July	U.S. National Security Act signed into law, creating Department of Defense, Central Intelligence Agency, and National Security Council.
2 September	Rio Pact signed between United States and South American nations (defense agreements).

1948

17 March	Brussels Treaty (Treaty of Economic, Social, and Cultural Collaboration and Collective Self-Defence) signed by United Kingdom, France, Belgium, Netherlands, and Luxembourg.
9 December	United Nations adopts Convention on the Prevention and Punishment of the Crime of Genocide.
10 December	United Nations adopts Universal Declaration of Human Rights.

1949

4 April	North Atlantic Treaty signed in Washington.
13 April	Agreement between the Governments of the United States, France, and the United Kingdom on Prohibited and Limited Industries in the Western Zones of Germany.

12 August	Geneva Convention signed in four parts: I (on Wounded and Sick Members of the Armed Forces in the Field); II (on Amelioration of Wounded, Sick, and Shipwrecked Members of Armed Forces at Sea); III (on the Treatment of Prisoners of War); IV (on the Protection of Civilians in Time of War).
29 August	USSR tests atomic bomb.
17 September	North Atlantic Treaty Organization (NATO) established.
November	United States and West European nations create the Coordinating Committee for Multilateral Export Controls (COCOM).

1950

25 May	Tripartite Arms Declaration signed by United Kingdom, France, and the United States regarding security in the Near East.

1951

10 July	Korean War cease fire talks begin.
1 September	ANZUS defense treaty signed by Australia, New Zealand, and the United States.
1 November	United States tests world's first hydrogen bomb on Bikini Atoll.

1952

Spring	UN Disarmament Committee created.
3 October	United Kingdom tests atomic bomb.

1953

18 November	UN Commission on Disarmament establishes the Subcommittee on Disarmament (which serves as the primary international disarmament negotiating forum from 1954 through 1957).
8 December	United States makes "Atoms for Peace" proposal to the UN General Assembly.

1954

12 January	United States announces policy of massive retaliation.
2 April	India calls for first moratorium on atomic testing.
21 July	Geneva Conference ends Indochina War, divides Vietnam.
30 August	U.S. Congress enacts Atomic Energy Act, amending 1946 McMahon Act, allowing peaceful sharing of nuclear knowledge.
8 September	Southeast Asia Treaty Organization (SEATO) established at Manila Conference.
23 October	Protocol to the Brussels Treaty (West Germany pledges not to produce, procure, or possess weapons of mass destruction, and is allowed to rearm conventionally).
December	NATO deploys nuclear weapons.

1955

4 February	Baghdad Pact signed between United Kingdom, Iran, Iraq, Turkey, and Pakistan (known as Central Treaty Organization, or CENTO, after 19 August 1959; in effect until 1979).
19 March	United States creates office of Special Assistant to the President for Disarmament.
10 May	USSR proposes atomic test ban.
14 May	Eastern Europe and USSR form Warsaw Treaty Organization (also known as the Warsaw Pact).
21 July	U.S. Open Skies proposal presented at Geneva Conference of Heads of Government (a U.S., UK, USSR, and French summit) (to allow aerial overflight and inspection of states parties).
8-20 August	First International Conference on Peaceful Uses of Atomic Energy held in Geneva.
4 November	Austrian State Treaty signed (restored Austrian neutrality; prohibited Austria from possessing special weapons).

1956

12 July	Indian Proposal to the Disarmament Commission to end nuclear weapons tests.

18 July	The Law of Land Warfare published in U.S. Army Field Manual FM 27-10 (forbidding certain means of waging warfare).
26 October	International Atomic Energy Agency created, based in Vienna.

1957

25 March	Treaty of Rome creates European Economic Community.
11 July	First Pugwash Conference begins, Pugwash, Canada.
2 October	Rapacki Proposal (by Poland) to establish a denuclearized zone in Central Europe (reiterated in 1958 and 1962).
4 October	USSR launches Sputnik, first orbiting satellite.
15 October	USSR and China sign Defense Technical Accord, providing China with help developing a Chinese atomic bomb.

1958

10 January	United States tests world's first intercontinental ballistic missile.
15 January	Petition presented to UN secretary general to stop nuclear testing (signed by 9,235 scientists).
March-August	United States and USSR introduce unilateral reciprocal nuclear testing moratoriums (lasting through September 1961).
8 April-21 Aug	Conference of Experts meets in Geneva to discuss verification of a nuclear test ban.
September	Surprise Attack Conference begins (through January 1959).
31 October	United States, United Kingdom, and USSR begin negotiations on a comprehensive test ban treaty (CTBT) as the Conference on the Discontinuation of Nuclear Weapons Tests begins in Geneva (through 1962 this forum serves as the primary venue for discussions on the partial test ban).

1959

January	United States proposes limited test ban for atmospheric testing.
1 December	Antarctic Treaty signed by 12 nations (demilitarized the continent); entry into force 23 June 1961.

1960

March	UN Ten Nation Conference on Disarmament established in Geneva (the name of this ongoing forum changed to the Eighteen Nation Conference on Disarmament in 1962, to the Conference of the Committee on Disarmament in 1969, and to the Conference on Disarmament in 1979). United States proposes a threshold test ban limiting nuclear tests to five kilotons.
13 February	France tests atomic bomb.
2 May	U.S. U-2 reconnaissance plane shot down over USSR; Soviets cancel Four-Power Paris Summit scheduled later that month.

1961

1 September	Nonaligned Movement meets in Belgrade, Yugoslavia.
26 September	United States passes Arms Control and Disarmament Act, assigning lead role for these activities to secretary of state and establishing U.S. Arms Control and Disarmament Agency.
24 November	UN Resolution on Nuclear Weapons (General Assembly Res. 1653).

1962

15 March	Soviet proposal for general and complete disarmament to the UN Eighteen Nation Disarmament Committee.
28 March	Polish proposal to UN Eighteen Nation Disarmament Committee for denuclearized and limited armaments zone in Europe (updated Rapacki Plan).

18 April	U.S. proposal to the UN for General and Complete Disarmament.
19 July	U.S. Nike Zeus antiballistic missile (ABM) test successfully intercepts ICBM in flight.
15-28 October	Cuban Missile Crisis.

1963

10 June	U.S., UK, and USSR begin nuclear test ban talks.
20 June	Hot Line Agreement signed by the United States and USSR in Geneva.
5 August	Limited Test Ban Treaty (LTBT) signed by United States, USSR, and United Kingdom in Moscow (banned nuclear weapon tests in the atmosphere, outer space, and underwater); 125 follow-on signatories; entry into force 10 October 1963.
7 August	UN Arms Embargo Against South Africa enacted (Security Council Resolution 181); reiterated in Resolutions 182 (1963), 418 (1977), and 558 (1984).
27 November	Preparatory Commission for the Denuclearization of Latin America begins.

1964

January	United States proposes program to UN Eighteen-Nation Disarmament Committee to halt nuclear arms race.
April	United States ceases production of highly enriched uranium for weapons purposes.
May	Soviets parade Galosh ABM missile; U.S. intelligence assumes large ABM system being built around Moscow.
21 July	Declaration of the Denuclearization of Africa (by Organization of African Unity).
16 October	Peoples' Republic of China tests atomic bomb.

1967

27 January	Outer Space Treaty signed by 67 countries (established principles regarding peaceful, non-

	military exploration and use of outer space and celestial bodies); entry into force 10 October 1967.
14 February	Latin American Nuclear Weapon Free Zone (Treaty of Tlatelolco) signed by 20 nations in Mexico City; entry into force 22 April 1968.
23 June	Glassboro Summit between the U.S. and USSR; began discussions leading to Anti-Ballistic Missile (ABM) and Strategic Arms Limitation (SALT) Treaties.
25 August	United Kingdom-USSR Direct Communication Link Pact signed in London (updated 31 March 1987).
18 September	United States declares intent to build Sentinel ABM system.
13 December	United States discloses it has tested multiple independently targetable reentry vehicles (MIRVs) on an ICBM.

1968

13 May	U.S.-North Vietnamese peace talks begin in Paris.
1 July	Treaty on the Nonproliferation of Nuclear Weapons (NPT) signed by 73 countries in Washington, London, and Moscow (eventually 187 members); entry into force 5 March 1970.
12 December	NATO adopts policy of flexible response.
19 December	UN Resolution on Human Rights (General Assembly Res. 2444); ruled that the sovereign right of war is not unlimited, demanded protection for noncombatants.

1969

14 March	United States cancels Sentinel and announces Safeguard ABM system.
17 November	SALT talks between United States and Soviet Union begin in Helsinki, Finland.
25 November	U.S. unilateral ban on biological weapons and BW research, and renunciation of lethal or incapacitating chemical weapons.

16 December	UN Resolution on Chemical and Bacteriological (Biological) Weapons.

1970

14 February	United States extends ban on biological weapons to include toxin weapons.
12 August	West Germany and USSR sign Moscow Treaty, formalizing post-World War II borders.
7 December	West Germany and Poland sign Warsaw Treaty, formalizing post-World War II borders.
16 December	UN Resolution on Protection of Civilians (General Assembly Res. 2675).

1971

11 February	Seabed Treaty signed by 63 nations in Washington, London, and Moscow (prohibits placement of nuclear or other weapons of mass destruction on or under the sea floor); entry into force 18 May 1972.
20 August	INTELSAT Agreement signed between United States and 10 other nations; currently 142 member states (regulates international telecommunication satellite procedures).
3 September	United States, United Kingdom, France, and USSR sign Quadripartite Agreement on Berlin.
3 September	Zangger Committee created, based in Vienna (33 nation agreement to voluntarily restrict nuclear-related exports).
30 September	Nuclear War Risk Reduction Agreement signed by United States and USSR in Washington (also called the Accidents Measures Agreement) (enhanced transparency, early warning, openness).
30 September	Hot Line Agreement signed between the United States and USSR in Washington (modernized and expanded the 1963 agreement).
16 December	India proposes Indian Ocean Zone of Peace to UN.

1972

29 March	Liability Convention signed by United States and USSR (assesses international liability for damage caused by space objects); entry into force 9 October 1972; currently 100 states parties and 2 international space agencies.
10 April	Biological and Toxin Weapons Convention (BWC) signed by 139 parties in Washington, London, and Moscow; entry into force 26 March 1975.
25 May	Prevention of Incidents at Sea Treaty signed between the United States and USSR in Moscow (rules to prevent misunderstandings).
26 May	Strategic Arms Limitation Treaty (SALT I) signed in Moscow by United States and USSR; includes Interim Agreement on Limiting Strategic Offensive Arms (limiting ballistic missile delivery vehicles and submarines) and Anti-Ballistic Missile Treaty, which limited strategic defenses (two sites, 100 interceptors each; amended by 1974 Protocol to one site). Entry into force 3 October 1972.
26 May	Standing Consultative Commission created in Geneva to monitor SALT treaties.
22 November	Conference on Security and Cooperation in Europe (CSCE) talks begin in Geneva and Helsinki.

1973

27 January	Vietnam peace agreement signed in Paris.
31 January	Mutual and Balanced Force Reductions (MBFR) begin in Vienna (unsuccessful measure to limit military forces in Europe; talks lasted through 1989).
22 June	Prevention of Nuclear War Agreement signed by United States and USSR in Washington (agreement to consult in times of crisis).
27 October	Arab-Israeli October War cease-fire signed.

1974

18 May	India tests atomic "device."
3 July	Threshold Test Ban Treaty (TTBT) signed by United States and USSR in Moscow (limited size of underground nuclear weapons tests to yields of less than 150 kilotons); entry into force 11 December 1990 (though observed by both sides prior to that date).
3 July	Protocol to the ABM Treaty signed in Moscow by the U.S. and USSR; limited each side to one strategic defensive site; entry into force 24 May 1976.
3 September	NPT Exporters Committee (also known as the Zangger Committee) founded to develop lists of nuclear equipment and material exports that trigger IAEA safeguards.
24 November	Vladivostok Agreement between U.S. and USSR presidents; sets numerical limits and terms of reference for SALT II treaty.
9 December	Eight Latin American nations adopt Declaration of Ayacucho, limiting armaments acquisition.

1975

14 January	Convention on Registration of Objects Launched into Outer Space signed; entry into force 15 September 1976; 44 signators.
22 January	United States ratifies 1925 Geneva Protocol outlawing use of poisonous gas and bacteriological warfare.
23 April	Nuclear Suppliers Group created (to restrict exports of sensitive technology).
May	First NPT Review Conference held in Geneva.
30 July-2 August	U.S.-Soviet summit meeting in Helsinki, Finland.
1 August	Helsinki Accords (also known as Helsinki Final Act) signed by 35 states (created the CSCE, which became the Organization for Security and Cooperation in Europe [OSCE] in December 1994).
26 December	United States completes destruction of all its biological weapons.

1976

28 May	Peaceful Nuclear Explosions Treaty (PNET) signed between the United States and USSR; entry into force 11 December 1990 (describes size and purpose of PNEs).
30 June	U.S. Arms Export Control Act passed.
July	Bilateral U.S.-Soviet chemical weapons talks begin in Geneva.
3 September	INMARSAT Agreement signed; entry into force 16 July 1979; 78 signators (regulates international maritime satellite communications).

1977

13 May	Presidential Directive PD-13 calls for Conventional Arms Transfer Talks to limit Soviet arms sales (talks collapse in 1979).
18 May	Environmental Modification Treaty (or Convention) (prohibits military or other hostile use of environmental modification techniques); entry into force 5 October 1978.
June	Indian Ocean Arms Limitation talks begin in Moscow, Washington, and Bern (talks suspended in 1979).
3 October	United States, United Kingdom, and USSR begin trilateral talks on Comprehensive Test Ban Treaty (CTBT) in Geneva.
10 October	United Kingdom-USSR Prevention of Accidental Nuclear War Agreement signed in Moscow.
18 November	U.S.-IAEA Safeguards Agreement signed in Vienna.

1978

16 January	U.S.-Soviet communications links using satellites established.
18 September	Camp David Accords signed by United States, Israel, and Egypt (addressing Arab-Israeli dispute).

1979

January	UN Committee on Disarmament changes name to Conference on Disarmament.
23 January	U.S.-Soviet Anti Satellite talks begin in Bern, Switzerland (talks suspended later in 1979).
18 June	Strategic Arms Limitation Treaty (SALT II) signed between United States and USSR in Vienna (limited strategic delivery vehicles to 2,400, with sublimits by category).
29 September	United States passes Export Administration Act (to limit export of sensitive technologies).
12 December	North Atlantic Treaty Organization (NATO) agrees on a dual-track strategy: simultaneously deploying intermediate-range nuclear force (INF) missiles and negotiating INF arms control with USSR.
18 December	Agreement Governing the Activities of States on the Moon and Other Celestial Bodies signed by 16 countries (none of them current or potential space-faring nations).
27 December	Soviet invasion of Afghanistan.

1980

4 January	President Carter withdraws SALT II Treaty from Senate consideration to protest Soviet invasion of Afghanistan.
3 March	Convention on the Physical Protection of Nuclear Material signed in New York (entry into force 8 February 1987).
May	Second NPT Review Conference held in Geneva.
2 July	United States ratifies 1977 agreement to adhere to IAEA safeguards.
16 October	China conducts last known atmospheric nuclear test.

1981

10 April	UN Convention Restricting Excessively Injurious or Indiscriminate Conventional Weapons (or Inhumane Weapons Convention) opened for signature, entry into force 2 December 1983. (Also

called Convention on Certain Conventional Weapons, or CCW.)

22 September	USSR proposes "no-first-use" pledge by super-powers to United Nations.
18 November	United States proposes "zero option" for elimination of all INF weapons.
30 November	U.S.-Soviet INF Negotiations begin in Geneva.

1982

9 May	U.S. proposes Strategic Arms Reduction (START) negotiations with Soviet Union.
29 June	START negotiations begin in Geneva.

1983

23 March	President Ronald Reagan announces U.S. plans to develop strategic missile defenses (Strategic Defense Initiative).
October-November	U.S. INF forces—Pershing II and ground-launched cruise missiles (GLCM)—deployed to Europe.
27 October	NATO's Montebello Decision to upgrade but reduce the number of short-range nuclear forces.
23 November	Soviet delegation walks out of INF talks in Geneva to protest deployment of NATO INF missiles.
8 December	START talks adjourn indefinitely.
15 December	MBFR talks adjourn indefinitely.

1984

17 January	Stockholm Conference on Confidence- and Security-Building Measures in Europe begins.
7 February	UN Committee on Disarmament changes name to Conference on Disarmement.
17 July	Hot Line Memorandum of Understanding between the United States and USSR, signed in Washington (updated 1963 and 1971 agreements).
12 December	Cameroon Initiative (UN resolution calling for denuclearization of the African continent, including South Africa).

1985

12 March	Nuclear and Space Talks begin in Geneva (United States and USSR); venue includes START, INF, and Defense and Space Talks.
June	Australia Group created by 15 countries (to curb transfer of chemical weapons precursors and technologies to the Third World).
August	U.S. Congress passes Pressler Amendment (restricts military sales to Pakistan unless it can prove it is not pursuing nuclear weapons).
6 August	Treaty of Rarotonga signed, creating South Pacific Nuclear Free Zone.
August-September	Third NPT Review Conference held in Geneva.
19-21 November	U.S.-Soviet summit meeting in Geneva.
29 November	Brazil and Argentina sign Joint Declaration on Nuclear Policy.
12 December	North Korea joins NPT.

1986

15 January	USSR proposes complete elimination of nuclear weapons by year 2000.
15 July	Prevention of Incidents at Sea Treaty signed by the United Kingdom and USSR in London.
22 September	Agreement on Confidence- and Security-Building Measures and Disarmament in Europe (also known as the Stockholm Agreement) signed by 35 states in Stockholm; entered into force January 1987.
26 September	Early Notification of a Nuclear Accident agreement signed in Vienna.
11-12 October	Reykjavik Summit between U.S. and Soviet presidents furthers progress toward strategic agreements, including INF.
17 November	Delhi Declaration urges comprehensive test ban treaty.
11 December	Brussels Declaration on Conventional Arms Control by NATO (which leads to the Conventional Forces in Europe Treaty in 1990).
19 December	USSR accepts in principle the U.S. demand for on-site nuclear test inspections in the Soviet Union.

1987

7 April	Missile Technology Control Regime established to limit risks of nuclear proliferation by controlling technology transfers in multiple categories (25 members).
15 September	Nuclear Risk Reduction Centers Agreement signed between the United States and USSR in Washington (to provide advance warning of missile tests and establish centers in both countries with communications links) after eight months of negotiations.
15 September	United States and USSR begin INF negotiations.
9 November	U.S.-Soviet negotiations on reduction and elimination of nuclear tests begins.
8 December	Intermediate-Range Nuclear Forces (INF) Treaty signed in Washington between the United States and Soviet presidents (calling for the global elimination of missiles with ranges of 500-5,500 kilometers, with intrusive verification requirements); entry into force 1 June 1988.

1988

26 January	U.S. On-Site Inspection Agency (OSIA) created within Department of Defense to handle INF verification and compliance duties.
16 March	Iraq uses chemical weapons in attack on Kurdish city of Halabja, killing 5,000.
14 April	Geneva Peace Accords signed by United States, USSR, Pakistan, and Afghanistan, ending Afghanistan War.
29 May-2 June	U.S.-Soviet summit meeting in Moscow.
31 May	Ballistic Missile Launch Notification Agreement signed by United States and USSR in Moscow.
August	United States closes its plutonium production facilities at the Savannah River Site.
7 December	U.S.-Soviet summit in New York.
7 December	USSR announces to United Nations its plan for deep unilateral conventional force reductions.
31 December	Indian-Pakistani Agreement Not to Attack Nuclear Installations signed in Islamabad.

1989

6 March	NATO and Warsaw Pact begin talks in Vienna on CFE Treaty.
12 June	Agreement on the Prevention of Dangerous Military Activities signed by the United States and USSR in Moscow.
18-22 September	International Government-Industry Conference Against Chemical Weapons held in Canberra, Australia.
23 September	Agreement on Notification of Strategic Exercises signed by the United States and USSR in Jackson Hole, Wyoming; entry into force 1 January 1990.
23 September	Memorandum of Understanding regarding data exchanges and inspections for Chemical Weapons Convention (CWC) and Agreement on Reciprocal Advance Notice of Major Strategic Exercises signed by the United States and USSR in Jackson Hole, Wyoming.
9-10 November	Berlin Wall falls.
December	Sole U.S. plutonium manufacturing facility at Rocky Flats, near Denver, Colorado, closes.
2-3 December	U.S.-Soviet summit meeting aboard Soviet ship *Maxim Gorky.*

1990

May	OSIA expands mandate to handle inspections for CFE, START, TTBT, and PNET treaties and chemical weapons agreements (and in July 1991, to support UNSCOM).
3 May	United States announces cancellation of NATO short-range nuclear forces modernization.
30 May-5June	U.S.-Soviet summit in United States.
1 June	United States and USSR sign Bilateral Destruction Agreement for chemical weapons.
July	United States calls for removal of nuclear artillery shells in Europe.
5-6 July	NATO summit in London declares that the Warsaw Pact is no longer an enemy.
2 August	Iraq invades Kuwait.
August-September	Fourth NPT Review Conference held in Geneva.

22 August	Joint Declaration of the Federal Republic of Germany and of the German Democratic Republic on Nonproliferation of Nuclear, Chemical, and Biological Weapons (in association with the reunification of Germany; this declaration was made at the NPT Review Conference).
September	Last U.S. INF missiles removed from Europe.
12 September	German Unification Treaty (also known as the Four Plus Two Treaty) signed in Moscow by the United States, United Kingdom, France, USSR, and West and East Germany (ending World War II).
9 September	U.S.-Soviet summit in Helsinki.
17 November	CSCE signs Vienna Document 90 on CSBMs.
19 November	Treaty on Conventional Forces in Europe (CFE) signed by 22 member nations of NATO and the Warsaw Pact (limited military equipment in different regions of Europe).
21 November	Charter of Paris for a New Europe signed to reflect end of the Cold War.
28 November	Argentine-Brazilian Joint Declaration on Nuclear Policy issued at Foz do Iguacú, Brazil (confidence building and data sharing).

1991

1 January	CSCE Vienna Document 1990 enters into force (regarding confidence and security building measures in Europe).
17 Jan-27 Feb	United States leads multinational military coalition to force Iraq to withdraw from Iraq (Operation Desert Storm).
29 January	United States changes its SDI program to Global Protection Against Limited Strikes.
March	United States ends plutonium reprocessing for nuclear weapons.
31 March	Warsaw Pact dissolved.
3 April	UN passes Resolution Prohibiting Iraqi Possession of Weapons of Mass Destruction, also creates UN Special Commission on Iraq (UNSCOM) to verify compliance (UN Security Council Resolution 687; reiterated in Resolutions 707 and 715, and 1441).

29 May	Middle East Arms Control Initiative to control the sale of conventional arms in the region proposed by United States.
9 July	Big Five Initiative on Arms Transfer and Proliferation Restraints signed in Paris by the United States, USSR, China, France, and the United Kingdom (reiterated in communiqué issued in London 1 October 1991).
10 July	South Africa joins the NPT.
18 July	Argentine-Brazilian Bilateral Accord on Nuclear Energy signed (also known as Guadalajara Agreement).
29 July-1 August	U.S.-Soviet summit in Moscow.
31 July	Treaty on the Reduction and Limitation of Strategic Offensive Arms (known as the Strategic Arms Reduction Treaty [START I]) signed between United States and USSR presidents in Moscow; treaty limits strategic delivery vehicles to 1,600 and warheads to 6,000 each.
27 September	Presidential Nuclear Initiative on nonstrategic nuclear weapons reductions and dealerting (Soviet and Russian presidents respond with parallel initiatives 5 October 1991 and 27 January 1992).
30 October	U.S.-Soviet summit in Madrid.
8 November	NATO announces new strategic concept and calls for significant reductions in substrategic forces.
14 November	Germany destroys all former East German SS-23 missiles.
27 November	U.S. Congress passes Nuclear Threat Reduction Act to help the former USSR transport, store, safeguard, and destroy nuclear weapons (this act created the Cooperative Threat Reduction [CTR] Program [also known as the Nunn-Lugar Program] in 1993).
4 December	Cartagena Declaration on the Renunciation of Nuclear Weapons by five South America states.
5 December	United States passes Missile Defense Act calling for early deployment of an ABM Treaty compliant ballistic missile defense system.
9 December	United Nations General Assembly Resolution 46/36L adopted, creates Transparency in Arma-

	ments (TIA) regime, including annual UN Register of Conventional Armaments.
13 December	Quadripartite Agreement on full-scope IAEA safeguards of Argentine and Brazilian nuclear installations.
21 December	USSR breaks up into 15 countries; Commonwealth of Independent States created.
25 December	Soviet Union formally dissolved after four months of turmoil.

1992

20 January	Joint Declaration on the Denuclearization of the Korean Peninsula signed by North and South Korea.
27-28 January	U.S. and Russia reach joint understanding on further strategic nuclear reductions, call for START II negotiations.
1 February	U.S.-Russian summit in Maryland; Camp David Declaration announces that the Cold War is over.
17 February	United States, Germany, and Russia agree to open International Science and Technology Centers in Moscow and Kiev.
February-March	All Soviet tactical nuclear weapons in Belarus, Kazakhstan, and Ukraine transferred to Russia.
24 March	Treaty on Open Skies (25 nation agreement to allow unarmed surveillance flights) signed in Helsinki.
9 March	Peoples' Republic of China joins NPT as nuclear weapons state.
May	Tashkent Conference of Commonwealth of Independent States to determine CFE Treaty limits by country.
1 May	Vienna Document 1992 enters into force (European CSBMs).
23 May	Lisbon Protocol (to START I) signed; admits Soviet successor states (Ukraine, Belarus, and Kazakhstan) as non-nuclear state parties to START limitations and Nuclear Nonproliferation Treaty.
15-19 June	U.S.-Russian summit in Washington.
18 June	United States and USSR agree on framework for START II treaty.

July	Helsinki CSCE Summit agrees to create Forum for Security Cooperation, based in Vienna.
13 July	United States announces it will no longer produce plutonium or highly enriched uranium for nuclear explosives.
17 July	Conventional Forces in Europe Treaty 1A signed in Vienna (limits personnel in Europe).
3 August	France joins NPT as nuclear weapon state.
23 September	Last U.S. nuclear test before Hartfield Amendment (signed 2 October) establishes unilateral moratorium on nuclear testing.
September	First meeting of U.S., Russia, and UK in Trilateral Working Group on biological weapons.

1993

3 January	START II Treaty ("Treaty on Further Reduction and Limitation of Strategic Offensive Arms") between Russia and the United States signed by both presidents in Moscow (treaty limits strategic nuclear warheads to 3,000-3,500 each, and eliminates MIRVed warheads and heavy ICBMs). Ratified by United States 26 January 1996 and by Russia 14 April 2000.
13 January	Chemical Weapons Convention (CWC) signed in Paris by 130 countries (bans production, acquisition, stockpiling, and use of chemical weapons); enters into force 29 April 1997.
January-October	U.S. Department of Defense conducts Bottom Up Review of national security policy.
5 February	Czech Republic and Slovakia agree to division of forces according to CFE Treaty limits on former Czechoslovakian state.
18 February	U.S. and Russia sign agreement to convert Russian highly enriched uranium to civil reactor use in the United States.
24 March	South Africa announces it had a clandestine nuclear weapons program since 1974 that built six nuclear devices.
3-4 April	U.S.-Russian presidents meet at G-7 summit in Vancouver, Canada; Vancouver Declaration calls for improved trade relations and enhanced cooperation in fields of science and technology.

April	First joint U.S.-Russian military maneuvers since World War II carried out in Siberia.
23 July	Belarus accedes to NPT.
December	United Nations passes resolution calling for negotiations leading to Fissile Materials Cutoff Treaty.

1994

12-15 January	U.S.-Russian summit in Russia.
14 January	United States, Russia, and Ukraine sign trilateral agreement by which Ukraine transfers inherited nuclear weapons on its soil to Russia.
25 January	CTBT negotiations begin in UN Conference on Disarmament in Geneva.
14 February	Kazakhstan joins NPT.
31 March	COCOM disbanded.
April	U.S. national laboratories begin lab-to-lab contacts with Russian and former Soviet laboratories to deal with fissile material protection, control, and accounting.
30 May	United States and Russia announce detargeting of strategic nuclear missiles. United Kingdom also detargets its missiles in separate agreement with Russia.
23 June	United States and Russia sign agreement on shutting down remaining Russian plutonium production facilities by 2000 (also called the Gore-Chernomyrdin Agreement.)
22 September	United States releases Nuclear Posture Review.
27-28 September	U.S.-Russian summit in Washington.
21 October	United States negotiates Agreed Framework with North Korea, promising economic aid and safe nuclear power in return for an end to Pyongyang's nuclear weapons program.
23 November	United States secretly removes highly enriched uranium from Kazakhstan (Operation Sapphire).
28 November	CSCE Vienna Document 1994 signed.
28 November	Global Exchange of Military Information agreement adopted by CSCE Forum for Security Cooperation; entry into force 1 January 1995. (Part of Vienna Document 1994.)

December	Convention on Security and Cooperation in Europe (CSCE) changes its name to the Organization for Security and Cooperation in Europe (OSCE).
1 December	IAEA begins monitoring excess U.S. fissile material (initially at Portsmouth Plant, Ohio).
5 December	Ukraine joins NPT as non-nuclear weapon state. (Ukraine completes transfer of all nuclear warheads to Russia on 1 June 1996.)
5 December	START I entry into force.

1995

23 March	Fissile Material Cutoff Talks begin in Conference on Disarmament, Geneva.
24 March	United States ratifies Convention on Certain Conventional Weapons.
17 April-12 May	NPT Extension Review Conference in New York; states parties reach consensus agreement to extend treaty indefinitely.
25 April	Kazakhstan completes transfer of all inherited Soviet nuclear ICBMs to Russia.
10 May	Moscow Summit; United States and Russian presidents sign joint statement on Transparency and Irreversibility of the Process of Reducing Nuclear Weapons.
13 October	Protocol to Conference on Certain Conventional Weapons bans the use of blinding laser weapons.
23 October	U.S.-Russian summit in Hyde Park, New York.
21 November	Dayton Accords reached establishing framework for peace in Bosnia and Herzegovina (treaty formally signed in Paris 14 December 2004).
15 December	Southeast Asian Nuclear Weapons Free Zone created via Bangkok Treaty, signed by 10 nations. (Entry into force 27 March 1997.)
19 December	Wassenaar Arrangement on export controls established by 28 nations.

1996

26 January	U.S. Senate ratifies START II treaty.
13 March	U.S.-Russian summit in Sharm al Sheikh, Egypt.

11 April	Pelindaba Treaty signed by 43 nations in Cairo, Egypt, creating African Nuclear Weapons Free Zone.
19-20 April	Nuclear Safety Summit meeting in Moscow.
8 July	International Court of Justice releases ruling on the legality of nuclear weapons use.
12 July	Wassenaar Arrangement on Export Controls for Dual-Use Goods and Technologies signed by 33 nations in Vienna.
25 July	Czechs destroy their SS-23 missiles.
10 September	United Nations adopts Comprehensive Test Ban Treaty (eventually 166 signatories). United States signs treaty on 24 September, but refuses to ratify it on 13 October 1999.
23 September	United States and Russia sign agreement delimiting strategic and theater ABM systems.
23 November	Belarus completes the transfer of Soviet ICBMs and nuclear warheads to Russia.

1997

January-December	United States conducts Quadrennial Defense Review (QDR).
January-December	U.S. National Security Panel conducts parallel study to Quadrennial Defense Review.
21 March	At Helsinki Summit U.S. and Russian presidents sign Joint Statement on Parameters for Future Reductions in Nuclear Forces and agree to begin START III talks once START II enters into force, with strategic warhead limits of 2,000-2,500; protocol verifying agreement signed in New York 26 September 1997.
25 April	United States ratifies Chemical Weapons Convention.
27 May	NATO-Russian Founding Act declares that NATO has no intention and no plan to station nuclear weapons on the territory of new members.
23 September	U.S and Russia sign Plutonium Production Reactor Agreement on closing or converting plutonium production reactors.
26 September	U.S. and Russia sign Memorandum of Understanding in New York to amend START II and

	ABM Treaty and extend ABM Treaty to cover Soviet successor states (Russia, Ukraine, Belarus, and Kazakhstan).
26 September	United States and Russia sign TMD/NMD demarcation agreement.
3 December	Mine Ban Covention (also known as the Ottawa Convention) opened for signature; entry into force 1 March 1999; over 125 states parties.

1998

19 January	Military Maritime Consultation Agreement signed by United States and China in Beijing.
27 February	Welch Report released warning against a "rush to failure" in U.S. ballistic missile defense program.
16 March	United States and Ukraine sign U.S.-Ukrainian Nonproliferation Agreement.
11-13 May	India tests atomic weapons.
28-30 May	Pakistan tests atomic weapons.
June	Global moratorium on nuclear testing.
8 July	UK announces nuclear reductions and detargeting of its remaining SLBMs.
15 July	U.S. Rumsfeld Commission report released on the growing nuclear, chemical, and biological weapons threat to the American homeland.
31 August	North Korea launches three-stage Taepo Dong missile.
1-3 September	U.S.-Russian summit in Moscow.
2 September	United States and Russian presidents sign agreement on the management and disposition of excess plutonium.
22 September	United States and Russia begin Nuclear Cities Initiative to provide nonmilitary work to Russian scientists and engineers.
1 October	U.S. Defense Threat Reduction Agency created by combining On-Site Inspection Agency, Defense Special Weapons Agency, and Defense Technology Security Administration.
31 October	Economic Community of West African States (ECOWAS) signs moratorium on the import, export, and manufacture of small arms and light weapons.

December	Iraq expels UNSCOM inspectors.

1999

12 March	NATO expands by adding three new members (Poland, Czech Republic, Hungary).
24 March	NATO launches 78-day air campaign to drive Serbia out of Kosovo (through 9 June).
April	U.S. Arms Control and Disarmament Agency eliminated; functions absorbed by U.S. State Department.
23 April	NATO releases new strategic concept at 50th anniversary summit in Washington.
July	U.S passes National Missile Defense Act calling for missile defense deployment at earliest opportunity.
13 October	U.S. Senate votes against ratifying Comprehensive Test Ban Treaty.
1 November	U.S.-Russian summit in Helsinki.
16 November	OSCE Vienna Document 1999 signed. Adapted CFE Treaty signed.
November	Welch Report on missile defenses released.

2000

January	U.S. Quadrennial Defense Review begins (completed 30 September 2001).
10 January	Russia announces new national security strategy with increased emphasis on nuclear weapons.
14 April	Russian Duma ratifies START II treaty.
14 April-19 May	Fifth NPT Review Conference in New York City.
3-5 June	U.S.-Russian summit in Moscow.
4 June	United States and Russia agree to dispose of excess weapons-grade plutonium. (The G-8 nations agree to fund this program at their 28 July 2000 summit.)
6 September	U.S.-Russian Millennium Summit in New York.
13 October	U.S. Senate refuses to ratify CTBT by vote of 51-48.
27 October	Slovakia destroys its SS-23 missiles.

2001

February	U.S. Department of Defense begins Nuclear Posture Review (completed 31 December 2001).
16 June	U.S.-Russian summit in Ljubljana, Slovenia.
25 July	United States rejects draft BWC Protocol on enhanced treaty compliance measures.
11 September	Terrorist attacks strike U.S. World Trade Center and Pentagon.
7 October	United States-led coalition begins air and special forces assault on Taliban and al-Qaeda forces in Afghanistan. Taliban regime falls on 18 December.
21 October	U.S.-Russian joint statement on alliance against international terrorism.
13 November	U.S. and Russian presidents agree at Crawford, Texas, to further unilateral cuts in strategic nuclear arsenals.
4 December	United States and Russia achieve START I reduction limits.
13 December	United States gives formal notice to Russia of intent to withdraw from ABM Treaty in six months in order to develop and deploy a missile defense system.

2002

13 May	United States withdraws from ABM Treaty.
31 May	United States and Bulgaria agree to destroy Bulgaria's remaining SS-23 and Scud missiles.
23-26 May	U.S.-Russian summit in Moscow.
24 May	United States and Russian presidents sign Strategic Offensive Reductions Treaty (SORT, or the Moscow Treaty) in Moscow.
28 May	NATO-Russia Council created.
19 June	United States and Russia sign deal on purchase of surplus Russian highly enriched uranium.
27 June	The G-8 countries agree to a Global Partnership Against the Spread of Weapons and Materials of Mass Destruction, and pledge $20 billion over the next 10 years to this effort (also called the "10 Plus 10 Over 10" agreement).
18 July	First test flight of U.S. airborne laser.

8 August	Inaugural flight of Open Skies Treaty; Russian reconnaissance overflights of United Kingdom.
20 September	White House releases new U.S. National Security Strategy, which highlights role of counterproliferation and preemption.
27 September	Central Asian NWFZ announced in Samarkand; member states include Kazakhstan, Kyrgyzstan, Tajikistan, Turkmenistan, and Uzbekistan.
1 October	United States begins dismantling its Peacekeeper ICBM force and converting some Trident nuclear submarines to conventional roles in accordance with the SORT Treaty.
5 October	North Korea admits it has had a secret nuclear weapons program.
23 October	Cuba accedes to the Treaty of Tlatelolco; joins NPT 4 November.
8 November	UN Security Council Resolution 1441 demands Iraqi compliance with WMD inspections and disarmament.
22 November	NATO extends membership offer to seven states: Estonia, Latvia, Lithuania, Slovakia, Slovenia, Bulgaria, and Romania.
27 November	UN inspectors return to Iraq for first time in five years (under the auspices of UNMOVIC).
11 December	White House releases National Strategy to Combat Weapons of Mass Destruction.
19 December	Russia begins operation of its first chemical weapons destruction facility.

2003

10 January	North Korea announces its withdrawal from the Nuclear Nonproliferation Treaty.
6 March	U.S. Senate ratifies SORT Treaty.
12 March	U.S.-Russian agreement to shut down Russia's last three nuclear reactors dedicated to producing plutonium.
19 March	United States-led coalition launches air and ground attack on Iraq. Baghdad falls on 9 April.
14 May	Russian Duma ratifies SORT Treaty.
September	Proliferation Security Initiative signed by 11 states in Paris.

22 September   Five-year old U.S.-Russian Nuclear Cities Initiative lapses.

10 November   IAEA issues a report charging Iran with violating its NPT obligations and pursuing a nuclear weapons capability.

2004

7-12 June   First Russian Open Skies overflight of the United States.

Introduction

"In the post-Cold War world, is arms control still relevant?" The very fact that this question has been raised by pundits, politicians, advocates, and academics reinforces the timeliness of a review of where "arms control" has come from and where it might be going across this period of global transition. Such a review reinforces that the concepts embodied at the core of arms control and disarmament have been present throughout recorded human history and that those concepts remain fully relevant today and into the future. The review also serves to remind us that it is we, the contemporary inhabitants of that historic development, who have redefined and considerably narrowed our perspectives on what the terms arms control and disarmament imply. That is the reason for the questions, and it prompts a review of how both the definitions of the terms and the conduct of the participants in the field have developed, why both arms control and disarmament remain very much alive and relevant today and into the future.

Disarmament

The classical practices underlying the term "disarmament" can be found almost as far back as the beginnings of recorded Western history. Early practices were largely postconflict impositions of limitations on military force by the victor upon the vanquished. However, there were also examples of efforts to avoid conflict by cooperating to demilitarize likely regions of contact and to restrict the use of new and destructive technologies. Such efforts are well documented, such as the 448 B.C. Athens-Persia Accord (or Peace of Callias) that demilitarized the Aegean Sea and the 202 B.C. Treaty or Zama between Rome and Carthage that imposed limits on Carthage's military capabilities, including the use of war elephants.

Efforts to impose some degree of order on interstate conflict have been a feature of international relations across the history of the Westphalian system. These efforts focused on the advance of legal standards toward just war that date from very early in the Christian era. An example here is the 989 Peace and Truce of God proclaimed in the Synod of Charroux, France, that established noncombatant status for civilians. These agreements also continue postconflict limitations on military force as well as efforts to prevent the use of poison gas and other severe technologies as they developed. An example here is the 1675 Treaty of Strassburg between France and Germany to outlaw poison weapons. A third area was a series of efforts to demilitarize colonial forces and avoid distant conflicts, such as the 1814 agreement between Great Britain and Spain restricting trade with rebels in Spain's American colonies.

The period of the late 19th and early 20th centuries was marked by dramatic increases in the lethality of warfare and a concomitant movement toward bounding the employment of new weapons. Efforts were made to ban the use of certain systems and munitions, to limit numbers of advanced systems deployed, and to restrict the geographic employment of forces. The 1868 St. Petersburg Declaration prohibited explosive projectiles such as "dum-dum" bullets, and the Second Hague Convention of 1899 outlawed chemical, bacteriological, and biological weapons. The 1922 Washington Naval Treaty limited the size of the fleets of signatory nations as well as attempting to defortify the Pacific Islands.

The impact of destructive technologies and practices during World War I spurred a flurry of activity across the interwar period to limit or prohibit weapons. Part of this activity was undertaken in the post-World War I organization, the League of Nations. Much of the focus fell on limiting battleships and other major naval combatants and on outlawing poison gas. While the overall effectiveness of many of these efforts can be questioned because of their failure to prevent or limit World War II, the establishment of an international process of disarmament negotiations left a strong legacy as foundation for post-World War II efforts.

Traditionally, then, "disarmament" was used to indicate the full range of historical endeavors to reduce and restrict military weapons and forces through a wide variety of means from cooperation to imposition. These efforts included the demilitarization or deconfliction of potential regions of conflict—both at home and in colonial areas. They included postconflict limitations on state forces and weapons, as well as attempts to limit and eliminate new and destructive technologies. And they included efforts to regulate the conduct of warfare, from determinations of noncombatant status to precepts of just and moral uses of armed force. The concept was broadly used as an umbrella under which all of these arrangements and means of implementation could reside.

Arms Control

The centrality of the concept of disarmament was supplanted by the term "arms control" early in the nuclear age. In the mid-1950s policymakers began rethinking an approach that had emphasized general and complete disarmament and to consider instead limited, partial measures that would gradually enhance confidence in cooperative security arrangements. Thus, more modest goals under the rubric of arms control came to replace the propaganda-laden disarmament efforts of the late 1940s and early 1950s. International security specialists began using the term arms control in place of disarmament, which they felt lacked precision and smacked of utopianism. The seminal books on the subject published in the early 1960s all preferred arms control as a more comprehensive term. Hedley Bull differentiated the two in his 1961 book as follows: disarmament is the reduction or abolition of armaments, while arms control is restraint internationally exercised upon armaments policy—not only the number of weapons, but also their character, development, and use.[1]

Just as advances in military technologies and lethal practices had spurred an increased focus on disarmament following World War I, World War II saw the introduction of what many described as the "ultimate weapon," as well as near-global technologies of delivery. Warfare had achieved truly total and global status simultaneously. With the failure of early proposals to either eliminate or internationalize control over atomic weapons, the focus shifted toward limiting their development and spread, and toward controlling their use and effects. Western academics and policy analysts soon realized that disarmament in the literal sense of eliminating nuclear weapons was not going to happen; these weapons had become a long-term reality of the international system. Thus, as they began examining these weapons and nuclear strategy, they adopted a preference for terminology that directly captured efforts to come to grips with "controlling" these weapons and bounding their use.

This perspective was perhaps best expressed by Thomas Schelling and Morton Halperin in their seminal 1961 book *Strategy and Arms Control* when they framed the arms control construct as follows:

> We believe that arms control is a promising . . . enlargement of the scope of our military strategy. It rests essentially on the recognition that our military relation with potential enemies is not one of pure conflict and opposition, but involves strong elements of mutual interest in the avoidance of a war that neither side wants, in minimizing the costs and risks of the arms competition, and in curtailing the scope and violence of war in the event it occurs.[2]

Arms control in the nuclear age was framed first as a component part of an overall military and national security strategy—as an instrument of policy and an adjunct to force posture, not a utopian or moral crusade. It captured the more cooperative side of policy, focusing not on imposition but on negotiation and compromise, recognizing the shared interest in avoiding nuclear conflict. And it was goal-oriented toward avoiding war, limiting the political and economic costs of preparing for war, and minimizing the consequences of any conflict. This was the construct of arms control as it was practiced during the Cold War in both multilateral and bilateral settings.

Arms Control in the Cold War

Multilateral efforts early in the Cold War sought to affect the control of nuclear weapons by bounding the physical scope of the weapons and limiting their testing and further technological development and proliferation. Multilateral agreements in the nuclear arena prior to the 1970s banned placing nuclear weapons in Antarctica, outer space, or the earth's seabeds. Regional "nuclear weapons free zones" were also established during this period in Latin America and later in the South Pacific, Africa, Southeast Asia, and Central Asia. Early restrictions on atmospheric testing were supplemented later by efforts to ban all atmospheric tests and eventually all weapons test explosions, even underground. The early multilateral efforts were capped by the 1968 Nuclear Nonproliferation Treaty (NPT) that sought to prevent future additions to the nuclear "club." These efforts framed nuclear control issues for further attention on a bilateral basis and established a framework for multilateral efforts extending to biological and chemical weapons, and to other arenas of both arms control and broader disarmament. The NPT also paid service to its disarmament heritage by containing a clause calling upon all nuclear weapons states to seek the eventual elimination of their nuclear arsenals.

With the completion of the Nonproliferation Treaty, the nuclear agenda for cooperative controls was narrowed to issues between the major nuclear powers. The primary arms control focus of the Cold War became centered on bilateral strategic controls between the United States and the Soviet Union, and the meaning of "arms control" subsequently narrowed even further to focus on the formal process. That process was characterized by three preliminary steps followed by a staged, four-part negotiation and implementation phase.

Formal Arms Control Negotiations

The preconditions were setting the agenda for negotiations, establishing a conducive level of mutual confidence, and inspiring self-assurance of the ability to achieve an adequate level of verification to allow strong consideration of a formal, binding agreement. The agenda was often set by progress in other negotiations, either multilateral nuclear efforts or bilateral relations outside of the nuclear arena, or by triggering events such as international crises that created a sense of urgency to pursue heightened cooperation in the nuclear relationship. In all cases, issues to be addressed in the formal process were defined and narrowed into a range that both sides found comfortable addressing. Formal negotiations were supplemented by, and all agreements prefaced by, a series of confidence-building efforts and agreements that established a cooperative base and comfort zone from which to proceed. And the essential enabler for all nuclear control agreements was the guarantee of adequate verification means, either within the negotiation process or via unilateral capabilities outside of the formal agreement itself.

Once the preliminary steps were taken (these could require a decade or more for a major round of agreements), the negotiation process could proceed toward an agreement. Formal talks were first established with large delegations representing the full range of affected agencies and functions on each side. These primary negotiations focused on both the substance of the agreement—with a central focus on equitable and stabilizing controls—and on its implementation. Years of effort and multiple, highly technical sidebar discussions were necessary, in most cases, to ensure that the eventual agreement and its implementation would hold no surprises for any party. Predictably, the talks would often hang up on a final series of points of contention, and a second stage—summitry between very senior officials, often chief executives, on each side—would be needed to reach final agreement. The third stage, the "endgame" (including the formal signing of the agreement), would be characterized by elevation to the highest government officials, much pomp and ceremony, and formal staging for both international and domestic political effect. The fourth and final stage consisted of implementation and compliance verification and monitoring. Formal mechanisms, often including elaborate procedural and even organizational structures, characterized the very last stage, although always supplemented by unilateral verification mechanisms or systems as the ultimate guarantor of faithful compliance by the other side.

The SALT Era

The bilateral United States-Soviet Union/Russia nuclear arms control effort continued across and beyond the Cold War. The first effort was one of process establishment and strategic limitations that led to the Strategic Arms Limitations Talks and ultimately resulted in the SALT I—with its adjunct Anti-Ballistic Missile (ABM) Treaty—and SALT II agreements. Cold War tensions and a dangerous and expensive nuclear arms race, whose potential ramifications had been made evident by the Cuban Missile Crisis, spurred both sides in the 1960s into an almost decade-long series of small cooperative measures and internal organizational steps toward bilateral cooperation on limiting future strategic systems growth and development. With the culmination of the major multilateral nuclear effort (the NPT) and the almost simultaneous attainment of sufficient capabilities in national technical means of unilateral verification, formal bilateral negotiations on SALT began in 1969 within the framework laid out at the 1967 Glassboro Summit. SALT I, signed in 1972, froze the total number of deployed intercontinental ballistic missiles on both sides and limited the total number of maritime strategic systems to be deployed over a five-year period. It also limited the development and deployment of future antiballistic missile systems and restricted defense technologies. Given the five-year life of the SALT I strategic system limitations, the two sides agreed on the outline of a follow-on agreement at the Vladivostok Summit in 1974. Subsequent detailed negotiations led to the culmination of SALT II in 1979, which placed an aggregate limit on deployed strategic launch vehicles and also limited the numbers of systems that could be equipped with multiple warheads. The first bilateral series, then, addressed limits on launch vehicles and strategic systems within the parameters of existing nuclear strategies and overall bilateral relations, and within the capability of the primary verification mechanism for SALT: national technical means of monitoring the other side.

The START Era

The second series of negotiations between the United States and the Soviet Union (and, after 1991, Russia) addressed force reductions through the Strategic Arms Reduction Talks—leading to the START I and START II treaties—and the elimination of an entire class of weapons through the Intermediate-Range Nuclear Forces (INF) Treaty. Beginning simultaneously with the first series of bilateral United States-Soviet Union negotiations, a broader series of East-West efforts addressed the reduction of tensions between the North Atlantic Treaty Organization (NATO) and the Warsaw Pact in Europe. While this effort addressed trans-European confidence-building measures and conventional force limitations, it also focused attention on the bilateral theater nuclear systems of the superpowers. Negotiations on these intermediate-range systems proceeded even while NATO decided to deploy the United States' intermediate-range missiles into Western European bases. By 1987, with the deployment well underway, the INF treaty negotiations came to fruition, and the missiles were withdrawn and destroyed by both sides. A key legacy of this agreement, in addition to its precedent for elimination of an entire category of weapon systems, was its reliance on on-site inspection teams to verify missile removal and destruction on the other side's territory. With on-site inspection as the essential supplement to national technical means now established, strategic systems reduction negotiations could proceed.

The START talks began in 1982 and proceeded across that decade alongside an extensive series of nuclear confidence-building measures addressing risk reduction and data sharing measures. The 1992 START I Treaty was significant in that it required measured reductions in both nuclear weapons and delivery vehicles, with intrusive verification provisions to ensure compliance. Events intervened in this second series of bilateral nuclear arms control, with changes of government leaders and even forms of government prompting new forms of arms control. Two controls that emerged were unilateral initiatives and cooperative threat reduction measures. The bilateral nuclear arms control process was so firmly established by the time of the dissolution of the Soviet Union in 1991 that a brief series of unilateral initiatives, begun by United States President George H. W. Bush and reciprocated, in turn, by outgoing Soviet leader Mikhail Gorbachev and incoming Russian President Boris Yeltsin, allowed the START process to continue to the 1993 START II Treaty. In this treaty both sides agreed to further reduce their nuclear arsenals. In addition, cooperative efforts succeeded in consolidating control and physical presence of Soviet nuclear systems into the Russian Republic and initiating a broad and shared effort to check the proliferation of former Soviet nuclear capabilities. At the 1997 Helsinki summit meeting both countries committed themselves to continue the strategic arms reduction process to even lower levels of nuclear warheads through a START III round that was later amended to become the 2002 Moscow Treaty (officially the Strategic Offensive Reductions Treaty, or SORT).

Multilateral Arms Control in the Later Cold War

Arms control was not solely focused on bilateral U.S.-Soviet strategic arms during the 1970s and 1980s, however. At the same time there was a parallel multilateral effort underway in multiple other fields, often led by the United Nations Conference on Disarmament or by regional organizations. These discussions were usually not as highly charged politically as the bilateral efforts, but they did achieve several notable accomplishments. For example, in 1972 the world agreed to ban the production, stockpiling, and use of biological and toxin weapons, and in 1993 they agreed to a similar convention on chemical weapons. NATO and the Warsaw Pact came to an agreement on conventional force levels, composition, and disposition in the Conventional Forces in Europe (CFE) Treaty in 1990. A Comprehensive Test Ban Treaty was signed in Geneva in 1996 (although it had not yet entered into force as of mid-2004), and discussions are still ongoing regarding a Fissile Materials Cutoff Treaty. Nuclear weapons free zones were declared in the South Pacific, Latin America, Africa, and Southeast Asia, essentially denuclearizing the entire Southern Hemisphere. A coalition of states and nongovernmental organizations led the effort to ban landmines in 1997. And several informal groupings of states were created to prevent the proliferation of weapons of mass destruction technologies—the Zangger Committee, the Australia Group, the Wassenaar Arrangement, and the Nuclear Suppliers Group among them.

Arms Control and Disarmament Today

The agenda of existing, active efforts in the arena of arms control and disarmament remains extensive. The United States and Russia each retain significant nuclear arsenals. During the Cold War other nations—initially Great Britain, France, and China—developed and deployed nuclear weapons, and today several other nations (India, Pakistan, Israel, North Korea, and possibly Iran) have joined or are seeking to join that nuclear club, either overtly or covertly. Remaining nuclear weapons arsenals and the potential for nuclear proliferation—whether materials, components, systems, weapons, or expertise—keep nuclear arms control on the agenda. Late Cold War efforts resulted in controls on major conventional weapons and systems in Europe, but a whole range of conventional arms remain outside of any effective controls. Other weapons with catastrophic potential—particularly biological and chemical—while subject to international controls and even bans, remain a threat for development and proliferation. And far-reaching technological developments have opened up entire new arenas of potential and actual military development, and concomitant arms control interest. Ongoing efforts—unilateral, bilateral, and multilateral; formal and informal; between nations and also including nonstate parties and interests in some cases—are addressing this wide agenda. Many of these efforts are centered in and around the United Nations Conference on Disarmament and its wide and varied agenda.

The extensive list of efforts and programs can be viewed as an umbrella of constituent components on a continuum of arms control and disarmament. "Disarmament" developed across the ages to imply the entire range of efforts, cooperative and imposed, to limit military capabilities or their deployment. "Arms control" was adopted to capture cooperative efforts to contain the nuclear dangers of the Cold War, and it subsequently narrowed to imply the drawn out, formal negotiation process addressing superpower strategic nuclear weapons. Against that very narrow and bilateral "arms control" arena, other and broader efforts continued in the multilateral arena aimed at limiting and even banning other weapons and systems, ranging from biological and chemical weapons to antipersonnel land mines. Because much of the focus here has been on eliminating classes of weapons and their use, this broad multilateral arena is often referred to as "disarmament," and many of these efforts reside in the United Nations Conference on Disarmament. If one retains this modern "disarmament" perspective and adds an "arms control" component under roughly the perspective of Schelling and Halperin, the entire range of unilateral, bilateral, regional, and multilateral efforts that is seen today is captured.

Directions in Arms Control and Disarmament

This brings the discussion full circle to the question "in the post-Cold War world, is arms control still relevant?" The answer here is that it is very much alive and that it retains high relevance, albeit in slightly altered—but no less important—forms.

First, one can project at least another two or more decades of the United States-Russia nuclear START/SORT implementation process, probably extending beyond the formal implementation and termination dates of the formal agreements. Recent unilateral and bilateral initiatives have led to additional reductions—now focused primarily on warheads and weapons—and further rounds of coordinated unilateral or bilateral reductions are certainly possible, as well. In addition, and perhaps even more significant, the cooperative effort to dismantle, control, and destroy the weapons-grade materials from literally thousands of weapons will continue with fits and starts. This is a massive, difficult, expensive, and often contentious process, and it will be compounded and extended with each new increment of cuts. The added factor of dealing with strategic defenses will broaden, extend, and further complicate this bilateral endgame, at least in the short term, but it also holds the potential—at least to some observers—of being the only route to the continued drawdown of the two strategic nuclear arsenals. In any case, it adds yet another dynamic to arms control. In addition, the United States and Russia have yet to address the additional nonstrategic nuclear weapons that are included in their arsenals. This will even further complicate bilateral arms controls. Finally, similar cooperative efforts to dismantle, control, and destroy former Soviet chemical and biological weapons and capabilities extend the scope and horizons of the bilateral strategic arms control effort. The highly formal Cold War bilateral arms control process will certainly be altered, but this series of arms control is far from over.

Second, one can expect a continuation of multilateral arms control and disarmament efforts, particularly toward halting and reversing the proliferation and development of nuclear, biological, and chemical weapons. Work remains to be done in fully implementing the NPT and the Comprehensive Test Ban Treaty, and in improving the implementation and extending the application of the Biological and Chemical Weapons Conventions. These efforts are very much alive.

Further, major regional arms control and disarmament efforts are just emerging. Europe has long addressed security cooperation, confidence-building, and conventional arms control issues, and that effort will continue as that region continues to stake out its identity and future course. Other regions have adopted nuclear weapons free zones, and some have established regional and subregional cooperative programs on a range of economic, political, and security issues. Today, with the emergence of new nuclear states in South Asia and with heightened proliferation concerns ranging from East Asia to the Middle East, efforts will be initiated and intensified to establish regional mechanisms for transparency and security. And one can also project other new and emerging arenas for arms control and disarmament, including existing efforts among some states and a number of nonstate actors to address controls or bans on small arms and land mines, at least academic discussion of controls on advanced conventional weapons, and emerging venues of military interest—and thus arms control interest—in space and cyberspace. All of these efforts are only in their infancy, implying continued interest in arms control for years to come.

Finally, one can expect a continuation and expansion of other efforts under the broad umbrella of arms control and disarmament focused around unilateral efforts, whether reciprocal or nonreciprocal. States have in the past undertaken self-limiting measures ranging from Switzerland's self-imposed neutrality to South Africa's dismantlement of its nuclear weapons program and capability, as well as destruction of much of its chemical and biological warfare capability. Others among today's nuclear states may find such unilateral disarmament in their interest, as witnessed by Libya's actions in late 2003 to disclose and dismantle its weapons of mass destruction development programs. Also within this category of unilateral efforts, and until broader efforts to control the proliferation and use of weapons of mass destruction bear fruit, states will pursue self-help counterproliferation programs, seeking to impose controls and limitations on the capabilities of others. These efforts too fit under the broad umbrella of arms control and disarmament.

International events beginning in late 2001 have had a profound effect on all dimensions of international relations. Global terrorism—including the specter of terrorists armed with chemical, biological, radiological, or nuclear weapons—and actions well outside of accepted norms of international behavior by rogue and failing states raise severe challenges to the foundations of cooperation and diplomacy that lie at the heart of arms control. History tells us that historical trends will continue—with some altered emphasis—over the long term. In the short term there is an increased emphasis on strengthened nonproliferation, as well as an expressed willingness to pursue active counterproliferation. On the part of the United States, this extends even to preemption. At the same time, there is also the ongoing and active agreement on the part of the United States and Russia to enact strategic nuclear weapons cuts to 2,000 or fewer warheads on each side, even after United States withdrawal from the ABM Treaty and a commitment to deploy strategic defenses. Given the historical record and the net effect of all of these trends, there is reason to believe that arms control and disarmament remain vital and relevant now and into the foreseeable future.

Human history is a chronicle of efforts to limit the potential and destructive results of warfare. Today, as modern technologies threaten massive suffering and even global destruction and human extinction, nations and individuals will continue to strive for humane and measured applications of force. As long as weapons remain tools of international relations, citizens of those nations will be involved in what we here have termed "arms control and disarmament." This field of international policy will remain viable and vital into the foreseeable future.

Notes

1. Hedley Bull, *The Control of the Arms Race: Disarmament and Arms Control in the Missile Age* (New York: Frederick A. Praeger, 1961).

2. Thomas Schelling and Morton Halperin, *Strategy and Arms Control* (New York: Twentieth Century Fund, 1961), 1.

The Dictionary

A

A-BOMB. *See* ATOMIC BOMB; FISSION WEAPON.

ABM TREATY. *See* ANTI-BALLISTIC MISSILE TREATY.

ACCIDENTAL LAUNCH. The release of a **strategic** weapon without central authorization. This event usually refers to the unauthorized launch of an **intercontinental ballistic missile** or **submarine-launched ballistic missile**.

ACCIDENTAL LAUNCH PROTECTION SYSTEM (ALPS). A limited-scope, **Anti-Ballistic Missile Treaty** (ABM) compliant defensive system designed to defend against a few missiles launched by accident or without authorization. ALPS was proposed in January 1988 as a near-term alternative to the **Ronald Reagan** administration's **Strategic Defense Initiative** (SDI) by Senator **Sam Nunn.** *See also* ACCIDENTAL LAUNCH.

ACCIDENTAL WAR. Any conflict that begins without premeditation by one or both sides. World War I, for example, began following a series of events that resulted from an assassination in Serbia. During the **Cold War**, accidental war usually referred to a conflict resulting from **accidental launch** of a missile and the subsequent military response by the target state.

ACCIDENTS MEASURES AGREEMENT (1971). Formally the "Agreement on Measures to Reduce the Risk of Outbreak of Nuclear War," this accord between the **United States** and the **Soviet Union** committed the signatories to improved weapon **safeguards,**

13

immediate notification of unexplained incidents or accidental detonations of **nuclear weapons**, and advance notification of missile launches in the general direction of the óther party. It was signed in Washington, D.C., on 30 September 1971.

ACCOUNTABLE WARHEADS. Strategic warheads subject to limits as specified in an **arms control agreement**.

ACHESON, DEAN (1893-1971). American diplomat and secretary of state under President **Harry S. Truman.** He served in the **U.S. State Department** during World War II under President **Franklin Roosevelt** and as secretary of state supported the concept of **containment** of the **Soviet Union** during the late 1940s. He was a leading proponent of **NSC-68**, which called for the military containment of the **USSR**.

ACTIVE DEFENSE. The attempt to protect one's society, forces, or territory by neutralizing or destroying an adversary's attempts to attack them. Also, the capabilities to detect, track, identify, intercept, and destroy or neutralize **warheads**, particularly warheads carrying **weapons of mass destruction**, delivered by airborne platforms, **ballistic missiles,** and **cruise missiles.** *See also* PASSIVE DEFENSE.

ACTIVE IMMUNITY. Immunity to a biological agent acquired from production of **antibodies** in response to the presence of antigens within an **organism.** *See also* PASSIVE IMMUNITY.

ACTIVE MATERIAL. Plutonium and selected uranium isotopes that can support a **fission chain reaction**.

ACTIVE QUOTA. The number of inspections one **state party** can conduct against another under the provisions of an **arms control agreement**. *See also* PASSIVE QUOTA.

ACUTE EFFECT. Symptom of short-term exposure to a hazardous material that causes a rapid crisis reaction for the exposed human.

ADENAUER, KONRAD (1876-1967). Chancellor of the Federal Republic of Germany from 1949 to 1963. He led the committee that wrote West Germany's new constitution (or Basic Law) following World War II, he was a staunch anticommunist and moved West

Germany firmly into the Western alliance system, including membership in the European Coal and Steel Community (the predecessor to today's **European Union**) and the **North Atlantic Treaty Organization** (NATO).

ADVANCED CRUISE MISSILE (ACM). A **stealth** follow-on to the **United States air-launched cruise missile**. An air-to-ground missile built by Raytheon and Boeing, it carries a nuclear **payload**, has a range of 2,000 miles, and was meant to be carried to its launch point under the wing of a **B-52 bomber**. The ACM (AGM-129A) was first introduced into the U.S. inventory in 1992.

ADVANCED MANNED STRATEGIC AIRCRAFT (AMSA). The early concept for a follow-on **United States strategic bomber** to replace the **B-52**. The plan was for a terrain-hugging penetrating bomber to fly below Soviet radar. The AMSA later became reality in the form of the **B-1 bomber**.

AEROSOL. Dissemination method for **chemical** and **biological weapons** that employs a suspension of very fine agent particles in a gaseous medium.

AFRICAN NUCLEAR WEAPON FREE ZONE. Created by the Treaty of Pelindaba, signed by 28 states in Cairo, Egypt on 11 April 1996. It established a **nuclear weapons free zone** for the African continent.

AGENCY FOR THE PROHIBITION OF NUCLEAR WEAPONS IN LATIN AMERICA (OPANAL). The implementing organization established for the Treaty of Tlatelolco, which enacted the **Latin American Nuclear Weapons Free Zone**.

AGENT. Any substance or force that causes change. Biological or chemical agents are used as weapons to cause catastrophic change, including incapacitation or death.

AGGREGATE CEILING. The combined total limit imposed by an **arms control agreement** on two or more different weapons or system components. An example is the **Strategic Arms Limitation Treaty** (SALT II) limit on the total number of **strategic** delivery systems allowed to each side, including **intercontinental ballistic**

missiles, **submarine-launched ballistic missiles**, and **strategic bombers**.

AGREED FRAMEWORK ON NORTH KOREA (1994). A cooperative **nonproliferation agreement** between the **United States** and the Democratic Peoples' Republic of Korea (**North Korea**) signed in October 1994. The United States and 11 other nations agreed to replace the North Korean graphite-moderated **nuclear reactors** with light-water reactors, increase political and economic relations, work toward a peaceful and **nuclear-weapons** free Korean peninsula, and strengthen international nuclear **nonproliferation**. In return, North Korea agreed to allow the international exposure, destruction, and monitoring of its nuclear weapons infrastructure. The measure fell apart in December 2002 when North Korea announced its intention to resume nuclear development efforts.

AGREEMENT. A formal written text resulting from **negotiations** that may or may not be legally binding. General agreements on principles do not carry the force of law, while agreements of formal and serious commitment intended to be binding are called **treaties**.

AGREEMENT ON CONFIDENCE- AND SECURITY BUILDING MEASURES AND DISARMAMENT IN EUROPE. *See* STOCKHOLM AGREEMENT.

AGREEMENT ON THE PREVENTION OF DANGEROUS MILITARY ACTIVITIES (1989). Following a number of accidental shootings and incidents in the early 1980s, and in the spirit of openness between the **United States** and the **Soviet Union** in the latter half of the decade, the two sides signed an agreement to improve military-to-military discussions, to enhance communications, to create areas of "special caution" where both militaries were working side by side during periods of heightened tension, and to avoid the use of dangerous lasers or electronic jamming with **command and control** networks.

AIR DEFENSE. Defense against airborne threats to one's country, forces, or allies. This can use aircraft, balloons, **surface-to-air missiles**, **directed energy weapons**, or other methods that prevent an adversary's air-delivered weapons from reaching their targets.

AIR-LAUNCHED CRUISE MISSILE (ALCM). An unmanned, self-propelled, air-launched vehicle that is capable of sustaining flight through aerodynamic lift across the majority of its flight path. The first U.S. ALCM (AGM-86) was built by Boeing. The project began in 1972 and had its first flight in 1976. It was developed in conjunction with the **Tomahawk cruise missile.** It had a range of 1,500 miles after being released by its **B-52 bomber** and could carry a conventional or **nuclear warhead.** ALCMs have been used by the **United States** in nearly all its recent conflicts.

AIR-TO-SURFACE BALLISTIC MISSILE (ASBM). A **ballistic missile** with a range in excess of 600 kilometers installed in an aircraft or on its external mountings and launched from that aircraft.

AIRBORNE ALERT. A state of aircraft readiness wherein combat-equipped aircraft are airborne and ready for immediate action. This usually refers to Operation Chrome Dome, when the **United States** maintained nuclear-armed manned **bombers** in an airborne status so as to ensure their survivability and to minimize their reaction time in response to nuclear attack. The **United States Air Force** maintained B-36, B-47, B-58, and **B-52 bombers** on continuous airborne alert from 1962 to 1968. Several high-profile accidents involving nuclear weapons on airborne alert attracted negative public attention, including B-52 crashes in Spain and Greenland.

AIRBORNE WARNING AND CONTROL SYSTEM (AWACS). A class of airborne command posts from which air threats can be detected and analyzed, and **air defense** responses can be directed. An example is the E-3 Sentry, a modified Boeing 707 with a large rotating radar dome attached to its fuselage, which was introduced to the **U.S. Air Force** in 1977.

ALLIED FORCE, OPERATION. The 1999 diplomatic and airpower campaign mounted by the **North Atlantic Treaty Organization (NATO)** against Serbia to force that state to stop its ethnic cleansing of Muslim Albanians in the province of Kosovo. This was the largest military conflict in Europe since the end of World War II, and the first time NATO had used military force out of its normal area of operations.

AMERICAN ACADEMY OF ARTS AND SCIENCES (AAAS). Founded in 1780, the American Academy of Arts and Sciences is an international learned society composed of many of the world's leading scientists, scholars, artists, business people, and public leaders. With a current membership of 4,000 American fellows and 600 foreign honorary members, the Academy has four major goals: promoting service and study through analysis of critical social and intellectual issues and the development of practical policy alternatives; fostering public engagement and the exchange of ideas with meetings, conferences, and symposia bringing diverse perspectives to the examination of issues of common concern; mentoring a new generation of scholars and thinkers; and honoring excellence by electing to membership men and women in a broad range of disciplines and professions. The Academy's main headquarters are in Cambridge, Massachusetts. It has also established regional centers at the University of Chicago and at the University of California, Irvine, and conducts activities in the United States and abroad.

AMERICAN ENTERPRISE INSTITUTE (AEI). The American Enterprise Institute for Public Policy Research is dedicated to preserving and strengthening the foundations of freedom—limited government, private enterprise, vital cultural and political institutions, and a strong foreign policy and national defense—through scholarly research, debate, and publications. Founded in 1943 and located in Washington, D.C., AEI is one of America's largest and most respected "think tanks." AEI research covers economics and trade; social welfare; government tax, spending, regulatory, and legal policies; U.S. politics; international affairs; and U.S. defense and foreign policies. The Institute publishes dozens of books and hundreds of articles and reports each year.

AMERICAN PHYSICAL SOCIETY (APS). The American Physical Society is the professional society for physicists in the United States, with more than 40,000 members. The principal functions of the APS are the publication of professional journals and arrangement of scientific meetings. On occasion, the APS produces reports on matters of public interest that require technical understanding and for which an impartial and authoritative analysis would be of particular use to the public and to policy makers. One such recent study was on the use of **directed energy weapons** for **missile defense**.

ANDROPOV, YURI (1914-1984). Leader of the **Soviet Union** during the period 1982-1984. He was appointed head of the KGB in May 1967. In 1973 Andropov became a full member of the Politburo.

Just days after **Leonid Brezhnev's** death (on 10 November 1982), Andropov became the Communist Party's general secretary. In the 15 months he ruled before his death, Andropov tried to improve the efficiency of the Soviet economy. His foreign policy stance reflected the Soviet status quo. During Andropov's tenure, he tried to persuade the Europeans not to allow U.S. President **Ronald Reagan** to station **Pershing missiles** in Germany. It was also during Andropov's time as Soviet leader that Soviet forces shot down a civilian South Korean airliner. Scholars debate whether Andropov would have proved to be a real reformer had he lived.

ANGLO-FRENCH PACT (1787). A bilateral **arms control agreement** that limited and equalized the size of the French and British navies following years of conflict between the two great powers of the eighteenth century.

ANGLO-GERMAN NAVAL PACT (1935). As part of the interwar naval limitations system, Germany and **Great Britain** signed a pact placing limits on the size and numbers of Germany's warships. The British hoped thereby to bring Germany into the European naval ratio system at a level that would not threaten the other naval powers; Germany hoped to prevent a naval **arms race** with Britain while still modernizing its fleet. Germany withdrew from the arrangement in April 1939.

ANTARCTIC TREATY (1959). The Antarctic Treaty was the first of the major post-World War II international **arms control treaties**, and set several major precedents for future **negotiations** and **agreements**. Signed in Washington, D.C., on 1 December 1959, it **entered into force** on 23 June 1961. The treaty recognizes that it is in the interest of all mankind to keep the Antarctic continent forever as a laboratory for peaceful purposes and prevent it from becoming the scene of international disputes. It therefore proscribes any measures of a military nature, military maneuvers, the building of any military base, and any nuclear explosion or the disposal of radioactive waste in the region, defined as the land mass south of 60 degrees latitude and attached ice sheets. Military forces may be used for scientific research or other peaceful purposes. All scientific and research stations are open at all times to outside inspectors and observers. Parties to the treaty do not, however, renounce their existing territorial claims to Antarctica. Treaty signatories include the **United States, USSR, United Kingdom,** Argentina, Australia,

Belgium, Chile, France, Japan, New Zealand, Norway, and South Africa. In effect, this treaty created the first **nuclear weapons-free zone** in the world.

ANTIBALLISTIC MISSILE (ABM). A defensive system designed to intercept and destroy **strategic ballistic missiles** on their inbound trajectory.

ANTI-BALLISTIC MISSILE TREATY (1972). "The Treaty between the United States of America and the Union of Soviet Socialist Republics on the Limitation of Anti-Ballistic Missile Systems" was signed by President **Richard Nixon** and Secretary General **Leonid Brezhnev** in **Moscow** on 26 May 1972. **Ratification** was advised by the U.S. Senate on 3 August 1972, and the treaty **entered into force** on 3 October 1972. Its purpose was stated in its preamble: "Effective measures to limit anti-ballistic-missile systems would be a substantial factor in curbing the race in **strategic** offensive arms and would lead to a decrease in the risk of outbreak of war involving **nuclear weapons.**" Article I prohibited the deployment of an ABM system for "the defense of the territory" or the provision of "a base for such a defense." The former prohibition included a nationwide defense, whether on land or sea or in air or space; the latter encompassed items such as powerful, **large phased-array radars** (LPARs), which are the long-lead-time items of a deployed land-based ABM system. The Treaty had unlimited duration, with five-year reviews.

The ABM Treaty came under increasing scrutiny and reconsideration in the late 1990s as the **United States** began seriously considering the deployment of a **national missile defense** system. The **William Clinton** administration hoped that **Russia** would be willing to renegotiate or modify the treaty to allow for modest defenses against **rogue states**, theater protection, and **accidental launch**, but Russia (indeed, most of the world community) seemed unwilling to risk eliminating the treaty. Many **arms control** advocates called the ABM Treaty "the cornerstone of strategic stability" in the international system. In May 2001 President **George W. Bush** announced that the United States would not be constrained by an outdated treaty that did not reflect the political realities of a world with new threats posed by rogue states armed with **weapons of mass destruction** and the means to deliver them against American territory. On 13 December 2001 the United States informed Russia that it would withdraw from the Treaty in six months in order to develop a missile defense system. The Treaty expired on 13 June 2002.

An antiballistic missile system was defined for treaty purposes as a system "to counter strategic ballistic missiles or their elements in flight trajectory," consisting of three components: ABM launchers, ABM interceptor missiles, and ABM radars. The word strategic was included to preserve the option of deploying antitactical or **theater ballistic missile defenses**. ABM components were defined as either "constructed and deployed for an ABM role" or of "a type tested in an ABM mode." These definitions were linked with Treaty prohibitions against the testing in an ABM mode of non-ABM systems such as **surface-to-air missile** systems.

The Treaty limited each side to two ABM deployment sites (later reduced to one site by the 1974 Protocol). The authorized deployment area, with a radius of 150 kilometers, was to be centered either on the national capital area or on an **intercontinental ballistic missile** (ICBM) field; each side had the right to switch the site one time. All deployed ABM components had to be located within the designated deployment area, and they must be fixed and land-based. The United States chose to locate its site at the Grand Forks, North Dakota, ICBM fields, while the USSR selected Moscow.

Provisions for ABM test ranges prohibited, among other things, ABM deployments in various locations around the country under the guise of test facilities. The numerical limitation of 15 launchers at an ABM test range reinforced this purpose. The United States had two ABM test ranges from which fixed land-based ABM components could be tested: White Sands, New Mexico, and Kwajalein Island in the Pacific.

The Treaty prohibited space-based, air-based, sea-based, and mobile land-based ABM systems and components. The ban covered development and testing as well as deployment. No restraints were placed on research that preceded field testing.

The Treaty imposed a ceiling of 100 ABM launchers and 100 ABM missiles at launch sites in the ABM deployment area. It prohibited certain capabilities of fixed land-based components, such as automatic, semiautomatic, or rapid-reload ABM launchers and launchers that could launch more than one ABM interceptor missile at a time. Agreed Statement E extended these prohibitions to ABM interceptors with more than one independently guided warhead. There were no limits on the range or velocity of the ABM interceptors.

The treaty limited the location of ABM radars to authorized ABM deployment areas or ABM test ranges. Early-warning radars constructed after the treaty entered into force were to be located on the periphery of the country and oriented outward. The periphery requirement assumed that a radar so located was vulnerable to military attack and therefore not strategically effective. The outward orientation was intended to prohibit the over-the-shoulder coverage necessary for an effective ABM radar providing coverage of incoming ballistic missiles within territorial boundaries. The explicit exceptions to these rules are radars for space tracking or for **national technical means** (NTM), which were not limited in terms of power, location, orientation, or other factors.

Provisions of the treaty were to be verified solely by national technical means; each party agreed not to interfere with the other's NTM and not to use deliberate concealment measures that would impede verification by NTM.

The United States and Russia signed a series of agreements on 27 September 1997 regarding demarcation between theater and national ballistic missile defenses and to allow Belarus, Kazakhstan, Russia, and Ukraine to succeed the **USSR** as **state parties** to the treaty.

The **Standing Consultative Commission** (SCC) was the forum that addressed compliance issues and on-going problems and challenges. It met in Geneva, Switzerland.

ANTIBODY. A protein produced in human blood or tissue as a reaction to the presence of a specific antigen that attacks **bacteria** and can neutralize an organic poison.

ANTIDOTE. That which counteracts the effects of a poison.

ANTISATELLITE WEAPON (ASAT). A weapon designed to attack satellites in orbit. An ASAT can be launched via **ballistic missile** or on a rocket from an aircraft. The **United States** and **Soviet Union** conducted several rounds of ASAT **negotiations** in 1978-1979, but without reaching any conclusion. The United States successfully tested a **Nike-Zeus missile** in an ASAT role in 1963 and fired an ASAT missile (called the air-launched miniature vehicle, or ALMV) from an F-15 Eagle in 1985. The ALMV program was cancelled in 1988.

ANTISUBMARINE ROCKET (ASROC). A U.S. ship-launched **ballistic missile** carrying an acoustic homing torpedo or nuclear depth charge used to destroy enemy submarines. The ASROC entered service in 1960. It had a range of six miles. Tactical **nuclear war-**

heads were removed from all **U.S. Navy** ships as a result of the 1991 **Presidential Nuclear Initiatives**.

ANTISUBMARINE WARFARE (ASW). Military activity undertaken to identify, track, and destroy enemy submarines.

ANTITACTICAL BALLISTIC MISSILE (ATBM). A defensive system designed to intercept and destroy short-range, **nonstrategic ballistic missiles** on their inbound path.

ANTITOXINS. Biological **antibodies** that counteract **toxins** in the body.

ANZUS TREATY. Australia, New Zealand, **United States** agreement on security cooperation. Signed in 1951, the three states agreed that an attack on one would be considered an attack on all three. The treaty remains in force, although the United States abrogated its responsibilities in 1986 after New Zealand refused to allow American nuclear-powered ships to enter its ports.

AREA DEFENSE. Broad protection of a larger geographic region as opposed to a specific target. *See also* POINT DEFENSE.

ARGENTINE-CHILEAN NAVAL PACT (1902). A bilateral **arms control agreement** to freeze and then reduce the naval strength of regional adversaries Argentina and Chile in order to avoid conflict.

ARMS CONTROL. One of a series of alternative approaches to achieving international security through military strategies, typically by applying restraints and limits on forces. Arms control is a process involving specific, declared steps by a state to enhance its security through implicit or explicit cooperation with other states. These steps can be **unilateral, bilateral,** or **multilateral**. It includes measures intended to reduce the likelihood of war, to limit the costs of preparing for war, and should war occur, to reduce the consequences. The term was invented and popularized by American and British security analysts in the late 1950s and early 1960s. During the **Cold War** the concept came to be identified with formal bilateral **negotiations** capped off by **treaty** signings at international **summit meetings** and the creation of systems of **inspection** and **verification** to ensure **compliance**. *See also* BULL, HEDLEY;

DISARMAMENT; HALPERIN, MORTON; SCHELLING, THOMAS.

ARMS CONTROL ASSOCIATION (ACA). The Arms Control Association, founded in 1971, is a national nonpartisan membership organization dedicated to promoting public understanding of and support for effective arms control policies. Through its public education and media programs and its magazine, *Arms Control Today*, the ACA provides policy makers, the press and the interested public with authoritative information, analysis, and commentary on arms control proposals, negotiations and agreements, and related national security issues. In addition to the regular press briefings that the ACA holds on major arms control developments, the Association's staff provides commentary and analysis on a broad spectrum of issues for journalists and scholars.

ARMS CONTROL AND DISARMAMENT AGENCY (ACDA). The principal **United States** government agency and focal point for all efforts dealing with arms control for nearly 30 years, ACDA was created by President **John F. Kennedy** in 1961. ACDA was a subdepartment within the **Department of State** but carried considerable political weight in its subject field. The agency was closed, and its functions incorporated into the State Department, in 1999.

ARMS EXPORT CONTROL ACT. A **United States** law initially passed in 1976, and updated regularly since, in response to congressional concerns over Middle East arms sales. It provides authorization for presidential control of the export of military equipment and services and prohibits firms from marketing dangerous technologies.

ARMS RACE. A situation in which two or more parties increase military strength and/or capability to either reciprocate or anticipate military increases by potential foes. This can become a continuing cycle of spiraling growth, ultimately increasing tensions and the chances that these forces might be used. A central feature of the **Cold War** and a primary target of **arms control** efforts between the **United States** and the **Soviet Union** was to limit and halt the nuclear arms race.

ARMS TRADE. The legal and illegal market for conventional and unconventional weapons between states, nonstate actors, and individuals. This includes sales, **arms transfers, gray market** transactions, and all other deals that result in weapons moving from one place to another. Often considered in negative terms, as when a group illegally obtains weapons for its own, often violent, purposes.

ARMS TRANSFER. The transfer of arms, including small arms, conventional heavy armaments, aircraft, ships, and so on, either by sale or grant.

ASPIN, LES (1938-1995). Congressman from Wisconsin and secretary of defense under President **William Clinton,** Aspin served as a leading defense intellectual in Congress prior to being picked for the senior **Department of Defense** position in 1993. In less than a year, he oversaw the transition of the U.S. military to a post-**Cold War** force, released the **Bottom-Up Review,** and pushed for the **North Atlantic Treaty Organization's Partnership for Peace** program. He resigned due to a combination of health concerns and public opposition to his leadership of the U.S. involvement in Somalia, and died shortly thereafter.

ASSURED DESTRUCTION. A policy adopted by both the **United States** and the **Soviet Union** during the **Cold War** to enhance **deterrence** of **strategic** attack on one's homeland by threatening the other side's destruction from a retaliatory **second strike.** Operationalizing this policy required both sufficient numbers of **nuclear weapons** and a deployment and use doctrine to provide a second-strike capability.

ASSURED VULNERABILITY. The foundational concept underlying **Cold War deterrence.** It is based on societal vulnerability and the belief that assured nuclear retaliatory capability provides deterrence. Rational states then avoid extreme provocation in cognizance of their vulnerability to retaliation. This concept required both sides to remain defenseless against attack. *See also* ACTIVE DEFENSE; MUTUAL ASSURED DESTRUCTION.

ASYMMETRICAL CUTS. Uneven reductions in numbers or categories of weapons. Asymmetrical cuts are features of many **arms control** treaties and are one way to enhance **confidence-building** and security measures between adversaries.

ATHENS-PERSIA ACCORD (448 B.C.). Also known as the Peace of Callias, this early **arms control** agreement was intended to demilitarize the Aegean Sea.

ATLANTIC CHARTER (1941). The Atlantic Charter was a joint declaration between the **United States** and **Great Britain** asserting that neither side sought any recompense nor territorial changes from World War II. Signed aboard a U.S. naval vessel on 12 August 1941, **Winston Churchill** and **Franklin Roosevelt** committed each other to peacefully and jointly resolving the world's problems following the war.

ATLANTIC TO THE URALS (ATTU). The traditional geographic area of interest in European **arms control**; "Greater Europe" in security terms. The concept of ATTU was particularly important as the region of concern in the 1990 **Conventional Forces in Europe Treaty** (CFE).

ATLAS MISSILE. Along with the **Titan missile**, the first generation of **United States intercontinental ballistic missiles** (ICBM) in the 1950s. The Atlas program was the top priority defense project in the late 1950s, as the United States rushed to match the **Soviet Union's** perceived lead in deploying intercontinental missiles. It went from full funding to first launch in two years. The first variants of this missile were above-ground launched, and they required liquid fueling just prior to launch. Built by Convair, they were first deployed in the western United States in 1958. The Atlas was retired from military service in 1965 as new, more reliable generations of ICBMs were deployed. The Atlas served as the rocket in the U.S. Mercury manned space program and launched early astronauts into orbit. Versions of the Atlas are still built by the Lockheed-Martin company and used for commercial space launches.

ATLEE, CLEMENT (1883-1967). Prime minister of Great Britain from 1945 to 1951, replacing **Winston Churchill** (and subsequently replaced by Churchill following the 1951 elections). A liberal internationalist, he favored closer relations with the **Soviet Union** and only reluctantly authorized the secret development (with help from the **United States**) of Britain's **atomic bomb**.

ATOMIC BOMB. A powerful explosive device based on energy from **uranium** or **plutonium fission**. First developed by the **United**

States and tested in New Mexico in July 1945. It was used on the cities of Hiroshima and Nagasaki, Japan, in August 1945. *See also* FISSION WEAPON; FUSION WEAPON; MANHATTAN PROJECT; TRINITY SITE.

ATOMIC ENERGY ACT (1947). Also known as the McMahon Act. This act placed the **United States atomic bomb** program under clear civilian control. The Act created the **Atomic Energy Commission** (AEC). The AEC was given sole responsibility for research and development, manufacture, and delivery of atomic weapons to the military, as well as civilian applications of atomic energy.

ATOMIC ENERGY COMMISSION (AEC). The principal **United States** government agency responsible for the design and production of **atomic bombs** following World War II. Created by the **Atomic Energy Act** of 1947, the AEC was subsequently (1970s) and briefly incorporated into the Federal Energy Agency, which in turn became part of the **Department of Energy**. *See also* NUCLEAR REGULATORY COMMISSION.

ATOMS FOR PEACE PROPOSAL. A proposal made in December 1953 by **United States** President **Dwight Eisenhower** in a speech to the **United Nations** General Assembly for the nuclear powers to provide an amount of **fissile material** to the control of an international organization that would oversee the use of that material by various countries for "peaceful" purposes such as power production and research. The proposal was initially rejected by the **Soviet Union**, but it eventually led to the formation of the **International Atomic Energy Agency** (IAEA).

AUSTRALIA GROUP. An **export control regime** formalized in June 1985 in response to the use of **chemical weapons** in the **Iran-Iraq War**. Its purpose was to monitor and control the trade in sensitive materials and technologies useful in the development of chemical and **biological weapons**. The 32 member states, all industrialized nations, assure that their national export control programs are fully consistent and compatible with the **Chemical Weapons Convention** and the **Biological Weapons Convention**. They drew up a control list of **dual-use** chemicals, facilities, equipment, and related technology that could have both commercial and military application. They meet annually in Paris to exchange data and coordinate actions. The group has no charter; it operates by consensus.

AUSTRIAN STATE TREATY. The 1955 vehicle by which states recognized the formal declaration of perpetual **neutrality** by Austria. Austria foreswore membership in any alliance, or the establishment of any foreign bases on its territory; it also promised not to pursue weapons of mass destruction.

B

B-1 BOMBER (Lancer). A nuclear-capable, four-engine, high-subsonic speed, intercontinental **United States strategic bomber** with variable geometry wings. Production of the B-1 was deferred by President **Jimmy Carter**, but the B-1 was put into production by President **Ronald Reagan**. Built by Rockwell, it first flew in 1974 and was delivered to the **U.S. Air Force** in 1985. One hundred were built. The United States agreed to convert the B-1 to a conventional-only bomber in the **Strategic Arms Reduction Treaty** (START II). Its first combat mission took place in the 1998 strikes against Iraq.

B-2 STEALTH BOMBER (Spirit). A **United States**, intercontinental, subsonic, four-engine **strategic bomber** that incorporates low-radar visibility technology. Built by the Northrop Grumman Corporation, it first flew in 1989 and was publicly unveiled in 1993. The B-2 was first used in combat operations in Kosovo (**Operation Allied Force**) in 1999. Twenty-one were built, at a unit cost of some two billion dollars each (when research and development costs are factored in).

B-52 BOMBER (Stratofortress). A **United States** subsonic, eight-engine intercontinental **strategic bomber** that serves today as an **air-launched cruise missile** launch platform. First flown in 1952, 744 in eight variants were built by the Boeing Company and delivered to the **U.S. Air Force** between 1955 and 1962. The B-52 was used extensively as a conventional bomber and **cruise missile** carrier in conflicts in Vietnam, the Gulf War, Kosovo, Afghanistan, and **Iraq.** It also served as the primary U.S. nuclear **alert** bomber during the **Cold War**. It has a range greater than 10,000 miles, is capable of in-flight refueling, and has a crew of six.

BACKFIRE BOMBER. A Soviet intercontinental-range, twin-engine, supersonic bomber. The Backfire was considered to be a **strategic**

bomber by the **United States** in the **Strategic Arms Limitation Treaty** (SALT) and **Strategic Arms Reduction Treaty** (START) **negotiations**. The Soviets/Russians claimed that it should be considered a medium bomber exempt from the treaty limits because of its restricted range without refueling. Resembling the American FB-111, it was designated the Tupolev Tu-26. Its production was limited by the SALT II Treaty.

BACTERIA. Simple, microscopic **organisms.** Some bacteria cause diseases, while others are essential to the production of **biological agents.**

BADGER BOMBER. An early **Soviet Union** medium-range nuclear bomber designated the Tupolev Tu-16. It had its first flight in 1952, and nearly 600 were produced.

BAKER, JAMES A. III (1930-). Secretary of the treasury and White House chief of staff during the **Ronald Reagan** administration, and secretary of state under President **George H.W. Bush**. Baker helped lead the world out of the **Cold War** in the early 1990s. Among his successes was signing a memorandum of agreement with Soviet Foreign Minister **Edouard Shevardnadze** in 1989 that laid out the parameters for the eventual **Chemical Weapons Convention.**

BALLISTIC MISSILE. A ballistic missile is a rocket that fires its engines and then allows momentum and gravity to carry its cargo to its intended target. It follows a trajectory without additional power after its initial thrust phase, relying on gravity and atmospheric drag to bring it back to earth. Most long-range ballistic missiles have two or more rocket motors, called stages, to sequentially propel the missile. Ballistic missiles are usually armed with one or more **nuclear warheads** inside a **reentry vehicle** that is aligned and released at the proper point in the missile's flight, and they operate beyond the earth's atmosphere for a portion of their flight. Recent technological advances have allowed ballistic missiles to become highly accurate. They were first developed by the **United States** and the **Soviet Union** in the late 1950s.

BALLISTIC MISSILE DEFENSE (BMD). The defense of one's territory, allies, or forces abroad against **ballistic missiles** launched from another country or from the sea. This is a class of systems designed to detect, track, and destroy ballistic missiles en route to their targets.

BALLISTIC MISSILE DEFENSE ORGANIZATION (BMDO). The **Department of Defense** organization that oversaw the development of the **United States' ballistic missile defense** system from May 1993 through January 2002. Successor to the **Strategic Defense Initiative Organization,** it was, in turn, succeeded by the **Missile Defense Agency.** BMDO's primary assigned mission was to focus on the development of **theater missile defense** capabilities.

BALLISTIC MISSILE EARLY WARNING SYSTEM (BMEWS). An early **Cold War United States** radar system consisting of large **phased array radars** located at Clear, Alaska; Thule, Greenland; and Fylingdales Moor, Great Britain. It was designed to provide **ballistic missile** attack warning in the event of a Soviet **intercontinental ballistic missile** attack. BMEWS would provide approximately 15 minutes warning to allow United States nuclear forces to respond prior to detonation.

BALLISTIC MISSILE LAUNCH NOTIFICATION AGREE-MENT (1988). A **confidence-building measure** agreed to between the **United States** and the **Soviet Union** to provide the other side 24-hours notice prior to the launch of any **intercontinental ballistic missile** or **submarine-launched ballistic missile**.

BANDWAGONING. A political theory that explains why a person or group joins forces with another person or group whose position appears likely to win a competition or election (or succeed in finalizing an **arms control negotiation** or **agreement**).

BARGAINING CHIP. A weapon system, existing or planned, that is bargained away, restricted, or deferred in **negotiations** in exchange for a concession.

BARRAGE. An employment tactic designed to overwhelm **active defenses** such as an **antiballistic missile** system by firing large numbers of weapons so that they all reach the defended area simultaneously.

BARUCH, BERNARD (1870-1965). American financier, politician, and diplomat, Baruch served as chief U.S. negotiator to the **United Nations** in the 1950s. *See also* BARUCH PLAN.

BARUCH PLAN. The proposal put forward by the administration of **United States** President **Harry Truman** in 1946 to eliminate all **nuclear weapons** and place the control of the development and use of atomic energy, including atomic materials, under an independent international authority under the auspices of the **United Nations**. It was also known as the Dumbarton Oaks Plan. Against the protestations of Secretary of State **Dean Acheson**, author of the plan, **Bernard Baruch** added provisions that the **Soviet Union** found objectionable, such as swift and sure punishment for those who violated the rules. The Soviet Union responded by calling for universal nuclear **disarmament**. In the end, the UN adopted neither proposal. The Soviet Union rejected the plan in 1949.

BASELINE INSPECTION. The initial inspection in implementing an **arms control agreement**, it establishes the foundation numbers and status against which future inspection results can be compared.

BASIC PRINCIPLES AGREEMENT (1972). A general **agreement** meant to codify the principles of **détente** between the **United States** and **Soviet Union** and a willingness to achieve normal relations with the Soviets on the basis of equality. President **Richard Nixon** insisted on both sides signing this at the **Moscow Summit** where he also signed the **Anti-Ballistic Missile Treaty** (ABM) and the **Interim Agreement on the Limitation of Strategic Offensive Arms** (together these two agreements were called the **Strategic Arms Limitation Treaty**, or SALT I).

BATTLEFIELD NUCLEAR WEAPONS. *See* NONSTRATEGIC NUCLEAR WEAPONS.

BEAR BOMBER. The mainstay **Soviet Union/Russian strategic bomber** introduced during the **Cold War** and still in service today. It was unusual in that it was not a jet; rather, it was powered by six turboprop engines. The Tupolev Tu-95 first flew in 1954; it had a range of 7,800 miles.

BELARUS. One of four republics of the **Soviet Union** in which **nuclear weapons**, components, and systems were present at the time of dissolution in 1991. All nuclear weapons were consolidated under Russian control in 1992.

BILATERAL ARMS CONTROL. Cooperative efforts and agreements between two **state parties**. During the **Cold War**, the central focus of **strategic** arms control efforts was the bilateral series of negotiations and agreements between the nuclear superpowers, the **United States** and the **Soviet Union**.

BILATERAL IMPLEMENTATION COMMISSION (BIC). The Bilateral Implementation Commission was first created in 1992 to serve as the governing body of the **Strategic Arms Reduction Treaty** (START II) **compliance** and **verification regime** between the **United States** and **Russia.** It met in Geneva, Switzerland. The Commission was reinstituted in 2002 to serve as the **implementation** forum for the **Strategic Offensive Reductions Treaty** (SORT). Meeting in Geneva, it held its first meeting with full delegations from both states in fall 2003.

BINARY CHEMICAL WEAPON. A weapon containing two separated chemical substances that mix together upon employment to produce a **chemical agent**. This design was considered far safer for handling and transportation than a traditional unitary warhead, since the **payload** was not toxic prior to firing.

BIOLOGICAL. Related to biology or life sciences.

BIOLOGICAL AGENT. A **microorganism** or **toxin** produced by a living **organism** that causes disease or incapacitation in humans, plants, or animals.

BIOLOGICAL DEFENSE. Measures taken to protect or defend against attacks employing **biological agents**. These measures can include such **passive defense** measures as inoculation, protective clothing and masks, or the use of counter agents.

BIOLOGICAL AND TOXIN WEAPONS CONVENTION (BWC). Building on the **Geneva Protocol** of 1925, which bans the use of chemical and biological weapons in war, the "Convention on the Prohibition of the Development, Production, and Stockpiling of Bacteriological (Biological) and Toxin Weapons and on Their Destruction" was signed on 10 April 1972 and ratified by the **United**

States Senate on 26 March 1975. It **entered into force** on the same date with an unlimited duration. The convention bans the development, production, stockpiling, and acquisition of **biological weapons** and the delivery systems of such **agents**.

An Ad Hoc Group met in several sessions between March 1992 and September 1993 to identify, examine, and evaluate potential methods of **verification**. Twenty-one potential verification measures, including **on-site inspections**, were identified and evaluated. It was clear that an effective verification **regime** would have to rely on several different measures. The need to protect sensitive commercial property and intellectual information was also identified.

The United States declared that it had destroyed all of its biological weapons by 26 December 1975. Yet it became increasingly clear that the Soviet BW program violated the BWC for years thereafter. President **Boris Yeltsin** admitted in 1992 that the **Soviet Union** had maintained a **biological weapon** program after the treaty entered into force.

In September 1992 trilateral negotiations between the United States, **United Kingdom**, and the **Russian Federation** began in an effort to resolve compliance concerns and improve verification methods. These talks became multinational in 1995 as efforts grew to develop a protocol to the BWC that would address verification and compliance issues. A special conference of the **state parties** to the convention in September 1994 ordered the creation of an ad hoc group to negotiate a legally binding verification and compliance protocol to the treaty. The ad hoc group began using a rolling text draft protocol in the summer of 1997. In March 2001 the BWC chairman released his own draft protocol, which was circulated for comment and consideration. In July 2001 a U.S. interagency review under the **George W. Bush** administration determined that the United States should not accept a protocol that could not prevent cheating. The November 2001 BWC review conference ended in disarray.

BIOLOGICAL WARFARE (BW). Biological warfare refers to the use of living organisms or toxins produced by living organisms as weapons against humans, animals, or plants. While the effects of a bioterrorist incident could have far-reaching ramifications, generally speaking these would be smaller in scale and would probably employ less sophisticated technology than in state-level BW programs. BW agents have already been utilized in modern-day acts of **terrorism,** albeit with relatively small impact in terms of total casualties (including both injuries and deaths). For example, several people died and a dozen others were infected in 2001 by anthrax spores that were mailed through the U.S. postal system by an unknown perpetrator.

Before renouncing the use of BW in 1969, the **United States** possessed a significant stockpile of **biological weapons** systems. The **Soviet Union** had at least a rudimentary program since the 1920s, and continued to develop BW agents and delivery devices long after pledging not to do so (from about 1975 to 1990). The Soviet Union researched, developed, and produced large quantities of potent BW agents including anthrax, smallpox, and plague for loading onto warheads that could hit U.S.-based targets (using **intercontinental ballistic missiles**). During the **Cold War,** the two **superpowers** had the capability of inflicting hundreds of thousands of biological casualties with the use of such weapons. Both countries, as well as many others who are party to the 1972 **Biological and Toxin Weapons Convention** (BWC), have agreed to ban the possession, research, and development of offensive biological weapons. But there exists today the possibility that other states could develop BW programs that could attain or even exceed the level of devastating potential once held solely by the United States and the former Soviet Union.

One would expect to have large numbers of casualties (in the thousands and even millions) caused by the large-scale delivery of BW agents suited for military (**counterforce**) or civilian (**countervalue**) targets. In fact, next to nuclear weaponry, biological weapons pose the greatest threat in terms of causing mass casualties. The major differences between nuclear warfare and BW include the lack of persistent contamination following the use of biological weaponry and the fact that biological munitions do not damage physical structures (such as buildings or other infrastructure). Biological weapons might be more accurately referred to as "mass casualty weapons" instead of **weapons of mass destruction** (WMD). *See also* CHEMICAL WARFARE; CHEMICAL WEAPONS.

BIOLOGICAL WEAPON (BW). Living **organisms** or materials derived from them used in a weaponized form to cause death or incapacitation.

BISHOPS' PASTORAL LETTER. Tensions within the Catholic Church between contrasting views over the legality of nuclear war resulted in the American Catholic bishops issuing a pastoral letter in May 1983, entitled "The Challenge of Peace." The American bishops condemned any policy that deliberately targeted noncombatants. They judged nuclear **deterrence** morally acceptable not as an end in itself but only as a stage toward progressive **disarmament**— a position articulated by Pope John Paul II in his message to the **United Nations** Special Session on Disarmament in 1982. They also opposed any policy of **first use** of **nuclear weapons**. This position was reaffirmed in 1993 by the American bishops in a new letter, also entitled "The Challenge of Peace."

BISON BOMBER. A **Soviet Union/Russian strategic bomber**, lighter than the **Bear bomber** but jet-engine powered.

BLACKJACK BOMBER. The most modern Russian **strategic bomber**, the Blackjack began flight tests in 1982 and came into operational service at the very end of the **Cold War**. Its design was much like the American **B-1 bomber**.

BLINDER BOMBER. A supersonic Soviet short-range bomber that entered the inventory in 1960, designated the Tupolev Tu-22.

BLISTER AGENT. Chemical warfare agents that damage tissue. A blister agent can affect the eyes, respiratory tract, or skin.

BLIX, HANS (1928-). Director general of the **International Atomic Energy Agency** from 1981 to 1997 following a career in the Swedish Ministry of Foreign Affairs, Blix was instrumental in dealing with Iraq's efforts to develop **nuclear weapons** and the world's attempts to prevent that, primarily through the **United Nations Special Commission on Iraq** beginning in 1991. Blix came out of retirement in 2000 to head up the **United Nations Monitoring, Verification, and Inspection Commission**.

BLOOD AGENT. Cyanide-based **chemical warfare agents** that block the transfer of oxygen from the blood into body tissue. They are fast acting and deadly to humans.

BOLT FROM THE BLUE ATTACK. A surprise attack that comes during a time of relatively low tension, thus increasing its shock effect. Such an attack would likely be designed to catch the target offguard and cripple its military capability. *See also* FIRST USE; PREEMPTION.

BOMBER. An aircraft that is capable of delivery of bombs and other weapons such as **cruise missiles**. Long-range bombers have an unrefueled range of greater than 6,000 miles, while medium bombers have unrefueled ranges in the category 3,500 to 6,000 miles, and short-range bombers fall below 3,500 miles.

BOMBER GAP. In the 1950s, the **United States**, under President **Dwight Eisenhower**, built its military strategy around its **strategic bomber** force. The arms buildup in the **Soviet Union** proceeded at a faster pace than had been anticipated in the West, and this resulted in the fear of a "bomber gap" in which American **strategic** forces would be insufficient to deter the Soviets. Eisenhower supposedly closed this perceived gap by increasing the size of the United States fleet of **B-52 bombers**. **John F. Kennedy** campaigned on this presumed gap in the 1960 presidential campaign, which was ultimately proved false after he took office.

BOOST PHASE. The initial phase of flight in the trajectory of a **ballistic missile** lasting from launch through the burnout of the engines of the final stage.

BOOST-PHASE INTERCEPT. Intercept of a **ballistic missile** during its initial phase of flight (while the missile's engines are burning). Missile defense systems aim toward **boost-phase** intercept whenever possible because the **ballistic missile** is most structurally vulnerable during the gravitational force loading that characterizes this phase. In addition, a **warhead** from a destroyed missile—if not itself destroyed—would fall back to earth close to its launch site.

BOOSTED FISSION WEAPON. Thermonuclear weapon in which the energy produced by the nuclear reaction is used to enhance the fission process rather than to directly produce the explosion, thereby greatly magnifying the energy of the explosion.

BOTTOM-UP REVIEW. A comprehensive review of **United States national security strategy** and military force structure for the post-**Cold War** environment. It was conducted by Secretary of Defense **Les Aspin** during the first year of the **William Clinton** administration (1993-1994). While the Bottom Up Review focused on macro strategy and conventional force structure, its companion **Nuclear Posture Review** reaffirmed a continuing role for **nuclear weapons** and recommended a post-Cold War nuclear force strategy and structure.

BRANDT, WILLY (1913-1992). Chancellor of West Germany 1969 to 1974, where he was the leading proponent of the policy of *Ostpolitik* and improved relations with East Germany and its neighboring **Warsaw Pact** states. In 1970 he concluded the **Warsaw Treaty** with Poland and a Moscow Treaty with the **Soviet Union**, both of which reduced **Cold War** tensions in Central Europe and furthered the process of **détente**. These efforts earned him the Nobel Peace Prize in 1971.

BRAZILIAN-ARGENTINE AGENCY FOR ACCOUNTING AND CONTROL OF NUCLEAR MATERIALS (ABACC). The "Agencia Brasileno-Argentina de Contabilidad y Control de Materiales Nucleares" is a bilateral agency created in the **Guadalajara Agreement** of 1991 to administer the **Joint System for Accounting and Control of Nuclear Materials** that was also established in the agreement.

BREAKOUT. The sudden and complete abrogation of an **arms control agreement** characterized by the large-scale deployment of controlled weapons so as to tip the military balance of power.

BREEDER REACTOR. A type of nuclear reactor that produces more **fissile material** than it consumes. Fissile material is produced both in the core and in neutron-receptive material around the core (a process known as "breeding"). This type of reactor uses liquid metals rather than water as a moderator. The **uranium** absorbs the neutrons produced by the fissile activity, creating more **plutonium** than is normally produced in a traditional water-cooled reactor. Plutonium, fissile uranium (U-235), and other **radioactive** elements can then be removed from the moderating rods through a chemical **reprocessing** process. Fast breeder reactors are located in Japan, **Russia**, and **India. France, Great Britain**, the **United States**, and **Kazakhstan** have all put an end to their fast breeder reactor programs.

BREZHNEV, LEONID I (1906-1982). Soviet Union leader during the period 1964-1982, a period largely characterized by **super-**

power strategic parity and **détente**. Brezhnev was the Soviet force behind the **Strategic Arms Limitation Talks** (SALT) and the **SALT I** treaty. He met **United States** President **Gerald Ford** at **Vladivostok, Russia**, in November 1974, forging a preliminary agreement for what became **SALT II** later in his tenure.

BRILLIANT PEBBLES. A midcourse **strategic defense** concept that became part of the **Ronald Reagan** administration's **Strategic Defense Initiative** and carried over into the **George H.W. Bush** plan for **Global Protection Against Limited Strikes**. The system consisted of thousands of autonomous interceptors in low-earth orbit that would independently intercept and destroy **ballistic missiles** en route to their target. With survivability provided by the large numbers and small size of the orbiting interceptors, brilliant pebbles systems were envisioned to stay in orbit for up to 10 years.

BRINKMANSHIP. The **United States/Soviet Union** practice of challenging the other side following advantageous changes in the **strategic** balance, seemingly pushing the challenged side to the "brink" of nuclear confrontation. After the **Cuban Missile Crisis**, this practice was replaced by serious **arms control negotiations**.

BRODIE, BERNARD (1910-1978). Considered the dean of American nuclear strategists during the **Cold War**, Brodie was affiliated with Yale University and the **RAND Corporation**. His 1946 book, *The Absolute Weapon*, was the first major work on nuclear strategy. While Brodie at times contributed to **counterforce** targeting and nuclear **warfighting strategy** arguments, at the beginning and end of his career he argued that **nuclear war** could not be won and that nuclear **parity** was the route to stable **deterrence**.

BROOKINGS INSTITUTION. A privately funded research and analysis organization (or "think tank") located in Washington, D.C. The Brookings Institution is particularly strong in political science, U.S. government and budgetary analysis, and international relations.

BRUSSELS DECLARATION ON CONVENTIONAL ARMS CONTROL (1986). In December 1986 the **North Atlantic Treaty Organization** (NATO) members agreed to meet with the **Warsaw Pact** to consider mutual military reductions in Europe from the **Atlantic to the Urals**. In so doing, NATO announced that it would only consider **arms control** if it improved the military situation of the Alliance by establishing stability at lower force levels. This declaration began the process that led to the 1989 treaty on **Conventional Forces in Europe.**

BRZEZINSKI, ZBIEGNIEW (1928–). Polish émigré to the **United States** who taught international relations at Columbia University. He became national security advisor under President **Jimmy Carter** and formed a hard-line anticommunist balance to the more liberal Secretary of State **Cyrus Vance.** Brzezinski was a key sponsor of **PD-59,** which called for an American military buildup in response to the Soviet invasion of Afghanistan in 1979.

BULGANIN, NIKOLAI (1895-1975). Soviet premier 1955-1958. A protégé of **Josef Stalin** and supporter of **Nikita Krushchev,** Bulganin was a career diplomat who led the Soviet delegation at the 1955 **Geneva Summit.**

BULL, HEDLEY (1932-1985). An early and seminal influence on **Cold War** thinking on **arms control** and **disarmament** in the nuclear age. His 1961 book, *The Control of the Arms Race: Disarmament and Arms Control in the Missile Age,* is considered one of the foundational works in the field and is widely credited with establishing the modern distinction between the control of arms and their effects (arms control), on the one hand, and the elimination of weapon systems (disarmament), on the other.

BUNDY, McGEORGE (1919-1996). National security advisor to United States Presidents **John Kennedy** and **Lyndon Johnson.** While in government Bundy was a supporter of Defense Secretary **Robert McNamara's** policy of **assured destruction.** After leaving government service Bundy later wrote in support of much smaller nuclear arsenals.

BUNDY, WILLIAM P. (1917–). Older brother of **McGeorge Bundy,** William was a career intelligence officer and diplomat whose role in the State Department helped shape American policy during the Vietnam War. After leaving government service he served as editor of the journal *Foreign Affairs* from 1972 to 1984.

BURT, RICHARD (1947–). Former reporter for the *New York Times.* Beginning in 1981 he served as Director of Politico-Military Affairs in the **Department of State**, Assistant Secretary of State for European and Canadian Affairs, and U.S. Ambassador to the Federal Republic of Germany from 1985 to 1989 during the **Ronald Reagan** administration. He was instrumental in negotiating the **Strategic Arms Reduction Treaties** (START I and II).

BUS. A small rocket that carries multiple **nuclear weapons** on top of a **ballistic missile**. The bus maneuvers after the **boost phase** of the trajectory to position each **warhead** at the correct point, velocity, and trajectory to strike its individual target.

BUSH, GEORGE H. W. (1924-). United States president from 1989-1993. Father of President **George W. Bush**. A former **U.S. Navy** pilot, his government career included service as director of the **Central Intelligence Agency** and vice president under **Ronald Reagan**. His administration oversaw the dissolution of the **Soviet Union** and the end of the **Cold War**, as well as the greatest reduction in the **strategic** nuclear arsenals of the two states, including the **Strategic Arms Reduction Treaties** (START I and II).

BUSH, GEORGE W. (1946-). United States president inaugurated in 2001. The son of President **George H.W. Bush**, his administration withdrew from the **Anti-Ballistic Missile Treaty** and refused to sign a verification protocol for the **Biological and Toxin Weapons Convention**, but it also negotiated the **Strategic Offensive Reductions Treaty** in 2002. His administration was known for its endeavors to halt the **proliferation** of **weapons of mass destruction** into the hands of such "**rogue states**" as **Iraq**, **Iran**, and **North Korea**, as well as from nonstate **terrorists**.

BUTLER, LEE (1939 -). Air Force general officer; last commander of **Strategic Air Command** and first commander of **Strategic Command** during the transition between the two commands in 1992. He became a staunch advocate of nuclear **disarmament** following retirement from the military in 1994.

C

CAMEROON INITIATIVE (1984). A call in the **United Nations** General Assembly for the UN to undertake a comprehensive review of its entire **disarmament** program. It called for more concrete roles by the UN. The net effect was to revitalize and energize UN **disarmament** efforts outside of the **superpower** nuclear arena.

CAMP DAVID ACCORDS (1978). An **agreement** brokered by **United States** President **Jimmy Carter** between **Israel** and Egypt that ended a three-decade state of war between those two nations. The United States guaranteed a rough military balance between the two sides, providing arms to both of the former antagonists.

CAMPAIGN FOR NUCLEAR DISARMAMENT (CND). A **peace movement** founded in New Zealand in 1959, with an Australia branch formed the following year. The CND was a leader in the opposition to the 1960s **nuclear testing** in the Southern Hemisphere, particularly by **France** and the **United Kingdom**. This process ultimately contributed to the declaration, in 1985, of the **South Pacific Nuclear Free Zone**. CND became active in Great Britain in the early 1980s opposition to the deployment of **intermediate-range nuclear forces** in Europe by both the **North Atlantic Treaty Organization** and the **Warsaw Pact**. *See also* TREATY OF RAROTONGA.

CANBERRA COMMISSION. The Canberra Commission on the Elimination of Nuclear Weapons was established as an independent commission by the Australian Government in November 1995 to propose practical steps toward a nuclear weapon-free world, including the related problem of maintaining stability and security during the transitional period and after this goal is achieved.

CARCINOGEN. A cancer-causing substance or **agent**.

CARNEGIE ENDOWMENT FOR WORLD PEACE. A U.S. research and analysis center located in Washington, D.C. An offshoot of the philanthropic Carnegie Endowment, it is particularly strong in studies of international affairs.

CARTER, JAMES EARL (JIMMY) (1924-). United States president from 1977-1981. He signed the **Strategic Arms Limitation Treaty** (SALT II), cancelled the **B-1 bomber** program and the enhanced neutron weapon (the **neutron bomb**), and negotiated the **Camp David Accords** between Egypt and **Israel** (1978).

CATALYSIS. Addition of a substance to increase the speed of a chemical reaction.

CATALYST. A substance that increases or decreases the speed of a chemical reaction, or causes a particular reaction to occur.

CATALYTIC WAR. A small-scale conflict that accelerates into a larger conflict involving a nuclear power, or a conflict between two powers precipitated by a third party.

CATO INSTITUTE. The Cato Institute is a nonprofit public policy research foundation founded in 1977 and headquartered in Washington, D.C. The Institute is named for Cato's Letters, a series of libertarian pamphlets that helped lay the philosophical foundation for the American Revolution. The Cato Institute seeks to broaden the parameters of public policy debate to allow consideration of the traditional American principles of limited government, individual liberty, free markets, and peace. Toward that goal, the Institute strives to achieve greater involvement of the intelligent, concerned lay public in questions of policy and the proper role of government.

C-CUBED (C3). See COMMAND, CONTROL, AND COMMUNICATIONS.

C-CUBED-I (C3I). See COMMAND, CONTROL, COMMUNICATIONS, AND INTELLIGENCE.

CENTER FOR NATIONAL SECURITY STUDIES (CNSS). A research and analysis center located at **Los Alamos National Laboratory**, New Mexico, which operated from 1986 to 1995.

CENTER FOR STRATEGIC AND INTERNATIONAL STUDIES (CSIS). One of the largest and most well-respected research centers in Washington, D.C., CSIS was founded in the early 1960s and has a staff of nearly 200 analysts. Its nonpartisan studies address the full spectrum of new challenges to national and international security, regional issues, governance, technology and public policy, international trade, and energy.

CENTERS FOR DISEASE CONTROL (AND PREVENTION) (CDC). A set of U.S. government-sponsored research laboratories that deal with diseases, viruses, biological agents, and pathogens. The CDC is empowered with releasing national warnings and restrictions upon confirmation of a dangerous biological situation. The CDC is based in Atlanta, Georgia.

CENTRAL AMERICAN ARMS PACT. A 1923 regional arms limitation pact, also known as the "Convention for the Limitation of Armaments," between Costa Rica, El Salvador, Guatemala, Honduras, and Nicaragua. The Pact was pushed by the **United States**, which wanted internal regional stability in support of general security for the Panama Canal. The Pact capped the size of the national armies of the parties and supported the development of national constabularies instead of standing military forces. It had only limited success.

CENTRAL ASIA NUCLEAR WEAPONS FREE ZONE. An agreement between Uzbekistan, **Kazakhstan**, Tajikistan, Kyrgyzstan, and Turkmenistan to ban all production, testing, and admittance of **nuclear weapons** into the region. The agreement was reached in October 2002 after five years of negotiations. This was the first **nuclear free zone** negotiated under the auspices of the **United Nations**. **Entry into force** was still on hold as of mid-2004, as the five Central Asian states were awaiting endorsement by the five **nuclear weapons states** before final treaty formalization.

CENTRAL INTELLIGENCE AGENCY (CIA). The United States' foremost national intelligence collection and analysis organization, headquartered in McLean, Virginia. The director of the CIA is a key member of the president's cabinet and sits on the **National Security Council.**

CENTRAL NERVOUS SYSTEM (CNS). The human system that controls mental and voluntary muscular activity, and coordinates involuntary muscular activity, including the brain and spinal chord.

CENTRAL TREATY ORGANIZATION (CENTO). The Central Treaty Organization was an alliance between Turkey, **Iran, Pakistan,** and **Great Britain** for mutual defense. It originated as the Baghdad Pact, signed by Turkey and **Iraq** in 1955. Later that year Great Britain, Pakistan, and Iran joined the alliance. Iraq withdrew after a revolution in 1958, and the headquarters of the alliance was moved to Ankara, Turkey. In 1959 the name was changed from

Baghdad Pact to Central Treaty Organization. The **United States** was closely associated with CENTO from its inception but did not become a full member. The alliance collapsed with the withdrawal of Iran, Pakistan, and Turkey after the Iranian revolution in 1979.

CERTAIN CONVENTIONAL WEAPONS CONVENTION (CCW). The "Convention on Prohibitions or Restrictions on Use of Certain Conventional Weapons Which May be Deemed to be Excessively Injurious or to Have Indiscriminate Effects" (also known as the Convention on Certain Conventional Weapons). It was opened for signature in 1981 and **entered into force** on 2 December 1983. The convention's purpose is to regulate conventional weapons that risk indiscriminate damage and injury to civilians or can cause unnecessary suffering. There are currently 88 **state parties** to the **treaty** that have agreed to one or more of the four protocols involving restrictions on the manufacture, stockpiling, and use of certain conventional weapons. The first three protocols cover nondetectable fragmentation weapons; mines, booby traps, and other devices; and incendiary weapons. During the 1995-1996 review conference, a fourth protocol was added addressing blinding laser weapons. A review conference in December 2001 discussed the possibility of expanding the convention to internal conflicts rather than its current focus on international conflicts. The review conference also examined inspection, compliance, and enforcement measures.

C-FOUR-ISR (C4ISR). *See* COMMAND, CONTROL, COMMUNICATIONS, COMPUTERS, INTELLIGENCE, SURVEILLANCE, AND RECONNAISSANCE.

CHAIN REACTION. Neutrons produced in a nuclear reaction induce subsequent **fission** reactions, thus creating a series of reactions that are sustained as long as each fission produces another fission.

CHAIRMAN OF THE JOINT CHIEFS OF STAFF (CJCS). The senior officer in the **United States** military. Prior to 1986, the chairman was largely "first among equals" of the committee of the chiefs of the military services. With the passage of the 1986 Goldwater-Nichols **Department of Defense** Reorganization Act, the chairman became the principal military adviser to the president and the secretary of defense. The Chairman's Joint Staff also became the principal representative body of the uniformed military within the United States government interagency process on all national security policy issues, including **arms control** and nuclear strategy.

CHALLENGE INSPECTION. A nonroutine, usually short-notice inspection requested by a **state party** as provided for in an **arms control agreement** of any facility in the territory of or in any other place under the jurisdiction or control of another state party. Such inspection may be requested as a result of a noncompliance concern of the requesting state party under the provisions of several current and emerging arms control agreements. Some agreements specify a right of refusal. Treaties that apply challenge inspections include the **Chemical Weapons Convention** (CWC) and the **Strategic Arms Reduction Treaty** (START I).

CHARTER OF PARIS FOR A NEW EUROPE. A 1990 declaration by the **Conference on Security and Cooperation in Europe** to encourage the development of post-**Cold War** peace and security in Europe and to encourage cooperation on economic and human rights issues. The Charter was a major instrument in easing the transition of Europe out of the Cold War.

CHEMICAL AGENT. A chemical substance intended to kill, severely injure, or incapacitate. Chemical agents include **blister, blood, choking, incapacitating,** and **nerve agents**. Specifically not included in this category are **riot control agents, herbicides,** and **flame agents**.

CHEMICAL AND BIOLOGICAL WARFARE (CBW). *See* BIOLOGICAL WARFARE; BIOLOGICAL WEAPONS; CHEMICAL WARFARE; CHEMICAL WEAPONS; CHEMICAL WEAPONS CONVENTION.

CHEMICAL WARFARE (CW). Chemical warfare is the use of toxic chemicals in battle. "Gas warfare" is a throwback to World War I-era terms such as "poison gas," because the earlier battlefield employment of chemicals was indeed in the form of gases. In the modern era, however, chemical compounds used in warfare or **terrorism** can take the form of liquids, solids, or gases.

As mass casualty weapons, chemicals cause death or injury by their poisonous effects. All CW **agents** have two main characteristics: they are very poisonous in small quantities (high toxicity), and they have physical attributes that are amenable for use in weapons on the battlefield. CW agents and their **precursors** often are relatively easy to manufacture and store.

Chemical weapons can be distinguished between the CW agent—the **toxic** substance itself in the form of solid, liquid, or gas—and the weapon used to deliver the agent (bomb, artillery shell, etc.). Thus, a delivery system such as an artillery shell becomes a chemical weapon when filled with CW agent.

Chemical **terrorism** refers to smaller-scale attacks upon civilians or governmental institutions; and like CW, chemical terrorism is a rare occurrence. In 1994-1995, however, a political-religious organization called the Aum Shinrikyo (Sect of the Supreme Truth) in Japan used sarin nerve agent, an extremely lethal chemical agent, in two major attacks that killed at least 19 people. Sarin is a standard military CW agent that was stockpiled by both the United States and the former **Soviet Union** during the **Cold War**. Tens of thousands of tons of CW agents are still in storage, mostly in **Russia** and the **United States**, but these stockpiles are scheduled for destruction under the terms of the 1992 **Chemical Weapons Convention** (CWC).

Although the basic idea behind CW is simple, in practice a chemical attack against a modern military force is an extraordinarily challenging undertaking. One might think that in this modern industrial era there must be hundreds of toxic chemicals that could be effectively used as a means of warfare. In actuality, few are effective enough to be used in a battlefield setting. During World War I, for instance, traditional poisons such as hydrogen cyanide failed to produce mass casualties. Through deliberate scientific research and a good deal of trial and error, several basic chemicals have been identified that could pose a significant battlefield or terrorist threat: **nerve agents** (e.g., sarin); **blister agents** (mustard, Lewisite); **blood agents**, (hydrogen cyanide); **choking agents** such as phosgene and perfluoroisobutylene; and psychoincapacitants. *See also* CHEMICAL WEAPONS; CHEMICAL WEAPONS CONVENTION.

CHEMICAL WEAPONS (CW). Chemical weapons include **toxic** chemicals and their **precursors**, munitions, and devices specifically designed to cause death or serious harm through the toxic properties of the chemicals. CW also includes equipment specifically designed for direct use in conjunction with the employment of chemical munitions and devices. Chemical weapons include **blister, blood,**

choking, **incapacitating**, and **nerve agents**. *See also* CHEMICAL WARFARE; CHEMICAL WEAPONS CONVENTION.

CHEMICAL WEAPONS CONVENTION (CWC). The "Convention on the Prohibition of the Development, Production, Stockpiling, and Use of Chemical Weapons and on Their Destruction" (also called the Chemical Weapons Convention) is a multilateral **agreement** to ban the production, possession, transfer, and use of **chemical weapons** by all parties to the Convention. It was negotiated by the 39 nations (with 36 additional nations in observer status) of the **Conference on Disarmament.** After 12 years of negotiation, the convention was signed in Paris on 13 January 1993 by 130 nations. The number of signatories had grown to 182 states as of mid-2004. The ratification debate in the U.S. Senate was rancorous, but the convention was ratified on 24 April 1997. **Entry into force** occurred on 29 April 1997, 180 days after the 65th state ratified the convention.

The convention bans the development, production, stockpiling, transfer, acquisition, and both retaliatory and **first use** of chemical weapons. It also prohibits a state from aiding any other state, regardless of whether it is a party to the convention, in the pursuit of treaty-banned activities, which effectively institutes a **nonproliferation regime**. Additionally, parties were required to declare all chemical weapons and facilities no later than 30 days after entry into force and to destroy all chemical weapons within 10 years of the entry into force. It requires declarations on the production of other types of **precursor** and dual-purpose chemicals.

The **verification** regime includes routine, intrusive **on-site inspections** of declared government chemical weapons facilities as well as civilian facilities that use certain chemicals that could be used or converted to make weapons. In addition, short notice **challenge inspections** may be conducted at any facility where a party suspects illegal activities. Inspectors will be allowed to visit the site and investigate whether or not banned activities are taking place. The CWC is implemented by the **Organization for the Prohibition of Chemical Weapons (OPCW)**, in The Hague, Netherlands.

The **United States** and the **Soviet Union** entered into two bilateral agreements regarding chemical weapons in order to facilitate the Chemical Weapons Convention. The **memorandum of understanding** (MOU), signed at **Jackson Hole, Wyoming**, in 1989, called for two phases of data exchanges and visits/inspections of facilities. Phase I was completed in December 1989, when the United

States and the USSR declared that they had 29,000 and 40,000 agent metric tons, respectively. Phase II called for more detailed exchange of information and more thorough inspections. The second agreement is the Bilateral Destruction Agreement (BDA), signed in Washington, D.C., on 1 June 1990. The BDA bans CW production, provides a schedule for the destruction of all chemical weapons, and allows for on-site inspections. In a series of summit meetings between President **Boris Yeltsin** and Presidents **George H.W. Bush** and **William Clinton**, several advances were made. Yeltsin committed Russia to abide by the existing agreements and signed implementing documents, including a timeline, for Phase II of the Wyoming MOU. Additionally, the schedule was altered to delay reduction to 5,000 agent tons until December 2004 (a date later extended yet again to 2007). Financial assistance to help Russia meet these deadlines was provided by the United States under the **Nunn-Lugar Act**. An additional agreement signed at Tashkent by some members of the **Commonwealth of Independent States** (CIS) (Azerbaijan, Armenia, **Kazakhstan**, Kyrgyzstan, Moldova, **Russian Federation**, Tajikistan, Turkmenistan, and Uzbekistan), commits these parties to similar goals regarding chemical weapons.

CHERNENKO, KONSTANTIN (1911-1984). Soviet Union general secretary 1984-1985. Chernenko was a protégé of **Leonid Brezhnev** and served as a conservative choice for General Secretary following the death of reform-minded **Yuri Andropov**.

CHERNOBYL. A series of four nuclear power facilities located on the **Ukrainian-Belorussian** border. It became infamous in spring 1986 when one of the reactors suffered a catastrophic meltdown, leading to the release of large amounts of **radiation** that spread across Europe. Thousands of local citizens and rescue workers died from radiation poisoning and associated longer-term illnesses, and much of the Belarus countryside remains uninhabitable to this day.

CHEYENNE MOUNTAIN. The underground **command and control** center for the **North American Aerospace Defense Command** (NORAD) near Colorado Springs, Colorado, built in the mid-1960s. NORAD has organizationally been assigned to the Air Defense Command, **U.S. Space Command**, and, since 2002, **U.S. Strategic Command**. Its mission is to monitor the skies over the earth to detect missile attacks against the United States and to track orbital debris in space. Its importance was reiterated following the attacks on the **United States** on 11 September 2001 and by its close relationship with the new unified command created in October 2003 to focus on homeland defense, **U.S. Northern Command**, also located in Colorado Springs.

CHINA, PEOPLES' REPUBLIC OF (PRC). The world's most populous country, China has been relatively isolated from the center of international political events for most of its history. Communist leader Mao Zhedong created modern China in 1949, in the aftermath of 20 years of war. Since his death in 1976, the country's leadership has attempted to integrate China within the larger international community. It has very little experience or participation in **arms control agreements** or **regimes**, but given that it is a nuclear power (since 1964), the largest power in East Asia, and potentially one of the world's leading economic superpowers, the world is beginning to take note of China.

CHOKING AGENTS. Chemical warfare agents that attack the respiratory tract, causing a "choking" effect and possibly death.

CHURCHILL, WINSTON (1874-1965). Prime minister of **Great Britain** during World War II (1940-1946) and again from 1951-1955, Churchill was one of the Western allies' greatest spokesmen and leaders. A career statesman, he coined the phrase "iron curtain" to describe the political wall that the **Soviet Union** had erected in Europe after the war. He continued to believe that Great Britain maintained **superpower** status long after the rest of the world had recognized the larger truth, yet this attitude led to the development of a British nuclear **deterrent** force.

CIRCULAR ERROR PROBABLE (CEP). The common measure of **accuracy** of a weapon system. Circular error probable is the radius of a circle around a target within which 50 per cent of the weapons aimed at that target will strike.

CIVIL DEFENSE. Defense of the civilian population from attack, normally by means of shelters or evacuation. *See also* PASSIVE DEFENSE.

CLINTON, WILLIAM (1946-). United States president from 1993-2001. During his administration the United States moved forward on the development of a **national missile defense system**, worked to normalize relations with **Russia**, established a **nuclear test moratorium**, and oversaw the **implementation** of the **Strategic Arms Reduction Treaty** (START I) and the Nunn-Lugar **Cooperative Threat Reduction program**. Clinton also met with Russian president **Boris Yeltsin** in 1997 to sign the **Helsinki Agreement**.

CLOSELY SPACED BASING. *See* DENSE PACK.

CLUSTER BOMB. One of a family of conventional weapon systems that dispenses large numbers of bomblets or mines, usually against area targets. These can be antipersonnel, fragmentary, delayed fuse, or magnetic.

COERCIVE ARMS CONTROL. Forcing a state or group to disarm or demilitarize as the result of losing a conflict. The winning power can instill whatever rules and restrictions it likes as a result. Examples include the demilitarization of the Rhineland imposed by the **Versailles Treaty** and the forcible disarmament of **Iraq** following Operation **Desert Storm** by the **United Nations Special Commission on Iraq** (UNSCOM).

COLD LAUNCH. A **ballistic missile** launch technique in which the missile is ejected from its **launch canister** by gas pressure, with engine ignition only after the missile is clear of the canister. This allows reuse of the undamaged launch canister.

COLD WAR. The period following World War II (beginning approximately 1948) until the dissolution of the **Warsaw Pact** in 1989 and the **Soviet Union** in 1991. This period was characterized by nuclear tension between the **United States** and the Soviet Union and theater tension between the **North Atlantic Treaty Organization** (NATO) and the Warsaw Pact. This tension was of such centrality that it became the defining characteristic of global international relations and the almost singular focus of **arms control** efforts. The United States deployed hundreds of thousands of troops and associated military hardware to Europe to face off the Soviet threat, and both sides engaged in "proxy wars" around the world in an attempt to get the upper hand in this game of international chess. *See also* NORTH ATLANTIC TREATY ORGANIZATION; WARSAW PACT.

COLLATERAL DAMAGE. Spillover effects from a military action or weapon that damages the population or nonintended property in the vicinity of the military target.

COLLECTIVE SECURITY. In a global sense, the idea that an intergovernmental body, normally understood to be the **United Nations** in the post-World War II world, employing forces provided by its member states can and will ensure global peace and security. In practice, nations were unwilling to surrender sovereign control over their armed forces to such collective control. On a regional, alliance scale collective security became the provision of the combined defense by one group of allied countries against another group of countries. This concept is perhaps best exemplified by the **North Atlantic Treaty Organization's** Article V, which states that an attack against one is an attack against all.

COMMAND AND CONTROL (C2). The system used to direct and control military forces in peace, crisis, and war. Command and control of **strategic** weapons is a critical dimension of nuclear **deterrence**, safety, security, and stability.

COMMAND, CONTROL, AND COMMUNICATIONS (C3). The system through which communication of orders and military directives, including the release of **nuclear weapons**, is accomplished.

COMMAND, CONTROL, COMMUNICATIONS, AND INTELLIGENCE (C3I). The information processing system that links threat detection and analysis to decision-making and the issuance and promulgation of response orders.

COMMAND, CONTROL, COMMUNICATIONS, COMPUTERS, AND INTELLIGENCE (C4I). A fully automated **command, control, communications, and intelligence** system.

COMMAND, CONTROL, COMMUNICATIONS, COMPUTERS, INTELLIGENCE, SURVEILLANCE, AND RECONNAISSANCE (C4ISR). An integrated and automated system designed to bring the data and capabilities from all relevant **detection** and warning, decision-making, and operational control systems to those authorized to make decisions and direct actions in **strategic** military operations.

COMMISSION ON NATIONAL SECURITY IN THE 21ST CENTURY. The U.S. Commission on National Security in the 21st Century, also known as the **Hart-Rudman Commission,** began work in 1998 and completed its three-volume study in 2001. While most analyses of national security have focused on U.S. military capabilities and on diplomatic efforts, the commission took a broader look. It considered technological advances, the education of America's youth, and commercial relationships as crucial to America's security. It looked at alternative futures for the **United States** and the world through 2025 and at the role the United States should play in that world, explicitly considering those nontraditional components of national security. The Commission's Phase III Report addressed a broad range of issues, from securing the national homeland to redesigning government institutions and examining human requirements for national security, including the role of Congress.

COMMITTEE ON THE PRESENT DANGER. Originally formed in 1950 by **Paul Nitze** to rally influential members of the academic, scientific, and diplomatic communities in the **United States** to support the goals of **NSC**-68. The committee was dissolved in 1953, but reenergized in 1976 to oppose **détente** and the liberal internationalist policies of the **Jimmy Carter** administration. The committee was made up of senior American government, industry, and academic leaders who opposed the **Soviet Union,** advocated nuclear superiority, and helped to create the concept of U. S. nuclear inferiority and the concept of **"window of vulnerability."** The committee expressed opposition to all types of **arms control**. It was a strong supporter of **Ronald Reagan's** candidacy for the presidency in 1980 and his platform of American military strength. Many of its members became leading political and military leaders during the ensuing 25 years, particularly during the Reagan, **George H.W. Bush,** and **George W. Bush** administrations.

COMMODITIES CONTROLS LIST. The **United States** has employed **export control** laws continuously since 1940. The first controls aimed to avoid scarcity of critical commodities during World War II. **Cold War**-era controls aimed mostly at preventing diversion of advanced technology to the Soviet bloc and **China**. Later, more and more controls aimed at changing behavior of foreign countries.

The most important of these laws include the **Atomic Energy Act** (1946), the **Arms Control Export Act** (1968), the International

Emergency Export Act (1977), and the Export Administration Act (EAA) of 1979. The Export Administration Act authorizes the president to control exports of U.S. goods and technology to all foreign destinations, as necessary for the purpose of national security, foreign policy, and short supply. The **Department of Commerce** administers the Export Administration Regulations, which implement the EAA, even though the EAA expired in August 1994. President **William Clinton** kept the EAA export controls in force since then by executive order under the International Emergency Economic Powers Act. Although this use of emergency powers has faced legal challenge from time to time, no challenge has succeeded. Regulated by the Commerce Department's Bureau of Export Administration are exports of **"dual-use"** advanced technology and materials having both military and civilian applications. The objective of national security controls was to maintain a qualitative weapons advantage for the United States against the former Soviet bloc and China, as well as to promote changes in its behavior of other countries. Most of the controls aim at halting **proliferation** of **weapons of mass destruction** and reducing support for **terrorism.**

By executive order in 1990, President **George H.W. Bush** vastly increased the scope of **export controls** aimed at halting proliferation of **nuclear, chemical,** and **biological weapons** and missiles. Bush's Enhanced Proliferation Control Initiative was a catch-all provision requiring an exporter to apply for a Commerce Department license on shipment of any goods that he or she knows could be used for proliferation of weapons of mass destruction, whether or not the items are otherwise controlled. The Commerce Department regulations also control exports of commodities in short supply. The export of crude oil carried on the Trans-Alaska Pipeline is controlled, as is that of crude oil and western red cedar harvested from federal or state lands.

Direct commercial sales of U.S.-origin defense products, components, technologies, and services are controlled by the International Traffic in Arms Regulations (ITAR), which are administered by the **Department of State** to implement the Arms Export Control Act. Those items requiring export licenses from the State Department's Office of Defense Trade Controls appear in the U.S. Munitions List in the ITAR. The **Department of Defense** Defense Technology Security Administration also reviews many of the applications. Any item on the Munitions List requires a license for export to all countries.

COMMON SECURITY. Common security is based upon a simple idea: to create a dynamic in which military force reductions build trust, and the trust in turn leads to further arms reductions, so that security is increased for all. President **Mikhail Gorbachev's** many initiatives of the late 1980s built on this theme, which was given a public boost by a report in 1982 from Swedish Prime Minister Olaf Palme. The results were apparent: **intermediate-range nuclear forces** destroyed, conventional forces reduced, and **strategic** nuclear forces reduced as well. Because the concept of "common security" seems to have had considerable success in reducing tensions between the superpowers, the question is insistently raised whether similar principles might apply in the Third World.

COMMONWEALTH OF INDEPENDENT STATES (CIS). An association of former republics of the **Union of Soviet Socialist Republics** (USSR). It was created in 1991 following the dissolution of the USSR.

COMPLIANCE. Those activities that support **implementation** of an **arms control agreement** without violating the provisions of that agreement. Finally, those activities that ensure existing and future programs are in accord with the obligations of an arms control agreement.

COMPLIANCE REVIEW GROUP (CRG). An ad hoc working group within the **United States Department of Defense** formed for each **arms control agreement** as required to conduct executive-level reviews of **compliance** issues.

COMPREHENSIVE TEST BAN TREATY (CTBT) (1996). A treaty that would bar any **nuclear weapon** test explosion in any environment. The concept of a comprehensive test ban can be found in the Preamble to the **Limited Test Ban Treaty**, signed in 1963. Later **negotiations** resulted in more restrictions on testing, such as those in the **Threshold Test Ban Treaty** and the **Peaceful Nuclear Explosions Treaty**. Trilateral negotiations between the **United States, United Kingdom,** and **Soviet Union** from October 1977 to November 1980 on a comprehensive ban ended without result. A reopening of the talks was then delayed until the **verification** issues of existing treaties could be resolved. Currently, four of the five nuclear powers (excluding the **People's Republic of China**) have enacted unilateral testing **moratoriums**. The U.S. moratorium was initiated by Congress on 4 September 1992 and was extended through 2001 by President **William Clinton**, and again indefinitely by President **George W. Bush**.

After initial consultation between the five nuclear powers, the First Committee of the **United Nations** General Assembly on 19 November 1993 approved a resolution by consensus that advocated a global **treaty** to ban all nuclear weapons tests. As urged by the UN resolution, the **Conference on Disarmament** created the Nuclear Test Ban Ad Hoc Committee of the Conference on Disarmament, which held several negotiating rounds beginning in 1994. The result was a treaty opened for signature on 24 September 1996. The United States was the first country to sign the CTBT. President Clinton signed the treaty at the United Nations in New York with the same pen President **John F. Kennedy** used to sign the 1963 **Limited Test Ban Treaty**. Yet in a major setback to the **arms control** community the U.S. Senate voted against **ratification** on 13 October 1999. The treaty will not **enter into force** until it is signed by all 44 of the states that possess nuclear power or research reactors; as of late 2004 some 33 of them had signed, and a total of 120 countries had ratified the treaty.

Despite not yet entering into force, the CTBT **verification** regime has moved forward with concrete steps. It includes a global network of hydroacoustic and seismic stations and infrared and radionucleide sensors, as well as the right to conduct **on-site inspections**. The treaty also established a new international organization in Vienna, the **Comprehensive Test Ban Treaty Organization** (CTBTO) to implement the treaty and oversee compliance. *See also* INTERNATIONAL MONITORING SYSTEM.

COMPREHENSIVE TEST BAN TREATY ORGANIZATION (CTBTO). The implementing body established for the **Comprehensive Test Ban Treaty**. The organization includes an Executive Council, a Technical Secretariat, and a pool of international inspectors drawn from member nations. Until the treaty **enters into force** this body is called the Preparatory Commission for the Comprehensive Test Ban Treaty Organization. Its headquarters are located in Vienna, Austria.

CONCEALMENT. The process of hiding a weapon or delivery system so that it can not be readily seen by **reconnaissance** or detected by technical means. It is most often associated with attempts to circumvent the responsibilities for openness and **compliance** in counting items restricted by an **arms control treaty**.

CONFERENCE OF THE COMMITTEE ON DISARMAMENT (CCD). Established by the **United Nations** as the single multilateral **disarmament** negotiating forum of the international community from 1969-1978. The CCD replaced the **Eighteen Nation Disarmament Committee;** it was subsequently replaced by the UN Committee on Disarmament from 1979-1983 and the **UN Conference on Disarmament** after 1983.

CONFERENCE OF EXPERTS (1958). During the period of the parallel development of the global **verification** system and the **Comprehensive Nuclear Test Ban Treaty** (CTBT) there were phases when the political process was in a deadlock. Nevertheless, scientific activities were carried on even with a political mandate. For some years, scientific activities kept up the momentum and prepared the ground for political progress. This was clearly the case with the Geneva Group of Experts (1958-1960) as well as the successor Group of Scientific Experts (since 1976) that formed the main basis for continuity until the CTBT negotiations started in 1993. The Geneva Conference of Experts met in July and August 1958, attended by representatives of the **United States**, **Great Britain**, Canada, **France**, the **Soviet Union**, Poland, Czechoslovakia, and Romania. They agreed on the technical characteristics of a control system to monitor a ban on **nuclear testing** in the atmosphere, under water, and underground. Their report proposed an elaborate network of land- and sea-based listening and recording posts, as well as aircraft **overflights**. They also recognized that **onsite inspections** would be necessary in some cases to confirm and differentiate explosions from earthquakes.

Several lessons can be drawn from the experience of the Geneva Group of Experts. For the first time, scientists were given an independent role in negotiating security issues before diplomats were able to negotiate. Scientists prepared the ground for **verification** and **implementation**, thus paving the way for future discussions on a **limited test ban** and, later, a comprehensive test ban.

CONFERENCE ON CONVENTIONAL WEAPONS. *See* CERTAIN CONVENTIONAL WEAPONS CONVENTION.

CONFERENCE ON DISARMAMENT (CD). *See* CONFERENCE OF THE COMMITTEE ON DISARMAMENT; UNITED NATIONS COMMISSION ON DISARMAMENT.

CONFERENCE ON DISARMAMENT IN EUROPE (CDE). The 1984-1986 multilateral forum for negotiations on security issues in Europe among the **United States,** the **Soviet Union,** and 33 European nations. The conference settled on a series of **confidence-building measures** involving advanced notification of large-scale military exercises. This was also known as the Stockholm Conference on Disarmament in Europe, or the **Stockholm Agreement.**

CONFERENCE ON SECURITY AND CONFIDENCE-BUILDING MEASURES AND DISARMAMENT IN EUROPE. *See* CONFIDENCE- AND SECURITY-BUILDING MEASURES; STOCKHOLM AGREEMENT.

CONFERENCE ON SECURITY AND COOPERATION IN EUROPE (CSCE). A 1975 multilateral conference of 35 nations that agreed on human rights, economic, and security measures for Europe, including **confidence-building measures** such as advanced notification of large military maneuvers. The CSCE became the **Organization for Security and Cooperation in Europe (OSCE)** in December 1994.

CONFIDENCE-BUILDING MEASURES (CBM). *See* CONFIDENCE- AND SECURITY-BUILDING MEASURES (CSBMs).

CONFIDENCE- AND SECURITY-BUILDING MEASURES (CSBM). As opposed to structural **arms control** measures designed to limit, reduce, or eliminate numbers of weapons systems, confidence- and security-building measures are intended to foster **transparency** and trust through purposely designed cooperative measures. CSBMs are intended to help clarify states' military intentions, reduce uncertainties about potentially threatening military activities, and constrain opportunities for surprise attack or coercion. Specific examples of CSBMs in the European context included an early precursor, the **Stockholm Agreement** of 1986.

The **Conference on Security and Cooperation in Europe** (CSCE)—as of December 1994, the **Organization on Security and Cooperation in Europe** (OSCE)—established a series of **agreements** and procedures designed to increase the security of members through increased military **transparency** and cooperation. The **Helsinki Final Act**, signed in 1975, was the first of these measures.

The CSCE later formed a subcommittee named the **Conference on Disarmament in Europe (CDE)**, which met from 1984-1986. One of the results of this conference was the **Stockholm Agreement**, which entered into force in January 1987 and expanded the requirements for notification and provided for observation of military activities. Members of the CSCE met from March 1989 to November 1990 in order to strengthen the existing CSBMs in line with the Stockholm Convention. The result was the **Vienna Document 1990**, which **entered into force** on 1 January 1991. The **Vienna Document 1992**, negotiated between 26 November 1990 and 4 March 1992, supplemented these measures and entered into force on 1 May 1992. The **Vienna Document 1994** was signed 28 November 1994, and **Vienna Document 1999** was signed 16 November 1999 and entered into force 1 January 2000. Each of the Vienna Documents updated and expanded the previous constraints on the 54 OSCE participants, including restrictions on the size and notification procedures for large-scale military activities in Europe. The **Vienna Document 1999** also provides for the evaluation and inspection of OSCE members' military facilities.

The OSCE's confidence-building regime, as established by the Vienna Documents, includes a number of existing measures, among them a 42-day advance notification of ground exercises involving more than 9,000 troops or 250 tanks or more than 3,000 airborne or amphibious assault troops; observation rights to all countries for ground maneuvers involving more than 13,000 troops or 300 tanks or more than 3,500 airborne or amphibious assault troops; limits on the number of exercises a country can conduct with more than 40,000 troops or 900 tanks (one every two years); limits on the number of exercises a country can conduct with 13,000-40,000 troops or 300-900 tanks (six per year, of which only three can involve more than 25,000 troops or 400 tanks).

In addition, each party may be inspected by any other party, but is only obligated to accept three short-warning inspections and 15 information **verification** inspections each year. Exchanges of military information that will be accurate for the following year are required every 15 December, including the location, manpower levels, major weapon systems employed, and commanding organizations for any unit at or above regiment/brigade level. States must extend invitations to air bases and demonstrations of new weapons and equipment. The **United States** has conducted over 220 inspections as part of this CSBM process.

At the July 1992 Helsinki Summit Meeting of the CSCE, a decision was made to form the **Forum for Security Cooperation (FSC)**. This organization, which meets weekly in Vienna, is tasked with carrying out follow-on **negotiations** to the **Conventional Forces in Europe Treaties** (CFE and CFE-1A) and the Vienna CSBMs. Additionally, this body oversees implementation, implementation assessment, discussion, and clarification of existing CSBMs.

CONFLICT PREVENTION CENTER. Part of the **Organization for Security Cooperation in Europe (OSCE)**, the Conflict Prevention Center was established in Vienna in 1990. At this time the OSCE also created a Secretariat in Prague, an Office for Democratic Institutions and Human Rights in Warsaw, and in December 1992, an office of Secretary General. During 1992, the decision to move from principle to action was most marked in a new Helsinki document which established a number of practical tools that help the OSCE work with the **North Atlantic Treaty Organization** (NATO), the **European Union** (EU), and other international bodies to defend human rights and manage the unprecedented changes now taking place in Europe. In particular, it sets out an ambitious role for the OSCE in **conflict resolution** and "preventive diplomacy." The OSCE is also an important framework for conventional **arms control** in Europe. The **Conventional Forces in Europe Treaty** (CFE) limits non-nuclear ground and air forces from the **Atlantic to the Urals**. A separate political agreement covers personnel in the same region. Through continued negotiation, **confidence-building measures** have been extended and higher expectations for treaty **compliance** and **verification** have been set.

CONFLICT RESOLUTION. Various methods, usually peaceful, of bringing an end to conflict between parties. Parties can seek resolution of disputes through **negotiation**, inquiry, mediation, conciliation, arbitration, judicial settlement, or regional agreements or arrangements. As a general rule the **United Nations** suggests that legal disputes be referred to the International Court of Justice. Determining the most effective means of accomplishing this goal is a major subfield of activity in international relations. *See also* UNITED NATIONS.

CONSEQUENCE MANAGEMENT. Ways and means of alleviating the short- and long-term physical, socioeconomic, and psychological effects of a chemical, biological, or nuclear attack. It describes the coordination of international, national, regional, and local assets to deal with the effects of such an attack. The term also includes preparatory work in response to a **weapon of mass destruction** threat.

CONTAMINATION. Presence of **biological** or **chemical warfare agents** or **radioactivity** in a form or amount that poses danger.

CONTAMINATION CONTROL. Measures taken to avoid, reduce, remove, or render harmless **contamination**.

CONTINUOUS MONITORING. Continuous, 24-hour, seven-day inspector presence at a specified facility to ensure **compliance** with an **agreement**. Several agreements, including the **Intermediate-Range Nuclear Forces Treaty**, the **Strategic Arms Reduction Treaties**, and the **Chemical Weapons Convention** incorporate continuous **monitoring** provisions in their inspection protocols.

CONTROLLED ITEM. A piece of hardware, software, technology, or military equipment that cannot be freely given, traded, or sold to another country. A controlled item often appears on a **"trigger list"** of items that are restricted by **export controls** of a nation or multinational group. *See also* AUSTRALIA GROUP; COORDINATING COMMITTEE FOR MULTILATERAL EXPORT CONTROLS; NUCLEAR SUPPLIERS GROUP; WASSENAAR ARRANGEMENT; ZANGGER COMMITTEE.

CONVENTION ON THE LAW OF THE SEA. *See* LAW OF THE SEA.

CONVENTION ON THE PHYSICAL PROTECTION OF NUCLEAR MATERIAL (1980). The Convention on the Physical Protection of Nuclear Material, signed in Vienna and New York on 3 March 1980, obliges contracting states to ensure the protection of nuclear material within their territory or on board their ships or aircraft during international nuclear transport. The convention entered into force 8 Feburary 1987.

CONVENTION ON THE PROHIBITION OF THE USE, STOCK-PILING, PRODUCTION, AND TRANSFER OF ANTIPER-SONNEL MINES AND ON THEIR DESTRUCTION. *See* MINE BAN CONVENTION.

CONVENTION RESTRICTING EXCESSIVELY INJURIOUS OR INDISCRIMINATE CONVENTIONAL WEAPONS. *See* CERTAIN CONVENTIONAL WEAPONS CONVENTION; LAWS OF WAR.

CONVENTIONAL ARMS CONTROL. Measures intended to limit, reduce, or constrain transfer of conventional (non-nuclear) weapons systems.

CONVENTIONAL ARMS TRANSFER TALKS (CAT). A series of negotiations between the **United States** and the **Soviet Union** across 1977 and 1978 that sought to limit conventional arms sales and transfers to other countries.

CONVENTIONAL FORCES IN EUROPE TREATY (CFE). The "Treaty on Conventional Armed Forces in Europe" (though more typically the Conventional Forces in Europe Treaty) was originally signed by the 16 members of the **North Atlantic Treaty Organiza-tion** (NATO) and the eight **Warsaw Pact** members on 19 Novem-ber 1990. However, due to the breakup of the **Soviet Union** and other changes in Europe, 30 states are now parties to the treaty. The area of application (AOA) for the CFE Treaty is commonly referred to as the **Atlantic to the Urals** (ATTU). For those countries that ei-ther do not fall within this area, such as the **United States** and Can-ada, or those that have territory extending outside of the AOA, such as **Russia**, Turkey, and **Kazakhstan**, the limits apply only to forces stationed in the ATTU zone. However, an agreed statement requires Russia to destroy 14,500 pieces of equipment that were moved east of the Urals during the negotiations. The CFE Treaty **entered into force** on 9 November 1992, with unlimited duration, to be reviewed after 46 months and at five-year intervals thereafter. The treaty only limits the amount of equipment in the AOA; troop limits were ad-dressed in follow-on negotiations that resulted in the second **Con-ventional Forces in Europe** (CFE-1A) document.

　　The Treaty divides Europe into two regions: the North Atlan-tic Treaty Organization and the members of the former Warsaw Treaty Organization, imposing conventional arms limitations equally to both. Each of the groups' total holdings are limited in five major categories: tanks, artillery pieces, armored combat vehicles (ACV), combat aircraft, and attack helicopters. Three of these categories were further defined as follows: artillery (guns and howitzers, mortars, and multiple launched rocket systems); ACVs (armored personnel carriers, armored infantry fighting vehicles, and heavy armament combat vehicles); and helicopters (specialized attack and multipurpose attack).

Sublimits were also placed on the most threatening ACV's, including armored infantry fighting vehicles and heavy armament combat vehicles. There is an additional grouping of equipment that is not limited by the treaty, yet is still subject to the treaty. The equipment in this category includes trainer aircraft, combat support and transport helicopters, river bridging vehicles, and armored vehicle look-alikes, all of which are subject to operational constraints and information exchanges.

Four nested zones were also created, each one encompassing the preceding zone plus adjacent territory or districts, resulting in a Russian Matrushka doll effect. Specific limits are placed on the ground equipment allowed in each zone, the smallest of which is the central zone. These limits allow for free movement away from, but not toward, the center of Europe, thus decreasing the threat of a surprise attack. Aircraft and helicopters, while limited in the AOA, are not affected by the zoning limits. Additionally, there were limits put on the number of forces that could be stationed in the so-called flank zone. This zone includes Armenia, Georgia, Azerbaijan, and Moldova, as well as the southeastern third of Ukraine and the Leningrad and North Caucasus military districts in the Russian Federation. This was done to prevent the Soviet Union (or Russia) from repositioning its forces previously located in Central Europe to the borders of Turkey and Norway, forcing them instead to be moved deep within Russia.

Although each group was left to decide for itself the equipment levels allotted to each country, limits on the amount a single country could possess are stated in the treaty. These single-party limits stress the importance of no one nation being able to dominate the continent. Additionally, restrictions were placed on the amount of equipment that one state could station on the territory of another. Before signing the treaty at the November 1990 summit meeting in Paris, both groups met separately to develop individual country limits. While the results of the North Atlantic Treaty Group's meeting in Brussels remains relatively unchanged, political events have significantly altered the agreement reached by the countries of the former Warsaw Pact in Budapest.

In May 1992 the eight members of the **Commonwealth of Independent States** (CIS) that had territory within the AOA met in Tashkent to decide how to divide the **Former Soviet Union's** allotment of equipment. Russia and Ukraine also agreed to sublimits within the Flank zone. Kazakhstan pledged not to station any of its forces west of the Ural River, thus in the AOA. Russia assumed responsibility for former Soviet forces outside the CIS, such as in Poland, Germany, and the Baltics. In a separate agreement, signed on 5 February 1993 in Prague, the Czechs and Slovaks agreed to a 2:1 split of the equipment allocated to the former Czechoslovakia.

All equipment was to be destroyed within 40 months (by 17 November 1995) except for a very limited number that can be converted to trainers, target drones, nonmilitary uses, or decommissioned. In the May 1996 CFE Review Conference the parties agreed to grant Russia exemption from this limit in certain areas of its flank regions until May 1999. Due to the ongoing conflict in Chechnya, however, Russia also failed to meet its obligations by this date.

The treaty allows for several methods of ensuring **compliance**, including **national/multinational technical means**, information exchanges, and **on-site inspections**, all of which are supervised by the Joint Consultative Group, based in Vienna. There are several types of inspections described in the treaty: announced inspections of declared sites, challenge inspections within a specified area (a country may refuse, but then a reasonable assurance of compliance is required), and inspections to verify the destruction or reclassification of equipment. The number of allowed inspections is based on percentages and varies depending on the type of inspection and the current phase of **implementation**.

At the 1 December 1996 Heads of State summit for the **Organization for Security and Cooperation in Europe** (OSCE) in Lisbon, states parties to the CFE agreed to revise the treaty. This goal was reiterated on 24 July 1997, when a plan was devised to set national maximum force levels for each signator rather than keeping collective limits on the original groups of states. A document revising the treaty in this manner was signed at the OSCE summit in Istanbul in November 1999. Entry into force of a "new" CFE Treaty will take place following ratification by all 30 OSCE states parties. However, the United States and its NATO allies have said that they will not ratify the treaty until Russia first complies with its new weapons limits and with the commitments Moscow made in the CFE Final Act. The act—a political, not legally binding, document concluded with the adapted treaty—set out additional commitments by CFE states-parties on future weapons deployments, including pledges by Russia to withdraw treaty-limited weapons from Georgia and Moldova. Early in 2002, Moscow declared that it had met the adapted treaty's weapons limits. NATO accepted the claim in July 2002 but repeated that Russia must still fulfill its commitments with regard to Georgia and Moldova before ratification. The original treaty therefore remains in effect.

CONVENTIONAL FORCES IN EUROPE TREATY 1A (CFE 1A). The "Concluding Act of the Negotiation on Personnel Strength of Conventional Armed Forces in Europe" was signed on 17 July 1992 and entered into force the same day. It is a politically, not legally, binding document and therefore is not subject to **ratification**. The goal of the **agreement** is to limit and/or reduce manpower levels in the area of application of the **Conventional Forces in Europe Treaty.** Each state sets its own limits. These are open to discussion, but not subject to **negotiation**. The CFE-1A treaty is of unlimited duration, but was reviewed after six months and at five-year intervals thereafter.

The personnel that are counted against the limits fall into several categories: land or air forces (including ground-based air defense) and the command and staff for these units; other forces that hold equipment limited under the CFE Treaty, including land-based naval aircraft and naval infantry forces; and coastal defense units and reserve personnel called up for full-time service for more than 90 days. Exempted are sea-based naval personnel, internal security units, and forces serving under **United Nations** command.

Personnel information is provided during preinspection briefings for CFE declared site inspections, or in response to inspectors' requests during a CFE **challenge inspection.**

CONVENTIONAL WAR. Conflict in which the weapons employed are limited to conventional weapons. No **nuclear, biological, chemical,** or **radiological weapons** are employed.

CONVENTIONAL WEAPONS. All weapons other than **nuclear, biological, chemical,** and **radiological weapons.**

COOPERATION. To work together toward a common end or purpose. In international relations, this usually refers to two or more states agreeing to move in concert toward a goal, which may include an **arms control treaty** or **agreement**, or the creation of a multinational consortium in pursuit of some end. Cooperative measures in an arms control sense usually mean actions taken by one side to enhance the other side's ability to verify **compliance** with the provisions of an agreement.

COOPERATIVE DEFENSE. Cooperative defense is often equated with alliances between multiple states, so that the "all-for-one and one-for-all" concept allows for a reduced threat and enhanced defensive capabilities. It can also refer to the shared risks and costs associated with joint development of a new defensive system or program. Cooperation lessens the risks to any one participant, and may enhance the overall security situation for all participants through the synergy of combined capabilities.

COOPERATIVE THREAT REDUCTION PROGRAM (CTR). In the fall of 1991 conditions in the disintegrating **Soviet Union** created a global threat to nuclear safety and stability. The **United States** Congress, recognizing a window of opportunity to materially reduce the threat from nuclear weapons in the **former Soviet Union** and the **proliferation** potential they represented, enacted the Soviet Nuclear Threat Reduction Act—also called the **Nunn-Lugar** legislation. Subsequently the program has expanded to include all **weapons of mass destruction** (WMD), assistance for defense conversion, and facilitating military-to-military contacts.

The CTR program currently provides assistance to reduce or eliminate the threat posed by the thousands of existing WMD and associated infrastructure remaining in the former Soviet Union. Primary program objectives are to accelerate WMD dismantlement and destruction while ensuring a strong chain of custody for **fissile material** transport and storage. These objectives also foster compliance with the **Strategic Arms Reduction Treaties**, the **Lisbon Protocol**, the **Nuclear Nonproliferation Treaty**, the **Chemical Weapons Convention**, and the January 1994 **Trilateral Agreement**. Through mid-2004, the United States had authorized over $4.4 billion for the program, and agreements were in effect in **Russia, Ukraine, Belarus,** and **Kazakhstan**.

A congressional report in 2000 recommended major increases in funding for CTR programs to deal with the "loose nukes" problem in the former Soviet Union. But President **George W.** **Bush's** first supplemental defense spending plan called for just the opposite: a one-third cut in the **Department of Energy's** funds for CTR and related programs. *See also* WEAPON OF MASS DESTRUCTION.

COORDINATING COMMITTEE FOR MULTILATERAL EXPORT CONTROLS (COCOM). A **North Atlantic Treaty Organization**-born cooperative effort to control technology exports, particularly dual-use technologies, and other military trade with the then **Soviet Union** during the **Cold War.** COCOM was in effect from 1949 to 1992, when it was replaced by the COCOM Cooperative Forum. COCOM was established in 1949 to control the export of **strategic** products and technical data from member countries to proscribed destinations. Members were Australia, Belgium, Canada, Denmark, **France,** Germany, Greece, Italy, Japan, Luxembourg, Netherlands, Norway, Portugal, Spain, Turkey, **United Kingdom,** and the **United States.** COCOM was abolished 31 March 1994. COCOM members established a new organization, the **Wassenaar Arrangement,** with expanded membership on 12 July 1996. Wassenaar focuses on **nonproliferation export controls** as opposed to East-West control of advanced technology.

CORRELATION OF FORCES. The Soviet military concept of the balance of power between the **United States** and the **Soviet Union.** The correlation of forces included the entirety of the set of economic, political, military, and social factors within the **superpower** relationship. This balance enabled **strategic arms control negotiations** when the nonmilitary factors created adequate offsets for the weapons limitations under discussion.

COUNTERFORCE. A targeting plan focusing on strikes against military targets. Also a nuclear strategy based on highly accurate weapons targeted so as to destroy the enemy's retaliatory or **second-strike capability.** Counterforce strategies and capabilities may be seen as destabilizing traditional **deterrence** by giving incentive to **first use** of **nuclear weapons** and providing the foundation for a perception that a **nuclear war** might be winnable. *See also* COUNTERVAILING; COUNTERVALUE.

COUNTERMEASURES. Use of devices and techniques in implementing **arms control agreements** in order to protect national security and business proprietary information while fulfilling **state party treaty** obligations. Also the use of **decoys** or distractions by an offensive weapon to throw off defenses during an attack, often considered when discussing ways for **ballistic missiles** to overcome **missile defenses**.

COUNTERPROLIFERATION. In general usage, any effort to block the spread of weapons or major system components to states or non-state actors not previously possessing those capabilities. Within **United States** government usage, the concept is operationally oriented toward efforts to counter the effects and consequences of **proliferation** after it has already occurred. In this sense, it includes the full range of efforts to combat the effects of proliferation, including diplomacy, **arms control**, **export controls**, and intelligence collection and analysis, with particular emphasis on assuring continued military capability when confronted by an adversary armed with advanced weapons or systems through proliferation. As a final resort, counterproliferation includes **active** and **passive defenses**, and preemptive or retaliatory military strikes. *See also* NONPRO-LIFERATION.

COUNTERPROLIFERATION INITIATIVE (CPI) (1993). A **United States Department of Defense** initiative to stress protection from proliferated weapons as a full partner to existing national and international programs and efforts designed to prevent **proliferation**. It incorporates prevention via denial, reassurance, **dissuasion**, and reversal, and it adds protection via **deterrence, active defense, passive defense,** and **counterforce**.

COUNTERVAILING. A nuclear strategy derived from **counterforce** capabilities that rejects explicit concepts of **warfighting** or war winning when applied to **nuclear weapons**. A countervailing strategy employs counterforce capabilities to provide a range of nuclear options in response to a wide range of provocations. It envisions a protracted nuclear conflict, and it focuses on denying the other side any possibility of success while holding out at least the possibility of military success in a nuclear conflict. A flexible nuclear strategy under the name countervailing strategy was adopted by the administration of **United States** President **Jimmy Carter** as an extension and slight expansion of the **limited nuclear options** strategy. *See also* COUNTERFORCE; COUNTERVALUE.

COUNTERVALUE. A targeting plan focusing on strikes against targets seen to be of high political, social, and economic value to the enemy. These targets are typically a state's population, its leadership, or specific economic or industrial sectors of its economy. Sometimes called a "city busting" strategy. Countervalue targeting does not require a high degree of accuracy. A countervalue strategy is designed to raise the stakes of war to an unacceptable level, thus deterring conflict. Countervalue targeting is a common characteristic of **second-strike capabilities**. *See also* COUNTERFORCE; COUNTERVAILING.

COUPLING. Asymmetrical provisions in **arms control agreements** that link action or restrictions in one area to reciprocal actions or restrictions in another area, either related or unrelated, as opposed to direct head-to-head actions or restrictions on a single class of weapons systems or other symmetrical concerns. This was an approach associated with the diplomacy of Secretary of State **Henry Kissinger** in the early 1970s. *See also* LINKAGE.

CRAWFORD, TEXAS. Home of **United States** President **George W. Bush.** His ranch was the site of numerous diplomatic visits during his presidency, including the initial agreement in November 2001 with Russian President **Vladimir Putin** on reduced **strategic** force levels (codified in the May 2002 **Strategic Offensive Reductions Treaty**), and to end the **Anti-Ballistic Missile (ABM)** Treaty.

CREDIBILITY. Both national power and **deterrence** calculations rely heavily on credibility, which can be defined as a combination of capability and will. Capability can be objectively measured in terms of systems, numbers, forces, but national will is a much more subjective factor. Others' beliefs, perceptions, and impressions of one's will form the degree of credibility that is attached to capability to form a **strategic** posture and its relative power and deterrent effect.

CRISIS PREVENTION. The attempt to defuse a situation marked by high tensions and the possibly of abrupt or decisive change instituted by one of the parties. Crisis prevention measures may include the use of direct diplomacy, enlisting another state or nonstate organization as an arbitrator, the establishment of direct communications links between states likely to face future crises, and so on.

CRISIS STABILITY. The situation in which the incentives for both sides of a crisis to first launch a nuclear attack are minimized.

CRITICAL MASS. The minimum amount of **fissionable material** that will allow a self-sustaining nuclear **chain reaction**, such as in a **nuclear bomb**.

CRUISE MISSILE. An unmanned, self-propelled vehicle that is capable of sustaining flight across the majority of its flight path using aerodynamic lift. It is a self-guided missile that flies at relatively low altitudes to avoid radar detection. It can carry either nuclear or nonnuclear warheads, and can be launched from the air, land, or sea. *See also* AIR-LAUNCHED CRUISE MISSILE; GROUND-LAUNCHED CRUISE MISSILE; SEA-LAUNCHED CRUISE MISSILE.

CUBAN MISSILE CRISIS. The Cuban Missile Crisis was a 10-day period in October 1962 in which the **United States** and the **Soviet Union** came close to war under the leadership of U.S. President **John F. Kennedy** and Soviet Chairman **Nikita Krushchev**. The USSR had tried to surreptitiously emplace **medium-range ballistic missiles** in Cuba to threaten the American homeland. When this was discovered through aerial **reconnaissance**, the United States refused to accept the situation and demanded the withdrawal of those missiles. The United States placed a naval blockade around Cuba and refused to allow additional Soviet ships to reach the island. Tensions were reduced when the Soviet Union gave in and removed its missiles. In return, the United States agreed to voluntarily remove its **Jupiter** MRBM missiles from Turkish bases. In one sense this could be considered a case of successful **coercive arms control**.

D

DAMAGE LIMITATION OR DAMAGE LIMITING. Strategies designed to limit or reduce the damage from a **strategic** attack. These strategies focus on or combine **passive defenses** such as hardening missile launch facilities, **active defenses** such as **antiballistic missile systems**, and **preemption** and **counterproliferation strategies** such as strikes against an adversary's offensive military capabilities. From the mid-1960s the dual objectives of **United**

States nuclear forces were to deter a nuclear attack through the maintenance of an **assured destruction** capability and to limit the destructiveness of an attack should one occur.

DATABASE. A detailed description of military forces and capabilities from both parties in an **arms control agreement** that is shared under conditions and in details specified in the agreement.

DATA DECLARATION. A report required by an **arms control** agreement on treaty-monitored activities, items, armaments, and equipment.

DATA EXCHANGE. The sharing of each side's **database** of military forces and capabilities as specified in an **arms control agreement**.

DAYTON ACCORDS (1995). The Dayton Peace Agreement ended the Yugoslav civil war that had raged since 1992. The **agreement** was initiated at Wright-Patterson Air Force Base, Dayton, Ohio, in late 1995 at the behest of Madeleine Albright, Secretary of State under U.S. President **William Clinton**. They were signed in Paris in December 1995 by Bosnia, Croatia, and the Yugoslav Republic (Serbia). Contact member nations agreed to oversee the **implementation** of the peace accords; these included the **United States**, **Great Britain**, **France**, Germany, and **Russia**. In addition, the **United Nations** agreed to create an international police task force for the region.

DEALERTING. The process of removing aircraft, missiles, or submarines from short-notice alert status. This is a **confidence-building measure** that lessens the possibility of **accidental nuclear war** due to misperception or faulty intelligence or information. The **United States** and **Russia** lowered the level of international tension in the early 1990s when they dealerted their aircraft and retargeted their missiles to the open oceans at the end of the **Cold War**.

DECAPITATION. A strategy focused on destroying the opponent's leadership and decision-making function early in a conflict, thereby disrupting the opponent's **command, control, and communication system** to confuse its direction of its military forces.

DECLARATION. A formal position or set of data regarding weapons or systems presented by one party, normally a nation-state, in an **arms control negotiation** as the starting point for discussion.

DECLARATION OF AYACHUCHO (1974). The six members of the Andean Group, created in 1969 for the purpose of subregional economic integration (Bolivia, Chile, Colombia, Ecuador, Peru, and Venezuela), plus two nonmembers (Argentina and Panama), undertook to create conditions permitting an effective limitation of armaments and putting an end to their acquisition for offensive purposes. The stated aim of these measures was to devote all possible resources to the economic and social development of the countries of Latin America.

DECLARATION ON THE DENUCLEARIZATION OF AFRICA (1964). A declaration adopted at the meeting of the Organization of African Unity, at Cairo, Egypt, in 1964, expressing the intent of the states of the region not to acquire nuclear weapons. This was the first regional declaration of this kind, and it was a first step toward the establishment of a **nuclear weapon free zone** in Africa.

DECLARATION OF SWISS NEUTRALITY (1815). The vehicle by which states recognized the formal declaration of perpetual **neutrality** by Switzerland. The declaration also provided guarantees by other European powers of the inviolability and integrity of Switzerland's territory.

DECLARATORY POLICY. The stated **strategic** weapons policy of a state. Declaratory policy gains its **credibility** and resulting **deterrent** effect from its perceived relationship to actual strategic posture and expected use.

DECLARED FACILITY OR SITE. Designated installation, factory, or plant declared by a **state party** to meet the requirements of an **arms control agreement**.

DECONTAMINATION. The process of neutralizing, removing, absorbing, or destroying **biological** or **chemical agents**, or removing **radiological** elements, from a person, object, or area.

DECOY. A facsimile weapon or system component intended to mislead or confuse an opponent's intelligence gathering or military attempts to counter or destroy the actual system.

DEFENSE AND SPACE TALKS. Begun in 1985, these **bilateral arms control negotiations** between the **United States** and the **Soviet Union** centered on **implementation** of the **Anti-Ballistic Missile Treaty** and related issues of **strategic defense** and space militarization. The talks ended with the signing of the **Strategic Arms Reduction Treaty** (START I) in 1991.

DEFENSE INTELLIGENCE AGENCY (DIA). The Defense Intelligence Agency is a U.S. **Department of Defense** (DoD) combat support agency and a member of the **United States** Intelligence Community. With over 7,000 military and civilian employees worldwide, the DIA is a major producer and manager of foreign military intelligence. It provides military intelligence to warfighters, defense policy makers, and force planners, in the Department of Defense and the Intelligence Community, in support of U.S. military planning and operations and weapon systems acquisition.

DEFENSE NUCLEAR AGENCY (DNA). A support command within the U.S. **Department of Defense** (DoD), the DNA's lineage derives from the **Manhattan Project** that produced the first **atomic bomb**. It carried out nuclear support responsibilities throughout the **Cold War**. Over the years, the name of the organization evolved from the Armed Forces Special Weapons Project in 1947, to the Defense Atomic Support Agency in 1959, to DNA in 1971, and to the Defense Special Weapons Agency in 1995. It became part of the **Defense Threat Reduction Agency** in 1998. The DNA's missions include: maintaining a center for nuclear technical expertise within DoD; conducting nuclear weapons stockpile support and serving as the lead DoD agency for national nuclear **stockpile stewardship programs**; performing nuclear and advanced weapons effects research and operational support; carrying out research and development to support U.S. government **implementation, compliance, and verification** of **arms control treaties** and **agreements**; researching and developing capabilities for military responses to the **proliferation** of **weapons of mass destruction**; supporting military warfighters in analyzing plans and response options for both nuclear and advanced conventional weapons; and carrying out DoD's **Cooperative Threat Reduction Program** projects.

DEFENSE SUPPORT PROGRAM (DSP). The Defense Support Program is a survivable and reliable satellite-borne system that uses infrared detectors to sense heat from **ballistic missile** plumes against the earth background, to detect and report in real-time missile launches, space launches, and nuclear detonations. DSP satellites have been the spaceborne segment of **North American Aerospace Defense Command's** (NORAD) tactical warning and attack assessment system since 1970. The satellites feed warning data, via communications links, to NORAD and **U.S. Strategic Command** (formerly **U.S. Space Command**) **early warning** centers within **Cheyenne Mountain,** Colorado. These centers immediately forward data to various agencies and areas of operations around the world.

DEFENSE THREAT REDUCTION AGENCY (DTRA). United States Department of Defense (DoD) agency founded in 1998 to serve as the DoD focal point for addressing **weapons of mass destruction proliferation.** The DTRA mission is to reduce the present threat and prepare for any future threat to the United States and its allies from **nuclear, chemical, biological,** conventional, and special **weapons** and technology transfers. It blends operational and technical expertise to understand, prevent, deter, and defend against these threats. DTRA was created by the consolidation of three existing government agencies into one: the **Defense Nuclear Agency,** the **On-Site Inspection Agency,** and the Defense Technology Security Administration.

DEFENSIVE ARMS CONTROL. Limitations placed upon a state's abilities to deploy effective defensive capabilities, such as **antiballistic missile systems.** Paired with **offensive arms control** since 1972, when the first **Strategic Arms Limitation Talks** (SALT I) treaty and **Anti-Ballistic Missile Treaty** were signed, establishing a stable nuclear **deterrent** regime between the **North Atlantic Treaty Organization** and the **Warsaw Pact.** For 30 years the ABM Treaty formed "the cornerstone of **strategic** stability," but the **United States** withdrew from it in 2002, citing its restrictions on the development of improved **theater** and **ballistic missile defenses** that the **United States** required to meet new threats in the post-**Cold War** era.

DEGAULLE, CHARLES (1890-1970). French general and president of France's Fifth Republic from 1955 to 1969. A conservative and

French nationalist, DeGaulle oversaw the development of an independent French nuclear capability and France's withdrawal from the military arm of the **North Atlantic Treaty Organization** (NATO).

DELHI DECLARATION (1985). A call to the **nuclear weapons states** to halt **nuclear testing** and conclude a **comprehensive test ban treaty**. This was the result of a conference of six nonaligned nations led by **India's** Prime Minister Rajiv Ghandi.

DELIVERY SYSTEM. The means or vehicle by which a **strategic** weapon is conveyed to its target. Common delivery vehicles include **ballistic missiles, cruise missiles,** and **bombers.**

DEMILITARIZATION. The process of reducing, restricting, or eliminating military organizations, weapons, systems, or materials from a state or nongovernment organization or from a geographic region. Well-known attempts at demilitarization include the demilitarization of the Rhineland, imposed on Germany during the 1920s and 1930s by the victors of World War I in the **Versailles Treaty**, and the search for and elimination of **weapons of mass destruction** in **Iraq** by the **United Nations** in the 1990s. *See also* COERCIVE ARMS CONTROL.

DEMILITARIZED ZONE. A buffer area between former or potential adversaries that is free from military units, weapons, or systems.

DENSE PACK. A basing mode considered in the late 1970s for the **United States Peacekeeper** (MX) **intercontinental ballistic missile** that would place as many as 100 missiles within a mile-long rectangle in **silos** hardened against nuclear blast. The theory was that unless all 100 missiles were struck simultaneously by an enemy **first strike**, the blast effects from the first missiles to arrive would destroy subsequent incoming missiles, providing protection to the remaining silos and their missiles. *See also* FRATRICIDE.

DENUCLEARIZATION. Eliminating or preventing the introduction of **nuclear weapons,** nuclear materials, or nuclear-powered vessels from a particular area. This can involve a **declaration** not to obtain or use nuclear weapons within a specified geographic region in return for international guarantees of political independence and territorial integrity. For example, the Treaty of Tlatelolco denuclearized

Latin America. Or it can involve the actual removal of such material, as for some of the members of the **Commonwealth of Independent States** (CIS) where Soviet equipment, weapons, and delivery vehicles were stored.

DEOXYRIBONUCLEIC ACID (DNA). The genetic foundation of all **organisms** and **viruses** except for a small category of viruses based on **ribonucleic acid.** Such viruses have the potential of being developed and used as **biological weapons,** possibly with the ability to target specific ethnicities or races.

DEPARTMENT OF COMMERCE. The cabinet department within the **United States** government responsible for implementation of international economic and trade policy. The Department of Commerce is the key executive agency developing national policy regarding **export controls** of weapons, military systems, and defense and **dual-use** technologies. *See also* COORDINATING COMMITTEE FOR MULTILATERAL EXPORT CONTROLS.

DEPARTMENT OF DEFENSE (DoD). The cabinet department within the **United States** government responsible for the military services, military policy, and military strategy. Headquartered in the **Pentagon,** Arlington, Virginia. Created by the National Security Act of 1947, DoD includes the three military departments (**U.S. Air Force, Army,** and **Navy**), the **office of the secretary of defense** (providing civilian oversight of the military), and the **Joint Chiefs of Staff** (representing the military services), as well as a number of agencies that report to the secretary of defense. Total manning for DoD and its direct reporting agencies, including both civilian and military personnel, is approximately three million men and women, and its annual budget for fiscal year 2005 is over $400 billion. *See also* DEFENSE NUCLEAR AGENCY; DEFENSE THREAT REDUCTION AGENCY.

DEPARTMENT OF ENERGY (DOE). The cabinet department within the **United States** government responsible for oversight of the nuclear power industry. Headquartered in Washington, D.C., DOE shares responsibility with the **Department of Defense** for **nuclear weapons** production and stockpile management. DOE is responsible for the national laboratories (including **Lawrence Livermore, Los Alamos,** and **Sandia National Laboratories**) and the **National Nuclear Security Agency** (NNSA).

DEPARTMENT OF HOMELAND SECURITY (DHS). One of the major executive branch organizations within the **United States** government responsible for all actions related to defending the American homeland from attack. The National Strategy for Homeland Security and the Homeland Security Act of 2002 served to mobilize and organize the **United States** to secure its homeland from terrorist attacks. One primary reason for the establishment of the Department of Homeland Security was to provide the unifying core for the vast national network of organizations and institutions involved in efforts to secure the nation. The department brought together many formerly independent government agencies, including the U.S. Coast Guard, the Immigration and Naturalization Service, and the U.S. Customs Service. It works with the **Department of Defense** and **U.S. Northern Command** to ensure the **homeland defense** of North America.

DEPARTMENT OF STATE. The State Department is the lead federal agency responsible for **United States** foreign affairs. The Department of State helps to shape a freer, more secure, and more prosperous world through formulating, representing, and implementing the president's foreign policy. One aspect of this foreign policy agenda is handled through the Bureau of Arms Control, which deals with **arms control** negotiations and **treaties**. In 1999 it absorbed the missions and organization of the previously independent **Arms Control and Disarmament Agency** (ACDA).

DEPLETED URANIUM. A form of **uranium** with a concentration of uranium-235 lower than that found in nature (0.711 percent). Depleted uranium is derived from spent atomic reactor fuel. It is essentially nonharmful to humans and is used in aircraft, ships, and conventional munitions because of its great density.

DEPLOYMENT. Fielding a military system in a ready to employ position and state.

DEPRESSED TRAJECTORY. Firing a **ballistic missile** with an initial launch trajectory of less than 45 degrees, thus reducing its maximum range while reducing its flight time to the target. The use of a depressed trajectory attack by nuclear submarines, for example, could minimize warning time for targets near the coastline in a surprise **first strike**.

DESERT SHIELD, OPERATION. The preparatory phase of deployment and advanced preparation for Operation **Desert Storm** as part of the Gulf War. This preparatory phase took place August 1990 to January 1991. *See also* DESERT STORM.

DESERT STORM, OPERATION. The employment phase of aerial and surface combat during the Gulf War. The **United States** led a multinational coalition that conducted a preliminary 100-day aerial combat phase that took place from January to March 1991 as a prelude to the 100-hour surface combat phase, resulting in the capitulation of **Iraq**. *See also* DESERT SHIELD.

DETARGETING. Sometimes also called **retargeting**, the process of removing coded flight and targeting instructions from a weapon system on alert in order to prevent the destruction of a target in the event of **accidental launch**. This served as a **confidence-building measure** when the **United States** and **Russia** detargeted their **intercontinental ballistic missiles** and **submarine-launched ballistic missiles** away from one another after the end of the **Cold War** (in 1994). The missiles of each country either have no targets, or the target coordinates were changed to open ocean areas in case of accidental launch. In most cases the real targets can be reloaded into the missile's guidance computer in a matter of minutes.

DETECTION. Determination of the presence of an **agent**, weapon, or system component.

DÉTENTE. A period of relative relaxation of tension and broad **cooperation** between adversaries. During the **Cold War**, there was a period of détente during the mid- to late-1970s—from the late stages of **United States** involvement in the Vietnam conflict until the introduction of Soviet combat forces in Afghanistan. This was the period of the **Strategic Arms Limitation Talks** (SALT) and conclusion of the **SALT I** and **SALT II** treaties.

DETERRENCE. Actions by one actor that cause a second, target actor to undertake an assessment of the costs and risks of an anticipated or contemplated course of action, with the outcome of that assessment resulting in a decision to avoid military force or militarily provocative action. In short, preventing an adversary from acting in a certain way.

DETERRENCE BY DENIAL. Nuclear **deterrence** by denial is based in traditional concepts of defense—the ability to deny an adversary success in its employment of its nuclear arsenal. Deterrence by denial depends on a credible capability for **damage limitation** through either **active** or **passive defenses** or a combination of both, and on a credible **counterforce** targeting capability. *See also* DETERRENCE BY PUNISHMENT.

DETERRENCE BY PUNISHMENT. In nuclear terms, **deterrence** by punishment underlies concepts such as **assured destruction** where the employment of one's nuclear capabilities is deterred by the credible capability of the other side to cause unacceptable damage to highly valued targets such as one's industrial base or population. Deterrence by punishment often implies employment of offensive forces against **countervalue** targets, such as cities, in an automatic response to attack. *See also* DETERRENCE BY DENIAL.

DETONATOR. A sensitive explosive device used to set off a weapon's high-explosive element, which in the right configuration can initiate the process leading to the explosion of a **nuclear weapon**. *See also* FISSION WEAPON; FUSION WEAPON; IMPLOSION DEVICE.

DIPLOMACY. The employment of **negotiation** and political and social instruments in international relations. Diplomacy seeks **agreements** and other peaceful solutions to issues of possible conflict or disagreement. Diplomats are protected under international law and practice from direct threats, bodily injury, or detention by the foreign power to which they are assigned.

DIRECTED ENERGY WEAPON. A class of weapons systems based on the projection of energy beams, such as **laser weapons** or **particle beam weapons**, to disable or destroy a target.

DISARMAMENT. Classically, the family of efforts to limit, reduce, control, and restrict military systems and means—an umbrella term for the widest range of cooperative measures. Later, the term **arms control** became synonymous with that broadest construct, and disarmament was seen in narrower terms as the elimination of a specific weapon or category of weapons or significant reductions in such systems as a prelude to eventual elimination. During the later

Cold War disarmament was often used to denote the utopian goal of world peace as opposed to military growth limits or other less complete mechanisms of arms control. *See* UNITED NATIONS CONFERENCE ON DISARMAMENT; WORLD DISARMAMENT CONFERENCE.

DISARMING FIRST STRIKE. The attempt to eliminate an adversary's **strategic** strike capabilities through a surprise, **preemptive** attack against its military forces, particularly its nuclear strike systems.

DISCRIMINATION. A measure of the capability of **surveillance** systems to distinguish **decoys** from actual weapon systems.

DISSUASION. Influencing another state or nonstate actor to desist from taking some action, or persuading that group not to pursue some course of action. Within military circles, a concept of increased emphasis within the **United States'** 2002 **National Security Strategy** as a means of dealing with other states and nonstate **terrorist** organizations. By dissuading such groups from pursuing their own **weapons of mass destruction** due to the fact that they could never match the United States in overall military power, the U.S. hopes to preclude having to **deter** or possibly defeat those groups at some future time.

DOBRYNIN, ANATOLY (1919-). Ambassador of the **Soviet Union** to the **United States** for most of the **Cold War** (1962-1986), he dealt with six U.S. presidents, from **John F. Kennedy** to **Ronald Reagan.**

DOUBLE BUILDDOWN. A 1983 proposal made by the **United States** at the **Strategic Arms Reduction Talks** (START) to reduce the most destabilizing weapons and to decrease substantially the level of United States and Soviet **strategic** arms. This concept envisioned the replacement of older weapons systems with new systems, but with a replacement ratio of less than one for one. Thus both sides would end up with an improved, though smaller, arsenal, achieving what an **arms control treaty** could not—nuclear reductions.

DOVE. A person who prefers **disarmament** and peaceful solutions to international disputes. *See also* HAWK.

DUAL-CAPABLE SYSTEM. A weapon system, such as the **cruise missile** that is capable of delivering either a **strategic** nuclear or conventional **warhead.**

DUAL-PURPOSE CHEMICAL. A chemical that is produced for purposes not prohibited by the **Chemical Weapons Convention** (CWC), may be stockpiled as a **chemical weapon** (CW), and may pose a risk to the objectives of the CWC by virtue of its physical, chemical, and toxicological properties being similar to those of CW. Several dual-purpose chemicals are listed in Schedules 2 and 3 of the CWC Schedules of Chemicals.

DUAL-TRACK DECISION (1979). The decision by the **North Atlantic Treaty Organization** (NATO) to deploy **intermediate-range nuclear forces** (INF) in European NATO states and simultaneously carry on negotiations with the **Soviet Union** to limit or eliminate this category of weapons in the theater. These parallel initiatives were successful, leading to the 1987 **INF Treaty.**

DUAL-USE COMPONENTS. Elements of systems that have both weapon and nonweapon uses. For example, some components have use in nuclear energy production and also in **nuclear weapons** processes; some chemicals have both commercial and weapons applications.

DULLES, JOHN FOSTER (1888-1959). Secretary of state to **United States** President **Dwight Eisenhower,** Dulles had earlier served on President **Woodrow Wilson's** staff at the **Versailles Treaty** Conference following World War I and as a delegate for President **Franklin Roosevelt** to the San Francisco Conference that established the **United Nations.** As secretary of state he announced the policy of **massive retaliation,** and he was a practitioner of **brinkmanship** diplomacy. With President Eisenhower, Dulles believed that a defense strategy that relied on **nuclear weapons** could provide effective **deterrence** while reducing the requirements for and costs of large conventional forces.

DUMB BOMB. Any nonprecision bomb; one without a precision guidance capability, and which relies on its initial release point, gravity, and momentum to reach its target. *See also* PRECISION-GUIDED MUNITION.

DUMBARTON OAKS PLAN. *See* BARUCH PLAN.

E

EARLY NOTIFICATION OF NUCLEAR ACCIDENT (1986). Following the debacle of the **Chernobyl** accident earlier that year, an international conference met in Vienna, Austria, in September 1986 and agreed to immediately notify other states and the **International Atomic Energy Agency** (IAEA) of any unplanned or accidental release of **radioactivity** from their territories, so that the radiological consequences could be minimized.

EARLY WARNING. Detection of an adversary attack very close in time to the launch or initiation of attack. Modern **early warning** systems include long-range radar and space-based **surveillance** systems interconnected into sophisticated **command, control, and communications** networks.

EIGHTEEN NATION COMMITTEE ON DISARMAMENT. **United Nations** negotiating forum from 1962-1968. Based in **Geneva**, Switzerland, the committee served as a central focus for discussions on multilateral **disarmament** and **arms control** initiatives in the early years of the **Cold War**. Its direct descendent is the **UN Conference on Disarmament**.

EISENHOWER, DWIGHT D. (1890-1969). United States president from 1953-1961. Eisenhower's administration was known for its emphasis on national security and its opposition to the **Soviet Union** during the early years of the **Cold War**. His "New Look" policy led to increased reliance on **nuclear weapons** to deter an adversary as a cost-saving measure. He introduced **intercontinental ballistic missiles** (ICBM) to the U.S. military. His administration signed the **Antarctic Treaty**. This was also an era that witnessed the creation of multiple defense alliances, including the **North Atlantic Treaty Organization** (NATO), the **Central Asian Treaty Organization** (CENTO), the Australia-New Zealand-United States Treaty (ANZUS), and the **Southeast Asian Treaty Organization** (SEATO).

ELECTROMAGNETIC PULSE (EMP). The burst effect from the release of electromagnetic energy. This pulse creates strong electrical and magnetic fields that can cause damage to unhardened electronic and electrical systems. It is a typical by-product of a nuclear explosion.

ELECTRONIC COUNTERMEASURES. Electronic defense systems and actions that block or confuse adversary **detection** and radar systems by generating electronic noise or false images.

EMBARGO. A prohibition of all trade with a particular country, usually imposed as a penalty or to extract some political or economic concession from the target state.

EMBARGO OF CHINA. Diplomatic decisions at the end of World War I to omit a statement of racial equality from the Covenant of the League of Nations as well as to allow Japan to retain the Shantung Peninsula exacerbated the volatile political situation in China. The victors tried to stabilize conditions and to solidify the Beijing government's power by imposing an arms embargo on the country. Though well-intentioned, the embargo did little to improve the situation. When Sun Yat-sen failed to secure arms from the West, he turned to the Russians for assistance. The resulting Sun-Joffe Agreement was a major factor in Sun's eventual victory in the political struggle. By 1929 the United States recognized Sun's successor, Chiang K'ai-shek, as the legitimate ruler of China and ended the embargo.

EMERGENCY ACTION MESSAGE. The command by a **United States** president that would release and authorize employment of **nuclear weapons**. This sophisticated **command and control** system was developed during the **Cold War** to ensure that all **Strategic Air Command** forces would receive such an order as expeditiously as possible.

ENCRYPTION. Encoding information for transmission to prevent those other than intended recipients (who would have appropriate decryption systems) from understanding the message. Sometimes called "scrambling" a message.

ENDEMIC. A process within which a disease is present in a natural, continuous, and widespread manner in a given geographic area and its population.

ENDURING FREEDOM, OPERATION. The U.S.-led multinational military coalition effort to remove the Taliban from power and destroy **al Qaeda** in Afghanistan in the fall of 2001. More broadly, the beginning of the global war on **terrorism** that followed the terrorist attacks on the **United States** on 11 September 2001.

ENHANCED PROLIFERATION CONTROL INITIATIVE (EPCI). **United States export control** initiative that extends formal export controls to enable the government to require an export license for any item, whether or not on the control list, if the exporter has been informed or has reason to believe that the item will be used—either directly or indirectly—in a **nuclear, missile, chemical, biological weapons,** or **ballistic missile** program.

ENHANCED RADIATION WEAPON (NEUTRON BOMB). A type of **nuclear weapon** designed to release a much higher proportion of its energy in the form of neutron **radiation** than other types of nuclear weapons. The intended effect is to destroy enemy forces while limiting the damage to structures. It was first designed in the **United States** at the **Lawrence Livermore National Laboratory** in the 1970s. The attempt to deploy the enhanced radiation weapon to **North Atlantic Treaty Organization** (NATO) forces in Europe in the late 1970s caused a popular uproar, which was exacerbated by the political repercussions for several allied governments when President **Jimmy Carter** cancelled the program after getting their support for the deployment.

ENRICHED URANIUM. Natural **uranium** processed to increase the concentration of the fissile isotope U-235 from its natural level of 0.7 percent to 3.5 percent or higher. This enrichment creates nuclear reactor fuel or **weapons-grade material** (typically enriched to at least 90 percent). *See also* HIGHLY ENRICHED URANIUM.

ENRICHMENT. Any one of several large industrial processes through which natural **uranium** is processed into **weapons grade material**. Enrichment methods include gaseous diffusion, electromagnetic isotope separation, gyroscopic, and calutron processes.

ENTRY INTO FORCE (EIF). A **treaty** or **agreement** taking effect; the date upon which all parties to a treaty must abide by its provisions. This usually occurs after some predetermined number of **sig-**

natories have **ratified** the treaty. The effective date of the treaty is referred to as its entry into force.

ENVIRONMENTAL MODIFICATION CONVENTION (1977). A multilateral **agreement** that was signed by 34 nations on 18 May 1977 and which **entered into force** on 5 October 1978. The **treaty** was an attempt to preempt the consideration of military planning for environmental modification techniques in the future. **State parties** agreed not to use environmental modification of widespread, long-lasting, or severe effects to destroy, damage, or injure another state party to the convention. This included a prohibition against the deliberate manipulation of the natural processes of the earth, the atmosphere, and outer space, including changes in the weather, the ozone layer, and the ionosphere, and upsetting the ecological balance of a region. As of mid-2004 some 51 states had signed the convention.

ENVIRONMENTAL PROTECTION AGENCY (EPA). The Environmental Protection Agency was created in 1970 when 15 federal departments were consolidated into one agency to reduce pollution and enhance the quality and protection of America's air, water, and landscape. Its task is to facilitate implementation of environmental regulations. In almost all cases, the laws the EPA enforces allow state agencies to implement their own regulations as long as the state's regulations are at least as stringent as the federal rules.

EPIDEMIC. A process within which a disease from outside a given area attacks a significant number of the population at one time with the rate of infection exceeding normal expectations for that population.

EQUIVALENT MEGATONNAGE (EMT). A measure of the destructive power of **nuclear weapons**. As one creates larger nuclear weapons, the destructive power does not increase arithmetically with the size of the **warhead's** yield. This measure compensates for the diluted area effect of the weapon in which increased yield produces destructive power at a ratio of yield to the two-thirds power. EMT is often used as an aggregate measure of the total explosive power in a state's arsenal.

ESCALATION. Raising a conflict to a higher level of violence or the widening of conflict to an expanded geographic scope. In **strategic**

terms, escalation implies the possibility of movement from **conventional weapons** to **nonstrategic nuclear weapons** or even to **strategic nuclear weapons**. It implies movement up the spectrum of conflict to more dangerous levels. Such movement is sometimes referred to as "climbing the escalation ladder."

ESSENTIAL EQUIVALENCE. The possession of forces and capabilities approximately equal in overall effectiveness to those of a specific opponent. Essential equivalence does not require numerical equality or a system-for-system balance, but implies that each side has equal effectiveness regardless of systems or numbers. The term was coined during the **Richard Nixon** administration in the early 1970s.

ETHNIC WEAPON. A **biological** or **chemical agent** designed to exploit genetic factors so as to specifically target members of a given ethnic group.

EURO-ATLANTIC PARTNERSHIP COUNCIL. The international coordination body within the **North Atlantic Treaty Organization** (NATO) that replaced the former **North Atlantic Cooperation Council** (NACC) in 1997. Its purpose is to enhance greater cooperative efforts and closer relations between the states of the **Former Soviet Union, Warsaw Pact,** and NATO. It brings together the allies and partners in a forum providing for regular consultation and cooperation. It meets periodically at the level of ambassadors and foreign and defense ministers. Heads of state and government of the 46 members can also meet, when appropriate, as they did in Washington in April 1999

EUROPEAN ATOMIC ENERGY COMMUNITY (EURATOM). An organization of the European Union, established in 1957 to coordinate and encourage nuclear power development in Western Europe and cooperatively manage Europe's nuclear resources. EURATOM established a common **safeguards agreement** with the **International Atomic Energy Agency** for the region.

EUROPEAN COMMUNITY (EC). *See* EUROPEAN UNION.

EUROPEAN FREE TRADE ASSOCIATION (EFTA). Formed in 1960 as a free trade area and as a counter to the European Community, EFTA members presently include only Iceland, Liechtenstein,

Norway, and Switzerland. The EFTA states have jointly concluded free trade agreements with a number of countries worldwide. Iceland, Liechtenstein, and Norway entered into the Agreement on the European Economic Area (EEA) in 1992, which **entered into force** in 1994. The current contracting parties to the EEA are, in addition to the three EFTA states, the **European Union** and the 25 EU Member States.

EUROPEAN UNION (EU). Upon the ratification of the Treaty of European Union, or Maastricht Treaty, in November 1993, the European Community (EC) changed its name to the European Union. The EC had been formed in 1958 with the Treaty of Rome that created the European Coal and Steel Community. Today the EU is an economic and political grouping of European nations, and other organizations (with the same member nations) with certain commonalities that enjoys a degree of supra-nationality, especially on economic and trade issues (less so for foreign affairs and security, though it is pursuing common policies in those areas, as well). The EU is also responsible for cooperation on justice and home affairs. Fifteen countries—Austria, Belgium, Denmark, Finland, **France**, Germany, **Great Britain**, Greece, Ireland, Italy, Luxembourg, the Netherlands, Portugal, Spain, and Sweden—are full members of the organizations of the EU. Ten additional countries joined the EU in 2004: Cyprus (Greek part), the Czech Republic, Estonia, Hungary, Latvia, Lithuania, Malta, Poland, Slovakia, and Slovenia.

EUROSTRATEGIC FORCES. One leg of the **North Atlantic Treaty Organizations' deterrent triad**, Eurostrategic forces were generally considered to be all tactical and **theater-range nuclear weapons** based in Europe and capable of being used against the **Warsaw Pact** countries. The other two legs of the triad were conventional forces and the U.S. **strategic** arsenal. These were sometimes called "forward-based systems."

EXECUTIVE AGREEMENTS. Agreements made between the heads of state or government of two or more states without the requirement of **ratification** by their counties' parliaments. While not as legally binding as a **treaty**, they are often treated in the same manner.

EXPORT CONTROLS. A mechanism of **nonproliferation** policy designed to prevent the international sale or transfer of specified weapons or delivery vehicles, or key components of those weapons and vehicles. Export controls can be unilateral or multilateral, depending on the incidence of the controlled weapons, vehicles, or components. *See also* AUSTRALIA GROUP; COMMODITIES CONTROLS LIST; COORDINATING COMMITTEE FOR MULTILATERAL EXPORT CONTROLS; LONDON GROUP; NUCLEAR SUPPLIERS GROUP; WASSENAAR ARRANGEMENT; ZANGGER COMMITTEE.

EXTENDED DETERRENCE. The **deterrent** posture of a country or coalition of countries projected to extend to protect allies, **neutrals**, or one's own forces on foreign soil. This is accomplished through guarantees of **escalation** or retaliation against an aggressor on behalf of a third-party state. The concept was most commonly associated with the American nuclear guarantee to the European members of the **North Atlantic Treaty Organization** (NATO) during the **Cold War**. Sometimes referred to as the "deterrent umbrella."

EXTREMELY LOW FREQUENCY (ELF). A type of communications that employs the low end of the frequency range to allow transmission through water to submerged submarines. Such transmissions are a necessary part of the **command, control, and communications system** for countries that employ **ballistic missile**-launching submarines as part of their **strategic** forces. In the **United States**, a large ELF transmission antenna for communication with submerged U.S. ballistic missile submarines was built in the Upper Midwest in the late 1970s.

F

FALLOUT. The **radioactive** particle debris produced by **nuclear weapons** detonations, particularly ground bursts. Extremely dangerous to living **organisms**, fallout is a long-lasting by-product of nuclear explosions that can affect large areas downwind of the target. *See also* STRONTIUM.

FAST BREEDER REACTOR. A **nuclear reactor** in which **depleted uranium** surrounds the core, allowing the conversion of material to **plutonium** via neutron capture, a process known as "breeding." This type of reactor relies on nuclear **fission** of a combination of plutonium and natural uranium, creating an intense flux of high-energy (thus "fast") neutrons.

FB-111 BOMBER (Aardvark). A U.S. medium-range, supersonic, swing wing bomber, capable of carrying **nuclear** or **conventional weapons**. A variant of the F-111 tactical fighter-bomber, the FB-111 was introduced in 1968 and sat on nuclear alert for **Strategic Air Command** at Plattsburgh Air Force Base, New York, and Pease Air Force Base, New Hampshire, during the 1970s and 1980s. It was retired in 1991.

FEDERAL EMERGENCY MANAGEMENT AGENCY (FEMA). FEMA is a formerly independent **United States** federal agency that has now been incorporated into the **Department of Homeland Security**. Its more than 2,600 full-time employees work in Washington, D.C., and at regional offices across the country. FEMA also has nearly 4,000 standby disaster assistance employees who are available to help out after disasters. Often FEMA works in partnership with other organizations that are part of the nation's emergency management system. These partners include state and local emergency management agencies, federal agencies, and the American **Red Cross**.

FEDERATION OF ATOMIC SCIENTISTS. An organization of disaffected nuclear scientists created after World War II, since grown into a public advocate of reason and diplomacy. It publishes the monthly *Bulletin of the Atomic Scientists*, a primary voice of the nongovernmental **arms control** community in the **United States**. The *Bulletin* was best known during the **Cold War** for its trademark "doomsday clock," the hands of which measured the editors' perception of the threat of **nuclear war** in terms of minutes prior to midnight.

FIRST-STRIKE CAPABILITY. The possession of weapons and delivery systems designed to undertake an initial, usually surprise attack on an adversary. Such a first strike would be designed to destroy or significantly limit the adversary's retaliatory capability, thereby winning the conflict in the first exchange, without retaliation against one's own territory or deployed forces.

FIRST USE. The initiation of nuclear conflict through the introduction of nuclear weapons in a conflict at any level or in any form. *See also* NO FIRST USE.

FISSILE MATERIAL (or FISSIONABLE MATERIAL). Any material that will undergo nuclear **fission**, which can serve as nuclear fuel for reactor operations or atomic weapons. This includes **enriched uranium** and **plutonium**.

FISSILE MATERIAL CUTOFF TREATY (FMCT). The idea of a **fissile material** production cutoff gained prominence from 1956 through 1969, when it became the basis for U.S. **arms control negotiations**. Limited success was realized in 1964 when the **United States, United Kingdom**, and the **Soviet Union** all announced reductions in the production of **weapon-grade fissionable materials**. The success of **superpower arms control** initiatives, a U.S. halt in production of fissile material, and President **William Clinton's** speech to the **United Nations** in September 1993 all provided the impetus for a new cutoff convention.

The **UN Conference on Disarmament** began preliminary discussions on a fissile material cutoff convention during its 1994 session. In tandem with these negotiations, technical discussions were held in Vienna, with assistance from the **International Atomic Energy Agency** (IAEA), to address technical and **verification** issues. Once the **Indian** and **Pakistani** nuclear programs became public knowledge in 1998, both dropped their resistance to a fissile material production ban, which had served as an obstacle to **negotiations**. The Conference on Disarmament reached a consensus on a negotiating mandate in 1998. Yet another obstacle is found in the desire by the **nuclear weapon states** (NWS) to address only future production of fissile material, whereas many **non-nuclear weapon states** (NNWS), including the Group of 21 "nonaligned" nations, wish to include limits on existing stocks of weapons-grade nuclear material.

FISSION. The process of bombarding nuclear nuclei with neutrons to split the nuclei, releasing both vast amounts of energy and more neutrons capable of splitting more nuclei. Fission was first successfully achieved in a squash court under the bleachers in the football stadium at the University of Chicago in 1943 by a team of physicists working under the auspices of the **Manhattan Project**. Fission is the underlying physical process allowing atomic explosions. *See* ATOMIC BOMB; FUSION.

FISSION WEAPONS. Nuclear weapons based upon the **fission** process of **uranium** or **plutonium**. Also called **atomic bombs**.

FIVE POWER TREATY (1922). *See* WASHINGTON NAVAL TREATY.

FLAME AGENT. A lethal or incapacitating burning gas or vapor that causes direct burn wounds, depletes oxygen, or creates heat, carbon monoxide, or some combination of these effects.

FLEXIBLE RESPONSE. A military strategy, first proposed by **United States** President **John F. Kennedy** and later adopted by the **North Atlantic Treaty Organization** (NATO) in 1967, based upon the ability to choose the means and level of response to a given provocation. Under flexible response, NATO could choose to respond to a challenge in kind—at the level and category of military challenge issued—or at other levels or in other forms. This strategy provided a basis for selective responses or, conceptually, for controlled **escalation** up the spectrum of conflict, including **first use** of **nuclear weapons** by NATO if it felt this would stop the conflict..

FLEXIBLE TARGETING. A policy that accepts the need for situational flexibility and the willingness to plan targets during a conflict, rather than merely having preplanned options that limit one's response. This concept, which has become more commonly accepted by the U.S. military in the post-**Cold War** era, differs significantly from the **Single Integrated Operations Plan** on which the **United States** relied during the Cold War. Instead of a single, massive, planned response to any enemy action, flexible targeting develops multiple operations plans that respond to a wide variety of possible enemy actions with appropriate, scaled actions.

FLIGHT TEST. An actual missile launch or aircraft flight undertaken for system development or reliability testing or for training of launch personnel or aircrews.

FORD, GERALD R. (1913-). United States president from 1974 to 1977. Ford became president upon the resignation of **Richard Nixon.** He met with Soviet Secretary General **Leonid Brezhnev** in Siberia in 1974 to sign the **Vladivostok Agreement,** effectively breaking an **arms control** logjam and laying the foundation for the **Strategic Arms Limitation Talks** (SALT).

FORMER SOVIET UNION (FSU). Those states that comprised the **Union of Soviet Socialist Republics** prior to its dissolution. The

Soviet Union was one of the world's leading powers from 1917 to 1991. It was succeeded by the **Russian Federation** and a number of states formed from former Soviet Republics, some of which joined together in the **Commonwealth of Independent States** (CIS).

FORUM FOR SECURITY COOPERATION (FSC). At the July 1992 summit of the **Conference on Security and Cooperation in Europe** (CSCE), the organization decided to form the 55-nation Forum for Security Cooperation. The Forum meets weekly in Vienna, Austria. It is tasked with carrying out follow-on negotiations to the **Conventional Forces in Europe Treaty**, the CFE-1A Treaty, and the **confidence and security building measures** (CSBMs) included in the **Vienna Documents**. Additionally, this body oversees **implementation**, discussion, and clarification of existing CSBMs. It is also expected to implement a work program to address concerns regarding **arms control**, **disarmament**, and CSBMs, to enhance consultation and cooperation among participating states regarding security matters, and to further the process of reducing the risk of conflict. The Forum aims to create an atmosphere of openness and **transparency** regarding military issues and to develop measures to reduce the risk of armed conflict.

FORWARD-BASED SYSTEMS (FBS). Military capability deployed outside of one's home country, closer and more responsive to an area of potential conflict. Forward basing cuts response time while also directly increasing potential military power and **credibility**.

FOUR POWER TREATY (1921). The Four-Power Treaty was signed in Washington on 13 December 1921 between the **United States, Great Britain, France**, and Japan. Its purpose was to respect the interests of the other parties in the Pacific Islands and to notify each of the other parties in the event that any other country launched an attack in the area. No promises were made to help, nor to restrain, anyone's freedom of action in the region.

FRACTIONAL ORBITAL BOMBARDMENT SYSTEM (FOBS). A weapon system that is delivered on a semiorbital trajectory, thus significantly reducing warning time and complicating **early warning surveillance** and response planning. The concept was considered in the 1960s but banned by the **Outer Space Treaty**.

FRACTIONATION. The division of a missile's total **payload** into multiple, separate **reentry vehicles**. *See also* MULTIPLE INDEPENDENTLY TARGETABLE REENTRY VEHICLE.

FRANCE. One of the largest and most important countries in Europe. A nuclear power, France is one of the five permanent members of the **United Nations** Security Council. It is a **signatory** to most international **arms control agreements**, although it delayed signing the **Nuclear Nonproliferation Treaty** (NPT) until 1992, allowing it to continue **nuclear testing** until that date. It is a member of the **North Atlantic Treaty Organization** (NATO), the **European Union** (EU), the **Organization for Cooperation and Security in Europe** (OSCE), and most other major international organizations. *See also* DE GAULLE, CHARLES.

FRANCO-PRUSSIAN TREATY (1808). Meeting in Thuringia, Germany, Russian Emperor Alexander I and France's Napoleon I signed an agreement that imposed limits on the size and capabilities of the Prussian army.

FRATRICIDE. In **strategic** terms, the destruction of one or more **nuclear weapons** by the nearby detonation of other nuclear weapons. Fratricide is a targeting consideration when launching multiple warheads at a single site or the targeting of closely spaced sites. *See also* DENSE PACK.

FREEZE. Proposals seeking a halt to the further development, testing, production, or deployment of selected weapons and their means of delivery. The term in practice normally refers to a freeze on **nuclear weapons** and delivery systems.

FUNCTIONALLY RELATED OBSERVABLE DIFFERENCES. Variations in selected mission-oriented features of specified weapon systems that can be monitored by **national technical means** to differentiate that system from other variants or systems that are otherwise similar. These differences and **verification** means are central to controlling **dual-use** and other closely related systems, and are one mainstay of modern, detailed **arms control agreements**.

FUSION. The process of combining nuclear nuclei to affect the release of vast energy. The **United States** successfully demonstrated fusion in an explosive device tested in the South Pacific in 1952. *See also* FISSION; FUSION WEAPON.

FUSION WEAPON. Two-stage weapon in which a **fission** reaction initiates and sustains a **fusion** process in materials such as tritium or deuterium, also called **hydrogen bombs**, H-bombs, or **thermonuclear bombs**. These produce huge quantities of energy, with no theoretical limit as to their size.

G

GENE. A sequence of nucleic acids within the **deoxyribonucleic acid** molecules representing the genetic code for the production of proteins in a cell.

GENERAL AND COMPLETE DISARMAMENT (GCD). A peace proposal calling for the elimination and abandonment of all military forces and weapon systems other than internal police forces. GCD was a popular goal of international antimilitary groups during the 1950s and was adopted by the **United Nations** as a long-term goal in 1959. *See also* TRANSNATIONAL PEACE MOVEMENTS.

GENERAL-PURPOSE FORCES. Conventional military forces that can be used in multiple scenarios on land, at sea, or in the air. General-purpose forces are those that do not use **nuclear, chemical,** or **biological weapons.**

GENEVA. Located in Switzerland, Geneva is the headquarters of many international organizations, including the Geneva office of the **United Nations,** the **UN Conference on Disarmament,** and the **International Committee of the Red Cross.** Previously Geneva hosted the **League of Nations.** Numerous bilateral and multilateral **arms control negotiations** have taken place in Geneva.

GENEVA CONVENTION (1949). The four parts of the Geneva Convention were all signed in Geneva, Switzerland, on 12 August 1949. Geneva Convention I deals with the "Amelioration of the Condition of the Wounded and Sick in Armed Forces in the Field." It builds upon the **Red Cross Convention** and designates persons taking no part in hostilities, such as those placed *hors de combat* by sickness, wounds, or detention, who shall be treated humanely. It lists prohibited actions by a belligerent. It also describes appropriate actions for caring for wounded and sick, of either side in a conflict. Convention II, the "Amelioration of Wounded, Sick, and Shipwrecked Members of Armed Forces at Sea," lays down similar rules. Convention III, "Relative to the Treatment of Prisoners of War," describes who can be a prisoner, outlines general protections for prisoners, and describes requirements for their humane treatment, including rules regarding their quarters, food, clothing, and hygiene and medical attention. Convention IV, "Relative to the Protection of Civilian Persons in Time of War," deals with identifying protected civilians, as well as detailing protections to be provided, including the sanctuary for hospitals.

The Geneva Conventions were buttressed by the **United Nations** General Assembly Resolution 2675 on the Protection of Civilians, adopted 9 December 1970. *See also* HAGUE CONVENTIONS.

GENEVA NAVAL CONFERENCE (1927). An international conference that attempted to achieve additional restrictions on warships, in line with those agreed at the **Washington Naval Conference** of 1921-1922 and the resulting Five Power Treaty. The Geneva meetings failed to make any progress.

GENEVA PROTOCOL (1925). The "Protocol for the Prohibition of the Use in War of Asphyxiating, Poisonous, or Other Gases, and of Bacteriological Methods in Warfare" was an attempt by the victorious powers of World War I to ensure that **chemical weapons** were never again used on the field of battle. Restrictions were imposed on Germany, Austria, Bugaria, and Hungary through the **Versailles Treaty**. They were codified in the **Washington Naval Treaty** of 1922 and the Geneva Protocol, signed by 29 nations 15 June 1925. It **entered into force** on 8 February 1928. The protocol was honored by most parties during World War II, but violations by **Iran** and **Iraq** in the 1980s led to an international conference in Paris in 1989 that resulted in the **Chemical Weapons Convention** (CWC). The **United States** did not ratify the protocol until 22 January 1975. As of mid-2004 the protocol had been signed by 135 nations.

GENOCIDE COVENTIONS (1948). The Convention on Genocide was among the first **United Nations** conventions addressing humanitarian issues. It was adopted in 1948 in response to the atrocities committed during World War II. The UN recognized that "genocide is an international crime, which entails the national and international responsibility of individual persons and states." The convention has been widely accepted by the international community and ratified by the overwhelmingly majority of states.

GEOSYNCHRONOUS ORBIT. Earth orbit at an altitude such that the satellite circles the earth at the same rate as the rotation of the earth—once per day. A satellite in geosynchronous orbit will maintain position over the same point on earth, allowing enhanced **surveillance**, warning, and communications capabilities. This only occurs when a satellite is placed in orbit directly over the equator at an altitude of 22,000 miles.

GLASNOST. The **Russian** word for "openness." It was coined by President **Mikhail Gorbachev** in the mid-1980s to reflect the **Soviet Union's** willingness to allow greater flexibility in the Soviet economy and society. This also resulted in improved relations with the West. This liberalization of foreign policy and loosening of restrictions was largely responsible for the nonviolent revolution within the **Warsaw Pact** that ended the **Cold War** in 1989.

GLASSBORO SUMMIT (1967). The **Lyndon Johnson-Alexei Kosygin** summit meeting at Glassboro, New Jersey, in the summer of 1967 was the first such conference since the disastrous meeting between **John F. Kennedy** and **Nikita Khrushchev** in April 1961. But it produced little of substance. Every time Johnson raised the crucial issue of **arms control**, Kosygin shifted the subject to the Middle East. Kosygin claimed the **United States** wanted to get rid of the **Soviet Union's antiballistic-missile defense system** while maintaining its sizable lead in offensive weapons. The only tangible result of the summit was to make final the terms of the **Nuclear Nonproliferation Treaty** (signed in 1968). Not until the following year did the two nations agree to initiate talks on **strategic-arms limitation talks** (SALT).

GLOBAL DEFENSE SYSTEM. A mutual system of **antiballistic missile defenses** proposed by Soviet President **Mikhail Gorbachev** to U.S. President **Ronald Reagan** at the October 1996 **Reykjavik Summit** in Iceland. In order to forestall the American **Strategic Defense Initiative** (SDI), Gorbachev proposed cooperative defenses linked to major reductions in offensive **strategic** weapons. This was also the name given to the space-based sub-system of **Brilliant**

Pebbles satellites within the **George H.W. Bush** administration's modified SDI program in 1991, which was called **Global Protection Against Limited Strikes** (GPALS).

GLOBAL PARTNERSHIP AGAINST WMD (2002). The "Global Partnership Against the Spread of Weapons and Materials of Mass Destruction (WMD)" is an initiative of the **Group of Eight** industrialized countries (the G8, which includes the **United States, United Kingdom**, Canada, **France,** Germany, Italy, Japan, and **Russia**) aimed at preventing terrorists from obtaining **weapons of mass destruction** by denying them access to material and personnel, primarily from Russia, that could be used for that purpose. At the 2002 G8 Summit in Kananaskis, Canada, the G8 countries committed to raise up to $20 billion over ten years to fund **nonproliferation** projects, primarily in Russia. Under the "10 plus 10 over 10" plan, the United States is to provide $10 billion, with the other half to come from the remaining G8 members over a 10-year period. The **European Union**, Norway, Sweden, Switzerland, Finland, and the Netherlands have subsequently agreed to support the plan. The program focuses on four priority areas: destroying **chemical weapons** stockpiles, dismantling decommissioned nuclear submarines, securing nuclear and **radiological** materials, and finding civilian employment for former weapons scientists. As part of the initiative, G8 leaders established nonproliferation principles, guidelines for projects, and a Senior Officials Group to coordinate partnership programs. The partnership incorporates preexisting programs as well as new initiatives.

GLOBAL POSITIONING SYSTEM (GPS). A 24-satellite constellation operated by the **United States Department of Defense** for navigation and precise geodetic position measurements. GPS data has also been harnessed to improve targeting capabilities of **precision-guided munitions** through an inexpensive strap-on kit called the joint direct attack munition, or JDAM.

GLOBAL PROTECTION AGAINST LIMITED STRIKES (GPALS). A "thin" **United States strategic** defensive system pursued by President **George H.W. Bush** from 1990 designed to stop a limited number of missiles, but not a full-scale **Russian** attack. This system was supported as defense against the acts of a single renegade Russian commander or of a state possessing only a very limited **nuclear weapon** and **ballistic missile** arsenal. GPALS represented a significant retrenchment from President **Ronald Reagan's** original **Strategic Defense Initiative**, but it still called for a large number of components relying on untested technologies. The GPALS system was to consist of 1,000 **Brilliant Pebbles** satellites and 500 to 1,000 ground- or sea-based ballistic missile interceptors that would destroy incoming **warheads** using **hit-to-kill** technology.

GOODBY, JAMES (1929-). Trained in engineering, James Goodby became a career U.S. diplomat and served with the U.S. **Atomic Energy Commission**, representing the **United States** at several international **arms control** and **disarmament negotiations**, including the **Strategic Arms Reduction Talks** (START), the **Conference on Disarmament in Europe** (CDE), and the Safe and Secure Dismantlement of Nuclear Weapons.

GORBACHEV, MIKHAIL (1931-). Soviet leader during the period 1985-1991. He introduced programs of economic restructuring (*perestroika*) and openness in public life (*glasnost*). His willingness to open the **Soviet Union** to the West led to increasing confidence among the members of the **Warsaw Pact**, closer relations between the two sides, and several **arms control treaties** that reflected this increasing trust (as well as the need to reduce defense spending in order to improve the Soviet economy): the **Intermediate-Range Nuclear Forces Treaty** (INF), the **Conventional Armed Forces in Europe Treaty** (CFE), the **Strategic Arms Reduction Treaty** (START I), and eventually, the end of the **Cold War**.

GOVERNMENT-INDUSTRY CONFERENCE AGAINST CHEM-ICAL WEAPONS (1989). At the initiative of the **United States**, 67 nations attended this international conference in Canberra, Australia, in September 1989. Chemical industry participants expressed their willingness to work for a global ban on **chemical weapons**, opposed the misuse of **dual-use** chemicals, committed their industry to dialogue with governments on **implementing** a **chemical weapons convention**, and accepted a self-policing role.

GRADUATED DETERRENCE. A nuclear doctrine that prescribes a sequential, measured response to enemy activities including the use of conventional forces as well as tactical and **strategic nuclear weapons**. First embodied in the 1950s and 1960s as part of American strategic doctrine, this concept has experienced renewed interest as a result of U.S. experiences in the global war on **terrorism**. Some even advocate the development of a new generation of more usable small nuclear weapons to allow for a full range of deterrent capabilities.

GRADUATED AND RECIPROCATED INITIATIVES IN TENSION REDUCTION (GRIT). Phrase coined by Charles Osgood, who developed a theory on the behavior of governments during the **Cold War.** GRIT contrasted with the prevalent belief by the **superpowers** during the 1960s in unilateral **escalation** for dealing with threats. The acronym GRIT also reflected the requirement for states to be determined and patient while waiting for responses to their unilateral moves to reduce tension, whether alone or as a prelude to formal **negotiations**. While the political, intellectual, and moral climate of the Cold War was not favorable to such unilateral actions, the **United States** and **Russian** presidents did engage in some successfully reciprocated unilateral initiatives in the early 1990s. *See* PRESIDENTIAL NUCLEAR INITIATIVES.

GRAVITY BOMB. A bomb that falls to earth under the force of gravity, without any other propellant. Gravity bombs are typically delivered by aircraft. They can hold conventional, chemical, biological, or nuclear explosives.

GRAY MARKET. Trade in weapons or weapons materials, systems, components, or materials under export or use controls in which the end-user or end-use is hidden or misstated. Illegal arms sales are often used to subvert formal **arms controls agreements**.

GREAT BRITAIN. *See* UNITED KINGDOM.

GROMYKO, ANDREI (1909-1989). Career politician and diplomat in the **Soviet Union**. He was the ambassador to the **United States** during World War II, ambassador to the **United Nations**, Soviet foreign minister from 1957-1985, and president of the **USSR** from 1985 until his death. One of the leading figures in the making of Soviet policy throughout the **Cold War**.

GROUND ALERT. The practice of maintaining aircraft in a state of heightened readiness at military bases, fully loaded with fuel, weapons, and their crews, prepared to launch on their **strategic** strike mission on extremely short notice.

GROUND-LAUNCHED BALLISTIC MISSILE (GLBM). A **ballistic missile** weapon-delivery vehicle that is launched from the ground.

GROUND-LAUNCHED CRUISE MISSILE (GLCM). An unmanned, self-propelled weapon-delivery vehicle that is launched from the ground and sustains flight through aerodynamic lift over most of its flight path. GLCMs with a range of 500-5,000 kilometers were deployed in Europe by the **North Atlantic Treaty Organization** (NATO) in the early 1980s, but were banned by the 1987 **Intermediate-Range Nuclear Forces Treaty** (INF). A variant of the **Tomahawk sea-launched cruise missile**, the GLCM was officially designated the BGM-109B. *See also* CRUISE MISSILE.

GROUP OF SEVEN/GROUP OF EIGHT (G-7/G-8). Since 1975, the heads of state or government of the principal industrial democracies have been meeting annually to deal with the major economic and political issues facing their domestic societies and the international community as a whole. The six countries at the first summit, held at Rambouillet, France, in November 1975, were **France**, the **United States**, **Great Britain**, Germany, Japan, and Italy. They were joined by Canada in 1976 and by the European Community in 1977. From then on, membership in the G7 was fixed, although 15 developing countries' leaders met with the G7 leaders on the eve of the 1989 Paris Summit, and the **Soviet Union** and then **Russia** has participated in post-summit dialogue with the G7 since 1991. Starting in 1994, the G7 has met with Russia at each summit (referred to as the P8 or Political 8). The 1998 Birmingham Summit saw full Russian participation, giving birth to the G8 (although the G7 continued to function alongside the formal summits).

The G7/8 Summit has consistently dealt with macroeconomic management, international trade, and relations with developing countries. Questions of East-West economic relations, energy, and **terrorism** have also been of recurrent concern. From this initial foundation the summit agenda has broadened considerably to include microeconomic issues such as employment and the information highway, transnational issues such as the environment, crime and drugs, and a host of political-security issues ranging from human rights through regional security to **arms control**.

GROUP OF 23. Term applied to the combined membership of the **North Atlantic Treaty Organization** (NATO) and the **Warsaw**

Pact as they met to discuss and finalize the **Conventional Forces in Europe** (CFE) and **Open Skies Treaties**, 1988-1990. Creation of the Group resulted from a U.S. proposal at a 1987 **Conference on Security Cooperation in Europe** (CSCE) session to break the CSCE membership into two groups: one involving all member states to work on **confidence- and security-building measures** and disarmament in Europe, and the other, the Group of 23, to deal with strengthening stability at lower levels of conventional forces.

GUADALAJARA AGREEMENT (1991). This accord between Argentina and Brazil served as a nuclear **confidence-building measure** and regulatory regime, allowing peaceful nuclear development while controlling **fissile materials** to preclude development of **nuclear weapons**. The agreement established the **Joint System for Accounting and Control of Nuclear Materials** and the **Brazilian-Argentine Agency for Accounting and Control of Nuclear Materials** to administer it.

GULF WAR (1991). *See* DESERT SHIELD; DESERT STORM.

GUN-TYPE NUCLEAR WEAPON. One of two basic types of **nuclear weapon** design. A gun-type design takes two otherwise subcritical masses of **enriched uranium** and throws them together in such a way as to create a critical event and an atomic explosion. This is usually done by using a heavy metal tube (such as a naval cannon with both ends plugged) and high explosives that hurl one mass into the other. First designed by the U.S. **Manhattan Project** in 1945, scientists and engineers were so certain that it would work the first time that it was not tested prior to being dropped on **Hiroshima**, Japan, on 6 August of that year.

H

H-BOMB. *See* FUSION BOMB; HYDROGEN BOMB.

HAGUE COMMISSION (1923). Six nations sent legal, diplomatic, and military experts to The Hague, Netherlands, for three months of discussions on the rules of air warfare in 1923. The final report listed 62 rules for the conduct of aerial warfare, many of them adapted from land or sea **laws of war**. In particular, the commission attempted to define legitimate targets for aerial bombardment and to minimize the risk to civilians.

HAGUE CONVENTIONS (1899, 1907). The Hague conventions were adopted in the Netherlands at the turn of the 20th century and represented one of the earliest multinational attempts at regulating war. Convention II (1899) limited sieges, bombardments, and injuring the enemy by pronouncing that the right of belligerents to adopt means of injuring the enemy is not unlimited. Specifically, the convention restricted the use of poisoned arms, to kill or wound "treacherously," to kill or wound soldiers who are surrendering, to declare that no quarter will be given, to employ weapons that cause superfluous injury, to misuse a flag of truce or the uniform of an enemy, to wantonly destroy property, to attack an undefended city, to attack without warning, or to pillage a city. Before sieges or bombardments all opportunities should be taken to warn the besieged authorities, and to protect cultural and scientific sites and hospitals. Convention IV (1907) reiterated those rules and added new restrictions, including the abolishment or suspension of laws relating to the citizens of a belligerent country. Further, it outlaws forcing the nationals of a hostile country to take part in the operations of war directed against their own country. *See also* GENEVA CONVENTION; ROERICH PACT.

HALPERIN, MORTON (1938-). One of the intellectual founders, with **Thomas Schelling**, of the term **arms control** in the early 1960s. A civil libertarian and government watchdog, Halperin was denied confirmation by Congress as assistant secretary of defense for democracy and human rights in 1993 (a post subsequently moved to the **National Security Council,** where he served for two years) under President **William Clinton.**

HAMMARSKJÖLD, DAG (1905-1961). Swedish statesman who served as secretary general of the **United Nations** from 1953 until his death in a plane crash in the Congo in 1961. His tenure witnessed the high point of UN influence in world affairs, both diplomatically and in terms of its military peacekeeping responsibilities.

HANFORD, WASHINGTON. Location of one of the first national nuclear laboratories created as part of the **Manhattan Project,** Hanford was opened in 1943 for the express purpose of creating **plutonium** from atomic reactors to use in the first **atomic bomb.**

Enrico Fermi designed the B Reactor, the world's first plutonium production reactor. This location was selected due to its isolation and to its proximity to a steady supply of cooling water and electricity provided by the Columbia River hydroelectric project. It produced enough for two bombs by 1945, the first used in the **Trinity Test**, the second dropped on **Nagasaki,** Japan. Today Hanford is home to Pacific Northwest Laboratories. It comprises some 560 square miles of grasslands north of Richland in central Washington.

HARASSING AGENT. A **chemical agent** that, while insufficient to kill, causes interference with normal activities and requires masking or other protective measures. An example would be tear gas.

HARD MOBILE LAUNCHER (HML). The Boeing Small **Intercontinental Ballistic Missile** (ICBM) Hard Mobile Launcher (HML) was a mobile, radiation-hardened vehicle designed to transport and launch the Small ICBM, unofficially called the "Midgetman." The HML could travel on or off-road. It could withstand moderate nuclear effects, and the trailer-mounted plow allowed the tractor to bury the launcher-trailer in the ground for additional protection from nuclear blasts. Development work ceased when the Small ICBM program was cancelled in the late 1980s.

HARD-TARGET KILL CAPABILITY. A weapon system's ability to destroy a **hardened target** through its accuracy, **yield,** and penetration capabilities.

HARDENED TARGET. Sites that are protected by physical construction means against the expected blast, heat, and radiation effects of **nuclear weapons**. Hardened sites are often used to protect **intercontinental ballistic missile silos** and their launch-control facilities. *See also* PASSIVE DEFENSE.

HARMEL REPORT. In 1967 the **North Atlantic Treaty Organization** (NATO) shifted to a policy of **flexible response**. At the same time, it released a companion report on improving political relations with the **Soviet Union**. The Harmel Report called for the Alliance to pursue a dual-track approach for dealing with the **Warsaw Pact**: on the one hand, military modernization and enhanced strategies; on the other, **arms control** and **confidence-building measures** to reduce tensions between the two sides.

HARMONIZATION. In the context of **arms control negotiations,** the attempt to reconcile differing positions held by the **state parties** on measures under consideration. This is a necessary step if the parties wish to achieve agreement and eventual **treaty** signing.

HART-RUDMAN COMMISSION. *See* COMMISSION ON NATIONAL SECURITY IN THE 21ST CENTURY.

HAWK. A person who believes that one must rely on military strength and strength-based **deterrence** for security and the resolution of international conflict. *See also* DOVE.

HAZARDOUS MATERIAL. A material that endangers life or property.

HEAVY BOMBER. A technical definition used in the **Strategic Arms Limitation Treaty** (SALT II) to refer to current and future **United States** and **Soviet** bombers equipped to carry nuclear bombs and/or **cruise missiles** and capable of carrying out intercontinental missions. The **Strategic Arms Reduction Treaty (START I)** gave heavy bombers a discounted counting rule for determining the total warheads in a state's **strategic** arsenal. A heavy bomber is typically the largest bomber in a country's inventory, with intercontinental range. The U.S. **B-1, B-2,** and **B-52** are heavy bombers currently in its inventory.

HEAVY ICBM. A technical definition used in the **Strategic Arms Limitation Talks Treaty** (SALT II) **negotiations** to include any missile heavier than the **Soviet** SS-19 **intercontinental ballistic missile** (ICBM). This was a concern to American negotiators because of the large **throw weight** and multiple **warheads** such a missile could carry; it could conceivably strike many targets simultaneously, thereby serving as an effective and destabilizing **first-strike** weapon.

HEAVY WATER REACTOR. A **nuclear reactor** that uses heavy water as moderator and/or coolant and natural **uranium** as fuel. These differ from the more common **light water reactors** that require **enriched uranium** to operate.

HELSINKI. Capital of the **neutral** nation of Finland and site of numerous bilateral and **multilateral arms control negotiations** and agreements during the **Cold War,** including the **Helsinki Final Act** that led to the creation of the **Conference on Security and Cooperation in Europe** (CSCE, later the **Organization for Security and Cooperation in Europe,** or OSCE).

HELSINKI ACCORDS. *See* HELSINKI FINAL ACT.

HELSINKI AGREEMENT (1997). Presidents **William Clinton** and **Boris Yeltsin** agreed on a "Joint Statement on Parameters on Future Reductions in Nuclear Forces" at their meeting in Helsinki, Finland, in March 1997. This statement underscored the requirement for ratification of the **Strategic Arms Reduction Treaty** (START II) by both countries and an agreement to begin negotiations on START III once START II **entered into force.** The goal of START III negotiations would be a ceiling of 2,000-2,500 **strategic warheads** by 31 December 2007. This date was also the extended deadline for START II eliminations. In order to ensure the irreversibility of these reductions, the new **treaty** was to include inventory **transparency** provisions and call for the destruction of **nuclear warheads.** The two sides also agreed to discuss **nonstrategic nuclear weapons** (tactical weapons and **sea-launched cruise missiles)** in a separate but parallel forum. And they agreed to the goal of making all START treaties unlimited in duration. The March agreement was codified in **memorandums of understanding** signed by the two presidents in New York on 26 September 1997.

HELSINKI FINAL ACT (1975). Also known as the Helsinki Accords. Signed in 1975, this was the first of a series of agreements and procedures designed to increase the security of the members of the **Conference on Security and Cooperation in Europe** (CSCE, later the **Organization for Security and Cooperation in Europe,** or OSCE). It was signed by the **United States,** Canada, and all European nations except Albania. In addition to recognizing existing borders and the need for economic cooperation, the act required advance notification of military maneuvers involving more than 25,000 troops. This agreement set the foundation for the complicated and increasingly intrusive measures that followed in the realm of **confidence- and security-building measures.**

HERBICIDE. A substance that kills or inhibits the growth of plants. Large quantities or prolonged exposure to herbicides can also prove detrimental to human health.

HERITAGE FOUNDATION. A Washington, D.C., think tank founded in 1973 that conducts research and educational activities to promote conservative public policies based on the principles of free enterprise, limited government, individual freedom, and strong national defense.

HIGH ALTITUDE NUCLEAR DETONATION (HAND). A nuclear explosion in outer space could lead to dramatically increased levels of **radiation** within the earth's magnetic field. This is a particular concern to the military and commercial space industries. A study by the **Defense Threat Reduction Agency** in 2001 concluded that one low-yield, high-altitude nuclear explosion could disable all satellites in low-earth orbit that were not specifically **hardened** against radiation.

HIGH LEVEL GROUP (HLG). An advisory body to the **North Atlantic Treaty Organization's** (NATO) **Nuclear Planning Group** (NPG). The NPG meets several times per year to consider aspects of NATO's nuclear policy and planning and matters concerning the safety, security, and survivability of **nuclear weapons.**

HIGHLY ENRICHED URANIUM (HEU). Highly enriched uranium is a man-made substance that increases the level of **fissile material** in natural uranium to the point where it can be used for atomic reactor fuel or **nuclear weapons**. In nature, uranium consists largely of two isotopes, U-235 and U-238. The production of energy in nuclear reactors results from the **fission** or splitting of the U-235 atoms, a process that releases energy in the form of heat. U-235 is the main fissile isotope of uranium. Uranium is typically highly enriched when its proportion of U-235 exceeds 20 percent. There are several methods of enriching uranium, all of which involve large, advanced industrial processes. *See also* ENRICHED URANIUM; ENRICHMENT; WEAPONS-GRADE MATERIAL.

HIROSHIMA. The Japanese city upon which the first **atomic bomb** was detonated, on 6 August 1945 in World War II by the **United States**. This marked the first use of a **gun-type device** design using **highly enriched uranium** as its **fissile material**.

HIT-TO-KILL. A concept related to **ballistic missile defense** that refers to the method of intercepting and destroying an incoming **warhead**. Hit-to-kill implies striking the incoming weapon with a counter-weapon, using the impact force of the collision to destroy the weapon. This differs from other types of interception techniques that rely on detonating an explosive warhead in close proximity to the incoming weapon. Sometimes referred to as "hitting a bullet with a bullet," it poses a significant technological challenge. Nonetheless, this approach forms the basis of the **United States'** 21st century missile defense program.

HOMELAND DEFENSE (HLD). The protection of one's home territory, usually a nation-state, against attack from outside aggressors or from within its borders. A subset of **homeland security**, homeland defense includes the mission of detecting, **deterring, dissuading**, or defeating an adversary and accomplishing **consequence management** and mitigation activities if the attack occurs. Within the **United States**, homeland defense is the responsibility of the **Department of Defense** and **U.S. Northern Command**, working closely with the **Department of Homeland Security**.

HOMELAND SECURITY (HLS). All actions taken to protect one's state and its people. Broader in scope than **homeland defense**, homeland security includes border controls, immigration policies, counterterrorism, protection of transportation networks, and so on. In the **United States** this responsibility rests with the **Department of Homeland Security**, which works closely with the Federal Bureau of Investigation and **U.S. Northern Command**.

HOMING DEVICE. A component of the terminal guidance system of a missile that detects the target and guides the missile to that target using electronic or mechanical servos and controls.

HORIZONTAL ESCALATION. The spread of weapons or conflict laterally to additional nation-states beyond those originally involved. This differs from vertical escalation, which is the increasing level of violence in a conflict, up to and including the introduction of **nuclear weapons** into a previously conventional fight.

HOST. An **organism** that serves as home to, and often as food supply for, a parasite such as a **virus**.

HOT AGENT. A **microorganism**, often airborne, that is extremely and lethally infectious—for example, the Ebola Virus.

HOT AREA OR HOT ZONE. An area that contains lethal, infectious **organisms** and that is unsuitable for human habitation or work.

HOT LINE AGREEMENTS (1963, 1971, 1984). In order to minimize the chances of miscommunication leading to miscalculation during times of emergency or increased tension, the first of three **agreements** between Washington and Moscow was signed in **Geneva** on 20 June 1963. Both sides agreed to a direct communications link between their capitals using telegraph-teleprinter terminals, duplex wire telegraph circuits, and radiotelegraph circuits, and procedures for sending nearly instantaneous messages in both languages. A revised **treaty** was signed in Washington on 30 September 1971 and **entered into force** immediately. The two countries agreed to a direct communications link encompassing two separate satellite communications systems and teleprinter terminals. A **memorandum of understanding** was signed by both parties on 17 July 1984 in Washington, which agreed to improve the direct communications links by establishing three transmission links employing INTELSAT satellites and modems, facsimile machines, and computers.

HUDSON INSTITUTE. A foreign policy and national security research center based in Washington, D.C. (where it moved in 2004 after 20 years in Indianapolis, Indiana). It was founded in 1961 in Croton-on-Hudson, New York, by **Herman Kahn** with the charter of thinking about the future in conventional ways.

HYDROGEN BOMB. A **nuclear weapon** that employs **fusion** to generate vast energy. Hydrogen bombs are also called "H-bombs" or **thermonuclear bombs**. Hydrogen bombs have much greater explosive power than fission, or atomic, weapons, which are used as the trigger or first stage in a thermonuclear explosion. The first stage ignites the **fissile material** surrounding it, leading to a greatly enhanced result. Weapons can be tailored to achieve specific effects, such as blast or radiation, and have no theoretical limit as to their size. The United States first tested a hydrogen device in 1952; it had a surprisingly high yield of ten megatons. *See also* ATOMIC WEAPONS, FUSION WEAPONS.

I

IKLE, FRED (1924-). Undersecretary of defense for policy in the **Ronald Reagan** administration. A founding member of the **Committee on the Present Danger** in the 1950s, Iklé also cochaired the bipartisan Commission on Integrated Long-Term Strategy, which published *Discriminate Deterrence* in January 1988. From 1973 until 1977 he served as director of the U.S. **Arms Control and Disarmament Agency** (ACDA).

IMMUNITY. Ability to resist or overcome infections, either due to active **antibodies** or other defenses.

IMMUNIZATION. Administration of a nontoxic antigen to convey **active immunity** or of an **antibody** to convey **passive immunity** and render one insusceptible to a **pathogen** or **toxin**.

IMPLEMENTATION. The management process that defines administrative practices and operational procedures used to ensure **compliance** with the provisions of **arms control agreements**.

IMPLEMENTING LEGISLATION. Legislative action to ensure application of specific **treaty** provisions and **verification** requirements by enactment into the domestic law of a **state party**. Failure to comply with the tenets of that treaty then subjects citizens and organizations to civil or criminal legal consequences.

IMPLOSION NUCLEAR WEAPON. A spherical nuclear device containing **fissionable material** of less than **critical mass** that has its volume suddenly reduced by chemical explosives-induced compression, thus creating a supercritical state producing a nuclear explosion. This is one of two basic designs for a nuclear weapon. Implosion devices normally use a core of **plutonium** surrounded by a ball of lithium deuteride and an outside tamper of **depleted uranium**. A focused shock wave generated by an outer layer of conventional high explosives compresses the core, which, when enhanced at the right moment by an injection of tritium, will cause the **fissile material** to go critical and create an atomic explosion. This type of weapon was designed by the **Manhattan Project** and first tested at the **Trinity Site** in New Mexico in July 1945. It was the same type of weapon later used on the city of **Nagasaki**, Japan. *See also* GUN-TYPE NUCLEAR WEAPON; HYDROGEN BOMB.

INCAPACITATING AGENT. A **chemical** or **biological agent** that renders its victims incapable of normal physical or mental action.

INCIDENTS AT SEA TREATY (1972). A bilateral agreement between the **United States** and the **Soviet Union**, signed in Moscow on 25 May 1972. The treaty was a **confidence-building measure** that attempted to limit the chances of conflict precipitated by an incident at sea. It obligated both parties to closely observe International Regulations for Preventing Collisions at Sea, to refrain from mock air attacks on ships, and to provide prior notification of planned activities that could pose hazards to shipping. It also established steps to avoid collision, safe distances to remain from the other side's formations, and standard international signals to use when maneuvering near one another. A 1973 protocol extended the ban on mock attacks to include those against nonmilitary ships.

INDIA. One of the two major powers of South Asia, and the second most populous country on earth with a population of over one billion, India is a secular Hindu state that has been in perpetual conflict with neighboring **Pakistan** since that country's creation in 1947. India has developed an indigenous **nuclear weapons** capability and **intermediate-range ballistic missiles** as potential delivery vehicles for **nuclear warheads**. It conducted an underground test of a nuclear device in 1974 and performed nuclear weapons tests in May 1998. India has not signed the **Nuclear Nonproliferation Treaty.** In terms of **deterrence** policy, nuclear strategy, **command and control** issues, and the like, Pakistan and India find themselves on a learning curve much like that experienced by the **United States** and the **Soviet Union** in the early years of the **Cold War.**

INDIAN OCEAN ZONE OF PEACE PROPOSAL. A proposal adopted by the **United Nations** General Assembly in 1971 that called on the **United States** and the **Soviet Union** to halt any expansion into the Indian Ocean region and to withdraw any military presence from the region. This proposal would, if fully enacted, limit external power presence and influence from the region while also discouraging regional states from military relationships with external powers. The proposal has not been fully implemented.

INDO-PAKISTAN JOINT COMMISSION (1982). Discussions between high-level officials from **India** and **Pakistan** to establish increased levels of talks and trade led to meetings in New Delhi between Prime Ministers Indira Gandhi and Mohammad Zia, which in turn began a series of talks that led to the establishment of the **South Asian Association for Regional Cooperation** (SAARC).

INERTIAL GUIDANCE. An onboard system of gyroscopes and electronics that directs the path of a **ballistic** or **cruise missile** by measuring acceleration and correcting the missile's trajectory within a given coordinate system.

INHUMANE WEAPONS CONVENTION (1981). *See* CERTAIN CONVENTIONAL WEAPONS CONVENTION.

INITIAL INSPECTION. The first on-site inspection of a **declared facility or site** to verify **declarations**, set the baseline standard for future inspections, and establish the departure point for future **verification** activities. *See* BASELINE INSPECTION.

INSPECTION. The attempt by one party to an **agreement** to verify compliance with the **treaty** using physical, electronic, seismic, or other **sensor** methods. Inspections using **national technical means** were first written into **arms control** agreements with the 1972 **Strategic Arms Limitation Treaty** (SALT I), and **on-site inspections** were first authorized as part of the 1987 **Intermediate-Range Nuclear Forces Treaty** (INF).

INSPECTORATE. A body of inspectors established to carry out **verification** activities under an **arms control treaty** or **agreement**.

INSTITUTE ON DEFENSE AND DISARMAMENT STUDIES. A **strategic** studies and security research center located in Cambridge, Massachusetts, established in 1980. It focuses on **arms control**, alternative defense issues, common security, and defense spending.

INSTITUTE FOR INTERNATIONAL STRATEGIC STUDIES (IISS). A London-based defense and analysis institute, best known for its publication series, including *Survival*, *Adelphi Papers*, and the annual *Military Balance*. One of the oldest and most prestigious of the international security think tanks, it was founded in 1958.

INSTITUTE FOR NATIONAL SECURITY STUDIES (INSS). A **U.S. Air Force** research center located at the Air Force Academy in Colorado Springs, Colorado. Founded in 1992, INSS pools funding from multiple government agencies and sponsors a large number of small research projects by military officers and civilian faculty members of military schools. Its staff publishes a series of occasional papers and books focusing on **arms control, counterproliferation**, Air Force policy, homeland defense, information operations, environmental security, and space.

INSTITUTE FOR NATIONAL STRATEGIC STUDIES (INSS). A U.S. **Department of Defense**-funded research center located at National Defense University, Washington, D.C. INSS was established in 1984 to provide policy research, analysis, and **strategic** gaming for the **Joint Chiefs of Staff**, DoD, the unified commands, and other U.S. government agencies on national security and defense issues; to support NDU's educational programs as well as professional military education; and to conduct outreach programs, including conferences and publications. INSS is host to the National Strategic Gaming Center and the Center for Counterproliferation Research.

INTERCONTINENTAL BALLISTIC MISSILE (ICBM). A category of land-based **ballistic missiles** with a range of 5,500 kilometers or more. Such missiles typically have two or three boost stages and depart the earth's atmosphere en route to their target. They can sometimes carry up to 18 individually targetable **warheads**, which separate from the **delivery system** prior to or during descent. Examples include the U.S. **Titan, Minuteman**, and **Peacekeeper**, and the Russian SS-9 and SS-18 missiles.

INTERGOVERNMENTAL ORGANIZATION (IGO). A formally chartered organization comprised of state governments. An intergovernmental organization operating within the bounds of its charter is given quasi-state status within the international system. Examples include the **North Atlantic Treaty Organization** (NATO) and the **United Nations**.

INTERIM AGREEMENT ON LIMITING STRATEGIC OFFENSIVE ARMS (1972). *See* STRATEGIC ARMS LIMITATION TREATY (SALT I).

INTERMEDIATE-RANGE BALLISTIC MISSILE (IRBM). A category of land-based **ballistic missiles** with a range of between 3,000 and 5,500 kilometers. Examples include China's CSS-2 missile. Most U.S. and Russian weapons in this category were eliminated by the 1987 **Intermediate-Range Nuclear Forces Treaty** (INF).

INTERMEDIATE-RANGE NUCLEAR FORCES (INF). A category of **ballistic missiles** and **cruise missiles** with ranges between 1,000 and 5,500 kilometers. This range proved of particular importance to Europe during the **Cold War** as the **North Atlantic Treaty Organization** (NATO) and the **Warsaw Pact** both deployed missiles in this category to threaten the other party. This entire category of weapons was declared illegal by the 1987 **Intermediate-Range Nuclear Forces** (INF) Treaty. Examples included the U.S. **ground-launched cruise missile** and **Pershing II missile**, and the Soviet SS-20 missile.

INTERMEDIATE-RANGE NUCLEAR FORCES TREATY (INF) (1987). The "Treaty between the United States and the Union of Soviet Socialist Republics on the Elimination of Their Intermediate-Range and Shorter-Range Missiles" provided for the complete elimination of all U.S. and Soviet intermediate-range (1,000-5,500 kilometers) and shorter-range (500-1,000 km) **ground-launched ballistic** and **cruise missiles**. The INF Treaty was signed on 8 December 1987 and ratified on 27 May 1988, with **entry into force** on 1 June 1988. The **treaty** was of unlimited duration, although the **inspection** regime only lasted 13 years.

Despite the fact that the final elimination of missiles was completed by 1 June 1991, the **on-site inspection regime** continued until the year 2001 to ensure compliance with the treaty. This included continuous monitoring of the missile final assembly facilities at **Magna**, Utah, and **Votkinsk**, Russia. On-site inspections of former missile operating bases and missile support facilities were allowed at a rate of 15 per year until 1996 and 10 per year until 31 May 2001. Some of these facilities are now located in successor states other than the **Russian Federation (Belarus, Ukraine, Kazakhstan**, Uzbekistan, Turkmenistan and Lithuania, Latvia, and Estonia) and states of the former **Warsaw Pact**. The **Special Verification Commission** (SVC) is the body tasked with overseeing **verification** and **compliance**; it is based in **Geneva**, Switzerland. Parties to the treaty included the United States and **Soviet Union** (Russia assumed successor status); Belarus, Kazakhstan, and Ukraine have also accepted inspections. The **United States** conducted over 511 inspections in Russia as part of the INF Treaty verification and compliance regime; similarly, Russia conducted 275 inspections in the United States.

INTERNATIONAL ATOMIC ENERGY AGENCY (IAEA). An organization chartered in 1956 under the auspices of the **United Nations** to promote peaceful uses of nuclear technology, prevent the **proliferation** of **safeguarded** nuclear materials, and regulate health and safety standards within the nuclear industry. Located in Vienna, Austria, the IAEA has actively attempted to halt the spread of materials useful in the development of nuclear energy and **nuclear weapons**.

INTERNATIONAL ATOMIC ENERGY LIST. *See* NUCLEAR SUPPLIERS GROUP.

INTERNATIONAL COMMITTEE OF THE RED CROSS. The "Convention for the Amelioration of the Condition of the Wounded and Sick of Armies in the Field" was signed in Geneva on 27 July 1929. This convention called for all wounded soldiers and officers to be cared for, respected, protected, and humanely treated by whichever side of the conflict finds themselves in charge of such wounded personnel. The winner of a battle agrees to search the field for wounded and dead, and show them all courtesy. Belligerents agree to forward to each other the names of wounded, sick, and dead taken or discovered by them, as well as personal effects found on the battlefield. They shall also honorably inter or cremate all bodies after determining their identities. The International Committee of the Red Cross implements this founding agreement, as well as providing other humanitarian assistance around the globe where needed. *See also* GENEVA CONVENTION.

INTERNATIONAL DATA CENTRE (IDC). A forum for obtaining technical information and sharing data from multiple parties, sponsored by the **International Atomic Energy Agency** (IAEA). It includes information and links to such sites as the International Nuclear Information System, the world's leading information system on the peaceful uses of nuclear science and technology. *See* NUCLEAR REACTION DATA CENTERS NETWORK.

INTERNATIONAL LIST. *See* COMMODITY CONTROLS LIST.

INTERNATIONAL MONITORING SYSTEM (IMS). The **regime** established to monitor and analyze 321 hydroacoustic and seismic listening stations and infrared and radionucleide **sensors** around the world to enforce the **Comprehensive Test Ban Treaty** (CTBT), which was signed in 1996 but has not yet entered into force. The IMS is headquartered in Vienna, Austria. *See also* COMPREHENSIVE TEST BAN TREATY ORGANIZATION.

INTERNATIONAL MUNITIONS LIST. An annual list of **export controlled items** required by the U.S. **Arms Export Control Act**. The list includes multiple areas, from small arms to **ballistic missile** components to computer equipment, covering the spectrum of items that could harm the **United States** if they fell in the wrong hands.

INTERNATIONAL SATELLITE MONITORING AGENCY. Proposed during the 1980s, such an agency would have provided general monitoring and **verification** capability under the auspices of the **United Nations** in order to help enforce **arms control agreements** and independently verify military dispositions.

INTERNATIONALISM. Cooperation among nations, particularly in the fields of politics and economics. Such cooperation reflects a liberal viewpoint on the value of enhanced exchanges between countries that promote improved international relations, a relaxation of tensions, and reduced prospects of conflict.

INTRUSIVE VERIFICATION. Inspections of an adversary's weapons systems to ensure **compliance** with an **agreement** or **treaty**. It may be undertaken when an allegation of noncompliance with an **arms control** agreement is made. Such **verification** involves a wide variety of verification techniques, including overhead photography and **on-site inspections** of specific sites.

INVIOLABLE. Secure from violation, or impossible to penetrate. In diplomatic terms, this usually refers to a sanctuary or protected person, such as an ambassador or a state's embassy; in **arms control treaties** it often refers to the sovereignty of a country's territory, airspace, and littoral waters.

IRAN. One of the largest and most influential countries in Central Asia, Iran was formed in 1935 from the old Persian Empire. For many years during the 20th century Iran was a secular state and solid ally of Western nations. It was a founding member of the **Central Treaty Organization** in 1959. In 1979 a fundamentalist Islamic revolution overthrew the government and cut all ties with the outside world for many years, while remaining a sponsor of **terrorism**. Iran fought an eight-year war against **Iraq** from 1980 to 1988 in which both sides attacked the other's capital and forces in the field with **ballistic missiles** and **chemical weapons**. Iran has recently admitted to developing atomic energy, and many fear it has **nuclear weapons** aspirations.

IRAQ. A large country in the Middle East and home of several major civilizations, Iraq was formed in 1921. It signed the Baghdad Pact with Turkey in 1955 and was a member of the forerunner to the **Central Treaty Organization** from 1955-1958. But upon the rise of Saddam Hussein to power in the 1970s Iraq took a wrong turn in international relations. It used **ballistic missiles, chemical weapons**, and possibly **biological weapons** against **Iran** during their 1980-1988 war, despite being a signatory to the **Geneva Convention**. In 1991 it threatened the use of **weapons of mass destruction** (WMD) against the Coalition that faced it during the Gulf War after Iraq had invaded neighboring Kuwait. **United Nations inspections** during the 1990s uncovered evidence of Iraqi WMD efforts, including **nuclear weapons** research (despite being a signatory to the **Nuclear Nonproliferation Treaty**). Citing Iraq's WMD efforts and ties to international **terrorism**, the **United States** led a new coalition in an invasion of Iraq in 2003 that overturned the Hussein dictatorship and eliminated the final vestiges of Iraq's chemical, biological, and nuclear programs. *See also* DESERT STORM, UNITED NATIONS SPECIAL COMMISSION ON IRAQ.

IRAQI FREEDOM, OPERATION. The U.S.-led multinational military coalition that invaded **Iraq** in March 2003 in order to overthrow the Saddam Hussein regime, eliminate any remaining vestiges of Iraq's programs to develop **weapons of mass destruction**, and install a democratic government. The initial conflict only lasted three weeks, but guerrilla activities against the coalition continued and increased over the following two years. Sovereignty was restored to the Iraqi government in June 2004.

ISRAEL. Independent Jewish homeland since 1948, Israel is a small country in the Middle East surrounded by Islamic enemies. As a result, Israel has fought several wars to ensure its existence and maintains an armed civil society. It is widely assumed, though not confirmed, that Israel has **intermediate-range ballistic missiles** and a substantial arsenal of **nuclear weapons**. *See also* ISRAELI-PALESTINIAN ACCORD; MIDDLE EAST PEACE TALKS.

ISRAELI-PALESTINIAN ACCORD (1994). Following election of the Rabin government in 1992 in **Israel**, Israelis and Palestinians began secret **negotiations** outside the framework of the negotiations being held in Washington, D.C., which were leading nowhere. The Israeli government had earlier refused to negotiate with the Palestine Liberation Organization (PLO), but it found that no progress could be made in Washington, because the supposedly independent Palestinian delegates had to refer every issue back to the Palestinian National Authority. So Israel decided to pursue a separate channel in secret, under the sponsorship of Norwegian mediators. The Oslo Declaration of Principles was the result of these negotiations, surprising the United States and the world, and paving the way for the **Middle East Peace process**. In this document, both sides recognized the rights of the other to exist as a people within the borders of Palestine/Israel and committed themselves to negotiating a permanent settlement and to improving relations between the two peoples. The agreement provides a framework for a solution, rather than a solution. It made possible a peace treaty with Jordan. The chief negotiators on both sides, Yasser Arafat and Yizhak Rabin, subsequently received the Nobel Peace Prize for their efforts. This agreement also provided that Israeli forces would withdraw from areas in the Gaza Strip and a small area around Jericho, in preparation for elections to be held for a Palestinian government. Despite high hopes, within seven years the accord had fallen apart and Israeli-Palestinian relations were once again tense.

ISRAELITE-PHILISTINE TERM OF PEACE (1100 B.C.). One of the earliest **coercive arms control agreements**. Imposed by force upon the loser in this conflict, it limited **Israel's** use of iron.

ITEM OF INSPECTION (IOI). Term used in the 1990 **Conventional Forces in Europe Treaty** (CFE) to identify those items of military concern that were to be counted in **compliance** with the terms of the treaty. Limits were placed on how many items of each category a country, a geographic region, and an alliance could have.

J

JACKSON HOLE, WYOMING. Site of several bilateral **arms control agreements** between the **United States** and **Soviet Union** near the end of the **Cold War**, most notably the September 1989 memorandum of understanding between U.S. Secretary of State **James Baker** and Soviet Foreign Minister **Edouard Shevardnadze** concerning **chemical weapons.**

JOHNSON, LYNDON B. (1908-1973). United States president from 1963-1969. The Johnson administration began the **Strategic Arms Limitation Talks** (SALT) with the **Soviet Union**, which led to the 1972 SALT I treaty. It also negotiated and signed the **Outer Space Treaty** (1967) and the **Nuclear Nonproliferation Treaty** (1968).

JOINT CHIEFS OF STAFF (JCS). The most senior officers of each of the four U.S. military services (**U.S. Air Force, Army,** Marine Corps, and **Navy**), plus a designated chairman of the Joint Chiefs from any of the services. The chairman is the senior military advisor to the president. JCS also refers to the Pentagon staff of some 1,400 military officers who support the chiefs with studies, war plans, and force preparation.

JOINT COMPLIANCE AND INSPECTION COMMISSION (JCIC). The organization created for **implementation** and **compliance** with the **Strategic Arms Reduction Treaty** (START I). Located in **Geneva,** Switzerland, it became the locus of questions over the treaty between the **United States** and **Russia.** *See also* BILATERAL IMPLEMENTATION COMMISSION; STRATEGIC ARMS REDUCTION TREATY (START II); STRATEGIC OFFENSIVE REDUCTIONS TREATY.

JOINT DECLARATION ON THE DENUCLEARIZATION OF THE KOREAN PENINSULA (1992). Signed on 20 January 1992 by the prime minister of the Republic of Korea (South Korea) and representatives of the Democratic People's Republic of Korea (North Korea), the declaration sought to limit the danger of nuclear conflict in the region by eliminating **nuclear weapons** from the Korean peninsula. The six-point agreement came into force on 19 February 1992. Both countries pledged not to "test, produce, receive, possess, store, deploy or use nuclear weapons" or to "possess nuclear **reprocessing** and **uranium enrichment** facilities." The agreement sought to regulate the use of nuclear energy to ensure that it was used for peaceful purposes and not for reprocessing or uranium enrichment. Under the terms of the agreement, a South-North Joint Nuclear Control Commission was created to implement an inspection regime in order to monitor **compliance** with the agreement. However, no **inspections** have been conducted under the terms of the agreement. This failure was overshadowed by the 1994 **Agreed Framework on North Korea**, in which North Korea pledged to implement the terms of the Joint Declaration and engage in North-South dialogue. The Joint Declaration subsequently became part of a wider diplomatic dispute between North Korea and the United States when it turned out that Pyongyang had secretly continued work on its nuclear weapons program.

JOINT NUCLEAR CONTROL COMMISSION. This is the **inspection** and **compliance** organization established in the 20 January 1992 **Joint Declaration on the Denuclearization of the Korean Peninsula.** The Commission was to inspect suspect facilities on both sides.

JOINT STRATEGIC TARGET PLANNING STAFF (JSTPS). The military organization located at **Strategic Air Command** Headquarters, Offutt AFB, Nebraska, during the **Cold War.** The JSTPS identified enemy targets, assigned weapons against those targets, deconflicted the flight paths of those weapons and their delivery systems, and designed the **Single Integrated Operations Plan** (SIOP) by which the **United States** would have prosecuted a **nuclear war** against the **Soviet Union.**

JOINT SYSTEM FOR ACCOUNTING AND CONTROL OF NUCLEAR MATERIALS (SCCC). The *Sistema Comun de Contabilidad y Control de Materiales Nucleares* was established in the **Guadalajara Agreement** of 1991 to provide for accounting for and controlling all nuclear materials in Argentina and Brazil. Its goal was to prevent diversion of those materials to **nuclear weapons** development or production. The **Brazilian-Argentine Agency for Accounting and Control of Nuclear Materials** was established to implement the SCCC.

JUPITER MISSILE. The first U.S. **intermediate-range ballistic missile** (IRBM), developed at Redstone Arsenal. Jupiter was liquid fueled. Development began in 1954, and its first flight was in 1957.

Originally planned for the **U.S. Army,** an executive decision in
1956 restricted the range of Army missiles, giving Jupiter (and all
follow-on **intercontinental ballistic missiles**) to the **U.S. Air
Force.** (That decision was rescinded two years later, allowing the
Army back into the IRBM business.) Jupiters were deployed to Italy
and Turkey in support of the **North Atlantic Treaty Organization**
(NATO) from 1960 to 1965. The United States used Jupiters in
Turkey as bargaining chips with the **Soviet Union** in order to get
the USSR to remove its IRBMs from Cuba during the 1962 **Cuban
Missile Crisis.**

JUST WAR DOCTRINE. The just war tradition was developed by
religious and secular scholars during the Middle Ages. Two distinct
considerations arose regarding justice and conflict: *jus ad bellum,*
the morality and legality of going to war, and *jus in bello,* the conduct of combatants during hostilities, providing limited protection
to innocent civilians and noncombatants in the hands of a belligerent. *Jus ad bellum* emphasizes the right of self-defense and the con-
demnation of acts of aggression, so it is much in line with modern
diplomacy, arms control treaties, and organizations such as the
United Nations. The questions of *jus in bello* are addressed in treaties and agreements such as **The Hague** and **Geneva Conventions.**
The success of both aspects relies on good faith and respect for
treaty obligations by nations. Debate over just war arose again during the Cold War with respect to the use of nuclear weapons. *See
also* BISHOPS' PASTORAL LETTER.

K

KAHN, HERMAN (1922-1983). A long-time analyst for the **RAND
Corporation** and the founder of the **Hudson Institute,** Kahn was
one of the United States' most prominent **strategic** thinkers of the
1950s and 1960s. Kahn's writing outlined a continuum of warfare
from diplomacy to total **nuclear war** that placed nuclear conflict as
just another rung on a continuous ladder of **escalation.** Kahn believed that nuclear wear could be fought and won. Critics argued
that nuclear war was qualitatively distinct from all other forms of
conflict, and that there was a definite line, or **threshold,** separating
conventional from nuclear conflict. That counter-argument formed
a basis for early **Cold War** strategic **arms control** efforts.

KAZAKHSTAN. One of four republics of the **Soviet Union** in which **nuclear weapons**, components, and systems were present at the time of dissolution. All nuclear weapons were consolidated under **Russia's** control in 1992.

KELLOGG-BRIAND PACT (1928). The landmark multilateral agreement between many of the World War I belligerents and rising interwar powers that renounced offensive war as an instrument of national policy. Also known as the **Pact of Paris**, it failed to achieve its stated goals.

KENNAN, GEORGE (1903-). The "father" of the **United States Cold War** doctrine of "containment" of the **Soviet Union**. Kennan, as director of the **Department of State** Policy Planning staff and as department counselor in the period immediately following World War II, argued against the development of the **hydrogen bomb**. He was also ambassador to the Soviet Union and author of the famous "Long Telegram" on the sources of Soviet conduct, which was published in *Foreign Affairs* under the pseudonym "X" in 1947.

KENNEDY, JOHN F. (1917-1963). **United States** president from 1961-1963. Kennedy continued the U.S. **strategic** arms build-up, faced the **Soviet Union** during the **Cuban Missile Crisis**, and created the **Arms Control and Disarmament Agency** to serve as the central organization for dealing with those issues within the U.S. government. His administration negotiated and signed the **Hot Line Agreement** (1963) and the **Limited Test Ban Treaty** (1963).

KHRUSHCHEV, NIKITA (1894-1971). Soviet secretary general of the Communist Party and premier of the **Soviet Union** from 1958-1964. His dramatic speaking style and willingness to push the **United States** to the brink of war on several occasions made him a caricature in the West of all that was bad about the Soviet Union and its ideology, yet he was responsible for the Soviets signing the first **arms control agreements** with the West, including the **Antarctic Treaty** (1959), the **Hot Line Agreement** (1963), and the **Limited Test Ban Treaty** (1963).

KILOTON. One thousand tons of trinitrotoluene (TNT) equivalent. The measure used to classify and measure the explosive yield of **nuclear weapons**.

KINETIC ENERGY WEAPON. A class of weapons systems that depend upon a destructive or disabling force from their collision with a target.

KISSINGER, HENRY (1923-). Professor at Harvard University, national security advisor and secretary of state to Presidents **Richard Nixon** and **Gerald Ford**, Kissinger was an early advocate of a strategy of **flexible response.** He believed in the **linkage** of seemingly disparate foreign policy issues and was also the architect of the **United States** policy of **détente** toward the **Soviet Union**, enabling the success of the **Strategic Arms Limitation Talks** (SALT) and the **Anti-Ballistic Missile Treaty** (ABM).

KOHL, HELMUT (1930-). Chancellor of West Germany during some of its most significant years, from 1982 until 1998. A firm Atlanticist, he nonetheless courted Soviet leader **Mikhail Gorbachev** in the mid-1980s in a process that eventually led to the reunification of East and West Germany, as codified in the "Two Plus Four" Treaty signed in Moscow in September 1990. The reunified Germany remained a member of the **North Atlantic Treaty Organization** (NATO) and the **European Union** after becoming the largest and wealthiest country in Western Europe.

KOREA, DEMOCRATIC PEOPLES' REPUBLIC OF (NORTH KOREA). Suspicions of ongoing **weapons of mass destruction** programs in the Democratic People's Republic of Korea (DPRK or North Korea) have been a focal point of international security concerns since the early 1990s. The Korean peninsula remains a volatile region decades after the Korean War, which ended in a ceasefire in 1953. Movement toward unification of North and South Korea has been slow and fraught with tension. The parties to the conflict never signed a peace agreement and remain technically at war with each other.

In the 1990s it became obvious that North Korea was violating its responsibilities under the terms of the **Nuclear Non-Proliferation Treaty** (NPT) by actively pursuing **fissile materials** in order to produce an **atomic weapon**. In addition, North Korea is assumed to have both **chemical** and **biological weapons** for use by its large military. The international community, including the **United States**, signed an agreement with the Pyongyang government promising food, fuel, and help building a safe nuclear electrical plant in return for an end to that country's pursuit of nuclear weapons. This agreement fell apart by the early 2000s when North Korea announced that it had several such weapons and was resuming its **plutonium** extraction and **reprocessing** activities, as well as withdrawing from the NPT. The DPRK is also a know **proliferator** of nuclear technology to other so-called **rogue states**. *See also* AGREED FRAMEWORK ON NORTH KOREA.

KOSYGIN, ALEXSEI (1904-1980). Soviet premier from 1964 to his death in 1980. He replaced **Nikita Khruschev** in that position, but eventually became the number two man in the Soviet leadership to **Leonid Brezhnev**.

KRASNOYARSK. A town in Siberia and the site of a major international confrontation in the early 1980s after the **United States** discovered that the **Soviet Union** had built a **large phased-array radar** facing toward the center of the country. Such a radar could ostensibly be used as part of a national **missile defense system**, which was forbidden under the terms of the 1972 **Anti-Ballistic Missile Treaty** (ABM).

KWAJELEIN. Pacific island site of 1960s deployment of a primitive **United States antisatellite weapon** system. It became the site of United States' **strategic** missile system tests and **antiballistic missile system** tests. *See also* NIKE-ZEUS ABM SYSTEM.

L

LANCE MISSILE. A short-range, mobile, tracked, U.S. tactical missile deployed as a battlefield support system by the **U.S. Army**. Lance could deliver a rocket at a range of 75 miles with either a conventional or **nuclear warhead**. It was also used by several other **North Atlantic Treaty Organization** allies, although its nuclear warheads were always kept under U.S. control. Developed in the mid-1960s, it was first deployed in 1972 and retired in the early 1990s. Over 2,000 were built. Plans for a follow-on to Lance were shelved by President **George H.W. Bush** in 1990. *See also* NONSTRATEGIC NUCLEAR WEAPONS.

LARGE PHASED-ARRAY RADAR (LPAR). *See* PHASED-ARRAY RADAR.

LASER WEAPONS. Weapons based on a coherent, intense beam of electromagnetic radiation of a set wave length. Lasers can heat up and destroy a target at great distances.

LATERAN COUNCIL DECLARATION (1123, 1139). One of the first instances of church involvement in military affairs; this decree confirmed the 989 **Peace of God** protecting noncombatants and outlawed the crossbow as an immoral technological advancement in weaponry.

LATIN AMERICAN NUCLEAR WEAPON FREE ZONE TREATY. Also known as Treaty of Tlatelolco, the "Treaty for the Prohibition of Nuclear Weapons in Latin America" was signed on 14 February 1967 in Mexico City, entered into force on 25 April 1968, and endorsed by the **United Nations** that December. It obligates **state parties** not to acquire or possess **nuclear weapons,** nor to permit the storage or deployment of nuclear weapons on their territories. The treaty was expanded in 1990 to include the Caribbean basin states. Cuba became the last of 33 eligible states to ratify the treaty on 26 October 2002. *See also* NUCLEAR FREE ZONES.

LAUNCH CANISTER (LC). The container used for transporting and storing an assembled **intercontinental ballistic missile** (ICBM). In some ICBM systems a launch canister can also be used for launching the missile.

LAUNCH ON WARNING (LOW). The launch of a retaliatory nuclear strike upon receipt of warning data that an adversary has launched an attack, before any **nuclear weapons** have actually detonated on one's territory. This is a controversial policy because of the risk of intelligence or **sensor** error and the consequent possibility that such a launch would actually initiate a war based on faulty data.

LAUNCH UNDER ATTACK (LUA). The launch of a retaliatory nuclear strike upon confirmation that at least one **nuclear weapon** has detonated on one's territory, but before absorbing a complete **first-strike** attack.

LAUNCHER. The platform from which a weapon is fired (examples include an **intercontinental ballistic missile** silo, a **submarine-**

launched ballistic missile launch tube, or an aircraft [oftentimes specifically a bomber] bomb bay or **cruise missile** mount).

LAW OF THE SEA. The **United Nations** Convention on the Law of the Sea was opened for signature in December 1982 but was not signed by the **United States** until 28 July 1994. It **entered into force** on 16 November 1994. U.S. reluctance to sign the convention was based on its potential restriction on possible future entrepreneurial deep sea mining ventures by the United States and other industrialized states. However, a separate but associated **agreement** adopted by the UN General Assembly on 28 July 1994 deals with these issues. Most countries of the world are **signatories** to the Law of the Sea. In addition to being of economic and environmental significance due to its definition of rights and obligations with regard to mining the ocean floor, the Law of the Sea also guarantees freedom of navigation and overflight.

The Law of the Sea established several specific zones with corresponding rights: archipelagic waters; territorial seas (which may extend out to 12 nautical miles from a state (as measured in accordance with the convention's procedures); territorial seas, over which state sovereignty prevails, including the airspace above them and the seabed and subsoil beneath them; and contiguous zones, which may extend out to approximately 24 nautical miles from the baseline. Within these zones, a coastal state can exercise limited control as necessary to prevent or punish infringement of its customs, immigration, and sanitary laws and regulations that occur within its territory or territorial sea. Exclusive Economic Zones (EEZ), which can extend out 200 nautical miles, are areas beyond and adjacent to the territorial sea.

The High Seas are seaward of the EEZ, and the convention elaborates the principles of freedom of the high seas that have developed over many centuries. However, the right to fish has been made subject to additional requirements.

The Continental Shelf is the seabed and subsoil beyond a state's territorial seas (but not the water or airspace above), which may extend out to 200 nautical miles from the baseline (as measured in accordance with the convention procedures) over which a state can exercise sovereign control. The seabed beyond national jurisdiction includes the seabed and subsoil beyond that of the Continental Shelf (essentially that under the high seas), which is not subject to state control, but which will be regulated by the convention and a separate associated agreement on deep sea mining.

International airspace begins at the outer limit of the territorial seas. Hence, sovereignty extends over territorial seas, as well as over all inland waters and land territory.

The convention's major provisions on navigation and overflight include the right of innocent passage (not including the right of submerged passage). Freedom of navigation and overflight through international straits is guaranteed for merchant ships, cargo ships, naval ships and task forces, submarines, and military aircraft.

All ships and aircraft enjoy right of archipelagic sea lanes passage through, under, or over sea lanes passage while transiting through, under, or over the waters of archipelagos and adjacent territorial seas via archipelagic sea lanes.

The convention does not recognize the right to establish military security zones. The convention protects and strengthens the principle of sovereign immunity for warships and military aircraft. Convention provisions on the protection and preservation of the marine environment do not apply to warships or military aircraft.

LAWRENCE LIVERMORE NATIONAL LABORATORY. One of the two national laboratories (with **Los Alamos**) primarily responsible for the design and development of **nuclear warheads**. Its focus has been physics and weapons effects, although in recent years the laboratory has attempted to broaden its charter. It is now a leader in **fusion** energy research, for example. It is located near Livermore, California, some 60 miles east of Oakland.

LAWS OF WAR. The laws of war are sometimes considered to include multiple restrictions and rules laid out in different agreements, to include the **Hague Convention**, the **Geneva Conventions**, and so on. The Law of Land Warfare was published in U.S. Department of the Army Field Manual FM 27-10 in 1956. It includes forbidden means of waging warfare, thus subscribing to the understanding that the right of belligerents to adopt means of injuring the enemy is not unlimited. In particular, it is forbidden to employ arms, projectiles, or material calculated to cause unnecessary suffering. The manual discusses atomic weapons, poisons, gases, chemical and bacteriological warfare, bombardments, sieges, and assaults.

In addition, UN General Assembly Resolution 1653 on **Nuclear Weapons**, passed on 24 November 1961, declared that any use of nuclear or **thermonuclear weapons** is contrary to the spirit, letter, and aims of the **United Nations** and in direct violation of the

UN Charter. The use of such weapons would be considered a crime against mankind and civilization.

The UN also adopted a Convention Restricting Excessively Injurious or Indiscriminate Conventional Weapons on 10 April 1981, which **entered into force** on 2 December 1983. It includes restrictions and rules governing the use of booby traps, mines, non-detectable fragments, incendiary weapons, and small caliber weapons systems. *See also* CERTAIN CONVENTIONAL WEAPONS CONVENTION.

LAYERED DEFENSE. An approach to **ballistic missile defenses** that provides multiple systems for defeating an attack at different altitudes or distances from one's home territory. Such a system may include, for example, **boost-phase** interceptors in the adversary's home region, midcourse interceptors using space-based or terrestrial launched rockets, and **point defense** using yet other types of interceptors.

LEAGUE OF NATIONS. Following the end of World War I, the Big Four powers (**Great Britain, France**, Italy, and the **United States**) met in a peace conference in Paris beginning in January 1919. The result was the first attempt at an international consortium to keep world peace. The League of Nations was established in **Geneva**, Switzerland, on 10 January 1920. It convened numerous conferences and adopted many conventions during the 1920s and 1930s that attempted to outlaw war, limit and reduce armaments, and control the arms trade. States agreed not to go to war with other **signatories** without first submitting their disputes to the League for arbitration, mediation, or inquiry. Despite its best efforts, the League was unable to prevent World War II from breaking out, and it was dissolved in 1946 in favor of its successor organization, the **United Nations**. The United States received particular criticism for leading the effort to create the League, but then refusing to ratify President **Woodrow Wilson's** signature and become a member.

LEAKAGE. The inability to prevent all weapons in a dedicated attack from successfully penetrating one's defenses. During the **Cold War**, leakage usually implied a small number of Soviet missiles breaking through **ballistic missile defenses**, no matter how robust those defenses appeared on paper.

LEHMAN, RONALD F. II (1946-). Director of the U.S. **Arms Control and Disarmament Agency** from 1989 to 1993 during the golden era of **strategic arms control negotiations**. In 1995 he was appointed to the President's Advisory Board on arms **proliferation** policy. He is director of the Center for Global Security Research at **Lawrence Livermore National Laboratory**.

LENINGRAD ABM SYSTEM. In the early 1960s U.S. intelligence identified some 30 locations surrounding Leningrad where Soviet **antiballistic missiles** were being placed. These were primarily the SA-5 surface-to-air missile. There is some speculation that the Leningrad system was indicative of a much larger, possibly nation-wide ABM system that the **Soviet Union** put in place slowly and secretly. *See also* MOSCOW ABM SYSTEM.

LETHAL AGENTS. Infectious or intoxicating **chemical** or **biological agents** that cause death to those exposed to them.

LIGHT WATER REACTOR. A common class of nuclear power reactor that uses **enriched uranium** as fuel, producing spent fuel that contains significant amounts of **plutonium**. The spent fuel can be processed into **weapons-grade material** for use in **nuclear weapons**. *See also* LOW-ENRICHED URANIUM; REPROCESSING.

LILIENTHAL, DAVID (1899-1981). Lilienthal first became involved in U.S. nuclear policy immediately after World War II, when he was asked to help prepare a report on the international control of atomic energy. Lilienthal had previously run the Tennessee Valley Authority. Together with a board consisting of industry leaders and a committee headed by Secretary of State **Dean Acheson**, Lilienthal put forward a radical proposal that came to be known as the Lilienthal-Acheson Report. It suggested that international control of atomic energy might work "if the element of rivalry between nations were removed." This could be done, the document proposed, by assigning "the intrinsically dangerous phases of the development of atomic energy to an international organization responsible to all peoples." This authority would have a monopoly on **uranium**; it would license the use of "denatured" **plutonium**, which is difficult to convert into an explosive; and it would spread its mines and factories around the world so that the benefits they brought would be dispersed. The report was adapted into a proposal that President **Harry Truman** asked **Bernard Baruch** to present to the **United**

Nations. The **Soviet Union** rejected the proposal in 1949. On 1 January 1947, President Truman established the **Atomic Energy Commission**, and he nominated Lilienthal to be its first chairman. *See* BARUCH PLAN.

LIMITED NUCLEAR OPTIONS. A mixed **counterforce** and **countervalue** nuclear strategy developed under the direction of **United States** Secretary of Defense **James Schlesinger** in 1974 that placed emphasis on a series of limited, controlled nuclear strikes on one or more of the adversary's leadership (**command and control**), military, and economic targets. This strategy took advantage of advances in **nuclear weapon** systems' accuracy and represented both a departure from the countervalue **mutual assured destruction** focus and provided the basis for further counterforce developments in the **countervailing strategy** that evolved from it.

LIMITED NUCLEAR WAR. War in which each side exercises restraint in the use of **nuclear weapons**, employing only a limited number of weapons on selected targets. This could be a specific target or a set of targets such as **command and control** centers or a particular industry. Such a war, advocates believed, would be controllable and winnable, leading to a political resolution short of the next step on the escalatory ladder: unrestricted global thermonuclear conflict.

LIMITED TEST BAN TREATY (LTBT). The "Treaty Banning Nuclear Weapon Tests in Atmosphere, in Outer Space, and Under Water" was signed on 5 August 1963 by the **United States**, the **Soviet Union**, and the **United Kingdom**. It entered into force on 10 October 1963 with unlimited duration. The **signatories** agreed not to carry out any **nuclear weapon test** explosion in the atmosphere, in outer space, under water, or in any other environment that would cause **radioactive** debris to spread outside the territorial limits of the state that conducted the test. As of mid-2004 there were 125 parties to the treaty. It is also called the Partial Test Ban Treaty (PTBT).

LINKAGE. A negotiation strategy that joins progress on **arms control** issues with the status of nonarms control issues such as human rights. The term first entered the popular lexicon during the late 1960s and early 1970s, when it was used to explain Secretary of State **Henry Kissinger's** attempts to solve international issues. In another usage, linkage refers to the security bond and assurances between the **United States** and its allies around the world.

LISBON PROTOCOL (1992). A protocol to the **Strategic Arms Reduction Treaty** (START I) signed in Lisbon, Portugal on 23 May 1992. This made START a five-nation multiparty treaty by obligating the former Soviet republics of **Belarus, Kazakhstan,** and **Ukraine** to become non-nuclear **state parties** to the **Nuclear Non-Proliferation Treaty** (NPT). The five states signed a follow-up agreement in Moscow two years later (the **Trilateral Agreement**) that furthered the process of **denuclearizing** these states and ensuring they joined the NPT.

LOCAL SEISMIC NETWORK (LSN). As part of the **Comprehensive Test Ban Treaty** (CTBT) an **International Seismic Monitoring System** was set up to **verify compliance** with the treaty's restrictions. In addition to the official monitoring system, regional networks developed for earthquake studies and basic research can provide a strong **deterrent** against clandestine testing.

LOCARNO TREATIES (1925). Signed 16 October 1925 by **Great Britain, France,** Germany, Italy, Czechoslovakia, and Poland. Germany, France, and Belgium agreed to accept each other's borders, set up by the **Treaty of Versailles.** This included the promise not to send German troops into the Rhineland and the acceptance that Alsace-Lorraine was permanently part of France. Britain and Italy agreed to ensure that all three countries kept to this agreement, including the use of military force, if necessary. In return, Germany was allowed to join the **League of Nations**. In a separate **treaty,** also signed at Locarno, France promised to defend Belgium, Poland, and Czechoslovakia if they were attacked by Germany, which would not guarantee its eastern borders. The treaty gave Germany international respect and equality for the first time since World War I and provided France and Belgium safety from German invasion. Unfortunately, these were only paper guarantees that were violated by Germany throughout the 1930s, resulting in the outbreak of World War II in 1939.

LONDON GROUP. An informal group of states that seeks to control the export of nuclear materials, equipment, and technology, allowing such exports only to states that adhere to **International Atomic**

Energy Agency (IAEA) safeguards. *See* NUCLEAR SUPPLIERS GROUP.

LONDON NAVAL CONFERENCES. Meetings held in 1930 and 1935-1936 as part of a larger effort during the interwar period to address the size, capabilities, and basing of fleets in an attempt to avoid the naval **arms race** and destruction associated with World War I. *See also* WASHINGTON NAVAL TREATY.

LONG-RANGE THEATER NUCLEAR FORCES (LRTNF). Long-range theater nuclear forces are **nuclear weapons** on delivery systems that can reach deep within an adversary's rear areas, including possibly its home territory. There is no firm distance at which short- or intermediate-range forces are considered LRTNF, but these weapons are shorter range than **strategic** intercontinental systems. Debate about long-range theater nuclear weapons rose to prominence in the late 1970s following the **North Atlantic Treaty Organization's** (NATO) decision to upgrade its capabilities by deploying **Pershing II ballistic missiles** and **ground launched cruise missiles** in response to the Soviet military build-up including the deployment of the SS-20 **intermediate range ballistic missile**. Alliance acrimony over the modernization of NATO's LRTNF added impetus to the rebirth of the **peace movement** within Western Europe and led to significant protests as individual NATO countries allowed these weapons to be deployed on their territory. Ultimately, all three systems together with the Soviet SS-4s and SS-5s were eliminated as part of the **Intermediate-Range Nuclear Forces Treaty** (INF).

LOS ALAMOS NATIONAL LABORATORY. Located in the mountains northwest of Santa Fe, New Mexico, Los Alamos was opened in 1942. It achieved fame as the home of the **Manhattan Project** of World War II that designed, developed, and tested the first **atomic bomb**. It remains one of the primary national laboratories responsible for weapon design. In recent years the laboratory has accumulated small versions of many of the processes required to develop a bomb as other laboratories and industrial facilities in the nuclear weapons infrastructure closed.

LOW-ENRICHED URANIUM (LEU). Uranium that is enriched to less than 20 percent of its fissile isotope, uranium-235. Low-enriched uranium is used to fuel **light-water reactors**. Most commercial power reactors require low-enriched uranium to function. Typical enrichments for these power plants are between 2 and 5 percent. Some fuels in research reactors, however, are enriched to nearly 20 percent to allow for more compact cores. Low enriched uranium is mainly produced by processing natural uranium at an **enrichment** plant. Mixing natural uranium with **highly enriched uranium** is another way to produce LEU.

M

MACMILLAN, HAROLD (1894-1986). Prime minister of Great Britain from 1957 to 1963. MacMillan negotiated the purchase of British **Polaris** submarines and **submarine-launched ballistic missiles** from the **United States** at the Nassau Meeting of 1962. During his tenure Great Britain retreated from much of its old colonial empire and began facing serious economic difficulties and increasing dependence on the United States as a junior partner.

MAGNA, UTAH. Location of a Hercules rocket motor production facility, which was used in the U.S. **Pershing II intermediate-range nuclear missile**, and therefore selected as a portal at which **Russian** observers maintained continuous inspection for 13 years as part of the **Intermediate-Range Nuclear Forces Treaty's on-site inspection** and **verification** provisions. One of two such designated sites, the other being the SS-20 production facility in **Votkinsk**, Russia.

MALENKOV, GEORGY (1902-1988). Soviet premier 1953-1955. Malenkov was a member of **Josef Stalin's** inner circle, but believed in reforms and peaceful coexistence with the West. His opposition to **Nikita Krushchev** led to his removal from the Politburo prior to the implementation of most of his proposed reforms.

MALTA SUMMIT (1989). Off the coast of Malta in a Soviet ship named the *Maxim Gorky*, U.S. President **George H.W. Bush** and Soviet leader **Mikhail Gorbachev** met on 2-3 December 1989, within weeks of the fall of the Berlin Wall to discuss the rapid changes in Europe. Bush expressed support for **perestroika** and other reforms in the Eastern bloc, and both men recognized the lessening of tensions that had defined the **Cold War**. No agreements were signed at the summit, but to some it marked the end of the Cold War.

MANAGED ACCESS. Means of controlling who can see intelligence or information, or who can physically enter a building or other site that is restricted for reasons of safety or security. This concept comes into play during **on-site inspections** for **treaty compliance** and **verification.**

MANEUVERING REENTRY VEHICLE (MARV). A **ballistic missile reentry vehicle** that can change its trajectory while en route to its target.

MANHATTAN PROJECT. Code name for the development of the first **atomic bomb** by the **United States** during World War II. At the time, it was the most expensive research and development program in U.S. history and was accomplished in complete secrecy. The program began in 1942 and led to the creation of much of the nuclear infrastructure that would sustain America's nuclear build-up during the **Cold War**, including the national laboratories at **Los Alamos**, New Mexico, **Hanford**, Washington, and **Oak Ridge**, Tennessee. The results of this project included the first **atomic test** at **Trinity Site**, New Mexico, in July 1945, and the bombs dropped on **Hiroshima** and **Nagasaki**, Japan, one month later.

MASSIVE RETALIATION. A nuclear strategy that emphasized full-scale nuclear retaliation for any type of aggression, no matter how small. This was the **United States'** nuclear strategy during the administration of President **Dwight Eisenhower** in the 1950s. The overwhelmingly unbalanced response was believed to enhance **deterrence**, but the concept lost favor once the **Soviet Union** developed its own nuclear arsenal and both sides could achieve **assured destruction.**

MATERIAL BREACH. A violation of an **arms control treaty** serious enough to constitute grounds for terminating or suspending an **agreement**, in whole or in part. The violation of a provision essential to the accomplishment of the object or purpose of the treaty.

MATERIALS UNACCOUNTED FOR (MUF). The small amount of **radioactive** material lost or imbedded in equipment during normal **nuclear reactor** operations.

MCNAMARA, ROBERT (1916-). American businessman and U.S. secretary of defense under Presidents **John F. Kennedy** and **Lyndon Johnson**. MacNamara led a major overhaul in the Pentagon's organization and its way of doing business, pushed for greater American involvement in Vietnam, and oversaw a large increase in **strategic nuclear weapons** systems. He later served as president of the World Bank and became a critic of nuclear weapons.

MEDIUM-RANGE BALLISTIC MISSILE (MRBM). A category of **ballistic missile** with a range between 1,000 and 3,000 kilometers.

MEGATON. One million tons of trinitrotoluene (TNT) equivalent. The measure used to classify the explosive yield **nuclear weapons**. One thousand times larger than one **kiloton.** The first **nuclear test** to exceed one megaton in yield was the **United States'** "Mike" shot, a **hydrogen bomb** test that took place in November 1952. (Its yield was approximately 10.5 megatons.)

MEMORANDUM OF AGREEMENT (MOA). Any legal understanding between heads of state or directors of different organizations that creates responsibilities between the signing parties. For example, an MOA may serve as a codified agreement between a military force and a host nation that outlines various rights and obligations between the parties.

MEMORANDUM OF UNDERSTANDING (MOU). In **arms control,** an attachment to an international **agreement** to expand or clarify provisions of the agreement between the **state parties** to the agreement.

MICROORGANISM. An **organism** of microscopic dimensions, often pathogenic (disease producing).

MIDCOURSE PHASE. The center segment of a **ballistic missile** trajectory. The midcourse phase follows the **boost phase** and precedes the **reentry phase**. This part of a missile's flight occurs in space. *See also* POST-BOOST PHASE.

MIDDLE EAST ARMS CONTROL INITIATIVE (1991). Initiated by President **George H.W. Bush** in a speech at the **U.S. Air Force** Academy, 19 May 1991, the Middle East Initiative was a unilateral endeavor with multilateral consequences. Bush hoped that the five major powers in the UN Security Council would show greater supplier restraint in arms sales to states in the region. By so doing he hoped to introduce more stability into the region and avoid potentially dangerous **proliferation** of advanced **conventional weapons** or **weapons of mass destruction**. Due to the economic realities of corporate sales and the requirement for new markets in the immediate post-**Cold War** years, however, the initiative had basically collapsed within a year of being proposed.

MIDDLE EAST PEACE TALKS. An ongoing, noncontinuous series of meetings between **Israel** and the neighboring Arab states to resolve differences and end the irregular warfare that has dominated this region since the late 1940s, when the state of Israel was created. Two of the highlights and rare successes of this process were the 1978 **Camp David Accords** and the 1994 **Israeli-Palestinian Accord.** *See* MIDDLE EAST ARMS CONTROL INITIATIVE.

MIDGETMAN MISSILE. A U.S. single-warhead **intercontinental ballistic missile** (ICBM), also called the Small Intercontinental Ballistic Missile (SICBM). Proposed in the early 1980s as a cost-effective replacement for the multiple warhead intercontinental ballistic missiles then being discussed in **arms control negotiations**, it was cancelled early in the research and development phase. The SICBM was designed to travel on a **hard mobile launcher** (HML). Midgetmen gave the **United States** a more survivable **deterrent** because of its light-weight design and mobility. The Midgetman HML was hardened against **radiation** and capable of traveling up to 55 mph. The SICBM program was cancelled in 1992.

MILITARISM. The glorification of martial attributes and military forces, or the central role some militaries play in the governments of their countries. Militarism can also refer to the expansionist or war-like tendencies of a state in its foreign affairs.

MILITARY CRITICAL TECHNOLOGIES LIST (MCTL). A detailed listing, prepared by the **United States Department of Defense** (DoD), of the technologies that DoD assesses as critical to maintaining superior military capabilities. It applies to all mission areas, with special emphasis on **weapons of mass destruction proliferation** controls. The list provides a technical foundation for United States export proposals, particularly those that fall under the **Wassenaar Arrangement**.

MINE BAN CONVENTION (1997). The "Convention on the Prohibition of the Use, Stockpiling, Production, and Transfer of Anti-Personnel Mines and on their Destruction" was opened for signature on 3 December 1997. It **entered into force** on 1 March 1999 following **ratification** by 40 states. The initial campaign that led to the convention was begun by a group of nongovernmental organizations, largely humanitarian groups that saw their work impeded by the indiscriminate use of mines. A significant number of nations came to support a ban, which was negotiated in Ottawa, Canada. After initial support and involvement in the negotiations, the **United States** refused to sign the **treaty** in order to preserve its ability to use mines to defend the border between North and South Korea. Several other mine-producing nations, including **Russia** and **China**, also refused to sign the treaty. But the United States has been a leader in other efforts to reduce or redress the effects of anti-personnel mines. It has sought improvements to this problem in the **Certain Conventional Weapons Convention** and through the **UN Conference on Disarmament**.

MINIMUM DETERRENCE. Minimum deterrence argues that a state only requires a relatively small number of retaliatory weapons in order to achieve a deterrent effect. According to this theory, the opposing state will not risk the destruction of even a handful of its cities and key centers, so deterrence can be achieved with a much smaller and less accurate nuclear arsenal. This is a construct of deterrence very different from the prevailing **Cold War** norm of assured **second strike** and **mutually assured destruction**. *See also* ASSURED VULNERABILITY; STRATEGIC SUFFICIENCY.

MINISTRY OF ATOMIC ENERGY (MINATOM). In January 1992, following the dissolution of the **Soviet Union**, the **Russian** Federation Ministry of Atomic Energy (MINATOM) was established by presidential decree. MINATOM replaced the Soviet Ministry of Atomic Power and Industry. MINATOM controls 151 production and research facilities. When it was created, MINATOM employed approximately one million people. The ministry has its own education and training institutes, export organization, and banks. MINATOM is responsible for the production of all Russian nuclear materials and the development, testing, and production of its **nuclear weapons**. MINATOM also is responsible for the elimination of nuclear warheads and nuclear munitions. Responsibility for decommissioned nuclear-powered submarines was transferred from the Ministry of Defense to MINATOM in late 1998. The ministry controls most of the weapons-usable **highly enriched uranium** and **plutonium** not contained in nuclear weapons. MINATOM also has responsibility for Russia's commercial nuclear power program, nuclear safety oversight, basic and applied research, and the conversion of military facilities to civilian uses.

MINUTEMAN MISSILE. A category of **United States silo**-launched **intercontinental ballistic missiles** (ICBM). First tested in February 1961 and deployed in 1962, over 1,800 Minuteman missiles were produced by the Boeing Company. A mainstay of U.S. **deterrence** strategy for 40 years, the Minuteman is a three-stage, solid fuel missile that launches from an underground silo with a range of 8,000 miles. It can carry **multiple independently targeted reentry vehicles.** The single-warhead Minuteman I was retired in 1969; the three-warhead Minuteman III is currently in service and deployed by the **United States Air Force** at widespread silo fields on three northern bases (Malmstrom AFB, Montana; Minot AFB, North Dakota; and F.E. Warren AFB, Wyoming). It is scheduled to be converted to a single-warhead missile as part of the **Strategic Arms Reduction** (START) agreements.

MISSILE DEFENSE ACT (1991). A U.S. congressional demand for the deployment of a **treaty** compliant **missile defense system** "by the earliest possible date allowed by the availability of appropriate technology or by fiscal year 1996." The act was followed by a substantial budget increase in missile defense. Together these steps represented an attempt at compromise on a polarizing issue in American politics, but it also showed that a consensus was growing in support of limited missile defenses.

MISSILE DEFENSE AGENCY (MDA). A major executive agency within the **United States Department of Defense**, the Missile Defense Agency is a direct descendent of the **Strategic Defense Initiative Organization** and the **Ballistic Missile Defense Organization**; it was renamed in 2002. Its mission is to develop and field an integrated **ballistic missile defense system** capable of providing a **layered defense** for the United States and its deployed forces, friends, and allies against ballistic missiles of all ranges in all phases of flight. MDA is responsible for research, development, testing, and evaluation. Using complementary interceptors, **sensors,** and battle management **command and control** systems, the planned missile defense system will be able to engage all classes and ranges of ballistic missile threats. Missile defense elements being developed and tested by MDA are primarily based on **hit-to-kill** technology.

MISSILE EXPERIMENTAL (MX). *See* PEACEKEEPER.

MISSILE GAP. A phrase popularized during the 1960 U.S. presidential elections. Candidate **John F. Kennedy** accused the **Dwight Eisenhower** administration of allowing the **Soviet Union** to increase its **intercontinental ballistic missile** (ICBM) force to such a degree that it had an overwhelming superiority over the **United States**. The Kennedy campaign used this supposed inequity to show that the Eisenhower administration was soft on national defense. Upon winning the election and entering office, Kennedy discovered that there was in fact a missile gap—but it was the United States that held the commanding lead. As a result, the United States decided to cap the size of its ICBM force at 1,054 missiles, a level it reached in 1965. The **Soviet Union** continued to increase its ICBM arsenal throughout the 1960s and 1970s without regard for America's unilateral halt to the ICBM race, until the Soviets reached a point where they had far superior numbers.

MISSILE TECHNOLOGY CONTROL REGIME (MTCR). In April 1987 the **United States**, Canada, **France**, West Germany, Italy, Japan, and the **United Kingdom** created the Missile Technology Control Regime to restrict the **proliferation** of missiles and missile technology. The MTCR is the only multilateral missile **nonproliferation regime**. It is a voluntary arrangement, not an international **agreement** or a **treaty**, among countries that have an interest in stopping the proliferation of missile technology. The regime develops export guidelines that are applied to a list of **controlled items** and implemented according to each nation's procedures. In January 1993 the MTCR Guidelines were expanded to restrict the spread of missiles and unmanned air vehicles with a range of at least 300 kilometers, capable of delivering a 500 kilogram **payload** or a **weapon of mass destruction**. The guidelines are sensitive to the fact that **ballistic missile** and space launch vehicle technology are virtually identical. They are designed not to impede a nation's space program as long as it does not contribute to the delivery of weapons of mass destruction. Membership in the MTCR is open to any country that commits to the principles of nonproliferation and has a record of effective **export controls**. As of mid-2004 the MTCR regime had 33 members, and additional states have agreed to unilaterally adhere to its guidelines and principles.

MOBILE INTERCONTINENTAL BALLISTIC MISSILE. An intercontinental ballistic missile (ICBM) that can be transported to a new location prior to launch, thus enhancing its **survivability** against destruction in a **first strike**. Given the size of ICBMs, this is no easy task. In addition to physical movement, the target coordinates and flight parameters must be reentered into the missile's computers before launch in order to ensure that it will reach its target.

MOBILE INTERCONTINENTAL BALLISTIC MISSILE LAUNCHER. A **launcher** for an **intercontinental ballistic missile** that can be moved, usually by road or by rail. Such a launcher is often reusable, ejecting the missile by compressed gas before the rocket engine ignites.

MONITOR. As a verb, to closely keep track of something in order to gain intelligence information or confirm **compliance** with the elements of an **agreement**. As a noun, the person or equipment that observes and analyzes a location or a category of equipment, munitions, or other item for the purpose of collecting data and verifying compliance.

MORATORIUM. The suspension of some activity; often, a policy to unilaterally stop a series of actions, such as **nuclear weapon testing**, **arms sales**, or arms production.

MORGENTHAU, HANS J. (1904-1980). Renowned thinker and author in international relations and security studies. His works during the early **Cold War** influenced the development of **deterrence** and **strategic** policy in the **United States**.

MOSCOW. Capital of the **Soviet Union** and **Russia**, and site of many arms control conferences and **treaty** signings since the end of World War II. Some of the most well known include the Moscow Summits of 1972 (which resulted in the **Strategic Arms Limitation Treaty**—the Interim Agreement on Offensive Weapons and the **Anti-Ballistic Missile Treaty**) and 2002 (where the presidents of the **United States** and Russia signed the **Strategic Offensive Reductions Treaty**, or Moscow Treaty).

MOSCOW ABM SYSTEM. Built during the **Cold War**, the world's only functioning **antiballistic missile** system (still active as of mid-2004), the Moscow system consists of 100 Galosh missiles that surround the Russian capital. The missiles carry **nuclear warheads** that are detonated in the vicinity of incoming **reentry vehicles**. U.S. intelligence first observed the system being built in 1963.

MOSCOW TREATY (2002). *See* STRATEGIC OFFENSIVE REDUCTIONS TREATY.

MOST-FAVORED NATION. A term in international economics. Most-favored nation status confers trade benefits and closer economic relations between two countries. The **United States** has used this economic tool as a reward or punishment for other states, thereby trying to further political or military goals. *See also* LINKAGE.

MULTILATERAL ARMS CONTROL. Cooperative efforts and agreements between more than two **state parties**. Much of the multilateral arms control focus today rests in the **Conference on Disarmament** under the auspices of the **United Nations**.

MULTIPLE INDEPENDENTLY TARGETABLE REENTRY VEHICLE (MIRV). Two or more **warheads** carried on a single **ballistic missile** that can be delivered to different targets. A warhead **bus** in the nose cone of the missile releases each warhead at the precise moment to achieve similar **accuracy** on multiple widespread targets. *See also* FRACTIONATION.

MUSKIE, EDMUND (1914-1996). American politician and secretary of state under President **Jimmy Carter** for one year, 1980-1981, following the resignation of **Cyrus Vance**. Formerly a senator from Maine, it was his job to try to get ratification of the **Strategic Arms Limitation Treaty** (SALT II)—a task overturned when Carter withdrew the treaty from Senate consideration. He later served on the Tower Commission that investigated the Iran-Contra affair during the presidency of **Ronald Reagan**.

MUTUAL ASSURED DESTRUCTION (MAD). The basis of **Cold War stability** and **deterrence**, mutual assured destruction is the state of nuclear balance where both superpowers have the capability to inflict unacceptable damage on the other through a **second strike** after having absorbed a **first strike** from the adversary. The primary incentives in this situation are to avoid direct conflict.

MUTUAL ASSURED SURVIVAL. A declaratory policy that relies on defenses to prevent destruction and damage from a nuclear strike. In this construct, the ability of defenses to render **strategic** nuclear forces ineffective would enhance **deterrence** of attack.

MUTUAL AND BALANCED FORCE REDUCTIONS (MBFR). A series of **negotiations** between the **United States**, the **Soviet Union**, and European nations from 1973 to 1989 that focused on limiting conventional military forces deployed by the **North Atlantic Treaty Organization** (NATO) and the **Warsaw Pact**. While the MBFR did not achieve a formal **treaty**, the experience gained through this long set of negotiations proved key to the success of the 1989 **Conventional Forces in Europe Treaty** (CFE).

MUTUAL RECIPROCAL INSPECTION AGREEMENT (MRI) (1994). The Mutual Reciprocal Inspection Agreement between the **United States** and **Russia** was signed in March 1994. The agreement committed the two countries to develop methods to confirm each other's inventory of **fissile material** created by the dismantlement of **nuclear weapons** and to carry out inspections of both inventories using those methods. This agreement is part of the **Safeguards, Transparency, and Irreversibility** effort, backed by U.S.-Russian summit declarations, to increase both governments' confidence in their knowledge of each other's nuclear weapons and fissile material stockpiles.

N

NAGASAKI, JAPAN. The city where the second **atomic bomb** was detonated, on 9 August 1945 in World War II by the **United States**. The bomb used was a **plutonium implosion device**.

NATIONAL AIRBORNE OPERATIONS CENTER (NAOC). The **United States** aircraft designated to carry the president and to serve as the command post from which retaliatory strikes would be directed in the event of a nuclear war. The NAOC (formerly called the National Emergency Airborne Command Post, or NEACP) has been called the "doomsday plane." Aircraft used for this mission included the Boeing 707 and, since 1980, four highly modified Boeing 747s based at Offutt AFB, Nebraska.

NATIONAL COMMAND AUTHORITIES (NCA). In the **United States,** the president and the secretary of defense (or their officially deputized alternates), are the only officials who can authorize the use of **nuclear weapons.** This concept of civilian control was formalized in the **National Security Act of 1947.**

NATIONAL DEFENSE PANEL (NDP) (1997). A commission of distinguished American thinkers and support staff established to review and make recommendations to the secretary of defense on the **Quadrennial Defense Review.** The NDP's report also provided an assessment of alternative force structures for the U.S. military through the year 2010.

NATIONAL EMERGENCY AIRBORNE COMMAND POST (NEACP). *See* NATIONAL AIRBORNE OPERATIONS CENTER.

NATIONAL INSTITUTE FOR PUBLIC POLICY (NIPP). A Washington, D.C.-based research center, NIPP is a small, private institute founded in 1981 to assess international and defense policies in the evolving **strategic** landscape. Its political leanings are generally conservative.

NATIONAL INTELLIGENCE ESTIMATE (NIE). A large-scale, authoritative assessment of a particular area of concern to the president, conducted by the **Central Intelligence Agency** (CIA).

NATIONAL MISSILE DEFENSE (NMD). National Missile Defense was the name of the U.S. **ballistic missile defense** program proposed by the **William Clinton** administration in the mid-1990s. It comprised a system of **antiballistic missile** weapons designed to defend the **United States** from missile attack. While no complete NMD system was finalized, proposed capabilities included land-, air-, sea-, and space-based systems.

NATIONAL MISSILE DEFENSE ACT (1999). An act by the U.S. Congress stating that it was the policy of the United States government to deploy an effective national **missile defense system** capable of defending the territory of the **United States** against limited **ballistic missile** attack as soon as technically feasible.

NATIONAL NUCLEAR SECURITY ADMINISTRATION (NNSA). The organization within the **United States** government responsible for the **nuclear weapons** stockpile. An executive branch agency, it falls under the **Department of Energy**. Its responsibilities include the **Stockpile Stewardship Program** and management of the national laboratories (including **Los Alamos**, **Lawrence Livermore**, and **Sandia**). Its mission is to enhance U.S. national security through the military application of **nuclear energy**; to maintain and enhance the safety, reliability, and performance of the United States nuclear weapons stockpile, including the ability to design, produce, and test, in order to meet national security requirements; to provide the **U.S. Navy** with safe, militarily effective nuclear propulsion plants, and to ensure the safe and reliable operation of those plants; to promote international nuclear safety and **nonproliferation**; and to reduce global danger from **weapons of mass destruction**.

NATIONAL RECONNAISSANCE OFFICE (NRO). Formed in August 1960 as the lead U.S. agency for satellite **reconnaissance** and to ensure that all parties were represented in overhead satellite collection and distribution. The NRO designs, builds, and operates the nation's reconnaissance satellites. NRO products, provided to an expanding list of customers like the **Central Intelligence Agency** (CIA) and the **Department of Defense** (DoD), can warn of potential trouble spots around the world, help plan military operations, and monitor the environment. It conducted its business in secrecy for many years, falling under the **U.S. Air Force** organizationally. But in 1992 its existence, and the location of its headquarters in Chantilly, Virginia, were made public.

NATIONAL SECURITY ACT OF 1947. The National Security Act of 1947 mandated a major reorganization of the foreign policy and military establishments of the U.S. government. The act created many of the institutions that presidents have since found useful when formulating and implementing foreign policy, including the **National Security Council** (NSC). The act also established the

Central Intelligence Agency (CIA), which grew out of the World War II-era Office of Strategic Services. The CIA serves as the primary civilian intelligence-gathering organization in the government. Later, the **Defense Intelligence Agency** became the main military intelligence body. The 1947 law also caused far-reaching changes in the military establishment. The War Department and Navy Department merged into a single **Department of Defense** under the secretary of defense, who also created the Department of the Air Force. However, each of the three branches maintained its own service secretaries. In 1949 the act was amended to give the secretary of defense more power over the individual services and their secretaries.

NATIONAL SECURITY AGENCY (NSA). The National Security Agency is the **United States'** cryptologic organization. It coordinates, directs, and performs highly specialized activities to protect U.S. information systems and produce foreign intelligence information. A high technology organization, the NSA is on the frontiers of communications and data processing. It is also one of the most important centers of foreign language analysis and research within the government. The NSA employs the country's premier codemakers and codebreakers. It is said to be the largest employer of mathematicians in the United States and perhaps the world, who contribute directly to the two missions of the Agency: designing cipher systems that will protect the integrity of U.S. information systems and searching for weaknesses in adversaries' systems and codes. Most NSA employees work at Fort Meade, Maryland.

NATIONAL SECURITY COUNCIL (NSC). The National Security Council was created as a result of the **National Security Act of 1947**. The Council itself includes the president, vice president, secretary of state, secretary of defense, and other members (such as the director of the **Central Intelligence Agency**), who meet to discuss both long-term problems and more immediate national security crises. A small NSC staff is recruited to coordinate foreign policy materials from other agencies for the president. Beginning in 1953 the president's assistant for national security affairs directed this staff. Each president has accorded the NSC with different degrees of importance and has given the NSC staff varying levels of autonomy and influence over other agencies such as the **Departments of State and Defense.** *See also* NSC-20/4; NSC-30; NSC-68; NSC-162/2; NSDD-13; NSDM-242; PD-59.

NATIONAL SECURITY STRATEGY. A broad outline of **United States** national security objectives, priorities, and programs openly published, nominally annually (as directed by Congress) by the president. Countering the **proliferation** and use of **weapons of mass destruction** has been an increasingly important theme in these documents since the end of the **Cold War**.

NATIONAL STRATEGIC TARGET LIST (NSTL). The National Strategic Target List is one of most closely guarded U.S. military secrets. The NSTL is a prioritized list of identified targeting points and planning functions that is used in conjunction with the National Strategic Targeting and Attack Policy and the **Nuclear Weapons Employment Policy** (NUWEP). During the **Cold War** the **Joint Strategic Target Planning Staff** (JSTPS) of the **Strategic Air Command** (SAC) developed and maintained the NSTL. The NSTL was developed to provide for the integration of committed forces for the attack of a minimum list of targets, the destruction of which would accomplish given objectives. Additionally, the NSTL was given the task of processing and analyzing target data. In August 1960 President **Dwight Eisenhower** approved SAC's request to prepare the first National Strategic Target List.

Target lists are kept classified because they provide information concerning current target selection criteria, strategy, intelligence sources and methods, and **nuclear weapons** effects. U.S. nuclear war plans have included a wide range of target types: military forces, bases, installations, and stockpiles; economic and industrial centers; political and administrative centers; and after 1950, Soviet nuclear forces. In 1961, the **Single Integrated Operations Plan** (SIOP) introduced greater flexibility into the U.S. **strategic** nuclear war plan. The NSTL has been divided into various target sets to provide the **National Command Authorities** with a range of options, such as withholding attacks against urban-industrial areas.

NATIONAL TECHNICAL MEANS (NTM). Highly sophisticated intelligence systems such as **surveillance** satellites and ground-based radars that can be used by one state to monitor another state's **compliance** with the provisions of an **arms control agreement**.

NAVY OFFICE OF TREATY IMPLEMENTATION. The Naval Treaty Implementation Program, Strategic Systems Programs, is responsible within the Department of the Navy for the development of plans and procedures to ensure compliance with **nonstrategic**

treaties and **agreements**. This office is staffed with senior military and civilian personnel who have expertise with treaty **implementation** and **compliance** planning, policy, and preparation for treaty **verification** activities.

NEAR EAST ARMS COORDINATING COMMITTEE (1950). In August 1949 the **United States, France,** and **Great Britain** announced a coordinated effort to regulate the flow of arms to the Middle East region. In May 1950, this Tripartite Declaration was formalized with the establishment of the Near East Arms Coordinating Committee. However, the extensive regional interests of all three powers in the region, the competition between them, and the failure to include other major suppliers, including the **Soviet Union,** weakened the effectiveness of this effort. The language of the declaration included significant loopholes, permitting the acquisition of arms "to maintain a certain level of armed forces to assure their internal security and their legitimate self-defense." The appropriate level for each state was left undefined, and this was exploited by both suppliers and recipients.

NEGATIVE SECURITY ASSURANCE. In 1978 U.S. Secretary of State Cyrus Vance told members of the **United Nations** that "The United States will not use **nuclear weapons** against any non-nuclear-weapons state party to the NPT (**Nuclear Nonproliferation Treaty**) or any comparable internationally binding commitment not to acquire nuclear explosive devices, except in the case of an attack on the **United States,** its territories or armed forces, or its allies, by such a state allied to a **nuclear-weapons state** or associated with a nuclear weapons state in carrying out or sustaining the attack." There have been calls to simplify this assurance, which the United States has rejected, citing the ambiguity as to America's response this leaves in the minds of states considering an attack on U.S. interests with other **weapons of mass destruction**.

NEGOTIATIONS. The formal process of two or more parties coming together to discuss areas of common interest in hopes of reaching agreement or coming to terms. A common approach to reaching **arms control treaties** and **agreements** is the international **negotiating** round.

NERVE AGENT. A substance that interferes with normal neurological function in humans, usually causing rapid and lethal effects.

NEUROTOXIN. A **toxic** substance that inhibits nervous system function, thereby causing paralysis or death.

NEUTRALITY. A decision by a nation-state to opt out of great power politics by refusing to choose sides in international relations. This was particularly true for certain states during the **Cold War**. Neutrality is a strong belief in many states of northern Europe, including traditional neutrals Switzerland, Sweden, Austria, and Finland.

NEUTRALIZATION. Forcing a state to accept neutral status, not aligned with any other states. This should be distinguished from **neutrality**, a voluntary choice by a state. Neutralization also refers to the chemical process of detoxifying a **chemical weapon** by combining it with another chemical, making the resulting mixture inert.

NEUTRALIZING THE STRAIT OF MAGELLAN (1881). The agreement by Chile and Argentina to divide the southern tip of South America, including Tierra del Fuego, and keep the strait between the Atlantic and Pacific Oceans **neutral** and open to passage by all. The **United States** mediated this agreement.

NEUTRON BOMB. *See* ENHANCED RADIATION WEAPON.

NEVADA TEST SITE. The **United States** atomic **testing** location located 65 miles northwest of Las Vegas, Nevada, adjacent to the Nellis Air Force Base training areas. A 1,350 square mile tract of desert and mountains, the test site was established in December 1950, and the first atomic test took place there one month later. The site was also used by **Great Britain** for most of its atomic tests. While still officially open, the site was placed in caretaker status following the 1992 U.S. **moratorium** on further nuclear testing. The 2004 defense budget called upon the **Department of Energy** to have the site ready for use for future nuclear testing within 18 months of a decision to do so. Hundreds of atmospheric atomic tests, and even more underground tests, were conducted here over the course of 42 years, testing **nuclear weapons** and weapons effects. The site also contains the Yucca Mountain site, being prepared for the long-term storage of highly **radioactive** nuclear waste materials.

NEW LOOK. The **national security strategy** of **United States** President **Dwight Eisenhower**. Promulgated in 1952, this policy change was an attempt to save money by relying on **Strategic Air Command** and its **nuclear weapons** rather than large standing conventional forces. The nuclear strategy component of the New Look was **massive retaliation**.

NIKE MISSILE. Designed as a **surface-to-air missile** (SAM) for the **U.S. Army**, the Nike series has played a role in the territorial defense of the **United States** since the 1950s. The first Nike Ajax battery site was built near Washington, D.C., in 1953. Eventually there were multiple such sites surrounding America's major cities and military bases. The entire system was very large: 40 Army battalions, each with four batteries of 9 to 12 launchers. The missile itself was large and nonmobile; it was a canard with a two-stage rocket booster that pushed it to speeds exceeding Mach 2 with a range of 25 miles. Built by Douglas Aircraft, it located its target by electronic links to a ground acquisition radar system. Over 16,000 missiles and 3,000 launchers were delivered, and many of these were shared with U.S. allies in Europe and the Far East.

The next generation of Nike SAM was called the **Hercules**. It entered service in 1958, and was a significant improvement over the Ajax. Reaching speeds of Mach 3.6 and altitudes of 150,000 feet, and was deployed to 73 Army battalions as well as overseas with U.S. allies. Over 25,500 Nike Hercules were built in the United States and, under license, in Japan. The system was phased out in the early 1970s, with plans to replace it with next-generation **Patriot** SAMs.

NIKE-ZEUS ABM SYSTEM. Nike Zeus was a technical leap beyond the **Nike Hercules** surface-to-air missile system, but made up only a small portion of the total Nike production. First test fired in 1959, its purpose was to serve as an **antiballistic missile** weapon. Successful intercepts using nuclear warheads against Atlas missiles over the Pacific proved valuable in the eventual **Safeguard** BMD system, but President **Dwight Eisenhower** decided in 1959 not to deploy Zeus, since its technology was too old. Instead, Safeguard was designed to use the **Spartan** and **Sprint** missiles, developed from the 1963 authorization to build a Nike X ABM system.

NITZE, PAUL (1907-2004). For over 40 years Nitze was one of the chief architects of U.S. policy toward the **Soviet Union**. He served as vice chairman of the U.S. Strategic Bombing Survey at the end of **World War II**. As head of policy planning for the **State De-**

partment (1950–1953), and principal author of a highly influential secret **National Security Council** document (**NSC-68**), which provided the **strategic** outline for increased U.S. expenditures to counter the threat of Soviet armaments. He has also served as secretary of the **U.S. Navy** (1963–1967), deputy secretary of defense (1967–1969), member of the U.S. delegation to the **Strategic Arms Limitation Talks** (SALT) (1969–1973), and assistant secretary of defense for international affairs (1973–1976). He was President **Ronald Reagan's** chief negotiator of the **Intermediate Range Nuclear Forces Treaty** (INF) (1981–1984). In 1984 he was named special adviser to the president and secretary of state on **arms control**.

NIXON, RICHARD (1913-1994). United States president from 1969-1974. Nixon established the **strategic** doctrine of **essential equivalence** with the **Soviet Union**, began the **strategic arms limitation talks**, and opened relations with the **Peoples' Republic of China** after many years of separation. His administration signed the **Seabed Treaty**, the **Accidents Measures Agreement**, the modernization of the **Hot Line Agreement**, the **Biological Weapons Convention** (BWC), the **Incidents at Sea Agreement**, and the **Strategic Arms Limitation Treaty** (SALT I).

NO FIRST USE. A nuclear doctrine committing a nuclear power not to be the first party within a conflict to resort to the use of **nuclear weapons**.

NON-ALIGNED MOVEMENT. A summit meeting of 25 Third World powers took place in Belgrade, Yugoslavia, in 1961. Its purpose was to promote the security and development of smaller states outside the channels dominated by the two **superpowers** and the former colonial powers. Led by Josip Tito of Yugoslavia, Abdel Nasser of Egypt, and Jawaharlal Nehru of **India**, the movement grew to 101 members at its 1983 meeting. It encouraged the formation of the **United Nations** Conference on Trade and Development (UNCTAD) in 1964.

NONCOMPLIANCE. Failing to abide by some aspect of an **arms control treaty** or **agreement**. This can be done willingly, by accident, or simply because a state is having difficulty meeting its commitments for financial or other reasons. When one party of an agreement is in noncompliance, the other parties may have legal recourse to abrogate or withdraw from the treaty themselves. *See also* COMPLIANCE.

NONDESTRUCTIVE EVALUATION METHODS. The technique of inspecting something without destroying or damaging it. The most common nondestructive evaluation (NDE) methods used to characterize materials and inspect products are visual, operator-dependent, subjective, and qualitative. Those methods can be slow, imprecise, and inconsistent—and quite unsuited for inspections required during **arms control inspections**. The national laboratories are therefore developing specially tailored evaluation methods that deliver exact, quantitative results. The methods use automated, digital, breakthrough technologies implemented through such techniques as computed tomography, digital radiography, ultrasonics, machine vision, and infrared thermography.

NONGOVERNMENTAL ORGANIZATION (NGO). Civil groups that do not act in the official capacity of a state government. Examples include multinational corporations and international charitable organizations, such as the **Red Cross**, as well as many groups focused more broadly on peace or more narrowly on issues such as **disarmament**.

NONLETHAL AGENT. An agent that incapacitates rather than causes death. Examples include tear gas and **vomiting agents**.

NON-NUCLEAR WEAPONS STATE (NNWS). A nation-state that did not possess **nuclear weapons** upon **entry into force** of the 1968 **Nuclear Nonproliferation Treaty** (NPT). This is merely a legal distinction; nuclear states such as **Israel, India,** and **Pakistan** would also be considered **non-nuclear weapons states** if they were to sign the NPT, because there were, and only can be, according to that treaty, five **nuclear weapons states**.

NONPROLIFERATION. In general usage, any effort to block the spread of weapons or major system components to those not previously possessing those capabilities. Within **United States** government usage, efforts to secure cross-governmental and international cooperation in the prevention of the spread of significant weapons capabilities from possessor states, and also cooperation from non-possessor states to refrain from obtaining such capabilities. *See also* COUNTERPROLIFERATION; PROLIFERATION.

NONPROLIFERATION TREATY (NPT). *See* NUCLEAR NON-PROLIFERATION TREATY.

NONSTRATEGIC NUCLEAR WEAPONS (NSNW). Also called tactical, theater, battlefield, or short-range **nuclear weapons**. Relatively small-yield and limited-range nuclear weapons and systems designed for use within a theater of operations rather than for intercontinental, or **strategic**, employment. Nonstrategic nuclear weapons typically refer to short-range weapons, including land-based missiles with a range of less than 300 miles and air- and sea-launched weapons with a range of less than 400 miles. Though NSNW constitute a large percentage of the arsenals of the **nuclear weapon states**, they are the least-regulated category of nuclear weapons covered in **arms control agreements**. The **United States** reduced its arsenal of such weapons by some 90 percent in the decade following the **Presidential Nuclear Initiatives** of 1991.

NORDIC BALANCE. An informal measure of the relationship between the Scandinavian countries and the **superpowers'** spheres of influence in northern Europe. During the **Cold War**, Iceland, Denmark, and Norway were members of the **North Atlantic Treaty Organization** (NATO). Finland's foreign and defense policies were strongly influenced by its proximity to the **Soviet Union**. And Sweden, which fell between these two groups geographically, chose to remain **neutral**. This balance was accepted by both sides, and neither side attempted to overtly change the balance in their favor, thus making the Nordic region one of relative calm and lowered tensions throughout the otherwise dangerously tense Cold War period.

NORTH AMERICAN AEROSPACE DEFENSE COMMAND (NORAD). The bilateral defense organization between the **United States** and Canada founded in 1957 that monitors global aerospace **surveillance** systems and directs the defense of the North American continent against attacks transiting air or space. Formerly known as North American Air Defense Command, NORAD is headquartered in **Cheyenne Mountain** Air Force Station, Colorado, and works closely with **U.S. Strategic Command** and **U.S. Northern Command** to ensure the defense of North America.

NORTH ATLANTIC COOPERATION COUNCIL (NACC). The establishment of the North Atlantic Cooperation Council in December 1991 brought together the member countries of the **North At-**

lantic **Treaty Organization** (NATO) and, initially, nine Central and Eastern European countries, in a new consultative forum. In March 1992 participation in the NACC was expanded to include all members of the **Commonwealth of Independent States** (CIS). In 1997 the **North Atlantic Cooperation Council** was replaced by the **Euro-Atlantic Partnership Council** (EAPC).

NORTH ATLANTIC TREATY ORGANIZATION (NATO). The security alliance formed by the **Washington Treaty** (also called the North Atlantic Treaty) on 4 April 1949 between the **United States**, Canada, and 10 Western European states to protect the member states against attack or aggression by the **Soviet Union**. Original members included Belgium, Canada, Denmark, **France**, **Great Britain**, Iceland, Italy, Luxembourg, the Netherlands, Norway, Portugal, and the **United States**. NATO's membership was expanded with the addition of Greece and Turkey in 1952; West Germany in 1955 (and the eastern Länder of reunified Germany in 1990); Spain in 1982; the Czech Republic, Hungary, and Poland in 1999; and a large group of former **Warsaw Pact** nations in 2004: Bulgaria, Estonia, Latvia, Lithuania, Romania, Slovenia, and Slovakia. Throughout the **Cold War** NATO faced off against the Soviet Union and the Warsaw Pact with massive numbers of men, equipment, and weapons (including **nuclear weapons**) in Central Europe. With the end of the Cold War NATO's mission broadened to include threats other than Russia, as well as **nonproliferation** and more active military intervention. The basic premise of the original treaty remains, however: **collective defense**. An attack on one constitutes an attack on all. *See also* WASHINGTON TREATY.

NORTH KOREA. *See* KOREA, DEMOCRATIC PEOPLE'S REPUBLIC OF.

NSC-20/4. A **United States National Security Council** study completed on 24 November 1948 and titled "U.S. Objectives with Respect to the USSR to Counter Soviet Threats to U.S. Security." It established basic United States security objectives that applied through 1954. It defined the **Soviet Union** as a "dangerous and immediate threat" and projected ceaseless Soviet **strategic** force advances that would allow rough parity with the United States by 1955.

NSC-30. A U.S. **National Security Council** study completed on 16 September 1948 and titled "United States Policy on Strategic Warfare." This study, approved by U.S. President **Harry Truman** while the Berlin crisis and airlift were underway, placed the release of **United States** atomic weapons firmly under the control of the president.

NSC-68. A U.S. **National Security Council** study completed on 14 April 1950 and titled "U.S. Objectives and Programs for National Security." The report reaffirmed and expanded on **NSC-20/4**, providing a foundation behind the decision to develop the **hydrogen bomb**. NSC-68 provided a basis for a policy of military **containment** of the **Soviet Union**, and called for arms development, not **arms control**.

NSC-162/2. A U.S. **National Security Council** study completed on 30 October 1953 and titled "Basic National Security Policy." It established the security policy of the administration of **United States** President **Dwight Eisenhower**, provided the defense program to build up the **Strategic Air Command's** capabilities to ensure a **massive retaliation** posture, and supported a need for the development of **early warning** and continental defense systems.

NSDD-13. A U.S. **National Security Council** directive issued on 19 October 1981 and titled "**Nuclear Weapons Employment Policy.**" It established the nuclear policy for the administration of **United States** President **Ronald Reagan**, continuing the emphasis established in **PD-59** on a **countervailing** strategy but expanding guidance on the conduct of protracted **nuclear war**.

NSDM-242. A U.S. **National Security Council** study completed on 17 January 1974 and titled "Policy for Planning the Employment of Nuclear Weapons." This study articulated the "Schlesinger Doctrine" that called for **limited nuclear options** against a wider range of targets, including **counterforce** targets, and in a range of graduated options.

NUCLEAR, BIOLOGICAL, AND CHEMICAL WEAPONS (NBC). Sometimes called special weapons or **weapons of mass destruction**, these weapons categories are the focus of most contemporary **arms control** and **nonproliferation** efforts. *See also* BIO-

LOGICAL WARFARE; CHEMICAL WARFARE; NUCLEAR
WEAPONS.

**NUCLEAR AND COUNTERPROLIFERATION DIRECTORATE
(HQ USAF/XON).** The **United States Air Force** organization
charged with Service responsibility for nuclear, **arms control,** and
counterproliferation policy and actions. Created in 1997 by combining several smaller offices in the Air Staff, it was moved under
USAF/XOS in a 2004 reorganization.

NUCLEAR DILEMMA. Nuclear weapons, in clear contrast to conventional weapons, simultaneously create both security and insecurity. Adding a new class or increment of nuclear weapons in fact
can destabilize the nuclear balance and create insecurity. At the
same time, not adding that new class or increment of nuclear weapons, if the other side is building its capability, will also destabilize
the balance and create insecurity. This condition created incentives
for **arms control** during the **Cold War.**

NUCLEAR FREE ZONES. There have been several efforts by both
international and regional organizations to ban or limit the use of
nuclear material in specific regions of the world. In addition to several regional **treaties,** three separate treaties, which have been
signed by almost all the nations of the world, prohibit nuclear materials from being stored or tested in outer space, on the seabed floor,
and in Antarctica.

Five regional nuclear free zones have already been established
through treaties, effectively making most of the Southern Hemisphere nuclear free. The **South Pacific Nuclear Free Zone,** was
created on 6 August 1985 with the signing of the Treaty of Rarotonga. It **entered into force** on 11 December 1986 and is a multilateral treaty that bans the stationing, manufacturing, testing, and
dumping of nuclear weapons or nuclear waste within the zone. The
issue of ship and aircraft traffic is left up to individual countries.
Nuclear testing is banned in the region. Not all five of the **nuclear
weapons states** have yet signed all of the protocols.

The **Latin American Nuclear Free Zone** was formalized in
the Treaty of Tlatelolco, signed in Mexico City on 14 February
1967 with entry into force 25 April 1968. The treaty bans the storage and testing of nuclear weapons within the **signatory** countries,
but does allow for the peaceful use of nuclear material. The treaty
has two protocols: one that obligates states with colonies to adhere

to the treaty and another that calls for NWS to recognize the zone. All Latin American and Caribbean states have ratified the treaty.

The Treaty of Pelindaba was signed on 11 April 1996 in Cairo, Egypt, creating the **African Nuclear Weapons Free Zone**. Entry into force awaits ratification by 28 African states.

The Treaty of Bangkok was signed 15 December 1995 to establish the **Southeast Asia Nuclear Weapon Free Zone**. Seven of the 10 regional states had to ratify the treaty before entry into force, which occurred on 28 March 1977. Its provisions cover foreign ships and aircraft transiting the region, but the **United States** has not recognized this treaty.

Still pending is the **Central Asia Nuclear Weapons Free Zone**, signed in October 2002 by five countries in the region under the auspices of the **United Nations** but which had not entered into force as of mid-2004. It requires endorsement by the five **nuclear weapons states** before that can happen.

The first treaty of this type, the **Antarctic Treaty**, was signed on 1 December 1959 in Washington, D.C., and entered into force on 23 June 1961. One of the first international arms control treaties, it demilitarized the continent, ensuring its use for peaceful purposes and scientific exploration.

Efforts are currently underway to establish additional nuclear or nuclear weapon free zones in the Middle East, South Asia, and the South Atlantic. *See also* OUTER SPACE TREATY; SEABED TREATY.

NUCLEAR HEDGE. A category of **nuclear weapons** that is placed in storage rather than being destroyed following removal from a state's **strategic** arsenal. The term was coined by the 1994 **Nuclear Posture Review** and identified those weapons being downloaded as a result of the **Strategic Arms Reduction Treaty** (START) but kept intact in storage facilities, available for redistribution to delivery systems should the need arise.

NUCLEAR ILLUSION. Lord Zuckerman, who was for many years chief scientific advisor to the British Government, expressed his view in a 1983 book that the modernization of **nuclear weapons** was often due not to a real military need, but rather to the zeal of scientists to invent new gadgets; the military was usually a ready customer for laboratory inventions. This belief has also been called "technological determinism."

Eighth Assembly of the League of Nations, 1927. Courtesy of the UNOG
Library, League of Nations Archives.

Secretary of State Dean Acheson signs the North Atlantic Treaty for the
United States, Washington, D.C., 4 April 1949. NATO Photo. www.nato.int/
multi/photos/1949/m490404a.htm.

President Dwight D. Eisenhower makes his "atoms for peace" proposal to the United Nations General Assembly, 8 December 1953. UN Photo. www.iaea.org/NewsCenter/Multimedia/Imagebank/SearchResult_Recor dInfo.jsp?page=433.

The U.S. and Soviet delegations meet for the first time as the Strategic Arms Limitation Talks (SALT I) begin in Helsinki, Finland, 17 November 1969. NATO Photo. www.nato.int/multi/photos/1998/ m980923.htm.

Soviet President Mikhail Gorbachev and U.S. President Ronald Reagan sign the Intermediate-Range Nuclear Forces Treaty in Washington, D.C., 8 December 1987. Photo courtesy of the Ronald Reagan Library.

British and U.S. delegations at NATO's Prague Summit meeting, November 2002. At the table, left to right: UK Secretary of State Jack Straw, Prime Minister Tony Blair, U.S. Secretary of State Colin Powell, President George W. Bush. NATO Photo. www.nato.int/pictures/2002/021121/b021121ak.jpg.

The first U.S. hydrogen bomb test, the Mike shot (10.5 megatons) on Enewetak Atoll, Marshall Islands, 31 October 1952. DTRA Photo. www.dtra.mil/press_resources/photo_library/CS/CS-2.cfm.

U.S. Army troops observing a tactical nuclear weapon test (code named Buster-Jangle Dog), Nevada Test Site, November 1951. DTRA Photo. www.dtra.mil/press_resources/photo_library/CS/CS-3.cfm.

USS *Cape St. George* launches a Tomahawk cruise missile from the Mediterranean Sea during Operation Iraqi Freedom, 23 March 2003. U.S. Navy photo by Intelligence Specialist 1st Class Kenneth Moll. www.news.navy.mil/view_single.asp?id =5606.

U.S. B-1 Lancer dropping conventional ordnance on a test range at Edwards AFB, California, October 2003. USAF photo by Steve Zapka. www.af.mil/photos/index.asp?galleryID=13.

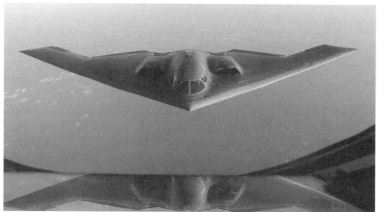

U.S. B-2 Spirit bomber returning from a mission over Iraq, refueling from a KC-135 Stratotanker over the Indian Ocean, 27 March 2003. USAF Photo by SSgt Cherie A. Thurlby. www.af.mil/media/photodb/photos/030327-F-203T-006.jpg.

U.S.–Israeli Arrow missile defense test launch at Point Mugu, California, July 2004. U.S. Missile Defense Agency Photo. www.acq.osd.mil/mda/mdalink/pdf/04fyi0013.pdf.

U.S. missile defense interceptor test launch, Kwajalein Atoll, July 2000. U.S. Missile Defense Agency photo. www.acq.osd.mil/mda/mdalink/ images/ift5_7.jpg.

CACTUS, the concrete radiological containment chamber over the Mike shot location, Enewetak Atoll, upon completion in 1979. DTRA Photo. www.dtra.mil/press_ resources/photo_library/CS/CS-2.cfm.

IAEA inspector checking a tree for depleted uranium shell fragments, Kosovo, November 2000. IAEA Photo by T. Cabianca. www.iaea.org/NewsCenter/Multimedia/Imagebank/SearchResult_RecordInfo.jsp?page=3.

UNMOVIC inspectors entering a site in Iraq, January 2003. UN Photo. www.iaea.org/NewsCenter/Focus/IaeaIraq/iraq_gallery/iraq_gallery10/pages/007.shtml.

NUCLEAR NONPROLIFERATION ACT (1978). The Nuclear Nonproliferation Act required countries receiving U.S. nuclear materials or technology or materials to accept so-called "full scope safeguards" by putting all of their national facilities under international **inspection**. In 1980, the **United States** terminated nuclear cooperation with India as a consequence of this law.

NUCLEAR NONPROLIFERATION TREATY (NPT). The "Treaty on the Non-Proliferation of Nuclear Weapons" obligates **nuclear weapons states** (NWS) parties to the treaty (the **United States, Soviet Union, United Kingdom, France**, and **China**) to three main principles: not to transfer **nuclear weapons** or control over such weapons to any recipient, directly or indirectly; not to assist, encourage, or induce any **non-nuclear weapon state** (NNWS) to manufacture or otherwise acquire such weapons, or seek control over them; and to actively work toward complete nuclear **disarmament**. Additionally, the NWS are required to assist the NNWS in the use of nuclear energy for peaceful purposes, including the benefits of **peaceful nuclear explosions**.

NNWS also agree to several provisions. They may not receive the transfer of nuclear weapons, or control over them. They are also prohibited from manufacturing, seeking help in manufacturing, or otherwise obtaining nuclear weapons. Although known to possess nuclear weapons, **Israel, India**, and **Pakistan** are officially NNWS according to the terms of this treaty.

The NPT was signed on 1 July 1968 and **entered into force** on 5 March 1970. The original duration called for a review after 25 years with the option to extend indefinitely or for a fixed period of time. At the 1995 Treaty Review Conference the states parties agreed to an indefinite extension of the **regime**.

All states must accept the **safeguards** negotiated with the **International Atomic Energy Agency** (IAEA), to prevent the diversion of nuclear energy from peaceful purposes to nuclear weapons. The IAEA is tasked as the treaty's **implementation** and **compliance** body; it meets in Vienna and is reinforced by two multilateral **export control** organizations: the NPT Exporters Committee (also known as the **Zangger Committee**) and the **Nuclear Suppliers Group**.

At the 1995 Review and Extension Conference in New York, the Treaty parties agreed to strengthen the review process. The review conferences will continue to take place every five years. A set of "Principles and Objectives for Nuclear **Nonproliferation** and

Disarmament" was agreed to, including the goal of achieving a **comprehensive nuclear test ban** by 1996. The treaty was extended for an indefinite period by consensus of the parties. Finally, the conference called upon the states in the Middle East to agree to the creation of a zone free of **weapons of mass destruction**.

The 2000 Review Conference in New York raised concerns over the potentially destabilizing effects of U.S. **missile defenses** on the NPT regime. The nuclear weapons states did agree to unequivocably seek "the total elimination of their nuclear arsenals, leading to nuclear disarmament," but no timeline for doing so was agreed upon.

NUCLEAR PLANNING GROUP (NPG). One of the major committees of the **North Atlantic Treaty Organization**, created in the early 1960s to coordinate nuclear **deterrence** and **warfighting** plans among Alliance members. All states except **France** participate in the NPG, although its agenda is dominated by the "big four" states: the **United States**, **Great Britain**, Germany, and Italy. Its principal subcommittee and source of many nuclear related studies is the **High Level Group**.

NUCLEAR POSTURE REVIEW (NPR) (1994, 2001). In 1994 the **United States Department of Defense** completed a major review of nuclear policy and posture entering the post-**Cold War** period. Given force and budget cuts, a much-altered threat picture, and the provisions of **Strategic Arms Reduction Treaties** (START I and II), the review affirmed a continuing **deterrent** role for a reduced arsenal of United States **nuclear weapons**. In 2001 the United States **Department of Defense** conducted a new Nuclear Posture Review to forecast nuclear policy and posture a decade after the Cold War. This resulted in significant changes to the United States' nuclear force posture, including the creation of a new **strategic triad** that would be made up of strategic strike assets (including the old nuclear triad of **bombers**, **intercontinental ballistic missiles**, and **submarine launched ballistic missiles**), strategic defenses, and an enhanced infrastructure. Some commentators saw the NPR as the executing document for the 2002 U.S. National Security Strategy, which included a greater emphasis on military **preemption** against adversaries.

NUCLEAR REACTION DATA CENTERS NETWORK (NRDC). The Nuclear Reaction Data Centers Network is a world-wide cooperation of nuclear data centers, under the auspices of the **International Atomic Energy Agency** (IAEA), established to coordinate the collection, compilation, and dissemination of nuclear data on an international scale. Dissemination of nuclear data and associated documentation to users is the primary goal of the network. In order to accomplish this goal, the following specific tasks are carried out: compilation of experimental nuclear data; bibliographic information; collection of evaluated nuclear data; exchange of nuclear data of all types among the centers; promotion of the development of special purpose evaluated data files; development of common formats for computerized exchange of nuclear data; coordinated development of computer software for managing and disseminating nuclear data; and documentation of current and future data needs in order to be able to meet changing user demands. There are currently 13 data centers active in the network.

NUCLEAR REGULATORY COMMISSION (NRC). The Nuclear Regulatory Commission is an independent U.S. government commission, created by the Energy Reorganization Act of 1974. The NRC is responsible for licensing and regulating the civilian use of nuclear energy to protect the public and the environment. The NRC also conducts public hearings on nuclear and **radiological** safety and on environmental and antitrust issues relevant to nuclear energy. A five-member commission heads the NRC. As part of the regulatory process, the NRC's four regional offices conduct inspection, enforcement, and emergency response programs for licensees within their borders, and investigate nuclear incidents.

Before the NRC was created, nuclear regulation was the responsibility of the **Atomic Energy Commission** (AEC), which Congress first established in the **Atomic Energy Act** of 1946. Congress replaced that law with the Atomic Energy Act of 1954. This act assigned the AEC the functions of both encouraging the use of nuclear power and regulating its safety. During the 1960s, an increasing number of critics charged that the AEC's regulations were insufficiently rigorous in several important areas, including radiation protection standards, reactor safety, plant siting, and environmental protection. By 1974 Congress decided to abolish the AEC. Supporters and critics of nuclear power agreed that the promotional and regulatory duties of the AEC should be assigned to different agencies. In passing the Energy Reorganization Act of 1974, Congress created the NRC and transferred all of the licensing and regulatory powers of the AEC to the new agency. The NRC began operations on 19 January 1975.

NUCLEAR RISK REDUCTION CENTERS AGREEMENT (NRRC) (1987). An **agreement** between the **United States** and the **Soviet Union** for each nation to establish a center to act as a clearing house for the exchange of information on current and future **arms control** agreement **compliance**, military maneuvers, and other activities such as missile launches and tests.

NUCLEAR AND SPACE ARMS TALKS (NST). A three-part series of negotiations between the **United States** and the **Soviet Union** begun in 1985 comprised of talks on military uses of space, **intermediate-range nuclear forces** (INF), and the **Strategic Arms Reduction Talks** (START). These talks led to the INF Treaty in 1987 and the START I treaty in 1992.

NUCLEAR SUPPLIERS GROUP (NSG). An informal group of 39 states that seeks to control export of nuclear materials, equipment, and sensitive technology by limiting said exports solely to states that adhere to **International Atomic Energy Agency** (IAEA) **safeguards** and **inspections**. Motivated by **India's** 1974 explosion of its first nuclear device, the founding members of the NSG began meeting in April 1975 to help implement the **export control** restrictions of the **Nuclear Nonproliferation Treaty** (NPT). Like the **Zangger Committee,** the NSG (also known as the London Club), adopted a **trigger list** of items related to **nuclear weapon** production. These guidelines were published by the IAEA in February 1978. The requirement for recipient states to agree to full scope safeguards has led to banning exports to **Israel, India**, and **Pakistan**. China is the only **nuclear weapons state** not a member of the NSG.

NUCLEAR TEST BAN. A formal international **agreement** that proscribes the detonation of an **atomic weapon** or device for any reason, including the test of a design or for stockpile assurance. *See* COMPREHENSIVE TEST BAN TREATY; LIMITED TEST BAN TREATY.

NUCLEAR TESTING. Detonating an **atomic weapon** or device in order to ensure it will work, or that a particular design feature functions correctly. Testing in the early years of the nuclear age was often conducted in the open atmosphere or underwater, but limits to that technique forced testing underground by the early 1960s. Thanks to reciprocated unilateral testing **moratoriums** by the **nuclear weapons states**, there have been no nuclear tests by any nation since **India** and **Pakistan** each conducted several tests in May 1998. The **United States** announced a moratorium on further testing in 1992, and a **Comprehensive Test Ban Treaty** has been signed by most nations, but not ratified by the United States.

NUCLEAR THREAT INITIATIVE (NTI). A charitable organization working to reduce the global threats from nuclear, **biological and chemical weapons**, NTI's mission is to strengthen global security by reducing the risk of use and preventing the spread of **nuclear, biological** and **chemical weapons**. NTI seeks to raise public awareness, serve as a catalyst for new thinking, and take direct action to reduce these threats. Founded in 2001, it has offices in Washington, D.C., and **Moscow**.

NUCLEAR THRESHOLD. The use of a **nuclear weapon** in a conflict would constitute "crossing the threshold" between conventional and **nuclear warfare**. The phrase was coined by **Henry Kissinger**. The nuclear threshold provides a significant psychological barrier that distinguishes traditional conventional warfare from nuclear catastrophe.

NUCLEAR WAR. War involving the use of **nuclear weapons** by one or both sides in a conflict. The penultimate type of military action on the spectrum of conflict intensity. *See also* NUCLEAR WINTER; SINGLE INTEGRATED OPERATIONS PLAN.

NUCLEAR WARHEAD. The component of a weapon system that delivers the package intended to disable or destroy a target. A nuclear warhead carries a nuclear explosive device, either a **fission** or **fusion weapon** (in the current **United States** arsenal, these are all **hydrogen bombs** of **implosion device** design). *See also* ATOMIC BOMB; PAYLOAD; REENTRY VEHICLE.

NUCLEAR WEAPONS. Weapons that involve an explosion based on a **chain reaction** involving the **fission** and/or **fusion** of atomic nuclei. A **nuclear weapon** is the combination of an atomic device encased in a compartment designed to achieve certain effects as a result of the atomic reaction, delivered to its target by a vehicle of some type ranging from an artillery shell to an air-delivered bomb to an intercontinental missile warhead. *See also* ATOMIC BOMB; GUN-TYPE DEVICE; HIGHLY ENRICHED URANIUM; HYDROGEN BOMB; IMPLOSION DEVICE; PLUTONIUM; URANIUM.

NUCLEAR WEAPONS EMPLOYMENT POLICY (NUWEP). The official **United States** government strategy for the use of **nuclear weapons** in deterrence and possible conflict. Developed by the **Office of the Secretary of Defense**, the NUWEP translates the highest level guidance from the president on nuclear weapons into direction for the U.S. military forces, in particular **U.S. Strategic Command**, which then determines targeting, timing, and deployment plans.

NUCLEAR WEAPONS FREE ZONES (NWFZ). Areas in which by agreement the production, deployment, and sometimes even the transit of **nuclear weapons** is prohibited. Most of the earth's Southern Hemisphere is covered by one of the extant NWFZs. *See also* AFRICAN NUCLEAR WEAPONS FREE ZONE; ANTARCTIC TREATY; CENTRAL ASIA NUCLEAR FREE ZONE; LATIN AMERICAN NUCLEAR FREE ZONE; NUCLEAR FREE ZONES; SOUTH PACIFIC NUCLEAR FREE ZONE; SOUTHEAST ASIA NUCLEAR WEAPON FREE ZONE.

NUCLEAR WEAPONS STATES (NWS). According to the **Nuclear Nonproliferation Treaty** (NPT), a state that openly possessed **nuclear weapons** on 1 July 1968. There were five such states: the **United States**, the **Soviet Union**, **Great Britain**, **France**, and **China**.

NUCLEAR WINTER. The potential ecological disaster following an exchange of **nuclear weapons** where the smoke and dust raised into the atmosphere from the bombing and subsequent fires could lead to a drop in global temperatures with large-scale effects, possibly blocking out the sun for years. This could lead to the demise of agriculture and possibly mass extinctions. The theory gained prominence in the international security community during the early 1980s.

NUNN, SAMUEL (1938-). An influential U.S. senator from 1972 to 1996 who served as one of the **United States'** leading thinkers on **arms control** and military strategy during the second half of the

Cold War. Among his notable contributions was cosponsoring the Nunn-Lugar **Cooperative Threat Reduction Initiative**. Upon retirement from the Senate, Nunn joined with media mogul Ted Turner to found the **Nuclear Threat Initiative**, a bipartisan think tank and advocacy organization.

NUNN-LUGAR PROGRAM. *See* COOPERATIVE THREAT REDUCTION PROGRAM (CTR).

O

OAK RIDGE, TENNESSEE. Site of the Oak Ridge National Laboratory and birthplace of **highly enriched uranium** (HEU). The first significant amounts of HEU were created at Oak Ridge's K40 plant during World War II as part of the **Manhattan Project**. The location was selected in part because of its proximity to the Tennessee Valley Authority, reflecting the need for massive amounts of electricity to run the **uranium enrichment** facility. Later the Y12 plant was added to build secondary components for **hydrogen bombs**. In the 1990s it served as a location for the dismantlement of surplus **atomic warheads** and storage of waste **fissile materials**.

OBJECTS OF VERIFICATION. A counting method for determining which units and equipment needed to be **verified** during the **implementation** of the **Conventional Forces in Europe Treaty** (CFE).

OBSERVER. A person representing a foreign country at a military exercise or **arms control inspection**. The observer is an official monitor and judge of the activities to ensure they subscribe to existing restrictions and guidelines.

OFFENSIVE ARMS CONTROL. Negotiations to halt or reverse the growth and spread of offensive weapons, such as **ballistic missiles, nuclear warheads,** and the like. Such efforts recognize the dangers of uncontrolled **arms races** that spiral to unnecessary levels. This represented the most common **arms control** approach in the **Cold War,** leading to such **agreements** as the **Strategic Arms Limitation Treaties** (SALT), the **Strategic Arms Reduction Treaties** (START), and the **Strategic Offensive Reductions Treaty** (SORT).

OFFICE OF THE SECRETARY OF DEFENSE (OSD). The principal staff element of the U.S. secretary of defense in the exercise of policy development, planning, resource management, fiscal, and program evaluation responsibilities. OSD includes the immediate offices of the secretary and deputy secretary of defense, under secretaries of defense, director of defense research and engineering, assistant secretaries of defense, general counsel, director of operational test and evaluation, assistants to the secretary of defense, director of administration and management, and such other staff offices as the secretary establishes to assist in carrying out assigned responsibilities.

OFFICE OF TECHNOLOGY ASSESSMENT (OTA). During its 23-year history from 1962 to 1995, the Congressional **Office of Technology Assessment** provided congressional members and committees with objective and authoritative analysis of the complex scientific and technical issues of the late 20th century. It was a leader in practicing and encouraging delivery of public services in innovative and inexpensive ways, including distribution of government documents through electronic publishing.

ON-SITE INSPECTION (OSI). A method of compliance verification involving visits by representatives of the other side of a bilateral agreement or of an international inspection authority to weapon production and deployment sites. On-site inspections became a common aspect of **strategic arms control treaties** negotiated during the **Cold War**.

ON-SITE INSPECTION AGENCY (OSIA). The U.S. organization responsible for ensuring foreign **compliance** with **arms control treaty** provisions. It was created in January 1988 to deal with the new **on-site inspection** requirements of the **Intermediate-Range Nuclear Forces Treaty.** The OSIA became a directorate within the new **Defense Threat Reduction Agency** (DTRA) in 1998.

ONE POINT SAFE. A modern **nuclear weapon** is designed with insensitive high explosives that can only be detonated in a controlled fashion by firing electronic detonators at several locations simultaneously. If the explosives surrounding the core of the weapon cannot be set off with, for example, a single rifle shot, they are considered to be "one point safe."

OPEN SKIES. A 1955 proposal by the administration of U.S. President **Dwight Eisenhower** for the **United States** and the **Soviet Union** to conduct aerial **inspections** of the other superpower primarily as a **confidence-building measure**. The concept was finally codified in a 1992 multinational **treaty** that established an aerial observation regime by **sensor**-equipped aircraft. The treaty **entered into force** in 2002, and flights began that same year.

OPEN SKIES TREATY. *See* TREATY ON OPEN SKIES.

OPERATION PLOWSHARE. A series of U.S. **underground nuclear tests** conducted in the 1960s and early 1970s as part of a set of experiments in **peaceful nuclear explosions**. Plowshare attempted to move large quantities of earth for the purpose of canal digging and other excavation work, to release trapped oil and natural gas deposits, and so on. The **Atomic Energy Commission** was seeking peaceful uses of nuclear weapons technology. The most striking reminder of Operation Plowshare is the Sedan Crater in the Nevada Test Site, 1,280 feet across and 320 feet deep. It was an experiment in the use of nuclear explosions for excavation, to dig canals or dredge harbors. The Sedan test detonated a 104-kiloton device 635 feet underground, displacing 12 million tons of earth. Tons of that sand became airborne fallout, and the process was deemed unsuitable for digging. Occasional Plowshare tests, 35 in all, continued until 1973.

OPPENHEIMER, J. ROBERT (1902-1967). A physicist at the University of California-Berkeley, Oppenheimer became director of the **Manhattan Project** and **Los Alamos Laboratory** during World War II. He led the development effort to create the first **atomic bomb**. He later served as a fellow at the Institute for Advanced Study in Princeton, New Jersey, and was a founding member of the **Pugwash conferences**.

ORGANISM. A complex structure of interdependent and subordinate elements whose relations and properties are largely determined by their function in the overall structure.

ORGANIZATION FOR THE PROHIBITION OF CHEMICAL WEAPONS (OPCW). Created in 1997 as the implementation and compliance body of the **Chemical Weapons Convention** (CWC). The OPCW has 158 members, a staff of 500, and is headquartered in The Hague, Netherlands. Its mission is to implement the provisions of the Chemical Weapons Convention in order to achieve a vision of a world both free of **chemical weapons** and in which cooperation in chemistry for peaceful purposes for all is fostered. Its ultimate aim is to contribute to international security and stability, to **general and complete disarmament**, and to global and economic development. To this end, it proposes policies for the implementation of the Convention to the Member States of the OPCW and develops and delivers programs with and for them. These programs have four broad aims: to ensure a credible, transparent regime to verify the destruction of chemical weapons and prevent their re-emergence in any member state, while also protecting legitimate national security and proprietary interests; to provide protection and assistance against chemical weapons; to encourage international cooperation in the peaceful uses of chemistry; and to bring about universal membership of the OPCW by facilitating international cooperation and national capacity building.

ORGANIZATION FOR SECURITY AND COOPERATION IN EUROPE (OSCE). The OSCE grew out of the **Conference on Security and Cooperation in Europe** (CSCE), which was renamed and revamped in December 1994. The OSCE is the largest regional security organization in the world with 55 participating states from Europe, Central Asia, and North America. It is active in **early warning, conflict prevention**, crisis management, and post-conflict rehabilitation. The OSCE approach to security is comprehensive and cooperative: comprehensive in dealing with a wide range of security-related issues including **arms control**, preventive diplomacy, **confidence- and security-building measures**, human rights, democratization, election monitoring, and economic and environmental security; cooperative in the sense that all OSCE states have equal status and decisions are based on consensus. The OSCE headquarters are located in Vienna, Austria. The organization also has offices and institutions located in Copenhagen, **Geneva**, The Hague, Prague, and Warsaw. It employs about 3,000 staff in 18 missions and field activities located in Southeastern Europe, the Caucasus, Eastern Europe, and Central Asia, working to facilitate political processes, prevent or settle conflicts, and promote civil society and the rule of law.

OSTPOLITIK. The West German diplomatic effort to enhance relations with East Germany during the **Cold War**. Literally "east politics," *Ostpolitik* was an attempt to created closer ties between the two parts of Germany. Its success was one factor in thawing relations during the 1970s and the development of **détente**. The ultimate goal and eventual outcome of *Ostpolitik* was the reunification of the Federal Republic of Germany and the German Democratic Republic, which occurred in 1990.

OTTAWA CONVENTION (1997). The conference that led to the **Mine Ban Convention**, outlawing the use of most types of antipersonnel land mines. This is of special note because the effort to create this convention was led not by nation-states, but by **nongovernmental organizations**. The **United States** refused to sign this convention, citing the need for continued use of land mines for the territorial defense of South Korea.

OUTER SPACE TREATY (1967). The "Treaty on the Principles Governing the Activities of States in the Exploration and Use of Outer Space, Including the Moon and Other Celestial Bodies" was negotiated primarily between the **United States** and the **Soviet Union**. It serves to limit the militarization of outer space and celestial bodies. Signed on 27 January 1967, the **treaty** prohibits any state from placing **weapons of mass destruction** in outer space or deploying them on celestial bodies. In addition, all celestial bodies are to be used solely for peaceful purposes and may not be used for military bases, fortifications, or weapons testing of any kind. It **entered into force** on 10 October 1967 with unlimited duration. There are currently 113 **signatories** to the treaty.

OVERFLIGHT. Using aircraft or satellites to ensure **compliance** with the provisions of an **arms control treaty**. Overflights avoid intrusive ground inspections, thereby precluding the need for complete trust between states parties to an agreement. A good example of cooperative overflights is the **Open Skies Treaty**. An example of noncooperative overflights would be the U.S. **reconnaissance** missions over Cuba during the **Cuban Missile Crisis**, and the regular **U-2** overflights of the **Soviet Union** in the late 1950s. These flights ended following Francis Gary Powers' plane being shot down by Soviet antiaircraft missiles, an event that also led to the collapse of a **summit meeting** in Paris between **Dwight D. Eisenhower** and **Nikita Khrushchev** in May 1960.

OVERHEAD SURVEILLANCE. Information gathering through the use of electronic or photographic means from aircraft or space vehicles that overfly the territory of another nation. This can be done surreptitiously, or in accordance with agreements such as the **Open Skies Treaty**.

P

PACIFISM. A personal conviction that renounces violence or the use of force, preferring to show one's beliefs through passive resistance and the force of moral logic. *See also* PEACE MOVEMENTS.

PACT OF PARIS (1928). A treaty between the **United States** and other major powers providing for the renunciation of war as an instrument of national policy. Signed in Paris, France, on August 27, 1928. *See also* KELLOGG-BRIAND PACT.

PACTS OF MAY (1902). A collection of **agreements** that defused the tense military situation between Chile and Argentina. Four agreements were signed: a protocol stating the international policy of both states; a general **treaty** of arbitration; a convention limiting naval armaments; and a decision on marking the boundary between the two countries. The pacts created a new spirit of rapprochement between the antagonists.

PAKISTAN. One of the two major powers of South Asia, Pakistan is a secular Islamic state that has been in perpetual conflict with neighboring **India** since its creation in 1947, including a civil war in 1971 that led to its eastern provinces becoming the independent state of Bangladesh. Pakistan developed an indigenous **nuclear weapons** capability to counter India's military force and conducted **nuclear tests** in May 1998. In terms of **deterrence** policy, nuclear strategy, **command and control** issues, and the like, Pakistan and India find themselves on a learning curve much like that experienced by the **United States** and the **Soviet Union** in the early years of the **Cold War**. *See also* PRESSLER AMENDMENT.

PALME REPORT. A 1983 report by Prime Minister Olaf Palme of Sweden that called upon the nations of Europe to engage in "**common security**." Institutionalists see cooperation as an alternative to the vicious cycle of threats, counter-threats, and misperceptions that arose in the **Cold War**. International **agreements** and institutions create norms that foster cooperation. In other words, "common security"—a term originally coined by West German Social Democrats—is possible even between adversaries.

PANTEX FACILITY. The **United States'** primary facility for dismantling and storing excess **nuclear warheads,** including those warheads designated as part of America's strategic hedge, located near Amarillo, Texas.

PARITY. The situation in which the balance of military capabilities in the arena under focus is roughly equivalent; a balance of power. During the **Cold War** this term usually referred to the balance of **strategic** nuclear forces between the **United States** and the **Soviet Union.** Parity was achieved by the Soviets in the late 1960s as a result of its massive strategic modernization program early in that decade, and the coincidental decision by the United States to freeze its nuclear arsenal at the numbers it had in 1965.

PARTIAL TEST BAN TREATY (PTBT). *See* LIMITED TEST BAN TREATY.

PARTICLE BEAM WEAPON. A type of **directed-energy weapon** (in the same category as lasers and microwaves), the particle-beam weapon generates its destructive power by accelerating sufficient quantities of subatomic particles or atoms to velocities near the speed of light and focusing these particles into a very high-energy beam that acts much like a lightning bolt. The **United States** has been pursuing such a weapon, possibly for basing in space, since the beginning of the **Strategic Defense Initiative** in 1982.

PASSIVE DEFENSE. An approach to defense with emphasis on protective measures such as hardening, sheltering, or dispersal. Within the **U.S. Department of Defense Counterproliferation Initiative,** it is "contamination avoidance (**reconnaissance**, detection, and warning), force protection (individual and collective protection and medical support), and decontamination." *See also* ACTIVE DEFENSE.

PASSIVE IMMUNITY. Immunity to a **biological agent** acquired from the introduction of an **antibody** to create a defense separate

from the natural immune system of the host. *See* ACTIVE IMMU-
NITY.

PASSIVE QUOTA. *See* ACTIVE QUOTA.

PATHOGEN. A bacteria, fungus, or **virus** that causes disease in humans, animals, or plants.

PAYLOAD. The deliverable weapon system package carried by a **delivery system**, or the carrying capacity of the delivery system.

PD-59. A U.S. **National Security Council** directive issued on 25 July
1980 titled "**Nuclear Weapons Employment Policy**." It formalized
United States nuclear policy late in the administration of President
Jimmy Carter into one based on a **countervailing** strategy.

PEACE MOVEMENTS. Popular protests against some aspect of military doctrine or operations. During the nuclear age, peace movements have predominantly opposed the role of **nuclear weapons**
and **deterrence** in national strategy. At times these movements
have grown to major public demonstrations, particularly during the
1950s and again in the early 1980s. The threat of global annihilation
seemed to generate a greater sense of urgency among those willing
to mobilize against the ultimate weapon. The movements seemed to
wane after reaching their high point in Europe about 1984, whether
out of exhaustion (following the failed attempt to block the deployment of U.S. and Soviet **intermediate-range nuclear missiles**
in Central Europe), or belief in the possibility of radical change, or
the success of **arms control treaties**. Examples of major peace
movements include the international **Pugwash conventions**, the
women who camped around the U.S. Air Force base at Greenham
Common, United Kingdom, during the 1980s to protest the deployment of **ground launched cruise missiles**, and the East German **Swords into Plowshares** movement of the 1970s and 1980s.

PEACE THROUGH STRENGTH. The national security position
held by Presidents **Ronald Reagan** and his successor, **George
H.W. Bush**, through the 1980s. This approach, resting on the bed-
rock of American ideals and emphasizing military power, was credited by many with forcing the **Soviet Union** to give up its **superpower** competition, thus ending the **Cold War**.

PEACE AND TRUCE OF GOD (989, 1150). Among the earliest **arms control agreements**, these decrees by the Catholic Church established the concept of protections for civilians in a noncombatant status in a conflict. It ended the idea of private wars then in common practice, and protected the church and its clerics, as well as citizens. These decrees led to the concept of **just war** and the protection of noncombatants.

PEACEFUL COEXISTENCE. A commonly used description of the relationship between the **United States** and the **Soviet Union** during the **Cold War**: one in which neither side trusted the other, but both sides adopted a wary, cautious stance that avoided open military conflict due to fears of uncontrolled **escalation** should conflict break out.

PEACEFUL NUCLEAR EXPLOSION (PNE). The uses of nuclear explosions for nonmilitary purposes such as mining and civil engineering. *See also* PEACEFUL NUCLEAR EXPLOSIONS TREATY (PNET).

PEACEFUL NUCLEAR EXPLOSIONS TREATY (PNET) (1976). The "Treaty between the United States of America and the Union of Soviet Socialist Republics on Underground Nuclear Explosions for Peaceful Purposes" was signed on 28 May 1976. As with the **Threshold Test Ban Treaty**, its protocol on the **verification** of compliance was not completed until 1 June 1990. The treaty **entered into force** on 11 December 1990. It allows **peaceful nuclear explosions** outside declared testing sites, but prohibits any individual explosion exceeding a yield of 150 **kilotons** (KT). Group explosions are limited to a yield of 1.5 **megatons**, provided that each individual explosion's yield can be verified and does not exceed 150 KT. The protocol to the PNET requires notification of explosions and allows for **on-site inspections** and other methods of measuring the yield of the detonation. The treaty had a duration of five years, with five-year extensions. It is still in effect.

PEACEKEEPER MISSILE. The name for the United States "missile experimental" (MX) **intercontinental ballistic missile**. The MX was designed to carry up to 14 **multiple independently targetable reentry vehicles,** but was deployed with 10 **warheads** and had a range of 8,100 miles. Peacekeeper was named after the famous six-shot revolver preferred by lawmen in the American West, the "gun that tamed the West," because of its supposed ability to quell Soviet ambitions once deployed. Research and development on the MX began in 1974, its first flight took place in June 1983, and it was deployed to F.E. Warren AFB, Wyoming, in 1986. The Peacemaker has four stages, three solid fuel and one liquid fuel, with greater range, payload, and accuracy than the **Minuteman** missile. Production was capped at 50 missiles in 1990 as a result of changes in the international security environment. In 2002 the United States began retiring Peacekeeper as part of its obligations under the **Strategic Arms Reduction** (START) treaties.

PEACEKEEPER RAIL GARRISON. One of several proposed deployment schemes for the **Peacekeeper intercontinental ballistic missile** (ICBM). The concept was to place the missile atop railroad cars that would shuttle 100 missiles between 1,000 hardened shelters built along railroad lines in the Western **United States**. This would complicate Soviet targeting efforts by requiring the **Soviet Union** to hit every shelter, not knowing where the missiles were actually hidden. The design would also allow panels in the shelter ceiling to be opened when necessary for Soviet satellite imagery to verify the total number of missiles in accordance with **arms control treaty** requirements.

PELINDABA, TREATY OF. *See* AFRICAN NUCLEAR WEAPON FREE ZONE.

PENETRABILITY. The ability of a weapon system to pass through, or penetrate, an **active defense** and reach its designated target.

PENETRATION AIDS. Systems, devices, techniques that enhance a weapon systems' **penetrability**. Examples include chaff, balloons, or decoys that would fool an **antiballistic missile system**.

PENTAGON. Headquarters of the **United States Department of Defense** (DoD) and its five branches of the military. One of the world's largest office buildings, with over 20,000 employees, it was built during World War II in the shape of a five-sided star in Arlington, Virginia (across the Potomac River from Washington, D.C.). "The Pentagon" is often used as shorthand for DoD or the military in discussions of American defense policy. It was damaged by an airliner used as a fuel-air explosive during the **terrorist** attacks on 11 September 2001.

PEOPLE'S REPUBLIC OF CHINA (PRC). *See* CHINA, PEO-PLES' REPUBLIC OF.

PERESTROIKA. Soviet economic and social policy of the late 1980s. *Perestroika* (restructuring) was the term attached to the attempts by **Mikhail Gorbachev** from 1985 to 1991 to transform the stagnant, inefficient command economy of the **Soviet Union** into a decentralized market-oriented economy. This movement, along with the parallel policy of *Glasnost* (openness) led to the end of the **Cold War** in the late 1980s and the dissolution of the **Union of Soviet Socialist Republics** in 1991.

PERLE, RICHARD (1942-). A powerful Washington insider since the 1980s when he served on the staff of Senator Henry Jackson, Perle became assistant secretary of defense for international security policy during the **Ronald Reagan** administration. He also served as foreign policy advisor for **George W. Bush** in the 2000 election campaign. Perle was generally opposed to **arms control negotiations** with the **Soviet Union** except when the **United States** could proceed from a position of strength. He coined the phrase "**zero option**" with regard to the early 1980's debate on **intermediate-range nuclear forces.** Because of his fixation on military power rather than diplomacy or new treaties, some European allies gave him the nickname "the prince of darkness."

PERMISSIVE ACTION LINKS (PAL). Locking mechanisms that prevent the use of a **nuclear weapon** without authoritative release. These are typically electro-mechanical devices, developed in the **United States** in the 1960s to ensure mechanistic control over **nuclear weapons** until such time as **national command authorities** gave the order for their use. In other words, PALs separate use of the weapon from possession of the weapon. The warhead cannot be armed until the proper enabling codes have been entered into the PAL device. The entire United States nuclear arsenal is now equipped with PAL devices.

PERSHING I. A mobile U.S. two-stage, solid fueled **ballistic missile** carrying a nuclear or conventional **warhead** and deployed in Europe and fielded by the **United States** and the West German *Luftwaffe.* Pershing I development began in 1958 by Martin Marrietta Corporation. Its first flight took place in 1960. Some 180 Pershing I's were deployed in Europe with a range of 450 miles.

PERSHING II. An improved version of the Pershing I, with greater range (800 miles), better accuracy, an earth-penetrating **warhead**, and enhanced mobility. The Pershing II was deployed in Germany in the mid-1980s, in part to counter the Soviet SS-20 intermediate-range nuclear missile, and was eliminated by the 1987 **Intermediate-Range Nuclear Forces Treaty** (INF).

PERSISTENCY. The characteristics of a **biological** or **chemical agent** that indicate the duration of its effects after dispersal and under given conditions. Persistency affects clean-up operations and is usually discussed in relation to follow-on military operations from the system, base, or ship that has been attacked by chemical or biological agents.

PERSISTENT AGENT. Generally, a **chemical agent** that registers a **persistency** of more than 24 hours.

PHASED-ARRAY RADAR. A radar system that is capable of targeting its electronic monitoring beams in multiple directions without mechanically repositioning an antenna. These radars have sufficient speed and accuracy to support **anti-ballistic missile systems** and were specifically limited by the **Anti-Ballistic Missile Treaty**. U.S phased-array radars will be upgraded and incorporated into a national **missile defense system** in the first decade of the 21st century.

PLUTONIUM (Pu). A **radioactive** element that releases vast amounts of energy in a nuclear explosion. Plutonium is highly **toxic** and is only produced as a waste product of nuclear reactors. It does not occur naturally. Plutonium has an atomic weight of 239. Separating plutonium from the spent **uranium** fuel that comes out of a nuclear reactor requires a large and complex industrial process called **reprocessing**.

PLUTONIUM PRODUCTION REACTOR AGREEMENT (PPRA) (1997). This confidence-building **agreement**, the result of the 1997 Gore-Chernomyrdin Commission, helped to slow the production of **fissile material**. It called for **Russia** to convert its remaining nuclear reactors capable of producing weapons-grade **plutonium** to nonplutonium types. The **United States** agreed to help pay for the costs of this conversion. Russia also promised to leave closed those reactors it had already shut down.

POINT DEFENSE. Localized protection of a specific individual target. *See also* AREA DEFENSE.

POLARIS. A two-stage, solid fueled, **submarine-launched ballistic missile** developed in the mid-1950s by the **United States**. It became operational in 1960 with a range of 2,880 miles and carried up to six **multiple independently targetable reentry warheads**. Polaris was carried by both U.S. and British Polaris-class submarines. The United States deployed 41 Polaris submarines carrying 16 missiles each; the **United Kingdom** had 4 Polaris boats.

POSEIDON. An evolutionary design based on the **Polaris submarine-launched ballistic missile** (SLBM). Poseidon was first tested in 1968. It was a two-stage, solid-fueled missile that could carry up to 14 **multiple independently targetable reentry vehicles**. Placed in service in 1971, it was deployed on 31 U.S. Polaris submarines.

POST-BOOST PHASE. The phase of a **ballistic missile's** trajectory from booster engine burnout to the initiation of the **reentry phase**. *See also* MIDCOURSE PHASE; REENTRY PHASE.

POUNDS PER SQUARE INCH (PSI). The measure used to represent the overpressure from a nuclear blast. PSI is used to predict the effects of a **nuclear weapon** and also to determine the ability of targets to withstand a nuclear blast—a measure of their **hardening**.

PRECISION-GUIDED MUNITION (PGM). A weapon with a guidance system that provides a high degree of **accuracy** in striking an individual target. Sometimes called "**smart bombs**," these may use laser sighting, video guidance, updates from **Global Positioning Satellites,** or other means to enhance their delivery **accuracy.** *See* DUMB BOMB.

PRECURSOR. A benign chemical that when combined with another substance produces a **chemical weapon**. Many precursors are **dual-use components** that are also found in common commercial applications.

PREEMPTION. Attacking another state or nonstate actor first when one believes that that adversary is about to attack one's own territory, people, or interests. Preemption is a long-standing policy that is generally considered legal under international law, presuming that the attacking state can provide evidence that it was merely thwarting an immediate danger from the state or actor it attacked first. It can serve as a form of **strategic** defense through offensive military action. The U.S. **National Security Strategy** published in 2002 expressly condones this type of attack if the **United States** feels imminently threatened by some other state or **terrorist** organization. The rationale of preemption played a role in the United States' decision to lead an international coalition in the war against **Iraq** in March 2002. *See also* PREVENTIVE ATTACK.

PREFERENTIAL DEFENSE. The ability of a defender to choose which of several valued items or sites it wishes to defend. This allows it to concentrate its defensive forces and fend off the attacker, who does not know which area has the greater defensive stance. This term is sometimes used when describing **ballistic missile defenses**. To protect an **intercontinental ballistic missile** field, for example, with a small number of defensive interceptors against a large volley of offensive missiles, the defender may accept that it can only save one or two silos. It will then write off the others and concentrate all its interceptors on missiles attacking that one silo. The attacker, not knowing which silos will be most heavily defended, must attack them all to attempt to destroy the **second strike** capability.

PREPROGRAMMED OPTIONS. A series of **command and control** options prepared in advance to minimize the chance of error or wrong decisions during periods of crisis. Such options were prepared for the president and other **national command authorities** during the **Cold War** for response to a Soviet **first strike** nuclear attack.

PRESIDENTIAL DECISION (PD). A major decision by a U.S. administration on national security strategy or related matters can be called a presidential decision (PD), a presidential decision directive (PDD), a presidential security decision memorandum (PSDM), or whatever other title a particular administration wishes to give it. Typically such decisions are rare, numbering but a handful each year.

PRESIDENTIAL NUCLEAR INITIATIVES (PNI). Between September 1991 and January 1992 there were a series of Presidential Initiatives by the presidents of both the **United States** and **Russia**

that significantly affected the nuclear force structure. Some of the measures were simply accelerations of those mandated by the **Strategic Arms Reduction Treaty** (START I), while others were incorporated into START II. However, there are additional binding actions that are not addressed in either treaty. In late 2001 the U.S. and Russian presidents agreed to additional unilateral but reciprocal reductions, which were later codified in the May 2002 **Strategic Offensive Reductions Treaty** (SORT).

On 27 September 1991, President **George H.W. Bush** announced that the United States would remove all U.S. **strategic bombers** and 450 **Minuteman** II **intercontinental ballistic missiles** (ICBM) from day-to-day alert; remove all **tactical nuclear weapons** on surface ships, attack submarines, and land-based naval aircraft slated for destruction or central storage; and cancel plans to develop a nuclear **short-range attack missile** (SRAM II), **Peacekeeper Rail Garrison** ICBM, and mobile portion of the **Small ICBM** (SICBM). He also proposed eliminating all U.S. and Soviet ICBMs with **multiple independently targetable reenty vehicles** (MIRV), and requested discussions on non-nuclear **anti-ballistic missile** (ABM) systems.

On 5 October 1991, President **Mikhail Gorbachev** responded by declaring similar reductions: **heavy bombers** and 503 ICBMs remained off alert; all tactical nuclear weapons on surface ships, attack submarines, and land-based naval aircraft removed for destruction or central storage; bomber nuclear arms and rail-mobile ICBMs placed in storage; SRAM, small mobile ICBM, and rail-mobile ICBM modernization and expansion programs cancelled; and seven SSBNs decommissioned. He also suggested reducing each side's nuclear arsenal to 5,000 warheads (below the START I limit of 6,000 warheads); and reducing **strategic** offensive arms by approximately one half. He suggested discussions on non-nuclear (ABM) systems and a one-year **moratorium** on **nuclear testing**.

In his State of the Union Address to the U.S. Congress on 28 January 1992, President Bush announced further reductions in the U.S. strategic forces to include limiting **B-2 Spirit bomber** production to 20 planes; limiting **Advanced Cruise Missile** production to 640; and canceling the **Small ICBM** and **Peacekeeper missiles** and the W-88 warhead for **Trident** missiles. Additionally, he stated that if Russia were to eliminate all MIRVed ICBMs, the United States would take the following actions to cut strategic **nuclear warheads** to approximately 4,700: eliminate Peacekeeper missiles; reduce Minuteman III missiles to one warhead per missile; reduce the number of **Trident** submarine warheads by one third; and convert a large number of strategic bombers to conventional use.

Russian Federation President **Boris Yeltsin** responded in a televised speech in Moscow on 29 January 1992. He stated Russia's intention to abide by all **arms control agreements** signed by the USSR, as well as his support for the **Nuclear Nonproliferation Treaty** (NPT), **the Missile Technology Control Regime** (MTCR), **the Comprehensive Test Ban Treaty** (CTBT), and the **Fissile Material Cutoff Treaty** (FMCT). He then made public additional reductions in strategic offensive forces of the **Commonwealth of Independent States** (CIS) and suggested several new U.S.-Russian initiatives, including the elimination of all **strategic ballistic missile submarine** patrols; reducing strategic nuclear warheads to 2,000-2,500; retargeting strategic offensive forces away from one another; reaching START limits three years early; and eliminating long-range nuclear SLCMs and new LRNAs.

In January 1994 Presidents **William Clinton** and Yeltsin agreed at the Moscow Summit that strategic forces under their control would be detargeted (no longer aimed at each other) by 30 May of that year. The **United Kingdom** took a similar initiative.

In November 2001 Russian President **Vladimir Putin** met with President **George W. Bush** in Washington, D.C., and **Crawford**, Texas. They wanted to overcome the stalemate that had arisen in strategic negotiations between their respective countries and accordingly agreed to further reductions in each side's nuclear arsenal. The two leaders established a goal of 1,700 to 2,200 long-range warheads on each side by the year 2012. Russia expressed its desire to formalize the deal in a treaty. Despite initial American reluctance, both sides signed the **Strategic Offensive Arms Reduction Treaty** (SORT), also called the Moscow Treaty, in Moscow on 24 May 2002.

PRESIDENT'S SPECIAL COMMITTEE ON DISARMAMENT. During the **Dwight D. Eisenhower** administration a special committee was established to coordinate and consider U.S. policies and their relationship to **United Nations disarmament** efforts. Topics discussed included **nuclear testing** and global disarmament proposals in the UN. *See also* DISARMAMENT; UNITED NATIONS CONFERENCE ON DISARMAMENT; UNITED NATIONS DISARMAMENT COMMISSION.

PRESSLER AMENDMENT (1985). A **United States** congressional restriction that forbade the sale of F-16s to **Pakistan** until such time as the U.S. administration could verify that Pakistan was not pursuing an indigenous **nuclear weapons** capability. The restriction was withdrawn in 2001 following Pakistan's public demonstration that it was a nuclear state in 1998 and the need for Pakistani support in the war on **terrorism** following the attacks of 11 September 2001.

PREVENTION OF NUCLEAR WAR AGREEMENT (1973). Signed in Washington 22 June 1973, the **United States** and the **Soviet Union** agreed that in any circumstance where there was a danger of nuclear confrontation, they would consult with each other in order to prevent such a conflict from occurring.

PREVENTIVE ATTACK. An attack launched against an adversary in anticipation of a planned attack by that adversary. Preventive attacks would be intended primarily as **damage limiting** attacks unless the preempting state possessed the **counterforce** capability to destroy the adversary's strike capability. Sometimes confused with **preemptive attacks**, which require a clear and present danger, preventive attacks are based on a longer-term assessment of an adversary's capabilities and intentions. A body of international opinion finds preventive wars unjustified in nearly all cases and therefore illegal under the **United Nations** charter. *See also* PREEMPTION.

PRODUCTION FACILITY. A nuclear reactor operated to produce nuclear **weapons-grade materials,** rather than being used simply for research purposes or to produce electricity.

PROLIFERATION. The spread of weapons—usually focusing on **nuclear, chemical**, and **biological weapons**—or major system components such as **ballistic missiles** to those not previously possessing those weapons. A number of international agreements have been adopted in an attempt to prevent proliferation, including the **Nuclear Nonproliferation Treaty** (NPT), the **Chemical Weapons Convention** (CWC), the **Biological and Toxin Weapons Convention** (BWC), and the establishment of numerous **nuclear weapons free zones.** Various bodies also monitor global proliferation and try to stem the trade in materials necessary to build weapons; these include the **Australia Group**, the **Nuclear Suppliers' Group**, the

Missile Technology Control Regime, and the Wassenaar Arrangement.

PROLIFERATION SECURITY INITIATIVE (PSI). The Proliferation Security Initiative is an informal, cooperative effort initiated by the United States in 2003 to interdict shipments of **weapons of mass destruction, ballistic missiles,** and related materials to states and nonstate actors of **proliferation** concern. In May 2003, the initiative was launched with eleven original members (Australia, **France,** Germany, Italy, Japan, the Netherlands, Poland, Portugal, Spain, the **United Kingdom,** and the **United States**). Canada, Norway, and Singapore joined in February 2004. Over 60 states have endorsed the initiative's objectives. In September 2003 members adopted legally nonbinding principles committing them to take measures to interdict transfers to states and nonstate actors of items of proliferation concern, including weapons of mass destruction, missiles, and related materials; to streamline related intelligence sharing; to strengthen relevant national and international law; and to take other specified steps to facilitate interdiction of proliferation-related cargoes.

PROMPTNESS. The ability of a weapon, or a country, to respond quickly to an attack or intelligence on a target and to destroy that target.

PROTOCOL ON EXISTING TYPES OF CONVENTIONAL ARMAMENTS AND EQUIPMENT (1990). The principal purpose of the protocol is to list, in an agreed format, all of those types of conventional armaments and equipment that are subject to the provisions of the **Conventional Forces in Europe Treaty** (CFE) and, in particular, specify which types of such armaments are limited by that treaty (i.e., subject to the numerical limitations set forth in the treaty). The protocol "fleshes out" the definitions set forth by clarifying which particular armaments and equipment within the area of application are covered by those definitions and thus are subject to the Treaty as of 19 November 1990, when the treaty was signed.

PSYCHOCHEMICAL AGENT. A **chemical agent** that distorts the perceptions and cognitive processes, leading to incapacitation. An example is D-lysergic acid diethylamide, popularly known as LSD. Sometimes considered as a potential **chemical weapon,** this type of agent was apparently tested by the **United States** on its military forces in the 1950s.

PUGWASH CONFERENCES. A series of over 150 meetings and activities originating in Pugwash, Nova Scotia (Canada), in 1957 based on the urgings of Albert Einstein and others for scientists to closely examine the ethical implications of their association with the **Cold War arms race**. The Pugwash conferences became a forum for scientists to cooperate on furthering and technically enabling the **arms control** process. *See also* PEACE MOVEMENTS.

PUTIN, VLADIMIR (1953-). Russian president first elected in 1999. A progressive leader who sought closer relations with the West, he accepted the **United States'** withdrawal from the **Anti-Ballistic Missile Treaty** in 2002, supported the United States in its war on **terrorism** following the 11 September 2001 attacks; and signed the **Strategic Offensive Reductions Treaty** (SORT) in **Moscow** in May 2002.

Q

QUADRENNIAL DEFENSE REVIEW (QDR). A congressionally mandated review and report of **United States** defense strategy conducted by the **Department of Defense** during the year following each presidential election. Reports were issued in 1997 and 2001. The QDR reports have resulted in modest changes in the fundamental defense strategies and associated force structures of the U.S. military services.

QUALITATIVE LIMITATIONS. Restrictions on the capabilities of weapon systems, as opposed to limits on numbers of system components (**quantitative limits**). Examples include limitations on missile throw-weight or **multiple independently targetable reentry vehicle** capability.

QUANTITATIVE LIMITATIONS. Restrictions on the numbers of weapon systems or key system components. Early **arms control treaties** of the **Cold War** tended to focus on qualitative numbers of weapons systems rather than later **agreements** that considered more **qualitative** measures.

QUEBEC AGREEMENT (1943). An agreement between the **United States, Great Britain**, and Canada to cooperate in the development of all atomic matters and to share in the results as the U.S. president saw fit. The other states agreed to defer to the United States as the leader in this effort.

R

RADAR. The acronym for "radio detection and ranging." Radar transmits radio waves and senses the return of those waves as they are reflected off of the target. Radar can often measure target characteristics such as distance, direction of movement, size, speed, and shape. Developed by **Great Britain** during World War II, it became one of the "secret weapons" that helped win the Battle of Britain.

RADIATION DETECTION EQUIPMENT. Devices used by **arms control verification** teams, nuclear material detection teams, and antiterrorist teams to detect **radiation** associated with **nuclear weapons** and radiological materials.

RADIOACTIVITY. Radioactivity is a broad term that refers to changes in the nuclei of atoms that release radiation. Radiation is an energetic ray or energetic particle. It is the disintegration or decay of the unstable nucleus of an atom, with the accompanying release of alpha and beta particles and gamma rays or neutrons. For ionizing radiation, the ray or particle has enough energy to cause changes in the chemical structure of the materials it strikes. These chemical structure changes are the mechanisms by which radiation can cause biological damage to humans. This means that a human body cell may be damaged if it comes into contact with the energy from a particle or ray released by radioactive decay. Radiation comes from many sources, some natural and some human-made. People have always been exposed to natural or background radiation. Natural sources of radiation include the sun, radioactive materials present in the earth's crust, in building materials, and in the air, food, and water. Some sources of ionizing radiation have been created by people for various uses or as by-products of these activities. These include nuclear power generation, medical diagnosis and treatment, and nuclear materials related to nuclear weapons. Radioactivity is extremely dangerous for all living things due to its negative impact on cells.

RADIOLOGICAL RELEASE. Unplanned emission of radiological material.

RAND CORPORATION. Created in World War II as the Research and Development (R and D) division of Douglas Aircraft, RAND became independent in 1948 and is today one of the largest and most respected American research centers. During the early **Cold War** it became a leading U.S. policy think tank, spawning many creative new ideas that became some of the central precepts and theories behind Cold War strategies, including nuclear policy and **deterrence**. RAND is located in Santa Monica, California, and Arlington, Virginia.

RAPACKI PLAN (1952). Named after Polish Foreign Minister Adam Rapacki, who proposed the creation of a denuclearized zone in Central Europe in the 1950s, including East and West Germany, Poland, and Czechoslovakia. He also suggested a nonaggression pact between the **North Atlantic Treaty Organization** (NATO) and the **Warsaw Pact.** His suggestions were rejected by the West, with the claim that the plan perpetuated the division of Germany and was too limited in scope. The **United States** was afraid it would create a serious military imbalance in Europe because NATO would be surrendering its nuclear advantage for conventional disadvantage.

RAROTONGA, TREATY OF. *See* SOUTH PACIFIC NUCLEAR FREE ZONE.

RATIFICATION. The process taken by a state's legislative body to approve a **treaty** signed by its executive office, thus legally binding the state to that treaty and its provisions. In the **United States**, treaties signed by the president must be approved by two-thirds of the Senate.

RATIONAL SUFFICIENCY. A nuclear policy based on the premise that **United States** nuclear capabilities in the 1970s were sufficient to deliver an unacceptable **second strike** on the **Soviet Union** after a Soviet **first strike**. United States **deterrence**, then, would have been assured without significant changes to its nuclear posture. The policy was considered, but never adopted, during the administration of President **Jimmy Carter**.

REAGAN, RONALD (1911-2004). United States president from 1981 to 1989. President Reagan is generally credited with having won the **Cold War** through his policies of confrontation with the **Soviet Union,** his massive military build-up, the proposal to develop a **ballistic missile defense** shield over America, and his willingness to outspend the other side in a new **arms race.** He also did much to restore America's sense of national pride during his tenure. Although known more for his confrontational style than for his commitment to **arms control,** during his administration the United States signed the **Intermediate-Range Nuclear Forces Treaty** (INF), the **South Pacific Nuclear Free Zone Treaty,** the **Prevention of Incidents at Sea Treaty,** the **Stockholm Agreement,** the **Ballistic Missile Launch Notification Agreement,** and the **Nuclear Risk Reduction Centers Agreement.** The United States also joined the **Australia Group** and the **Missile Technology Control Regime** during Reagan's presidency.

REALISM. One of the major theories in international relations, realism posits a perspective of pessimism about human nature; the need for an individual, and a nation-state, to be self reliant; and a belief in a balance of power in the international system. Realism contrasts with liberalism as a mind set that frames how one thinks about international politics.

REASONABLE SUFFICIENCY. The **strategic** doctrine of the **Soviet Union** under President **Mikhail Gorbachev.** Reasonable sufficiency of forces would be enough to defend the Soviet homeland from attack, but not enough to engage in offensive actions beyond its borders. The implication for nuclear forces was that only sufficient capability to destroy **United States** cities (a **countervalue** capability) was needed.

RECIPROCOL AGREEMENTS. The decision by two or more countries to undertake a series of actions both sides deem to be in their mutual interests. This can be a negotiated series of alternative moves by two states or a unilateral response to a first move by another state.

RECONNAISSANCE SATELLITES. Space-based machines that orbit the earth at high speed and high altitude and utilize photographic or electronic monitoring equipment in order to monitor and detect the activities of states, militaries, groups, or individuals.

RED CROSS CONVENTION. *See* INTERNATIONAL COMMIT-
TEE OF THE RED CROSS.

REENTRY PHASE. The final leg of a **reentry vehicle** during its
flight path. The reentry phase covers the period from the end of the
mid-course phase, through atmospheric reentry, until impact with
the earth. This phase generally lasts about one minute for a reentry
vehicle launched by a **ballistic missile**.

REENTRY VEHICLE (RV). The component of a **ballistic missile**
system that holds the **warhead** and delivers it to the target during
the terminal or **reentry phase** of the trajectory.

REGIME. A regime represents a voluntary commitment by a state or
states to comply with a set of agreed principles that bind behavior.
In the realm of **arms control**, a regime represents an **agreement** by
two or more states to limit the production and retention of specific
arms to a specific quantity, as well as the methods agreed to by the
signatories to ensure **compliance.**

REGIONAL ARMS CONTROL. Programs designed to restrict the
proliferation or expansion of conventional or unconventional arms,
or to achieve some other agreed military goal, within a specific
geographic region, rather than globally.

REGISTER OF CONVENTIONAL ARMAMENTS. Established in
1992 by the **United Nations** in order to increase transparency in
armaments, the Register calls upon all member states to voluntarily
inform the United Nations about the import and export of conventional arms, which are defined as battle tanks, armored combat vehicles, large-caliber artillery, combat aircraft, attack helicopters,
warships, and missiles and missile launchers. Member states are
also asked to provide an annual report on their military holdings,
procurement through domestic production, and relevant policies.

RELIABILITY. The level to which one can have faith or confidence
that something or someone will do what is expected of it or them. In
security terms, this usually refers to the percentage likelihood that a
weapon will function as designed. The term can also refer to the degree to which one can count on a partner in an alliance to support
you in a crisis.

RELOAD CAPABILITY. The turnaround time for a reusable missile launcher to load and fire a second missile after an initial missile launch.

REPROCESSING. The process through which **uranium** and **plutonium** are separated from spent nuclear reactor fuel, either for use as further reactor fuel or as materials for use in **nuclear weapons**. Reprocessing entails a large industrial process and represents a major financial commitment by a state to the production of plutonium.

RESTRICTIONS ON EXCESSIVELY INJURIOUS CONVENTIONAL WEAPONS. *See* CERTAIN CONVENTIONAL WEAPONS CONVENTION.

RETARGETING. *See* DETARGETING.

RETRIBUTIVE MEASURES. Sanctions imposed by a state, a group of states, or an international organization against an offending state or group of states because of an apparent violation of an **agreement**. Such measures can be economic, diplomatic, or military.

REYKJAVIK SUMMIT (1986). Meetings held in October 1986 at Reykjavik, Iceland, between Soviet General Secretary **Mikhail Gorbachev** and U.S. President **Ronald Reagan**. They addressed nuclear arms reductions, the future relationship of offensive and defensive weapons, and the place in **arms control** of Reagan's **Strategic Defense Initiative**. Reagan proposed the elimination of all offensive **ballistic missiles** within 10 years, and Gorbachev reciprocated by proposing to eliminate the even larger category of all **strategic** weapons. While no **agreement** was reached in Reykjavik, such forward thinking is credited with unlocking the **Cold War**-style **arms control negotiations** under way between the two countries and leading to great strides in this field within several years.

RIBONUCLEIC ACID (RNA). A nucleic acid similar in structure to a single strand of **deoxyribonucleic acid** (DNA), the building block of life. RNA is a chain made up of nucleotides that is found mostly in the cytoplasm of cells, rather than the nucleus. RNA delivers DNA's genetic message to the cytoplasm of a cell where proteins are made. Some **viruses**, such as HIV, carry RNA rather than DNA.

The DNA of certain ethnic or racial groups may be the future target of "designer" **biological weapons**.

RIDE OUT. The policy of absorbing a **first strike** when under nuclear attack, then assessing the situation before responding with one's own **second-strike** retaliatory attack. This can be a policy choice in order to confirm the nature and reality of an attack before unleashing a nonrecallable missile response of one's own. It requires a substantial secure second-strike capability to be successful.

RIOT CONTROL AGENT (RCA). Defined by the **Chemical Weapons Convention** (CWC) as any chemical that can rapidly produce in humans sensory irritation or disabling physical effects that disappear within a short time following termination of exposure. Because most RCAs can also be used militarily as **chemical weapons**, the line between a legitimate police tool and an illegitimate antipersonnel weapon has remained blurred. The "**Geneva Protocol** for the Prohibition of the Use in War of Asphyxiating, Poisonous or Other Gases, and of Bacteriological Methods in Warfare" further defined the difference between RCAs and chemical weapons as a difference in application. It allows for the use of RCAs in order to maintain order in prisons, quell disturbances on the streets, protect rear-echelon personnel from disturbances, and to rescue people from hostile areas. This issue came to the forefront of public discussion in 2003 when the **United States** occupying forces in **Iraq** wanted to use RCAs to quell certain situations following the end of the war there.

RISK ASSESSMENT. The process a state undertakes when making a decision regarding security choices. Also the risks as understood by a potential participant in an **arms control regime**. This includes the political stability of the actors, the likelihood and ability of either side to abandon its obligations to its advantage, and the relative advantage gained by both sides should the regime be agreed to.

ROERICH PACT (1935). The "Protection of Artistic and Scientific Institutions and Historic Monuments, Inter-American Agreement" was signed in Washington, D.C., on 15 April 1935, and **entered into force** on 26 August 1935. The concept was first raised at the 1933 International Conference of the American States held in Montevideo, Uruguay. The proposal was initiated by the **United States'** Roerich Museum. The parties agreed that immovable monuments that form the cultural treasure of peoples, including monuments, museums, scientific, artistic, educational, and cultural institutions are considered **neutral**, and as such protected and respected by belligerents. Such places shall be designated by a flag, and a list of such sites will be deposited with the Pan-American Union.

ROGUE STATES. Nation-states that do not subscribe to the normal rules of accepted international behavior, conducting such activities as seeking **weapons of mass destruction**, harboring **terrorist** organizations, or violating the rules of international law and diplomacy. The term was coined during the late 1990s in the administration of U.S. President **William Clinton**, but quickly disavowed as an official designation in U.S. government pronouncements. In his 2002 State of the Union address, however, President **George W. Bush** indirectly accredited the term by announcing that the **United States** was particularly concerned about a so-called "axis of evil" that included the rogue states **Iraq**, **Iran**, Libya, and **North Korea**.

ROME-CARTHAGE TREATY (201 B.C.). This treaty was imposed after Rome's defeat of Carthage at the end of the third Punic War. Carthage gave up its Spanish conquests, agreed to limit its military forces, and became a dependent ally of Rome.

ROOSEVELT, FRANKLIN D. (1882-1945). United States president for four terms (1933 to 1945) during the Great Depression and World War II, and arguably one of the leaders who most changed the face of American society with his progressive social programs. With **Winston Churchill** and **Josef Stalin**, Roosevelt led the Western allies to victory in World War II and planned for a postwar ear of peace and prosperity under the benevolent oversight of a **United Nations**. He ordered the beginning of the **Manhattan Project** to beat the Germans in developing the world's first **atomic bomb**.

ROSTOW, EUGENE (1913-). American lawyer, professor, and diplomat, who served as director of the **Arms Control and Disarmament Agency** from 1981-1983. In 1976 he joined with **Paul Nitze** to reinvigorate the **Committee on the Present Danger**. His younger brother Walt Rostow served as National Security Advisor to President **Lyndon B. Johnson** from 1966 to 1969. Both were conservative, anticommunist **hawks**.

RUMSFELD, DONALD (1932-). Secretary of defense under two presidents: **Gerald Ford** (1974-1976), when Rumsfeld was the youngest secretary of defense in American history, and **George W. Bush** (2001-), when Rumsfeld had the ironic distinction of then becoming the oldest secretary of defense in U.S. history. He oversaw the war on **terrorism** beginning in the fall of 2001, including Operation **Enduring Freedom** in Afghanistan and Operation **Iraqi Freedom** in Iraq. He also led efforts to transform the U.S. military into a 21st century fighting force.

RUSH-BAGOT AGREEMENT (1817). One of the first **arms control treaties,** and the first to which the **United States** was a **signatory,** Rush-Bagot was an agreement between the young United States and the **United Kingdom** shortly after the War of 1812 to **demilitarize** the North American Great Lakes.

RUSK, DEAN (1909-1994). American diplomat and **hawkish** secretary of state under President **John F. Kennedy** from 1961 to 1969. Rusk held the longest incumbency of any secretary of state during the **Cold War.** He was known for coining the phrase that the **United States** had stood "eyeball to eyeball" with the **Soviet Union** during the **Cuban missile crisis.**

RUSSIA. The largest republic and core culture of the **Union of Soviet Socialist Republics,** it regained its sovereignty when the USSR was dissolved in 1991. It remains the world's largest nation in geographic terms and its second largest nuclear power after the **United States.** It also maintains stockpiles of **chemical** and **biological weapons** in violation of international treaties to which it is a party. However, under the leadership of presidents **Boris Yeltsin** and **Vladimir Putin** Russia has been more active in **arms control negotiations** than was the old **Soviet Union.**

S

SAFEGUARD ABM SYSTEM. The first **antiballistic missile** (ABM) system to be deployed within the **United States.** The program began as the **Nike X** system in 1963. The system had two interceptor missiles: **Spartan,** built by McDonnell Douglas and a direct outgrowth of the **Nike Zeus** ABM interceptor, for exo-atmospheric hits, and **Sprint,** built by Martin, a quick-accelerating, hypersonic vehicle for last-chance endoatmospheric defense. Both carried **nuclear warheads**. The missiles were interconnected with a series of high power radars and a battle management control system.

In 1967 Secretary of Defense **Robert McNamara** announced that rather than a nation-wide ABM defense, the United States would instead deploy a 'thin" system to defend against the new Chinese **intercontinental ballistic missile** (ICBM) threat. Initially named the **Sentinel** system, in 1969 the name reverted to Safeguard. President **Richard Nixon** ordered the deployment of Safeguard to defend the **Minuteman** missiles based at Grand Forks Air Force Base, North Dakota. The 1972 **ABM Treaty** had limited each country to 100 ABM launchers (at one site, according to the ABM Treaty's 1974 Protocol), and Safeguard's capabilities were therefore limited. Safeguard became fully operational on 1 October 1975, but was deactivated by Congress the next day. Tactical operation was terminated in November 1975, and decommissioning began in February 1976.

SAFEGUARDS. A system of domestic and international **inspections** of the control and handling of materials as provided for in **treaties** and **agreements**.

SAFEGUARDS, TRANSPARENCY, AND IRREVERSIBILITY (STI). A series of talks between Presidents **William Clinton** of the **United States** and **Boris Yeltsin** of **Russia** in January 1994. These talks focused on the need to ensure that **fissile material** from eliminated **warheads** would not be recycled into new weapons.

SAFETY. A device designed to prevent accidents, such as a lock on a firearm preventing accidental firing. This is as true of **nuclear weapons** as it is of a small handgun. Modern safety devices for atomic warheads are called **permissive action links**. They not only prevent a warhead from accidentally exploding in case of accident or damage, but they require a special code from designated persons who have the predelegated authority to unlock the weapon and allow it to be detonated. More generally, safety differs from security of a weapon, which is its protection against theft or capture.

ST. PETERSBURG DECLARATION (1868). An early attempt to control the consequences of war should it occur, the St. Petersburg Declaration prohibited the use of so-called "dum-dum" bullets.

SAKHAROV, ANDREI (1921-1989). Soviet physicist who helped develop the **Soviet Union's hydrogen bomb** in the early 1950s. He subsequently became a human rights activist, winning the Nobel Peace Prize for his efforts.

SALT I and II TREATIES. *See* STRATEGIC ARMS LIMITATION TALKS; STRATEGIC ARMS LIMITATION TREATY I AND II.

SALVAGE FUSING. Equipping a weapon system with a destruction system designed to activate upon attack by a defensive system. Salvage fusing is suggested as a partial counter to an **antiballistic missile** system, as the detonation of one of the first incoming missile warheads in a stream of attack could complicate follow-on interceptions, as well as potentially cause some physical or electromagnetic damage to the defender.

SAMOS SATELLITE. SAMOS (Satellite and Missile Observation System) satellites were developed by the **United States** during the late 1950s and were first launched in October of 1960. SAMOS satellites were the first overhead photography satellites capable of transmitting their images electronically, although they also possessed capabilities to deliver film to earth using small **reentry vehicles**.

SAMPLING AND ANALYSIS. Chemical sampling and analysis is used by occupational health and safety professionals to assess workplace contaminants and associated worker exposures. The validity of an assessment is based, in part, on the procedures used for sample collection and analysis, and data interpretation. Such sampling includes the search for radiological, chemical, and biological **agents**.

SANDIA NATIONAL LABORATORIES. Opened in 1949 as part of the infrastructure required to manufacture and support the **United States' nuclear weapons** program. **Nuclear warheads** were designed by **Los Alamos** or **Lawrence Livermore** National Laboratories, but in both cases the next step was for Sandia to engineer the **delivery system** for the weapon. Sandia has two primary facilities: a large laboratory and headquarters in Albuquerque, New Mexico, and a smaller laboratory in Livermore, California. It is operated by the Lockheed Martin Corporation for the United States **Department of Energy's National Nuclear Security Administration**. In addition to designing and manufacturing over half of the required components of modern nuclear weapons, Sandia researches and develops technologies for counterterrorism, **homeland defense**, and nuclear **nonproliferation.**

SANTIAGO NAVAL CONFERENCE (1923). Officially named the Fourth Pan American Conference, delegations from all the American states met in Santiago, Chile, in 1923. This conference led to a wide range of agreements on trademark regulations, document publication, health and education regulations, and the establishment of fact-finding commissions to investigate disputes within the region.

SARY SHAGAN TEST RANGE. Situated within the Betpak-Dala desert, near Lake Balkhash in **Kazakhstan**, Sary Shagan is the testing ground for **Russian** antiaircraft defense, **antiballistic missile defense** (ABM), and **antisatellite** systems. In August 1956 the Soviet Union began to develop an antiballistic missile (ABM) system. To test such a system, it decided that the location of the test range was to be in Sary Shagan. A successful ABM test was undertaken in 1961. The 1972 **ABM Treaty** specified Sary Shagan as the only allowable site for the **Soviet Union** to conduct ABM tests. Although it is situated in Kazakhstan, some facilities are still leased to Russia and other former Soviet republics.

SATURATING. The intensive shelling or bombing of a military target to achieve total destruction. The term is normally applied to aerial bombardment, as in World War II, or the attempt to overcome **ballistic missile defenses** with an overwhelming number of **nuclear warheads**.

SCHELLING, THOMAS C. (1921-). A highly respected authority in multiple fields, Dr. Schelling's most well-known contribution came in 1961 when he and **Morton Halperin** published a book that defined the new field of **arms control**. Arms control, they said in *Strategy and Arms Control*, had three objectives: to reduce the chances of war occurring, to minimize the consequences if a conflict broke out, and to reduce the costs of preparing for war. These guidelines have served the arms control and policy-making community for more than 40 years.

SCHLESINGER, JAMES R. (1929-). U.S. secretary of defense (1973-1975), chairman of the **Atomic Energy Commission** (1971), secretary of energy (1977-1979), and director of the **Central Intelligence Agency** (1973) in the **Richard Nixon** administration. A nuclear expert with experience as an analyst at the **RAND Corporation**, he devised the "Schlesinger Doctrine," which changed **strategic** nuclear strategy from **massive retaliation** to a more nuanced **warfighting** approach that utilized **limited nuclear options** and **counterforce targeting**.

SCHULTZ, GEORGE P. (1920-). Former dean of the University of Chicago School of Business, he became chairman of the Council of Economic Advisors under President **Richard Nixon** and secretary of state under President **Ronald Reagan** (1982-1989). He engineered the negotiations surrounding Reagan's **"zero option"** policy, which led to the 1987 **Intermediate-Range Nuclear Forces Treaty**.

SCIENTIFIC RATIONALISM. A model for physicists to share in political power and shape debates about the role of science in society. They use science as a model for political action, such as calling for increased democratization, decentralization, and competitiveness in scientific and political culture and organization.

SCOWCROFT COMMISSION. President **Ronald Reagan** appointed a Commission on Strategic Forces in January 1983, chaired by Lieutenant General Brent Scowcroft. The commission was charged with assessing the new challenges to the **United States' deterrent** and **missile defense** capabilities. The Commission's report, issued on 6 April 1983, concluded that the United States' **strategic** deterrent was sound and would remain so without **strategic defenses**, as long as it continued to develop and deploy small single-warhead **intercontinental ballistic missiles** (ICBM) to supplant the multiple-warhead missiles and smaller submarines with fewer missiles aboard to succeed the 24-missile **Trident** boats deployed at the time. The report also recommended the immediate deployment of 100 **Peacekeeper** missiles in existing **Minuteman** silos to demonstrate national will and to compensate for the retirement of **Titan II** ICBMs.

SCUD MISSILE. A medium-range **ballistic missile** of Soviet design and direct descendent of the German V-2 rocket of World War I. Widely distributed through sales and production agreements, it can carry conventional, **chemical**, **biological**, or **nuclear warheads**, and has a range of up to 300 miles. First designed in 1957, there are now three variants (A, B, and C). Its first combat use came in the 1973 Yom Kippur War between **Israel** and Egypt. Currently some 19 countries have Scuds (or related missiles) in their inventory.

SEA- (OR SHIP- OR SUBMARINE-) LAUNCHED CRUISE MISSILE (SLCM). An unmanned, self-propelled, sea-, ship-, or submarine-launched air-breathing vehicle that is capable of sustaining flight through aerodynamic lift across the majority of its flight path. First designed in 1974, the United States' version is called the **Tomahawk**, capable of delivering either a conventional or **nuclear warhead** over a range of 2,300 miles.

SEABED TREATY (1971). The "Treaty on the Prohibition of the Emplacement of **Nuclear Weapons** and Other **Weapons of Mass Destruction** on the Seabed and the Ocean Floor and in the Subsoil Thereof" was signed by the **United States** and the **Soviet Union** on 11 February 1971 and **entered into force** on 18 May 1982. Like the **Antarctic Treaty,** the **Outer Space Treaty,** and the various **nuclear weapon free zones,** the Seabed Treaty seeks to prevent the introduction of international conflict and nuclear weapons into an area previously free of them. Negotiations over the treaty, however, took several years, as interest in the sea floor was growing among many nations as the science of oceanography advanced. The treaty outlaws a party placing weapons of mass destruction on or in the seabed beyond a 12-mile coastal zone. Review conferences have been held every five to seven years.

SECOND-STRIKE CAPABILITY. The capability to launch a retaliatory attack after sustaining a nuclear **first strike**. A secure second-strike capability requires a party to hold enough residual offensive **strategic** capabilities (usually nuclear) to destroy the state that initiated the war after first absorbing an attack. This capability can be enhanced through **hardening**, dispersal, heightened alert, or other means.

SECURITY. Freedom from danger, or the sense of personal safety. In international affairs, security refers to the military relationship between countries and the sense of safety a population feels within its borders. Security also refers to positive control over **nuclear weapons** to ensure they remain in the proper hands and cannot be stolen or used without the proper authorization.

SECURITY ASSISTANCE. Providing money, arms, or other materiel to another state or nonstate actor that allows that entity to enhance its military situation. This is most commonly a transfer between nations. Security assistance arrangements were intimately involved in the relationship between the **North Atlantic Treaty Organization** (NATO) and the **Warsaw Pact** during the **Cold War,** and to an even greater degree with allies or potential supporters in the Third World.

SELECTIVE OPTIONS. A nuclear targeting policy, first used by the **United States** in the late 1970s, that allowed it to apply its nuclear forces in a more discriminate manner, rather than simply launching an all-out **massive retaliation** strike. Selective options were the result of a move toward a more flexible response and a somewhat more flexible **single integrated operations plan.**

SENATE ARMED SERVICES COMMITTEE. A 25-member committee of the **United States** Senate that is charged with the study and review of matters relating to the common defense policy of the United States. This includes air and space military activities, the **Department of Defense**, the Armed Services, military nuclear energy, naval petroleum reserves, and the **strategic** and critical materials necessary for the common defense of the United States.

SENATE FOREIGN RELATIONS COMMITTEE. A 19-member committee of the **United States** Senate that participates in the shaping of American foreign policy by discussing and reviewing **treaties** and diplomatic appointments. The Committee also discusses the goals of American foreign policy and the strategies to be undertaken to achieve them.

SENATE SELECT INTELLIGENCE COMMITTEE. A 17-member committee of the **United States** Senate that oversees and studies the activities and programs of the United States' intelligence community. It also submits reports and proposals to the Senate concerning the activities and programs being undertaken by the U.S. intelligence community. The committee monitors the activities of the U.S. intelligence community to ensure that such activities conform with the Constitution and laws of the United States.

SENIOR DEFENSE GROUP ON PROLIFERATION (DGP). A **North Atlantic Treaty Organization** (NATO) body, founded in

1994 to address alliance defense issues associated with the **proliferation** of **weapons of mass destruction** and the means for their delivery.

SENSOR. A device that receives and responds to an external stimulus. The military uses sensors to conduct intelligence, **surveillance**, and **reconnaissance** gathering on other states or military bodies. A remote sensor can also be used to monitor **compliance** with an **arms control treaty**.

SENTINEL ABM SYSTEM. Plans to replace the **Nike antiballistic missile** system with Sentinel were announced by Secretary of Defense **Robert McNamara** on 18 September 1967. Sentinel reflected a change in American **strategic** fears to focus on a newly nuclear **China**. Sentinel was to consist of 13 sites in the **United States** and would have cost $5 billion, not counting research and development, daily operations, or maintenance. As public demonstrations against the program increased, and the conflict in Vietnam drew funds from Sentinel, construction of the system was halted in 1968. In February 1969, President **Richard Nixon** suspended Sentinel. It was replaced by a thin defensive shield called **Safeguard**, but that, too, was deactivated in 1975.

SHEVARDNADZE, EDOUARD (1928-). Appointed to be foreign minister of the **Soviet Union** by **Mikhail Gorbachev** in 1985. Shevardnadze promoted an arms-reduction policy that accepted unequal cuts in **superpower** arsenals. He oversaw preliminary negotiations for the **summits** between Gorbachev and **United States** President **Ronald Reagan** in **Geneva** in 1985 and **Reykjavik** in 1986, in which unprecedented **arms control agreements** were discussed. Following the collapse of the Soviet Union, he was elected president of Georgia in November 1995 and reelected in 2000. He resigned from the presidency in November 2003.

SHORT-RANGE ATTACK MISSILE (SRAM). A nuclear air-to-surface weapon system designed for battlefield use to destroy ground forces and air defenses, carried by U.S. **B-52 bombers**.

SHORT-RANGE BALLISTIC MISSILE (SRBM). A **ballistic missile** with a range of less than 1,000 kilometers.

SHROUDING. Screening or hiding the **warhead** of a delivery system or the **payload** of a missile behind some type of opaque cover, in order to prevent a competitor from possibly learning something of value by seeing the payload or warhead design.

SIGNATORY. A party, usually a nation-state (called a **state party**), to an **arms control treaty** or other international **agreement**.

SILO BASING. The technique of placing **intercontinental ballistic missiles** in prepared, **hardened** holes in the ground from which the missile can be launched. Silo basing allows for hardening of the silo itself, thereby enhancing the **survivability** of the weapon, and removes the weapon from the effects of weather—a consideration for the two states that aimed these weapons at one another in the early **Cold War**, since most missile silo fields are located in regions of severe Continental climates.

SINGLE INTEGRATED OPERATIONS PLAN (SIOP). The **United States'** nuclear targeting and strike plan, updated annually by the staff of **Strategic Air Command** (and, since 2002, by **U.S. Strategic Command**, or STRATCOM). Coincident with the 1994 **Nuclear Posture Review**, STRATCOM was in the middle of a major initiative to revise the nuclear war planning process. A new "adaptive" scheme replaced the old fixed war plan preparation process, which required nearly a year and a half lead time to produce the SIOP. In December 1992 a 10-person Strategic Planning Study Group was formed to develop a flexible, globally-focused, war-planning process known as the Strategic War Planning System. The group developed procedures for what they now call "a Living SIOP," a real-time nuclear war plan, one that can receive virtually instantaneous warfighting commands.

SITE DEFENSE. *See* POINT DEFENSE.

SMALL ICBM. *See* MIDGETMAN MISSILE.

SMART BOMB. *See* PRECISION-GUIDED MUNITION.

SMITH, GERARD C. (1914-1994). Assistant secretary of state and head of the Policy Planning Staff in the U.S. **State Department** from 1957 to 1961, and later chief of the U.S. delegation to the **Strategic Arms Limitation Talks** (SALT I) from 1969 to 1972.

From 1977 to 1980, he was ambassador at large and special presidential representative for **nonproliferation** matters.

SOLID-FUEL MISSILE TECHNOLOGY. A rocket or missile that is launched by igniting a solid core of fuel embedded in the missile body. Solid fuel has a number of advantages over liquid fuel. Solids do not require complicated engines or plumbing, but rely on sophisticated chemistry and strong casings to withstand the intense pressures that they generate. They can fire much faster, and accelerate more quickly at liftoff, but cannot be throttled in flight—once it is "lit," it is not coming back or slowing down until the fuel is used up. Missiles using solid fuel can be stored in a fueled configuration, which makes preparation to fire much faster. Recognizing these advantages, the **United States** switched its **intercontinental ballistic missile** fleet from liquid to solid fuel versions when it introduced the **Minuteman** in the early 1960s. **Proliferation** of solid fuel missile technology has continued, as many **rogue regimes**, such as **Iran** and **North Korea,** have pursued solid-fuel missile capabilities.

SOUTH AFRICA, REPUBLIC OF. In 1993 South Africa announced that it had had a covert **nuclear weapons** program for several decades that led to the development and production of six nuclear **warheads**. It also declared that it had voluntarily destroyed those weapons and the infrastructure required to create a nuclear arsenal in order to join the **Nuclear Nonproliferation Treaty regime**.

SOUTH ASIAN ASSOCIATION FOR REGIONAL COOPERATION (SAARC). Founded in 1983, SAARC is comprised of the seven South Asian countries of Bangladesh, Bhutan, **India**, the Maldives, Nepal, **Pakistan**, and Sri Lanka. SAARC is an international organization through which regional powers are able to discuss common problems and issue common position statements on issues of international **arms control** and **disarmament**.

SOUTH PACIFIC NUCLEAR FREE ZONE (1985). Also known as the Treaty of Rarotonga, the treaty was negotiated under the auspices of the South Pacific Forum. The pact declares the South Pacific a **nuclear-weapons-free zone**, prohibiting the manufacture, acquisition, possession, deployment, stationing, and testing of **nuclear weapons** within the region. There are 11 parties to the treaty, including Australia and New Zealand.

SOUTHEAST ASIA NUCLEAR WEAPONS FREE ZONE. The Treaty of Bangkok was signed by Brunei Darussalam, Cambodia, Indonesia, Laos, Malaysia, Myanmar, Philippines, Singapore, Thailand, and Vietnam on 15 December 1995. This established **a nuclear weapons free zone** across much of Southeast Asia, prohibiting the development, acquisition, storage, or testing of any **nuclear weapon**.

SOUTHEAST ASIA TREATY ORGANIZATION (SEATO) (1954-1977). An alliance organized in 1954 under the Southeast Asia Collective Defense Treaty by representatives of Australia, **France**, **Great Britain**, New Zealand, **Pakistan**, the Philippines, Thailand, and the **United States**. SEATO was created following the French withdrawal from Indochina. It later approved the United States' entry into Vietnam. Headquartered in Bangkok, Thailand, SEATO was composed of the military forces of its member states. Unable to intervene in Laos or Vietnam due to French and Pakistani refusal to approve American activity in Vietnam and SEATO's rule of unanimity, the future of the organization was in doubt by 1973, and SEATO was ultimately disbanded in 1977.

SOVIET NUCLEAR THREAT REDUCTION ACT. Enacted by the United States in 1991, and sponsored by Senators **Sam Nunn** and Richard Lugar, it was renamed the **Cooperative Threat Reduction (CTR) Program** in 1993. CTR has spent billions of dollars in assisting the countries of the former **Soviet Union** to destroy their **nuclear, biological, and chemical weapon** stockpiles and associated infrastructure, and establish verifiable **safeguards** against the **proliferation** of those weapons.

SOVIET UNION. *See* UNION OF SOVIET SOCIALIST REPUBLICS.

SPACE ARMS CONTROL. The prevention of the militarization of space through international **agreements**. Existing **arms control** agreements that control the use of space include the 1967 **Outer Space Treaty**, which precludes any country from placing **weapons of mass destruction** in orbit or on any celestial body and declares that the exploration of other worlds must be for peaceful purposes, without the intent of placing fortifications or military uses.

SPACE-BASED SENSORS. Sensors mounted on satellites that monitor environmental data, military activities, and other phenomena that can be detected from space. Space-based sensors form important aspects of **early-warning** systems, **ballistic missile defense** systems, military monitoring **regimes,** and **disarmament** oversight programs.

SPACE COMMAND. *See* U.S. SPACE COMMAND.

SPACE MINE. An **antisatellite weapon** comprised of a satellite equipped with an explosive charge that can be maneuvered into the vicinity of a target satellite and detonated.

SPACE SURVEILLANCE. The **reconnaissance** and intelligence gathering activities from satellites or vehicles in outer space. This can include photographic or electronic means of gathering intelligence information about another state and its activities.

SPARTAN ABM MISSILE. Spartan was the first line of defense in the 1960s-era **Safeguard antiballistic missile** defense system. A direct descendent of the **Nike Zeus** missile, Spartan was built by McDonnell Douglas. It had a range of 465 miles, and could intercept and kill an incoming **intercontinental ballistic missile (ICBM) reentry vehicle** in the exoatmosphere using a nuclear warhead. It was deployed to the Safeguard site in North Dakota in 1975, but deactivated several months after it was declared operational. *See also* SPRINT ABM MISSILE; NATIONAL MISSILE DEFENSE.

SPECIAL COMMISSION ON DISARMAMENT PROBLEMS. *See* PRESIDENT'S SPECIAL COMMITTEE ON DISARMAMENT; UNITED NATIONS DISARMAMENT COMMISSION.

SPECIAL NUCLEAR MATERIAL (SNM). Defined in Title I of the **Atomic Energy Act** of 1954 as **plutonium, uranium**-233, or uranium enriched in the isotopes uranium-233 or uranium-235. Uranium-233 and plutonium do not occur naturally but can be formed in nuclear reactors and extracted from the highly radioactive spent fuel by chemical separation (**reprocessing**). Uranium-233 can be produced in special reactors that use thorium as fuel. Plutonium is produced in reactors using U-238/U-235 fuel. Uranium enriched in uranium-235 is created by an **enrichment** facility.

SPECIAL VERIFICATION COMMISSION (SVC). A bilateral commission formed by the **United States** and the **Soviet Union** in 1987 under the **Intermediate-Range Nuclear Forces Treaty** (INF) to resolve questions on implementation of the treaty and to enhance the treaty's effectiveness. The Special Verification Commission is similar in purpose to the **Standing Consultative Commission**, but its focus is limited to the INF Treaty.

SPITZBERGEN CONVENTION (1920). A successful early example of negotiated international **demilitarization**. In the early 1900s a dispute arose between Norway, Sweden, Holland, and **Great Britain** as to ownership of the Spitzbergen Islands in the Barents Sea. The Spitzbergen (or Svalbard) Treaty of 1920 awarded the islands to Norway on the condition that they be permanently defortified. Prior to this decision the islands had been considered a no-man's land where all countries had equal commercial and economic rights, but no country had sovereign custody.

SPOT SATELLITES. SPOT (from the French, *Satellite Pour l'Observation de la Terre*) is a remote sensing satellite developed by the French National Space Centre. The first (SPOT 1) was launched in February 1986, and SPOT 2 followed in 1988. SPOT carries the High Resolution Visible **sensor**, circles the earth in a sun-synchronous retrograde orbit at an altitude of 500 miles, and can be over the same spot on earth every 26 days.

SPRINT ABM MISSILE. The quickest accelerating missile ever built, the Sprint was the last-chance defender of the **Safeguard ballistic missile defense** system. Built by Martin, it had a range of 25 miles and carried an **enhanced radiation warhead** (neutron bomb) and reached a speed of Mach 10 within five seconds of being launched. Its first test flight was in 1965, and it was deployed in the Safeguard site near Grand Forks, North Dakota in 1975—where it was deactivated the next day. *See also* NIKE ZEUS ABM SYSTEM; SPARTAN ABM MISSILE.

SPUTNIK. The world's first artificial satellite. Launched by the **Soviet Union** on 4 October 1957, Sputnik was about the size of a basketball, weighed 183 pounds, and took about 98 minutes to orbit the earth on its elliptical path. The launch of Sputnik frightened many Americans by raising the threat of instantaneous attack from space by **intercontinental ballistic missiles**. The **United States** subsequently rushed to keep up technologically. Sputnik thus sparked the space race and placed the Soviet Union in the forefront of a deepening **Cold War** and accelerating **arms race**.

SPY-IN-THE-SKY SATELLITES. Space-based **surveillance** satellites that use electronic and photographic technologies in order to monitor the activities of potential adversaries, their dispositions, and their communications.

STABILITY. In international relations, a situation wherein all countries are satisfied with the status quo. A period of stability is notable for an absence of crises or conflicts. In **strategic** affairs during the **Cold War**, stability meant a roughly equal balance of power between the two major **superpowers**, the **United States** and the **Soviet Union**, where **mutual assured destruction** was understood and neither side was tempted into a **first strike** against the other.

STALIN, JOSEF (1879-1953). Leader of the **Soviet Union** during the period 1929 to 1953, Joseph Stalin was in charge of Soviet policies during the early phase of the **Cold War**. Some would argue that his intransigence toward the West, the experiences of World War II, his subsequent desire for a militarily strong Soviet Union with a large geographic buffer zone, and his pursuit of a Soviet **atomic weapons** capability were in large part responsible for setting off the Cold War.

STANDING CONSULTATIVE COMMISSION (SCC). A bilateral commission formed by the **United States** and the **Soviet Union** in 1972 in accordance with the **Strategic Arms Limitation Treaty** (SALT I), later incorporated into SALT II (1979) to resolve questions of **compliance** and to establish procedures for **implementation** of the treaty. The SCC met in **Geneva**, Switzerland. *See also* SPECIAL VERIFICATION COMMISSION.

STAR WARS. *See* STRATEGIC DEFENSE INITIATIVE.

START I and II TREATIES. *See* STRATEGIC ARMS REDUCTION TREATIES.

STATE PARTY. A nation-state member of an arms control **treaty** or **agreement,** and bound to the requirements and restrictions thereof.

STEALTH. The use of both structural design and special materials to shield weapon systems from radar detection. The best known examples include U.S. aircraft such as the F-117 Nighthawk and the **B-2 Spirit bomber**.

STIMSON, HENRY (1867-1950). Secretary of war under President William Howard Taft, governor general of the Philippines from 1927 until 1929, secretary of state under President Herbert Hoover, and secretary of state and secretary of war under Presidents **Franklin Roosevelt** and **Harry Truman**. After the Japanese invasion of Manchuria in 1932, he issued a declaration that the **United States** would not recognize any situation or **treaty** that might impair U.S. treaty rights or that was brought about by means contrary to the **Kellogg-Briand Pact**. This policy came to be known as the Stimson Doctrine. At the end of World War II, Stimson argued in favor of the use of **atomic weapons** on Japan and took Kyoto off the target list for atomic attack due to its culturally significant heritage. Stimson was known for his pragmatic idealism and nonpartisan internationalism in U.S. foreign policy.

STOCKHOLM AGREEMENT (1986). A landmark **agreement** that reduced suspicion and improved confidence among European states. The agreement resulted from two years of discussions in Stockholm, Sweden. It clearly pointed to the coming end of the **Cold War**, as states on both sides of the Iron Curtain found that they had less to fear from their neighbors than they had thought. Following the Stockholm **Conference on Confidence- and Security-Building Measures and Disarmament in Europe**, most Western and Eastern European states, including the **Soviet Union**, who with the **United States**, agreed to refrain from the threat or use of force, agreed to the prior notification of military movements, and authorized observers at their own field exercises and some onsite inspections. *See also* CONFIDENCE AND SECURITY BUILDING MEASURES.

STOCKHOLM INTERNATIONAL PEACE RESEARCH INSTITUTE (SIPRI). Founded in 1966, and funded primarily by the Swedish government, SIPRI is an international independent research institute that conducts scientific research on questions of conflict and cooperation that are of importance for international peace and security. It publishes the highly regarded annual *SIPRI Yearbook*.

STOCKPILE. A country's total arsenal of a weapon system or combination of weapon systems, both deployed and in storage.

STOCKPILE STEWARDSHIP. Stewardship includes **nuclear weapons testing** and science-based weapons experimentation that ensures the **safety, reliability**, and performance of a nation's nuclear stockpile.

STOCKPILE STEWARDSHIP PROGRAM (SSP). A **United States Department of Energy** program for the management and care of the U.S. nuclear arsenal in the post-**Cold War** era. Begun in 1993, the Stockpile Stewardship Program uses advanced computer software to replace **nuclear testing**, which has not been authorized since the testing moratorium put in place by President **George H.W. Bush** in 1992. Stockpile stewardship includes **nuclear weapons** testing and science-based weapons experimentation and ensures the **safety, reliability**, and performance of the nation's nuclear stockpile. The research and development of the technologies required for stockpile management are included under stockpile stewardship.

STRATEGIC. Of or relating to the capability to apply one's military power to bear directly on that which an adversary holds most dear—usually its homeland. This implies global military capability, as opposed to theater or tactical capabilities that apply only to an adversary's military forces within a theater or on a battlefield. The term strategic is also often used as a synonym for nuclear-capable forces.

STRATEGIC AIR COMMAND (SAC). The branch of the **United States Air Force** within which the United States' **intercontinental ballistic missiles** and long-range **bombers** were assigned during the **Cold War**. SAC was the leading proponent of **strategic** offensive weaponry and the **strategic** air defense of North America from 1947 until it became **U.S. Strategic Command** in June 1992. It was also responsible for the **Single Integrated Operations Plan** (SIOP) and maintained the **Joint Strategic Target List**. In the early days of the Cold War, under the command of such well-known aerospace advocates as General Curtis E. LeMay, SAC was given a disproportionately large share of the entire U.S. defense budget in order to build America's strategic sword and shield to oppose the **Soviet Union**.

STRATEGIC ARMS LIMITATION TALKS (SALT). The series of negotiations between the **United States** and the **Soviet Union** conducted between 1969 and 1979 aimed at limiting both sides' **strategic** forces. These talks produced the 1972 **Strategic Arms Limitation Treaty** (SALT I, which officially consisted of the Interim Agreement on Strategic Offensive Arms and the **Anti-Ballistic Missile Treaty** (ABM), and in 1979 the second **Strategic Arms Limitation Treaty** (SALT II).

STRATEGIC ARMS LIMITATION TREATY (SALT I) (1972). "The Interim **Agreement** Between the **United States of America** and the **Union of Soviet Socialist Republics** on Certain Measures with Respect to the Limitation of Strategic Offensive Arms" was signed on 26 May 1972 in **Moscow** and was the result of the first series of **Strategic Arms Limitation Talks**, which lasted from November 1969 to May 1972. The agreement froze the number of **strategic ballistic missile launchers** (1,054 for the United States and 1,618 for the Soviet Union) and prohibited the conversion of older launchers to accommodate modern heavy **intercontinental ballistic missiles** (ICBMs). An increase in **submarine-launched ballistic missiles** (SLBMs) was allowed provided an equal number of land-based launchers were destroyed. The **United States** was authorized up to 710 SLBMs while the **Soviet Union** was allowed 950. Mobile ICBMs were not covered by the agreement.

The agreement was perceived as a holding action and its duration was limited to five years in the hope that a more comprehensive agreement would be reached. The U.S. Congress passed a joint resolution on 30 September 1972 supporting the agreement, instead of just the Senate ratification. It **entered into force** on 3 October 1972.

STRATEGIC ARMS LIMITATION TREATY II (SALT II) (1979). The "**Treaty** Between the **United States of America** and the **Union of Soviet Socialist Republics** on the Limitation of Strategic Offensive Arms" resulted from talks lasting from November 1972 until 18 June 1979, when the treaty was signed in Vienna. The treaty placed limits on **ballistic missiles** and their **launchers**, but did not require the reduction of such items. Each country was limited to 2,250 launchers, with a sublimit of 1,320 launchers for missiles with **multiple independently targetable reentry vehicles** (MIRV). MIRVed ballistic missiles were limited to 1,200, of which only 820 could be **intercontinental ballistic missiles** (ICBMs). In addition, new ICBMs were limited to carrying 10 **warheads** each, while **submarine-launched ballistic missiles** (SLBMs) were allowed to carry up to 14 warheads. Lastly, the treaty prohibited space-based **nuclear weapons**, fractional orbital missiles, and rapid reload missile launchers.

A protocol to the treaty was signed at the same time and was to remain in effect until 31 December 1981. The protocol prohibited the deployment of **ground-launched cruise missiles** (GLCMs) and **sea-launched cruise missiles** (SLCMs) with a range of over 600 kilometers, as well as mobile ICBMs. Additionally, MIRVd GLCMs and SLCMs with a range over 600 kilometers could not be tested.

President **Jimmy Carter** submitted the treaty to the Senate immediately following the signing, but due to political considerations and the Soviet invasion of Afganistan, he was forced to remove it from consideration in January 1980. Since the treaty was never ratified, it became a politically, not legally, binding agreement. On 27 May 1986, President **Ronald Reagan**, after citing Soviet violations, declared that the United States would no longer abide by the limits of the SALT agreements. The United States exceeded those limits on 28 November 1986.

STRATEGIC ARMS REDUCTION TALKS (START). The series of negotiations between the **United States** and the **Soviet Union** (and later **Russia**) begun in 1982 to seek reductions in both sides' **strategic** forces. These talks produced the 1991 **Strategic Arms Reduction Treaty I** (START I) and the 2000 **Strategic Arms Reduction Treaty II** (START II), as well as progress toward a **Strategic Arms Reduction Treaty III.**

STRATEGIC ARMS REDUCTION TREATY I (START I) (1991). "The **Treaty** between the **United States** and the **Union of Soviet Socialist Republics** on the Reduction and Limitation of **Strategic** Offensive Arms," which was signed on 31 July 1991, reduced the number of U.S. and former Soviet strategic offensive arms—**intercontinental ballistic missiles** (ICBMs), **submarine-launched ballistic missiles** (SLBMs), and **heavy bombers**—to 1,600 each and attributed **warheads** (an agreed upon number of warheads that are associated with each weapon system) to 6,000. There were additional sublimits for attributed warheads: 4,900 warheads on deployed ballistic missiles and 1,100 warheads on deployed mobile ICBMs. The former **Soviet Union** was also limited to 154 deployed

heavy ICBMs (down from 308 before the treaty), each carrying 10 warheads. In addition, an aggregate limit of 3,600 metric tons was placed on **ballistic missile** throw-weight. The treaty also provides for the right to reduce (download) the number of warheads attributed to three existing types of ICBMs and SLBMs. No single type may have more than 500 downloaded warheads, with a sublimit of four warheads downloaded per missile. Overall no more than 1,250 warheads may be downloaded at any one time.

Warheads carried by heavy bombers, including those in long-range, nuclear **air-launched cruise missiles**, would be counted at a discounted rate. Especially significant was the discounted rate for penetrating bombers, which counted as only one warhead regardless of how many missiles they were capable of carrying. Politically binding side agreements also limited the number of deployed nuclear **sea-launched cruise missiles** (SLCM) and the number of Soviet **Backfire bombers**.

An extensive series of **on-site inspections** and an exchange of locational and technical data for all systems, with regular updates, complemented each party's **national technical means** (NTM) to monitor **compliance** with the treaty. An additional important **verification** measure was the agreement to exchange telemetric information from all test flights of ICBMs and SLBMs, including the equipment necessary to interpret the data. The **Joint Compliance and Inspection Commission** (JCIC) was tasked with monitoring compliance with the treaty and has been meeting in Geneva since 1991.

On 23 May 1992, a protocol was signed in Lisbon that made START I a five nation, multiparty treaty instead of a bilateral treaty. The protocol and appended presidential letters obligated **Belarus, Kazakhstan**, and **Ukraine** to become **non-nuclear weapon state parties** to the **Nuclear Nonproliferation Treaty** (NPT). This provision had been mandated by the U.S. Senate's START I ratification bill. On 14 January 1994 in **Moscow**, the presidents of Ukraine, the Russian Federation, and the United States signed the Trilateral Agreement, which promised Ukraine financial and security assistance as a means of persuading its Parliament to ratify START I and the NPT. This occurred on 3 February 1994, and on 5 December 1994 Ukraine deposited its instruments of ratification for the NPT, allowing START I to **enter into force**. Its duration was 15 years, with an option to extend at five year intervals. Treaty limits were officially reached by all parties on 5 December 2001.

STRATEGIC ARMS REDUCTION TREATY II (START II) (1992). In 1991 and 1992 President **George H.W. Bush** and Russian President **Mikael Gorbachev** made a series of **Presidential Nuclear Initiatives** reducing nuclear stockpiles and lowering the alert status of several weapon systems. These set the foundation for a Joint Understanding at the June 1992 summit between Presidents Bush and **Boris Yeltsin** in Washington, D.C. The Joint Understanding called for the elimination of all **intercontinental ballistic missiles** (ICBMs) with **multiple independently targetable reentry vehicles** (MIRVs) and deep cuts in **submarine-launched ballistic missiles** (SLBMs), forming the basis of the "Treaty Between the **United States of America** and the **Russian** Federation on Further Reduction and Limitation of **Strategic** Offensive Arms" (START II). This treaty was signed at the 3 January 1993 **Moscow Summit** by Presidents Bush and Yeltsin. It relied heavily on START I for definitions, procedures, and **verification** and, as such, could not legally **enter into force** before START I. It will remain in force as long as START I does. The United States Senate ratified START II on 26 January 1996, and the Russian Duma did so on 14 April 2000, at which point the treaty entered into force.

The eliminations are to take place in a two-phase process. Within seven years of the treaty's entry into force, each side must reduce its deployed strategic forces to 3,800-4,250 attributed **warheads,** within which the following sublimits apply: 1,200 warheads for MIRVed ICBMs, 650 warheads for heavy ICBMs, and 2,160 warheads for SLBMs. Phase Two limits were to have been reached by the year 2003. At that time each party must have reduced its deployed strategic forces to 3,000-3,500 attributed warheads, within which the following sublimits apply: zero warheads for MIRVed ICBMs, 1,700-1,750 total warheads for SLBMs, and elimination of all heavy ICBMs. At the March 1997 **Helsinki Summit** Presidents **William Clinton** and Yeltsin agreed to extend the time for START II **implementation** and reductions to 31 December 2007. Systems to be eliminated under this treaty must be deactivated, however, by removing their warheads by December 2003. Because the treaty did not enter into force until April 2000, both phases were to be completed simultaneously.

In order to reach the lower warhead ceilings, the downloading procedures identified in the START I treaty have been modified. The Russian Federation is allowed to download 105 SS-19 ICBMs by five warheads, leaving only one warhead per missile (all other downloading is still limited to four warheads per missile). Additionally, the overall ceilings on the aggregate numbers of downloaded warheads were removed. As a result, any missile that was previously equipped with six warheads or more, except the SS-19s, must be destroyed, while those equipped with five or less may be retained, provided they are downloaded to only one warhead.

Since the treaty eliminates the entire class of heavy ICBMs (SS-18), special provisions were made regarding the reuse of that hardware. All of the missiles and their launch canisters may be converted to space-launch vehicles, while up to 90 of the silos may be converted to launch single-warhead ICBMs. Any nonconverted equipment must be destroyed.

The treaty also has several provisions regarding bombers. The **B-2 Spirit** must now be exhibited and is inspectable, whereas under START I, the B-2 was subject to neither condition unless it was tested or equipped with long-range nuclear **air-launched cruise missiles** (ALCMs). A one time reorientation of up to 100 nuclear **heavy bombers** to a conventional role is allowed without adhering to the START I conversion procedures as long as they were never accountable as ALCM-equipped heavy bombers. The United States chose this option for its **B-1 bomber** fleet. Additionally, conventional and nuclear bombers must be based separately and crews separately trained and have differences observable by **national technical means** and visible during inspection. The treaty also removes the "discount" provisions from START I bomber warhead counting rules but allows an increased number of bombers to be retained. START II also specifically provides the right to change the number of nuclear warheads the treaty attributes to a bomber if there is a visible change in the plane's configuration. Approximately 1,300 warheads may be attributed to bombers in each country, depending on the number of ICBMs and SLBMs retained by each party.

Although this treaty built on START I, some additional verification measures were included. START II significantly increased the number of **on-site inspections**, mostly relating to the retention of converted Russian heavy ICBM (SS-18) silos and the conversion of heavy bombers. The compliance regime is governed by the **Bilateral Implementation Commission**, which meets in **Geneva**, Switzerland.

STRATEGIC ARMS REDUCTION TREATY III (START III). Following the rapid success of the START I and II treaties and other **arms control agreements** in the early 1990s, hopes ran high that the logical next step would be for the two superpowers to conclude a START III **treaty**, further reducing the numbers of nuclear missiles, aircraft, submarines, and **warheads**. Many observers predicted that warheads would, in fact, be the focus of the next **strategic** arms control treaty, since previous regimes dealt with delivery platforms. The 1997 **Helsinki Agreement** between Presidents **William Clinton** and **Boris Yeltsin** included an outline of likely discussion points in the next round of strategic arms control talks. However, the changing international security environment made such a formal treaty appear, to some observers, to no longer be necessary. Accordingly, in December 2001 U.S. President **George W. Bush** and Russian President **Vladimir Putin** agreed to further reduce their strategic arsenals to 1,700-2,200 warheads by the year 2012. This agreement was codified in the two-page **Strategic Offensive Reductions Treaty** (SORT, also known as the Moscow Treaty) in May 2002, which effectively eliminated the need for further considerations of START III talks.

STRATEGIC BOMBER. An air-breathing bomber that can deliver **nuclear weapons** at intercontinental range. **United States** examples have included the B-36, B47, **B-52**, FB-111, **B-1**, and **B-2**. **Soviet Union/Russian** examples have included the **Backfire**, **Badger**, **Bear**, and TU-160.

STRATEGIC COMMAND. *See* U.S. STRATEGIC COMMAND.

STRATEGIC DEFENSE INITIATIVE (SDI). The program launched under U.S. President **Ronald Reagan** in March 1983 to develop a **ballistic missile defense** system for the **United States** that would overturn the situation of **mutual assured destruction** with the **Soviet Union** and held the promise, according to Reagan, of making **nuclear weapons** "impotent and obsolete." Also called "Star Wars" by its detractors, the SDI program emphasized exotic weaponry, including **directed energy weapons** and space-based systems. It became the largest and most expensive defense program in U.S. history, but some historians argue that it helped end the **Cold War** by posing to the Soviet Union the potential of a defensive **arms race** that, according to this theory, the Soviets recognized they could not win and that would bankrupt their already teetering economy. President **George H.W. Bush** maintained an interest in SDI but reduced its size and goals, changing the name to **Global Protection Against Limited Strikes** (GPALS). In 1993 under President **William Clinton** its focus shifted to **theater missile defenses**, and its organizational name changed accordingly to the **Ballistic Missile Defense Organization**. Another name change occurred in 2001 following the election of **George W. Bush**, as BMDO's status was elevated and it became the **Missile Defense Agency**. Following the U.S. withdrawal from the **Anti-Ballistic Missile Treaty** in 2002, a rudimentary missile defense system was finally deployed at locations in Alaska, California, and at sea in late 2004. *See also* SAFEGUARD; SENTINEL; STRATEGIC DEFENSE INITIATIVE; STRATEGIC DEFENSES.

STRATEGIC DEFENSE INITIATIVE ORGANIZATION (SDIO). The SDIO was created in 1983 to manage all **strategic defense** programs, including research, development, testing, and funding. As an organization that reported directly to the secretary of defense, it was based in the **Pentagon**. In 1993 its name was changed to the **Ballistic Missile Defense Organization**, and in 2002 it became the **Missile Defense Agency**. Its mission has remained essentially the same, although with less emphasis on space-based systems and more on tactical ballistic missile defenses. *See also* STRATEGIC DEFENSE INITIATIVE.

STRATEGIC DEFENSES. Strategic defenses are those systems a country employs to protect its territory and population from adversary attack against the homeland. Typically such defenses have included navies, coast guards, air defenses, and antiballistic missile interceptors. They are defensive measures meant to protect a nation or region against incoming threats. Strategic defenses typically cover a larger geographic region than tactical or point defenses. *See also* STRATEGIC DEFENSE INITIATIVE.

STRATEGIC MODERNIZATION. An active upgrade to one's **strategic** forces. The administration of **United States** President **Ronald Reagan**, for example, early in his first term (1981-1985) undertook a strategic modernization effort that included all three legs of the **Triad**, and also added **strategic defenses**.

STRATEGIC NUCLEAR DELIVERY VEHICLE (SNDV). Those military weapon delivery systems designed to carry **strategic nuclear warheads** to their target. These systems include **intercontinental ballistic missiles, submarine-launched ballistic missiles,** and **bombers**.

STRATEGIC NUCLEAR WEAPONS. Nuclear weapons delivered at intercontinental ranges by **strategic nuclear delivery vehicles**. These include **intercontinental ballistic missiles, submarine-launched ballistic missiles**, and gravity bombs and **air launched cruise missiles** carried by **heavy bombers**.

STRATEGIC OFFENSIVE REDUCTIONS TREATY (SORT) (2002). The latest in a series of offensive **strategic nuclear weapons treaties** between the **United States** and the **Soviet Union**. Also known as the Moscow Treaty, it was signed in **Moscow** on 24 May 2002. It is the shortest bilateral **arms control** treaty ever signed, at two pages in length. Its brevity is meant to reflect the changed relationship between the two countries, which are now strategic partners rather than adversaries, a major change since the **Cold War**. The principle elements of the treaty had been agreed by Presidents **George W. Bush** and **Vladimir Putin** at the **Crawford Summit** in November 2001. It commits both parties to continued reductions in their strategic nuclear arsenals, with a target of 1,700 to 2,200 deployed strategic **warheads** by 2012. There are no provisions for **verification, inspections,** or **compliance,** nor does it require the parties to destroy the warheads they remove from deployed status. This treaty essentially took the place of a third **Strategic Arms Reduction Treaty** (START III).

STRATEGIC STUDIES INSTITUTE (SSI). The Strategic Studies Institute is the **U.S. Army's** institute for geostrategic and national security research and analysis. Its primary function is to provide direct analysis for the Army and **Department of Defense** leadership and to act as a bridge to the wider **strategic** community. SSI is located at the U.S. Army War College in Carlisle, Pennsylvania. Its military and civilian staff hosts numerous annual conferences and publishes a wide range of studies and analytical reports.

STRATEGIC SUFFICIENCY. Having a **strategic** posture that provides for the perception and resulting rational decision on the part of an enemy that you have achieved the credible **capability** of **assured destruction**. This enables the type of **deterrence** you are seeking (**minimum deterrence** or **mutual assured destruction**).

STRATEGIC SUPERIORITY. Having a **strategic** posture that, as opposed to **strategic sufficiency**, provides the perception in the enemy that you are clearly stronger and more capable than required to simply maintain a given balance. Such unilateral or one-sided tips to the balance, as valuable as it may seem to the country that holds such superiority, are seen as destabilizing until a new balance is achieved.

STRONTIUM. One of the **radioactive fission** materials created in the operation of a **nuclear reactor**. One of its isotopes, Strontium 90, is produced by **fallout** from an atomic blast and has a half-life of 28 years; accordingly, it can contaminate property or the food chain for decades.

SUBMARINE, BALLISTIC MISSILE (SSBN). Nuclear powered ballistic missile submarines are traditionally referred to as SSBN (Ship, Submersible, Ballistic, Nuclear). These submarines carry and launch **submarine launched ballistic missiles** (SLBMs). Five nations have SSBNs: the **United States**, the **Russian Federation**, the **United Kingdom**, **France**, and **China**. For the United States, the original SSBN submarine force consisted of forty-one **Polaris** submarines, with the first, the USS *George Washington*, commissioned on December 30, 1959. Later SSBNs in the fleet included the **Poseidon** and **Trident** class boats.

SUBMARINE-LAUNCHED BALLISTIC MISSILE (SLBM). **Ballistic missiles** carried aboard and launched from submarines. SLBMs represented truly dramatic leaps in technology when they were designed in the late 1950s. The first SLBM deployed by the **United States Navy** was the **Polaris**, placed aboard the Polaris class nuclear powered submarine in 1960. Submarine-launched ballistic missiles are generally considered the most survivable **second-strike** weapon system.

SUBMARINE PROTOCOLS (1922). A set of rules and procedures developed at the 1922 **Washington Naval Conference** for submarines to follow when attempting to capture a merchant vessel. The protocols were reiterated in the 1930 and 1936 **London Naval Conferences**. *See also* WASHINGTON TREATY.

SUBMARINE ROCKET (SUBROC). A submarine-launched missile that acts as a nuclear depth charge. After launch from a submarine's torpedo tubes it transitions to an aerial trajectory for most of its route before the atomic depth charge separates and reenters the water near its target. It has a range of 35 miles. All U.S. nuclear submarines can carry up to several SUBROCs. Development of the missile began in 1955, and it was first deployed in 1966. It was converted to a conventional warhead following the **Presidential Nuclear Initiatives** of 1991.

SUFFICIENCY. *See* STRATEGIC SUFFICIENCY.

SUMMIT MEETING. A formal gathering of heads of state or government, often held for the purpose of negotiating or signing a **treaty** or **agreement**. Notable summit meetings of recent decades include the **Malta Summit** of 1989, the **Washington Summits** of 1949 and 1999, and the 1996 **Reykjavik Summit**.

SUPERPOWER. A nation-state with immense strength in all aspects of national power—economic, military, geographic, and diplomatic—that far exceeds any other state's power by those same measures. The first two superpowers were the **United States** and the **Soviet Union** following World War II (although one could argue that historically the Roman and British Empires represented early superpower states). Since the Soviet Union's dissolution and the end of the **Cold War** in the early 1990s, the United States assumed the mantel of the world's only superpower (sometimes called by the French term "hyperpower").

SURETY. The broad category of safety, security, and use control of **nuclear weapon** that ensures such weapons remain in the hands of the proper authorities.

SURFACE-TO-AIR MISSILE (SAM). A defensive weapon system in which ground-launched missiles are employed against airborne threats, including aircraft and **cruise missiles**.

SURPRISE ATTACK CONFERENCE (1958). An unsuccessful **Cold War arms control** conference in which, however, for the first time a state proposed the use of satellite imagery (**national technical means**) to monitor and **verify arms control regimes**.

SURVEILLANCE. Visually or electronically monitoring the physical state and activity of a geographic location or a specific unit. Such surveillance can be conducted by persons, remote **sensors**, aircraft, or satellites.

SURVIVABILITY. The ability of armed forces and civilian communities to withstand attack and continue to function effectively.

SWORDS INTO PLOWSHARES. The motto of the unofficial East German **peace movement** in the early 1980s. Led by the Lutheran Church, the movement took this motto not only for its Biblical origins (from a passage in the Old Testament book of Isaiah: "They will beat their swords into plowshares and their spears into pruning hooks. Nation will not take up sword against nation, nor will they train for war anymore."), but because the **Soviet Union** was unable to criticize it, since the phrase appeared on the side of a statue that had been presented to the **United Nations** by the Soviet Union and which showed a peasant hammering his sword into a peaceful implement.

T

TACTICAL NUCLEAR WEAPONS. *See* NONSTRATEGIC NUCLEAR WEAPONS.

TECHNOLOGY TRANSFER. The process by which existing knowledge, facilities or capabilities developed under federal research and development funding are utilized to fulfill public and private needs, or more generally, the sale or giving away of technical knowledge to a state that has not developed it. Such transfers are often referred to in a negative manner, particularly if the recipient state plans to use the technology against another state. Although this process can be very simple or quite complex, it basically involves a technical resource (such as a federal laboratory), a user (e.g., a small business), and some interface connecting the two. Technology transfer includes a range of formal and informal cooperative agreements between technology developers and technology seekers. In addition, technology transfer involves the transfer of knowledge and technical know-how as well as physical devices and equipment.

TELEMETRY. The data transmitted electronically from a missile in flight to ground stations to allow assessment of the missile's flight performance. Telemetry is generally limited to use in flight tests rather than during military employment.

TELLER, EDWARD (1908-2003). Generally considered the "father of the **H bomb**." Teller was a Hungarian physicist who had emigrated to America and was invited to be a member of the **Manhattan Project** in the early 1940s. He later became director of **Lawrence Livermore National Laboratory**. Teller pushed for the development of a more powerful "super" or hydrogen **fusion weapon**, eventually succeeding in 1952 with the first test of a U.S. fusion device.

TERMINAL PHASE. The final segment of a **ballistic missile** trajectory. During the terminal phase the **reentry vehicle** enters the atmosphere and delivers the **warhead** to the target.

TERRORISM. Indirect, asymmetrical, psychological warfare. Terrorism is notoriously difficult to define. Within government documents and the academic literature each agency or author defines terrorism to meet their particular objectives. However, within the context of this dictionary, most relevant definitions would highlight that terrorism applies calculated violence in ways designed to elicit a political response. Further, the violence is applied to generate fear within a target population so that that population, not the terrorist, presses governments for the desired political action.

Regardless of the definition, terrorism poses significant challenges to **arms control** and **disarmament**. First, the very basis of effective arms control and disarmament is acceptance of international law, norms, and standards, including the need for **compliance** and **transparency**. Terrorism rejects every aspect of that foundation. Second, arms control and disarmament lies in the state system: sovereign entities coming to bilateral and multilateral agreements and working together for **implementation** and **verification**. The world of terrorism is one of **rogue states**, failed or failing states, and nonstate actors. It lies outside of the international system and its acceptable modes of interaction.

Third, and perhaps the most important challenge today, is that even as the world sees the dangers of the **superpower** nuclear confrontation begin to wane, it also sees a rising security challenge as potential terrorist access to **weapons of mass destruction** increases. For just two examples, the Japanese terrorist group Aum Shinrikyo experimented with a range of **chemical** and **biological agents**, and it employed sarin gas in the Tokyo subway system. The global network al-Qaeda, by all reports, has an active program seeking chemical, biological, nuclear, and radiological capabilities.

Fourth, the basis for effective arms control and disarmament has been international cooperation and multilateral action. One arena of focus has been action to prevent the **proliferation** of weapons of mass destruction that heighten the terrorism threat. However, the inability of the international community to totally prevent the transfer of all weapons components and precursors, coupled with 21st century terrorist actions, has led some states to move toward unilateral action in terms of prevention and **preemption** of mass effects terrorism. Regardless of the justification for action, this move toward unilateralism also challenges the foundations of cooperation and unified action that lie at the heart of traditional arms control and disarmament.

TEST BAN. A restriction or **moratorium** that by international **agreement** precludes the field testing of a weapon or category of weapons. Usually used in reference to **atomic** or **nuclear weapons**, or **fissile material** experiments. *See also* COMPREHENSIVE TEST BAN TREATY; THRESHOLD TEST BAN TREATY.

TESTING MORATORIUM. A voluntary commitment by a state not to test a particular weapon or category of weapons (such as **nuclear weapons**) for a specific length of time. A state will sometimes make this commitment in hopes of reciprocal action by its adversary.

THATCHER, MARGARET (1925-). British politician and **hawkish** prime minister of **Great Britain** from 1979 to 1990. Her tenure aligned with the rise of other conservative leaders within the Western alliance, including **Ronald Reagan** and **Helmut Kohl**. Together these leaders oversaw the end of the **Cold War** and the demise of the **Soviet Union**. During Thatcher's rule the **United Kingdom** fought a war against Argentina over the Falklands Islands (1982).

THEATER HIGH-ALTITUDE AIR DEFENSE SYSTEM (THAAD). A U.S. Army missile capable of shooting down short- and medium-range **ballistic missiles** in flight using hit-to-kill technology. Fired from a truck-mounted launcher, THAAD is comprised of a single rocket booster with a separating kill vehicle and on-board radar that seeks out its target. Its first tests began in 1995; it is not yet fielded.

THEATER MISSILE DEFENSE (TMD). Antimissile weapons designed to defend a specific geographic area from missile attack. TMD would be deployed to protect U.S. troops overseas, the forces and territory of U.S. allies, and **neutral** countries during times of conflict. Such systems are not designed with protection of the American homeland as their primary mission. While no complete TMD system has been finalized, research and development has advanced on several land-, air-, and sea-based systems for the **United States**, including **Patriot, Theater High-Altitude Air Defense System** (THAAD), Airborne Laser, and Aegis. *See also* STRATEGIC DEFENSES.

THEATER NUCLEAR FORCES (TNF). *See* NONSTRATEGIC NUCLEAR WEAPONS.

THERMONUCLEAR BOMB. *See* FUSION WEAPON; HYDROGEN BOMB; TELLER, EDWARD.

THOR MISSILE. An **intermediate-range nuclear missile** developed by the **U.S. Air Force** and built by Douglas Aircraft. First delivered in 1956, only 10 months after the contract was awarded, Thor represented possibly the fastest major research and engineering project in American military history. Similar to the **Jupiter** IRBM, but operating out of a fixed location, Thor was deployed to **Great Britain** from 1959 to 1965.

THRESHOLD STATES. Nation-states that are close to the technical capability of developing and deploying **nuclear weapons**. There are usually political reasons a state does not cross the threshold to full-scale development of nuclear capabilities, even if it has the technological and financial resources to do so.

THRESHOLD TEST BAN TREATY (TTBT). The "Treaty Between the **United States** of America and the **Union of Soviet Socialist Republics** on the Limitation of Underground **Nuclear Weapons** Tests" was signed by the United States and **Soviet Union** on 3 July 1974. It prohibits signatories from the **underground testing** of nuclear weapons with a yield greater than 150 kilotons (KT) at declared testing sites. Due to U.S. concerns about possible Soviet violations of the treaty, negotiations were undertaken from 1987 to 1990 to strengthen the methods of **verification** and to address the possibility of accidentally exceeding the 150 KT limit. The resulting protocol requires notification of explosions and provides various options for measuring the yield of the explosions, including **on-site inspection** for tests with a planned yield greater than 35 KT.

The United States has only one declared testing site, located in Nevada. The former USSR maintained two testing sites, one within the **Russian Federation**, the other in **Kazakhstan**.

The treaty **entered into force** on 11 December 1990. It has a duration of five years, with five-year extensions, and is currently in force.

THROW WEIGHT. The maximum weight of the **payload** a missile can deliver over a selected range and trajectory, including the weight of the **warheads**, the **reentry vehicles**, and any other components associated with weapon delivery.

TITAN MISSILE. Along with the **Atlas** missile, the first generation of **United States intercontinental ballistic missiles** in the late 1950s. Built by the Martin Company in Denver, Colorado (later Martin Marietta, and still being manufactured there for commercial satellite launch purposes by Lockheed Martin), these missiles were above-ground launched. They required liquid fueling just prior to launch. The Titan I had its first test flight in 1959 and was deployed in 1963 at six bases within the continental United States. All Titan Is were retired by 1966, replaced by its larger successor, the Titan II, which first flew in 1961. It had a range of 9,325 miles and carried the largest nuclear **warhead** ever designed by the United States, the W-53, on a Mark-6 **reentry vehicle**, with an explosive yield of nine megatons. **Strategic Air Command** deployed 54 Titan IIs at three locations: Davis-Monthan AFB, Arizona; McConnell AFB, Kansas; and Little Rock AFB, Arkansas. All the Titans suffered from operational problems, primarily due to their use of liquid fuel. They were retired in 1987.

TLATELOLCO, TREATY OF. *See* LATIN AMERICAN NUCLEAR WEAPON FREE ZONE.

TOLERANCE. In weapons terms, tolerance refers to the degree of precision to which a weapon or system is manufactured, and the degree to which it can be moved from its operational specifications and still function. In biological terms, an organism can build up tolerance to a particular drug (or chemical or biological agent) such that a greater than normal dose is required to achieve the desired effects. Tolerance is sometimes used in **arms control** to refer to the allowable level of flexibility in conforming to the provisions of an **agreement**.

TOMAHAWK MISSILE. A winged **cruise missile**, capable of being launched from submarines, ships, or aircraft, the Tomahawk is primarily deployed by the **U.S. Navy**. It was first tested in 1976 and can carry either a conventional or nuclear **payload**. A variant of the Tomahawk was deployed to Europe in the mid-1980s as the **ground-launched cruise missile**. *See also* AIR-LAUNCHED CRUISE MISSILE.

TOXIC. Capable of causing death, incapacitation, or permanent harm to living organisms.

TOXICITY. A subjective measure of how **toxic** a given substance is.

TOXIN. An inert **toxic** substance derived from living **organisms** or from synthetic manufacture.

TRANSNATIONAL PEACE MOVEMENTS. International popular movements, often secular, union-based, and socialist, which call for an end to war or to a specific weapons program. Adherents sometimes travel to other countries in order to participate in demonstrations against perceived militarism and injustice. The first international secular peace organization was the League of Brotherhood, founded in 1847. The focus of peace movements has ranged from being organized around specific weapons (such as machine guns, **chemical weapons**, and **nuclear weapons**), to postwar efforts to clean up the environment, to conflict resolution, to the abolition of war itself through legal avenues or cultural campaigns. Antislavery, democratic, and human-rights movements have also focused on state-sanctioned violence. The most active recent periods of such peace movements occurred in the early 1950s as a result of the rise of atomic arsenals in the **United States** and the **Soviet Union,** in the early 1980s in opposition to the deployment of **intermediate-range nuclear forces** in Europe, and in 2003 to protest the war in **Iraq**. *See also* PEACE MOVEMENTS.

TRANSPARENCY. The exchange of information, access to facilities, and cooperative arrangements undertaken to provide observation and **verification** of defense-related activities. Enhancing the degree of transparency is often viewed as a political **confidence-building measure.**

TRANSPORTER ERECTOR LAUNCHER (TEL). A wheeled or tracked vehicle capable of carrying a mobile **ballistic missile** to its launch location and then raising it to a vertical position prior to launch. The best known was the TEL developed by a German company for the U.S. **ground-launched cruise missile** (GLCM) that was deployed in Europe in the mid-1980s. This system was eliminated by the 1987 **Intermediate-Range Nuclear Forces Treaty** (INF).

TREATY. Agreement of formal and serious commitment intended to be legally binding. *See* NEGOTIATIONS.

TREATY OF BANGKOK. *See* SOUTHEAST ASIA NUCLEAR WEAPONS FREE ZONE.

TREATY BANNING NUCLEAR WEAPONS TESTS IN THE ATMOSPHERE, IN OUTER SPACE, AND UNDER WATER. *See* LIMITED TEST BAN TREATY.

TREATY BETWEEN THE UNITED STATES OF AMERICA AND THE RUSSIAN FEDERATION ON FURTHER REDUCTION AND LIMITATION OF STRATEGIC OFFENSIVE ARMS. *See* STRATEGIC ARMS REDUCTION TREATY (START II).

TREATY BETWEEN THE UNITED STATES OF AMERICA AND THE UNION OF SOVIET SOCIALIST REPUBLICS ON THE LIMITATION OF STRATEGIC OFFENSIVE ARMS. *See* STRATEGIC ARMS LIMITATION TREATY (SALT II).

TREATY BETWEEN THE UNITED STATES OF AMERICAN AND THE UNION OF SOVIET SOCIALIST REPUBLICS ON THE LIMITATION OF UNDERGROUND NUCLEAR WEAPONS TESTS. *See* THRESHOLD TEST BAN TREATY.

TREATY BETWEEN THE UNITED STATES AND THE UNION OF SOVIET SOCIALIST REPUBLICS ON THE REDUCTION AND LIMITATION OF STRATEGIC OFFENSIVE

ARMS. *See* STRATEGIC ARMS REDUCTION TREATY (START I).

TREATY BETWEEN THE UNITED STATES OF AMERICA AND THE UNION OF SOVIET SOCIALIST REPUBLICS ON UNDERGROUND NUCLEAR EXPLOSIONS FOR PEACE-FUL PURPOSES. *See* PEACEFUL NUCLEAR EXPLOSIONS TREATY.

TREATY ON CONVENTIONAL ARMED FORCES IN EUR-OPE. *See* CONVENTIONAL FORCES IN EUROPE TREATY.

TREATY ON THE NONPROLIFERATION OF NUCLEAR WEAPONS. *See* NUCLEAR NONPROLIFERATION TREATY.

TREATY ON OPEN SKIES (1992). The Treaty on Open Skies was signed in Helsinki on 24 March 1992 by 27 members of the **North Atlantic Treaty Organization** (NATO) and the former **Warsaw Pact**, plus Finland and Sweden. The **United States** ratified it on 3 November 1993. Each participating state has the right to conduct, and the obligation to receive, overhead flights by unarmed fixed-wing observation aircraft. Each aircraft is authorized to carry pano-ramic, still frame, and video cameras; infra-red scanning devices; and side-looking synthetic aperture radars. Normally the inspecting party will provide the aircraft used in the overflight; however, the host nation may require that one of its aircraft be used. Prior to their use, all aircraft and sensor suites must undergo certification inspec-tions. The number of flights each country can conduct and must re-ceive is limited on the basis of negotiated annual quotas. The United States' quota is 42 overflights per year; however, during the first three years only 31 are permitted annually. Any state may ac-quire the data from any overflight.

The **treaty entered into force** on 1 January 2002 after the fi-nal two states (**Russia** and **Belarus**) deposited their instruments of ratification. There are currently 30 parties to the treaty. The treaty is of unlimited duration with an initial review after three years and at five-year intervals thereafter.

TREATY OF PARIS (1956). The peace treaty that ended the Crimean War also demilitarized the Black Sea, including both the **Russian** and Turkish coastlines that front it.

TREATY OF PELINDABA. *See* AFRICAN NUCLEAR WEAPON FREE ZONE.

TREATY ON THE PRINCIPLES GOVERNING THE ACTIVI-TIES OF STATES IN THE EXPLORATION AND USE OF OUTER SPACE, INCLUDING THE MOON AND OTHER CELESTIAL BODIES. *See* OUTER SPACE TREATY.

TREATY ON THE PROHIBITION OF THE EMPLACEMENT OF NUCLEAR WEAPONS AND OTHER WEAPONS OF MASS DESTRUCTION ON THE SEABED AND THE OCEAN FLOOR AND IN THE SUBSOIL THEREOF. *See* SEABED TREATY.

TREATY OF RAROTONGA. *See* SOUTH PACIFIC NUCLEAR FREE ZONE.

TREATY OF ST. GERMAIN (1919). The peace **treaty** between the victorious Allied powers and Austria at the end of World War I. The Treaty of St. Germain established Austria's borders (as well as adjusting the borders of several neighbors and creating additional new states, including Hungary, Czechoslovakia, and Yugoslavia) as the Austro-Hungarian empire broke apart. Signed 10 September 1919 in Paris, it was a peace and **disarmament** treaty forced upon the losing side.

TREATY OF TLATELOLCO. *See* LATIN AMERICAN NUCLEAR WEAPON FREE ZONE.

TREATY OF VERSAILLES (1919). The Treaty of Versailles was signed in **France** on 28 June 1919. Its primary purpose was to de-militarize Germany following World War I. It put Germany under the Allies' thumb, demilitarized the Rhineland, limited the size and capability of German military forces, fortifications, and naval and aerial forces. It also demanded German reparations to its former enemies. History now shows that such repressive measures do not necessarily work. World War II began just 20 years later—largely as a result, say many analysts, of German revulsion to the strict lim-its imposed by the Versailles Treaty.

TRIAD. The collective description of the three major component cate-gories of **United States** and **Soviet Union** nuclear forces: **intercon-**

tinental ballistic missiles, **submarine-launched ballistic missiles**, and **strategic bombers**. The purpose of having such disparate delivery means for **strategic nuclear weapons** was to ensure that at least one method would survive in the event of an adversary's sneak attack. Technological advances might allow an adversary to subvert or overcome one leg of the triad, but the odds were against that happening against all three legs.

In the 2002 **Nuclear Posture Review** the United States unveiled a new strategic triad. In the reformulation of this classic term, the United States now considers the military offensive strike capabilities to form one leg of the triad (bombers, missiles, and submarines); the other two legs are strategic defenses and an enhanced infrastructure that supports the first two legs.

TRIDENT. The newest and largest class of U.S. nuclear **strategic missile submarine** (SSBN), capable of carrying up to 24 **submarine-launched ballistic missiles** (SLBM), each tested with up to 14 **multiple independently targetable reentry vehicles** (MIRV) carrying **nuclear warheads**. The **Strategic Arms Reduction Treaty** (START I), however, limits the total number of **warheads** that the SSBN fleet can carry, as well as the number of MIRVed warheads allowed on each missile. The **United States** Trident fleet consists of 18 boats, the first launched in 1981. **Great Britain** has also purchased four Trident submarines for its **strategic** nuclear **deterrent** mission.

The Trident also identifies the SLBM missile that is loaded on to the boat. Two variants of Trident missile have seen service in the U.S. and British fleets: the C-4 (Trident I) and D-5 (Trident II). The C-4 was initially deployed on the **Poseidon** and Trident submarines that had carried the Poseidon missile, but the D-5 was installed solely on Ohio-class Trident submarines. The latter is much improved, with greater range (up to 4,500 miles) and accuracy. The first eight Trident SSBNs are being retrofitted to carry the Trident II missile. In addition, four early Trident boats are being converted to conventional roles as guided missile submarines (SSGN) in order to meet military needs of the post-**Cold War** era and to comply with the warhead limits in the 2002 **Strategic Offensive Reductions Treaty**.

TRIGGER LIST. A compilation of items that, due to their advanced or sensitive nature, are restricted from sale or transfer to certain states by **export controls**. Trigger lists are used by national export control agencies and with such multinational groups as the **Nuclear Suppliers Group**, the **Wassenaar Arrangement**, and the **Australia Group**.

TRILATERAL AGREEMENT (1994). An agreement between the **United States, Russia,** and **Ukraine** signed in **Moscow** on 14 January 1994 that promised Ukraine financial and security assistance as a means of persuading its parliament to ratify the **Strategic Arms Reduction Treaty** (START I) and the **Nuclear Non-Proliferation Treaty** (NPT). Ukraine did sign both treaties on 3 February 1994 and ratified them on 5 December of that year, thus allowing START I to **enter into force**.

TRINITY TEST. The world's initial test of an **atomic bomb**. The 14 July 1945 test by the **United States** was the fulfillment of the goals of the **Manhattan Project** and was conducted at a test site code-named "Trinity" in the New Mexico dessert. The success of this **plutonium implosion device** led directly to the employment of a similar bomb on **Nagasaki**, Japan, three weeks later. (The bomb dropped on **Hiroshima** was a **gun-type nuclear weapon** that used **uranium**, which had not been previously tested.)

TRIP WIRE. A method of warning of the approach of prey or an enemy. The concept was extrapolated to American military forces based in Germany during the **Cold War**. The idea was that these forces would be the first to verify an assault by Soviet or **Warsaw Pact** forces into the **North Atlantic Treaty Organization** (NATO) territory and would lead to more serious consequences, including potential **escalation** to **nuclear weapons** use by the West in order to stop the attack.

TRIPARTITE DECLARATION (1950). In an effort to further stabilize the Middle East Armistice Agreements, and to control the flow of arms to the region, on 25 May 1950 **France, Great Britain,** and the **United States** signed an **agreement** not to supply weapons to a state harboring aggressive designs. They also agreed to take action both within and outside the **United Nations** to prevent any change in the armistice lines. *See also* NEAR EAST ARMS COORDINATING COMMITTEE.

TRUMAN, HARRY S. (1884-1972). U.S. president from 1945-1951. Truman became president upon the death of **Franklin Roosevelt**

just prior to the end of World War II. As president, Truman oversaw the first use of **atomic weapons** on Japan, the beginnings of the **Cold War,** the creation of the **North Atlantic Treaty Organization** (NATO), and the Korean War.

TURKISH STRAITS PACTS (1805-1936). During the 19th century international affairs often revolved around "the eastern question," in which the competition for influence and power in the Middle East led most major world powers to the straits between the Mediterranean and Black Seas. **Russia** wanted to restrict passage to the Black Sea, while most other powers wanted unfettered access. In 1805, the Ottoman Empire granted to the Russian Navy special permission to pass through the Turkish Straits as both empires fought Napoleon. In 1833 the Turks closed the straits to all but Russian vessels. The 1841 Convention of the Straits closed them to all warships provided Turkey was at peace. Following the Crimean War, in 1856 the **Treaty of Paris** instituted a regime that demilitarized the Black Sea, the straits, and the Turkish and Russian shores. Russia repudiated the Treaty following the Franco-Prussian War in 1870. The 1871 Pontus Treaty closed the straits to all foreign warships. This situation lasted until they were reopened following World War I. The Turks were unhappy with the initial peace treaty and renegotiated their position in the Treaty of Lausanne in 1923, which recognized freedom of navigation during peacetime. An International Straits Commission was created under the auspices of the **League of Nations.** In 1936 Turkey received permission to remilitarize the straits in the face of the League of Nation's failure to provide its protection.

TWO-TRACK DECISION. *See* DUAL-TRACK DECISION.

TYPHOON SUBMARINE. A Soviet nuclear-powered missile-launching submarine first deployed in the early 1980s. The size of a World War II aircraft carrier, the Typhoon carried a large number of **submarine-launched ballistic missiles** that could reach North America while the boat was sitting in its home port. Following the end of the **Cold War,** Typhoons have seen service as supply vehicles for **Russia's** Arctic Ocean ports.

U

U-2 AIRCRAFT. A U.S. high-altitude, single-engine **reconnaissance** aircraft capable of carrying multiple sensors for a considerable period aloft. One of the earliest "spy planes," the U-2 first flew in 1955. With upgrades, it has been in the **U.S. Air Force** inventory ever since. It can fly as high as 70,000 feet. In one famous incident a U-2 carrying Frances Gary Powers was shot down over the **Soviet Union** in 1960 and the pilot put on trial for espionage. During the 1962 **Cuban missile crisis** it was U-2 photos that provided the proof of Soviet missile deployments.

UKRAINE. One of four republics of the **Soviet Union** in which **nuclear weapons**, components, and systems were present at the time of the USSR's dissolution in 1991. According to an agreement with **Russia** and the **United States** in 1994, all of those nuclear weapons were consolidated under Russia's control by 1996 and Ukraine acceded to the **Nuclear Nonproliferation Treaty** as a **non-nuclear weapons state**.

UNACCEPTABLE DAMAGE. The degree of damage anticipated from an enemy **second strike** that would be sufficient to deter one from launching a **first strike**.

UNDERGROUND EXPLOSIONS. Originally employed during the 1960s by the **United States** and **Soviet Union** in an attempt to obscure **nuclear weapon tests** and eliminate atmospheric pollution and **radiation** caused by atmospheric tests. *See* UNDERGROUND TESTING.

UNDERGROUND TESTING. Intentionally exploding weapons (normally **nuclear weapons**) to test some aspect of their design or to confirm the reliability of the stockpile by testing a randomly selected weapon. Such testing was originally done outdoors, but the **Limited Test Ban Treaty** of 1963 drove testing underground to preclude the escape of **radiation**. Testing was further limited to explosions of less than 150 kilotons yield by the 1974 **Threshold Test Ban Treaty**. The **United States** and **Great Britain** conducted most of their underground nuclear tests at the **Nevada Test Site**; the **Soviet Union** had underground test facilities on the island of Novya Zemyla in the Arctic Ocean.

UNEXPLODED ORDNANCE (UXO). The ammunition, artillery shells, bombs, missiles, and other explosive material held by a military but unused during a conflict and left on the battlefield. The abandonment of unexploded ordnance is associated with the injury and death of innocent civilians, as they accidentally set off the weaponry while cleaning up the battlefield after the conflict.

UNILATERAL INITIATIVES. Self-limiting measures taken by one party on its own volition, not as a result of a finalized formal **agreement**, that reduce tensions. Such measures, normally conservative in scope, are intended to evoke a reciprocal response from other parties and thus create a climate and trend toward easing of tensions. *See* PRESIDENTIAL NUCLEAR INITIATIVES; UNILATERAL RECIPROCAL CUTS.

UNILATERAL RECIPROCAL CUTS. Self-limiting measures taken by one party not as a requirement of a formal **agreement** but in positive, reciprocal response to another party's **unilateral initiative**.

UNION OF SOVIET SOCIALIST REPUBLICS (USSR). *Soyuz Sovetskikh Sotsialisticheskikh Respublik*, or *CCCP* in Cyrillic, more commonly known as the **Soviet Union**. Formed after the Bolshevik Revolution in 1918. While officially a union of 15 socialist states, the USSR was dominated by **Russia.** After the end of World War II, Communist Party Chairman **Joseph Stalin** solidified the USSR's effective control over Eastern Europe by establishing the **Warsaw Pact.** For the next 50 years, the Soviet Union would lead Eastern Europe in the **Cold War** against the United States and the **North Atlantic Treaty Organization** (NATO). Because of the immense destructive power of **nuclear weapons**, and following several decades of unconstrained growth in each side's nuclear arsenal, the USSR and **United States** entered into a series of **arms control regimes** that limited the offensive and defensive capabilities of both sides. These moves stabilized the situation between the two powers and created a relationship based on **mutual assured destruction** (MAD). Although the USSR fought a series of "proxy-wars" with the United States in Korea and Vietnam, MAD was stable and secure enough to prevent an all-out nuclear holocaust that both sides had at one time assumed was inevitable. Because of its planned economy, the USSR grew increasingly incapable of keeping up with the West economically or military. The Cold War ended in 1989 and the Soviet Union was dissolved in 1991.

UNITED KINGDOM (UK). The United Kingdom of Great Britain and Northern Ireland is a mid-sized European power and one of the world's five declared nuclear powers, or **nuclear weapons states**. During the 19th century Great Britain was arguably the world's leading power, but its status and strength diminished considerably following the two world wars of the 20th century. A permanent member of the **United Nations** Security Council, Britain was a partner in the **United States Manhattan Project** and had tested its own **nuclear weapons** by 1952. It is a signatory of nearly every major international **arms control treaty**, is a member of the **North Atlantic Treaty Organization** (NATO), and is one of the United States' closest allies.

UNITED NATIONS (UN). The global intergovernmental organization that was created in 1945 with the signing of the UN Charter. Maintaining the peace is its principal goal. Its major bodies include a General Assembly consisting of all member states and a more exclusive Security Council with five permanent members: **China**, **France**, **Russian Federation**, the **United Kingdom**, and the **United States**, as well as an additional 10 rotating members from the general membership. The UN's headquarters are located in New York City. Its primary **arms control** organization is the **Conference on Disarmament** (CD). Many of the current arms control **treaties** and **regimes** began as discussion items in the UN's hallways, in discussions of the General Assembly's **Disarmament Commission**, or at the CD in **Geneva**.

Article 1 of the UN Charter gives the United Nations the responsibility for bringing about by peaceful means, and in conformity with the principles of justice and international law, adjustment or settlement of international disputes or situations that might lead to a breach of the peace. The member states have a duty to resolve their disputes by peaceful means. This principle, from Article 2 of the United Nations Charter, has since been incorporated into general or customary international law and reaffirmed in various precedents, including the 1970 UN General Assembly Friendly Relations Declaration. Parties can seek resolution of disputes through means of their choosing, including **negotiation**, inquiry, mediation, conciliation, arbitration, judicial settlement, or regional agreements or arrangements. As a general rule the UN suggests that legal disputes be referred to the International Court of Justice (ICJ). The four principal organs of the UN for conflict resolution include the ICJ, the General Assembly, the Security Council, and the Secretariat. The General Assembly is meant to be a discussion forum, whereas the Security Council acts as the executive agency for actively intervening in a situation, should the members decide that is necessary. The secretary-general may also elevate any situation to the appropriate agency if he deems it is serious enough to merit attention.

A common method for dealing with **proliferation, disarmament**, and regional disputes has been to create a regional organization under UN auspices. These include the **Organization for Security and Cooperation in Europe** (OSCE), the Dayton Framework Agreement for Peace (based on the **Dayton Accords**), the Organization of American States, and the Economic Community of West African States (ECOWAS). In addition, the United Nations family includes numerous organizations dedicated to topical issues, such as the Food and Agriculture Organization and the **World Health Organization**.

UNITED NATIONS ARMS EMBARGO. In December 1977 the **United Nations** passed Security Council Resolution 421 in an effort to extend political and military pressure on South Africa by putting in place an international arms embargo. This resulted from a growing international outcry against South Africa's refusal to abandon its racist policies known as apartheid.

UNITED NATIONS CONFERENCE ON DISARMAMENT (CD). The Conference on Disarmament is the independent negotiating body of the **United Nations** for **arms control treaties**. It is one of three international **disarmament** forums (with the **UN Disarmament Commission** and the UN General Assembly **First Committee**), but the only body that negotiates treaties. The conference consists of 66 members, including all five **nuclear weapon states**. Additionally, numerous nations are allowed to participate as nonmembers. It has been meeting under different names since its creation in 1954: the Subcommittee on Disarmament (1954-1960); the Ten-Nation Committee on Disarmament (1960-1962); the **Eighteen-Nation Committee on Disarmament** (1962-1968); the Conference of the Committee on Disarmament (1969-1978); and finally the Conference on Disarmament (1979-). Although they maintain an open agenda, participants normally discuss **weapons of mass destruction, conventional weapons**, reduction of military budgets and armed forces, and **confidence-building measures**. Most of the work on these topics is accomplished in *ad hoc* committees. The CD is located in **Geneva**, Switzerland.

UNITED NATIONS DISARMAMENT COMMISSION (UNDC). A committee within the **United Nations** General Assembly that includes all UN member states. Created in 1952 as a committee of the Security Council, its role was enhanced and its membership made universal following the 1978 **UN Special Session on Disarmament**. It is a deliberative body that meets in regular session to consider all aspects of global **disarmament** issues, including nuclear disarmament, space arms control, **nuclear weapons free zones**, conventional **arms transfers**, **verification** and **compliance** issues, the **proliferation** of **weapons of mass destruction**, **confidence and security building measures**, **transparency**, and other disarmament proposals from the member states. The UNDC has no specific agenda. Its mandate is to consider and make recommendations on various problems in the field of disarmament and to follow up on relevant decisions. Its recommendations are decided primarily by consensus and are made to the General Assembly.

UNITED NATIONS FIRST COMMITTEE. One of six **United Nations** General Assembly committees. The First Committee handles **disarmament** and international security matters including the regulation of armaments. The First Committee considers topics that are also the subject of **negotiations** elsewhere, such as the **Comprehensive Test Ban Treaty**, **chemical weapons**, **biological weapons**, conventional arms sales, an **arms race** in outer space, and related topics. Each year it passes some 50 resolutions on these subjects, providing an opportunity for the international community to debate and register opinions and positions on all disarmament questions under discussion.

UNITED NATIONS MONITORING VERIFICATION AND INSPECTION COMMISSION (UNMOVIC). The **United Nations** Security Council established the United Nations Monitoring Verification and Inspection Commission on 17 December 1999 to undertake the responsibilities of the **United Nations Special Commission on Iraq** (UNSCOM). Following Iraqi insistence, UNSCOM withdrew its staff from **Iraq** on 16 December 1998, and ceased to function. UN Security Council Resolution 1284 created UNMOVIC to dissuade Iraq from its program to acquire **weapons**

of mass destruction (chemical, biological, and nuclear weapons and missiles with a range of more than 150 kilometers), and to operate a system of ongoing monitoring and verification with the International Atomic Energy Agency (IAEA). UNMOVIC was to check Iraq's compliance with its obligations not to develop or possess weapons prohibited to it by the UN Security Council. From its creation until 27 November 2002, UNMOVIC carried out no inspections due to Iraq's refusal to cooperate with inspection teams. On 16 September 2002, however, following UN Resolution 1441, Iraq decided to allow the return of UNMOVIC and IAEA inspectors without conditions. Inspections resumed on 27 November 2002. UNMOVIC produced an interim report to the Security Council on 9 January 2003, after completing 250 inspections. In making the report, Hans Blix noted that the Iraqi's most recent declaration to UNMOVIC was incomplete and left many questions unanswered. UNMOVIC evacuated its staff from Iraq on 17 March 2003, following Iraq's rejection of President George W. Bush's ultimatum to disarm. On 19 March a U.S.-led coalition invaded Iraq to eliminate suspected Iraqi WMD and missile programs and remove Saddam Hussein from power.

UNITED NATIONS REGISTER OF CONVENTIONAL ARMS. The United Nations General Assembly adopted Resolution 46/36L on 9 December 1991. Entitled "Transparency in Armaments" this resolution established an annual Register of Conventional Arms. UN member states were requested to provide data every calendar year on imports and exports of weapons in seven categories. These included the five categories found in the Conventional Forces in Europe Treaty (CFE) (tanks, armored combat vehicles, artillery pieces, attack helicopters, and combat aircraft) as well as warships and missiles/missile launchers. No verification provisions accompanied the resolution, but its sponsors hoped that increased transparency would encourage restraint by both buyers and sellers and would lead to public pressure on those states that supported irresponsible or destabilizing arms transfers.

UNITED NATIONS SPECIAL COMMISSION ON IRAQ (UN-SCOM). The United Nations Special Commission on Iraq was established in 1991 in order to enforce the peace agreement that ended the Persian Gulf War. Saddam Hussein, the dictator of Iraq, had agreed to destroy a long list of weapons and the capabilities to produce them. UNSCOM was formed to assist the International

Atomic Energy Agency (IAEA). Its mandate was to provide evidence of the destruction, removal, or demilitarization of Iraq's nuclear facilities and **ballistic missiles** with a range greater than 150 kilometers, including the **launchers**, production, related major parts, and repair facilities of such missiles. UNSCOM also was charged with undertaking a **monitoring** program to ensure that Iraq could never reconstitute its chemical, biological, and nuclear arsenal. After 83 inspections over seven years, UNSCOM was forced to leave the country and curtail its inspection mission in December 1998. In December 1999 the UN Security Council adopted Resolution 1284, replacing UNSCOM with the **United Nations Monitoring Verification and Inspection Commission**.

UNITED NATIONS SPECIAL SESSIONS ON DISARMAMENT. In 1959, the **United Nations** General Assembly adopted Resolution 1378 stating its hope for the early achievement of **general and complete global disarmament** under effective international control. The General Assembly has had three follow-up Special Sessions on Disarmament so far: in 1978, 1982, and 1988. While the first Special Session ended with an **agreement**, subsequent sessions have been unable to reach similar conclusions.

UNITED STATES AIR FORCE (USAF). The aerospace component of the **United States** armed forces. The nation's **intercontinental ballistic missiles, strategic bombers,** and **air-launched cruise missiles,** as well as most of its **nonstrategic nuclear weapons, strategic defenses,** and **national technical means,** are developed, maintained, and deployed by the U.S. Air Force. *See also* AIR-LAUNCHED CRUISE MISSILE; ATLAS MISSILE; B-1 BOMBER; B-2 BOMBER; B-52 BOMBER; HEAVY BOMBER; MINUTEMAN MISSILE; PEACEKEEPER MISSILE; PEACE-KEEPER RAIL GARRISON; NATIONAL AIRBORNE OPERATIONS CENTER; NATIONAL EMERGENCY AIRBORNE COMMAND POST; NUCLEAR AND COUNTERPROLIFERATION DIRECTORATE; STRATEGIC AIR COMMAND; TITAN MISSILE; U-2 AIRCRAFT.

UNITED STATES OF AMERICA (USA). The **United States** is the leading global **superpower**. It developed the world's first **atomic weapons** in 1945 as a result of the **Manhattan Project**, and emerged from World War II as one of the two leading nations on earth. It faced the **Soviet Union** through the **Cold War**, which required a large investment in **weapons of mass destruction** in order to deter what it saw as Soviet expansionist tendencies and a burgeoning weapons arsenal of its own. Beginning in the 1960s both states initiated a series of formal **arms control negotiations** that led to limits on both offensive and defensive **strategic** weaponry and formalized the strategic relationship with the Soviet Union known as **mutual assured destruction** (MAD). This approach lasted until the end of the Cold War in 1989. While the United States has typically been a leading proponent of new arms control initiatives, in recent years it has taken a more unilateral path to national security. As a result, it has withdrawn from the **Anti-Ballistic Missile Treaty**, refused to ratify the **Comprehensive Test Ban Treaty**, and blocked a verification protocol to the **Biological and Toxin Weapons Convention**. At the same time it continues to pursue reduced levels of strategic nuclear weapons with **Russia**, signing the **Strategic Offensive Reductions Treaty** in 2002.

UNITED STATES ARMY (USA). The primary land-based component of the **United States** Armed Forces. Thousands of **nonstrategic nuclear weapons** of multiple types were developed, maintained, and deployed by the U.S. Army from the early 1950s until the early 1990s. Today's Army has no nuclear mission, but remains involved in **arms control verification** and **compliance**. *See also* GROUND-LAUNCHED CRUISE MISSILE; JUPITER MISSILE; LANCE MISSILE; NIKE MISSILE; NIKE-ZEUS ABM SYSTEM; PERSHING I MISSILE; PERSHING II MISSILE.

UNITED STATES NAVY (USN). The maritime component of the **United States** Armed Forces. The nation's **submarine-launched ballistic missiles, sea-launched cruise missiles**, and some **nonstrategic nuclear weapons** are developed, maintained, and deployed by the USN, primarily on its fleet of ballistic missile submarines. *See also* NAVY OFFICE OF TREATY IMPLEMENTATION; POLARIS; POSEIDON; SUBMARINE ROCKET; SUBMARINE-LAUNCHED BALLISTIC MISSILE (SLBM); SUBMARINE, BALLISTIC MISSILE (SSBN); TRIDENT; TOMAHAWK MISSILE.

UPPSALA DECLARATION ON NUCLEAR FREE ZONES. At an international seminar in Uppsala, Sweden, in September 2000, some 50 renowned scholars, peace activists, and diplomats called for the creation of more **nuclear weapon free zones** around the globe, particularly in Northeast Asia, South Asia, the Middle East, and Central Europe. *See also* NUCLEAR-WEAPON FREE ZONES; PEACE MOVEMENTS.

URANIUM (U). A natural **radioactive** element used, in various forms, as a fuel for nuclear power reactors or as a base material for **nuclear bombs**. Found in many countries around the world, its value is marginal in natural form. In order to be useful as a weapon it must first be **enriched** through a complex industrial process.

U.S. NORTHERN COMMAND (USNORTHCOM). A **United States** unified command responsible for the **homeland defense** of North America and the Caribbean. Created in 2002, it was declared fully operational on 11 September 2003, two years after the terrorist attacks on the United States that began the global war on **terrorism**. Located in Colorado Springs, Colorado, USNORTHCOM has a two-fold mission: to provide military protection of its area of responsibility (including **deterrence, dissuasion**, detection, and defeat of adversary attacks) and to provide military assistance to civil authorities upon their request in order to help with consequence management. It coordinates its actions with the **Department of Homeland Security**.

U.S.-SOVIET BILATERAL AGREEMENT OF 1990. At the **Washington Summit** in June 1990 the **United States** and **Soviet Union** agreed to a number of bilateral understandings that had been discussed at the 1989 **Malta Summit**, including a **chemical weapons** destruction plan that formed the basis for the eventual **Chemical Weapons Convention** (1993); a series of **nuclear testing** protocols dealing with **verification** measures, including **on-site inspections**; a renewed commitment to the peaceful uses of atomic energy; and a series of additional educational and cultural exchange programs.

U.S. SPACE COMMAND (USSPACECOM). U.S. Space Command (USSPACECOM) was created as a unified command in 1985 to serve as the organizational focus for all U.S. military space activities, including nuclear launch warning, military **surveillance** and communications satellite control, and testing and evaluation. Originally headquartered at Peterson AFB, Colorado, it also uses nearby Schriever AFB (originally the test bed facility for the **Strategic Defense Initiative**) and **Cheyenne Mountain** (home of the **North American Aerospace Defense Command**, or NORAD), as well as many other far-flung sites around the world. In October 2002 USS-PACECOM was absorbed into **U.S. Strategic Command** in Omaha, Nebraska.

U.S. STRATEGIC COMMAND (USSTRATCOM). The **United States** military's unified command that plans for and would employ **nuclear weapons** systems upon the authenticated order of the **National Command Authorities** in the event of total war. Created in June 1992, USSTRATCOM was the successor organization to **Strategic Air Command**, which had held the same missions since 1947. USSTRATCOM includes military servicemen from all the services, but primarily from the **U.S. Air Force** and **U.S. Navy**, the two services that own the **strategic** nuclear delivery systems (**heavy bombers, intercontinental ballistic missiles**, and **submarine-launched ballistic missiles**). In 2002 USSTRATCOM absorbed **U.S. Space Command** (USSPACECOM) and its missions of global warning and assessment, as well as the responsibility for integrating global **missile defense**. USSTRATCOM is based at Offutt AFB, Omaha, Nebraska.

V

VACCINE. A preparation made from weakened or dead **bacteria** or **viruses** that causes the human body to produce **antibodies** that provide **immunity** to that **organism**.

VANCE, CYRUS (1917-). American diplomat and secretary of state under President **Jimmy Carter**, 1977-1980. Vance emphasized "quiet diplomacy," **détente**, and closer relations with the **Soviet Union**. He helped successfully achieve the **Camp David Accords** between Israel and Egypt in 1978 and the **Strategic Arms Limitation Treaty** (SALT II) in 1979.

VECTOR. The **organism** that carries and transmits a **virus** or other **microorganism**. Also the path of a disease used to trace its origin and determine whether it is of natural development or is the result of a biological attack.

VERIFICATION. Monitoring and evaluating a party's **compliance** with provisions of an **arms control agreement**.

VERIFICATION COORDINATING COMMITTEE (VCC). A committee consisting of all members of the **North Atlantic Treaty Organization** (NATO) that deals with matters of conventional **arms control implementation** and **verification**.

VERSAILLES TREATY. *See* TREATY OF VERSAILLES.

VERTICAL ESCALATION. The theory that, in conflicts between two nuclear powers of roughly equal capability, the conflict will quickly escalate from using conventional weapons to using **nuclear weapons**. This is visualized as a vertical climb up the ladder of escalation.

VIENNA CENTER FOR CONFLICT PREVENTION (CPC). Established in 1990 by the members of the **Conference on Security and Cooperation in Europe** (CSCE), since renamed the **Organization on Security and Cooperation in Europe** (OSCE). The CPC supports OSCE missions in the field, facilitates information exchanges as agreed under certain **confidence- and security building measures**, and organizes the annual meeting that assesses implementation of **Vienna Document** commitments.

VIENNA DOCUMENTS (1990, 1992, 1994, 1999). *See* CONFERENCE ON SECURITY COOPERATION IN EUROPE ; CONFIDENCE- AND SECURITY BUILDING MEASURES.

VIRUS. A submicroscopic **agent** that can infect animals, plants, and bacteria but can only reproduce within a host. Also a computer program that can infect and corrupt individual computers and networks.

VLADIVOSTOK ACCORD (1974). An understanding between President **Gerald Ford** and Chairman **Leonid Brezhnev**, signed at a summit meeting in Vladivostok, **Soviet Union**, which established the basic numerical framework for the **Strategic Arms Limitation Treaty** (SALT II)—although it took an additional five years of **negotiations** to arrive at that formal **agreement**.

VOMITING AGENT. A chemical **agent** that causes a strong irritation in the upper respiratory tract resulting in irritation to the eyes as well as violent, uncontrollable sneezing, coughing, nausea, and vomiting, often for up to several hours.

VOTKINSK, RUSSIA. A small city in Russia's Ural Mountains and the location of the **Soviet Union's** production facility for its SS-20 **intermediate-range nuclear missiles**. One of the two portal monitoring facilities (the other being the Hercules rocket plant in **Magna, Utah**, in the **United States**) as declared in the 1987 **Intermediate-Range Nuclear Forces Treaty** (INF). Beginning in June 1988, U.S. inspectors from the **On-Site Inspection Agency** spent 13 years monitoring the movement of equipment in and out of the Votkinsk machining facility to ensure that the Soviets (and later, Russians) were in **compliance** with the INF Treaty.

VULNERABILITY. The inability of a unit, a geographic area, or a population center to prevent an attack or to absorb a direct or indirect attack while retaining its effectiveness or viability. A vulnerable society without **strategic defenses** was deemed a requirement for **stability** through **mutual assured destruction** during the **Cold War**.

W

WALK IN THE WOODS. An informal meeting to exchange possible negotiating positions that could lead to an agreement in stalled **arms control negotiations**. The first occurred between the U.S. and Soviet ambassadors at the **Intermediate-Range Nuclear Forces** talks in Geneva in 1982. After the Soviets pulled out of the **Nuclear and Space Talks** in 1984, the **United States** instituted a series of informal bilateral discussions between the two chief negotiators that led to a return to formal **negotiations**. These informal discussions earned the sobriquet "walks in the woods" to denote their unusually casual approach to a normally staid series of formal talks.

WALTZ, KENNETH (1924-). Author and academic at the University of California whose writings on **deterrence** and nuclear forces have had considerable influence on American thinking. In the early 1990s he proposed a contentious thesis that the world would be safer if more countries had **nuclear weapons**, because it would enhance multilateral deterrence. **Proliferation**, therefore, was not necessarily a bad thing.

WARFIGHTING STRATEGY. A nuclear strategy that focuses on fighting and winning a nuclear war. This contrasts with a focus on maintaining and furthering **deterrence** and **strategic stability**.

WARHEAD. The component of a weapon system that disables or destroys the target. Warheads can be nuclear, biological, chemical, radiological, or conventional high explosive.

WARNKE, PAUL (1920-2001). Undersecretary of defense during the **Lyndon B. Johnson** administration. A **dove** who argued against stockpiling **nuclear weapons**, Warnke was the chief U.S. negotiator in the **Strategic Arms Limitation Talks** with the **Soviet Union** and headed the **Arms Control and Disarmament Agency** under President **Jimmy Carter.**

WARSAW PACT. The **Cold War** Eastern European security alliance formed as a counter to the **North Atlantic Treaty Organization** (NATO) in 1955 and disbanded with the dissolution of the **Soviet Union** in 1991. Its member states were Bulgaria, Czechoslovakia, East Germany, Hungary, Poland, Romania, and the **Soviet Union**.

WARSAW TREATY (1970). A treaty signed on 7 December 1970 between Poland and West Germany that recognized the Oder-Neisse Line as the formal border between Poland and Germany. In return, Poland allowed the repatriation of 300,000 ethnic Germans from former German territory. This was one of the concrete results of West German Chancellor **Willy Brandt's** policy of *Ostpolitik.*

WARSAW TREATY ORGANIZATION (WTO). *See* WARSAW PACT.

WASHINGTON NAVAL CONFERENCE. The 1921-1922 meetings that resulted in **negotiation** of the **Washington Naval Treaty** (also called the Five Power Treaty).

WASHINGTON NAVAL TREATY (1922). The Washington naval limitation system included the 1922 Washington Naval Treaty and the **London Naval Treaties** of 1930 and 1936 (and the 1937 protocols). The Washington Treaty (also called the Five Power Treaty) was signed on 6 February 1922 by the **United States, United Kingdom, France,** Italy, and Japan. It limited naval armaments, specifically capital class ships, according to a specific matrix that assigned total allowable metric tons of displacement to each **state party**. The **treaty** attempted to regulate warfare by limiting the lethality of the weapons allowed (battleships and aircraft carriers); their size; and their weaponry (gun caliber size). It included detailed lists (by name) of which ships were to be allowed, which must be scrapped, and which could be built. The 1936 treaty included extensive provisions for advance notification and the exchange of information.

WASHINGTON SUMMIT. There have been several major international **summit meetings** held in Washington, D.C. Among the more important recent such meetings were the **Washington Naval Conference**, 1921-1922; the **North Atlantic Treaty Organization** (NATO) founding meeting, which led to the **Washington Treaty**, signed 1949; and the NATO Summit which resulted in the New Strategic Concept in 1999.

WASHINGTON TREATY (1949). Also called the North Atlantic Treaty, it was signed by 12 states in Washington, D.C., on 4 April 1949 in a move that created the **North Atlantic Treaty Organization** (NATO). The treaty calls for common defense between the member nations; an attack on one is considered an attack on all. NATO was created primarily to meet the expansionist and belligerent aims of the **Soviet Union** in Europe. The original signatories were Belgium, Canada, Denmark, **France**, Iceland, Italy, Luxembourg, the Netherlands, Norway, Portugal, the **United Kingdom**, and the **United States**. NATO has since grown to 26 states (as of mid-2004).

WASSENAAR ARRANGEMENT. On 18 December 1995, 28 nations met in Wassenaar, The Netherlands, to set up an export control organization known as the "Wassenaar Arrangement on Controls for Conventional Arms and Dual-Use Goods and Technologies." This post-**Cold War** successor **agreement** to the **Coordinating Committee for Multilateral Export Controls** (COCOM) was designed for broadened management of international trade in **proliferation**-sensitive materials. This was the first agreement to address both **conventional weapons** transfers and **dual-use** goods and technologies. It calls upon states to exchange data, notify other parties of violations of the controlled items list, and coordinate export licenses. Participation is voluntary. It does not automatically target exports to a specific state, but does seek to limit exports to states that represent a serious concern to the Wassenaar Arrangement participating states.

The participants agree to implement controls on technologies and conventional weapon systems from two lists: the List of Dual-Use Goods and Technologies, and the Munitions List. The lists are updated regularly. As of mid-2004 there were 33 member states.

WEAPON OF MASS DESTRUCTION (WMD). The term weapon of mass destruction was originally coined by the **Soviet Union**. While it has been widely used since the early 1960s, there is no standard definition as to its meaning. Most definitions of WMD consist of listing types of **biological, chemical, radiological,** or **nuclear weapons**. These four types of weapons can affect large areas and large numbers of people, especially when compared to **conventional weapons** targeted at specific soldiers, vehicles, or buildings. In addition, all four kinds of weapons can produce effects that spread far beyond their original target area and **contaminate** a large area for a long time after their use. *See also* BIOLOGICAL WEAPONS; CHEMICAL WEAPONS.

WEAPONIZATION. The specific manufacture of a **biological agent** for use as a **biological weapon**. Also the engineering process of mating a nuclear explosive device with its delivery system.

WEAPONS-GRADE MATERIAL. Material possessing the qualities needed to produce **nuclear weapons**; for example, **plutonium** or weapons-grade **highly enriched uranium** is at least 90 percent Uranium-235. *See also* ENRICHMENT; REPROCESSING; URANIUM.

WESTERN EUROPEAN UNION (WEU). The Western European Union was established by the Brussels Treaty of 1948. Member states are Belgium, Luxembourg, **France**, the Netherlands, Germany, Portugal, Greece, Spain, Italy, and the **United Kingdom**. Its primary functions were subsumed into the **North Atlantic Treaty Organization** (NATO) from 1949 until 1984, when the WEU was reborn as a form of collective Western European defense against the **Soviet Union** that was not dependent on control by the **United States**. The WEU has since engaged in various security and humanitarian relief programs in the Adriatic Sea, the Danube River, Mostar, Albania, Croatia, the Persian Gulf, and Kosovo.

WILSON, WOODROW (1856-1924). U.S. president from 1912 to 1920, he led the **United States** during World War I and was critical in shaping the **Treaty of Versailles,** which ended that conflict. He was also one of the founders of the post-war **League of Nations.** To his bitter disappointment, the United States did not follow his lead and ratify or join the League, which historians now claim was one reason it failed to prevent World War II.

WILSONIANISM. (Also called Wilsonism.) A belief in the progressive democratic principles held by **Woodrow Wilson,** including the right of national self-determination of all people.

WINDOW OF VULNERABILITY. A theory popular in the early 1980s that the **strategic** balance between the **United States** and the **Soviet Union** was shifting measurably in favor of the USSR, possibly leading that country to calculate that its best chance for success at a **first strike** attack had come and would not be replicable in the future. Such a situation would be destabilizing and could lead to war. To prevent this window from opening and tempting the Soviets, some American analysts thought, the United States had to deploy new weapons immediately. *See also* COMMITTEE ON THE PRESENT DANGER.

WORLD HEALTH ORGANIZATION (WHO). The World Health Organization, the **United Nations'** specialized agency for health, was established on 7 April 1948. The WHO's objective, as set out in its Constitution, is the attainment by all peoples of the highest possible level of health. Health is defined in the WHO's Constitution as a state of complete physical, mental, and social well being and not merely the absence of disease or infirmity. The WHO is governed by its 192 member states through the World Health Assembly.

WORLD DISARMAMENT CONFERENCE (1932-1934). An attempt to develop a general **disarmament treaty** that embraced all states and all categories of forces and weapons, while at the same strengthening the collective security system of the **League of Nations.** Sixty one nations participated in the **Geneva** meetings, at the time the largest gathering in the history of disarmament. The conference broke up after Adolf Hitler came to power in Germany, rejected the proposals, and began a rearmament program.

WORLD WAR I (1914-1918). The first truly modern conflict and in some perspectives merely the first half of a war that lasted over 30 years. More than eight million people were killed and over twenty-one million injured during World War I, which lasted for four years and took place primarily in Europe. World War I erupted at a time when advances in modern technology and logistics (such as railroads) created a synergistic effect, leading to mass human carnage. The use of a relatively new invention, the machine gun, and the ability to transport thousands of soldiers to the front contributed heavily to the high death rate. Although World War I is remembered for the advent of modern "gas warfare," bullets, bombs, and shells were responsible for most of the death and destruction suffered during the war.

The magnitude of casualties and loss from this conflict led to a movement to try to control war in the future, an effort that influenced international relations for a generation. This included limitations on types of weapons used (the **Geneva Protocol** on **chemical warfare**, the **Washington and London Naval Conferences**), a greater appreciation for national sovereignty (the Rapallo Treaty and the break-up of the Austro-Hungarian Empire), attempts at **coercive arms control** (the **Versailles Treaty** with its military restrictions on Germany and demilitarization of the Rhineland), and a more general approach to ensuring global peace through a commitment to peaceful conflict resolution and organizational initiatives (the **Kellogg-Briand Pact** and the **League of Nations**).

WORLD WAR II (1939-1945). World War II began with Germany's invasion of Poland in September 1939, although that was just the culminating event of a series of conflicts and aggressive foreign policy by several states during the 1930s. The first war fought on a truly global scale, the primary participants were Germany, Italy, and Japan on the Axis side (states ruled by fascist dictators) and the **United States, United Kingdom, France, China**, and most of the rest of the free world on the Allied side. The **Soviet Union** began the war as a partner with Germany but switched to the Allied side following Germany's surprise invasion of Russia in 1941. In many ways World War II can be seen as a continuation of unsatisfied national desires left over from **World War I**, including overly stringent restrictions on Germany imposed by the **Versailles Treaty**. Some 40 million people were killed during the war, which was fought primarily in Europe and North Africa, in the islands of the South Pacific, on the ocean seaways using submarine warfare, and in the skies over the major belligerents.

No state used gas warfare on European battlefields during World War II, despite several countries having large stockpiles of advanced **chemical weapons** at their disposal. The memories of horrific chemical attacks during World War I and the universally agreed proscriptions against their use apparently had some effect on the decisions whether to instigate gas or germ warfare. In the Pacific, however, Japan used biological and chemical agents against the Chinese military and civilians during the war.

The United States initiated the top secret **Manhattan Project** in September 1942 to build an **atomic bomb** before Germany could develop its own **nuclear weapon**. The undertaking was a massive and costly project engaging many top U.S., Canadian, and British scientists. After overcoming substantial scientific, technical, and practical obstacles, the project produced the weapons that were used on **Hiroshima** and **Nagasaki**, leading to Japan's surrender in August 1945. (Germany had surrendered in May 1945, before the bombs were ready.) The use of atomic weapons against two Japanese cities brought a rapid conclusion to hostilities in the Pacific. However, the development and use of atomic weapons, ushering in the nuclear age and a four-decade nuclear stand-off between the United States and the Soviet Union in the **Cold War** has remained the object of political, policy, and moral debate.

Allied success in this conflict led to the creation of the United Nations in yet another effort to prevent future wars of such magnitude. In addition, the development of nuclear weapons and other advanced technologies during the war led to a series of efforts to control or eliminate these weapons over the following decades, including **arms control treaties**, **peace movements**, and calls for global nuclear **disarmament**.

X

X-RAY LASER. A **directed-energy weapon** theoretically capable of shooting down air and space threats as part of a **ballistic missile defense** system. The concept of x-ray lasers began in the 1970s, when physicists realized that laser beams amplified with ions would have much higher energies than beams amplified using gases. Nuclear explosions were even envisioned as a power supply for these high-energy lasers. That vision became a reality at the time of the **Stra-**

tegic Defense Initiative of the 1980s, when x-ray laser beams initiated by nuclear explosives were generated underground at the **Nevada Test Site**. **Lawrence Livermore National Laboratory** produced the first laboratory demonstration of an x-ray laser in 1984.

Y

YELLOW RAIN. A lingering mystery of the **Cold War**. In September 1981 U.S. Secretary of State Alexander Haig accused the **Soviet Union** of supplying trichothecene mycotoxins (poisonous compounds made by fungal molds that infect grain), popularly known as yellow rain, to the Communist regimes in Vietnam and Laos for use as a **chemical weapon** in counterinsurgency warfare. Leading American scientists challenged the U.S. government's evidence for these allegations, however, and the controversy was never fully resolved. Some scientists claim that yellow rain is a natural yellow substance, perhaps bee feces, that occurs as a mist or as dew-like deposits and that resembles pollen. The U.S. government has never retracted its claim.

YELTSIN, BORIS (1931-). **Russian** president from 1991 to 1999, Yeltsin oversaw the transition period immediately following the **Cold War** for the Russian side. During his tenure Russia signed the **Strategic Arms Reduction Treaties** (START I and II) and undertook major **Presidential Nuclear Initiatives** with the **United States** with respect to **non-strategic nuclear weapons**.

YIELD. A measure of the force of a nuclear blast, usually expressed in terms of equivalency in tons of TNT. *See also* KILOTON; MEGATON.

Z

ZANGGER COMMITTEE. An informal group of over 30 states that seeks to restrict the export of nuclear materials, equipment, and technology solely to states that adhere to **International Atomic Energy Agency** (IAEA) **safeguards** and **inspections**. The Zangger Committee was formed in September 1974 to establish guidelines for implementing the export control provisions of the **Nuclear Non-**

Proliferation Treaty. Its official name is the **NPT Exporters Committee**.

The **"trigger list"** of relevant technologies compiled during meetings of the Zangger Committee is used as a guideline for nuclear export to apply to both members of the committee and to other suppliers. The committee developed a so-called trigger list of materials and equipment that triggers safeguards by the IAEA, items that might otherwise be used to develop a nuclear explosive. These include **plutonium**, **highly enriched uranium**, reactors, **reprocessing** and **enrichment** facilities, and associated equipment and supplies. The list is updated regularly. There are currently 34 states on the Zangger Committee, all of which (with the exception of **China**) are also members of the **Nuclear Suppliers Group**. *See also* WASSENAAR ARRANGEMENT.

ZERO OPTION. A nuclear **arms control negotiation** option that eliminates all of the weapons or system components under discussion.

ZONES OF PEACE. Internationally recognized and protected regions housing cultural or environmental highlights, or a group of people that are to be protected from normal political and military concerns.

Bibliography

This bibliography reflects a broad selection of literature addressing two of the core conceptual constructs of the Cold War: arms control and disarmament. For nearly three generations, policy development and intellectual advancement in the field of international relations have focused on the role of arms control and used the specialized language developed for that purpose.

The concept and theory of arms control was developed in the late 1950s and early 1960s by a small number of academic study groups meeting in the United States and Great Britain. The three seminal works on arms control, all published in 1961, were the results of these team efforts. *Strategy and Arms Control*, by Thomas Schelling and Morton Halperin (New York: Twentieth Century Fund, 1961), reflected the findings of a 1960 Summer Study group organized under the auspices of the American Academy of Arts and Sciences. This group of some 50 leading academic and professional intellectuals met for several sessions over the course of the summer near Boston, and their discussions led to several follow-on studies, one of which resulted in the Schelling and Halperin book. The basic premise of their book was that "cooperative arrangements with adversaries could have the same objectives as sensible military policies in reducing the likelihood of war." The authors were influenced by the work of another member of the summer study, Donald G. Brennan, who served as editor of *Arms Control, Disarmament, and National Security* (New York: George Braziller, 1961). Similarly, *The Control of the Arms Race: Disarmament and Arms Control in the Missile Age*, by Hedley Bull (New York: Frederick A. Praeger, 1961), was based on a series of symposia held at Oxford University and a conference by the Institute for Strategic Studies held at Worcester College, Oxford, in September 1960. These three works form the essential basis for understanding modern arms control theory.

It was not long after the first works on arms control were published that the literature was co-opted by the fields of strategic studies and international security. This was primarily an American preoccupation; European analysts focused more on disarmament, peace studies, and the like. Key works in arms control include the books and selected articles on the following list, in which we have attempted to identify the best, most comprehensive works in each category of this bibliography. The reader will note that many of these works were written in the early 1990s, when optimism about the future of arms control reached its zenith as a result of the dissolution of the Union of Soviet Socialist Republics and the end of the Cold War. By the late 1990s and early 2000s the total number of arms control publications had dropped drastically, and the theme of most of them was the demise of arms control as a viable concept in international relations. Whether this reversal of attitude is warranted is yet to be seen.

General Overview

For a general background and understanding of arms control, start with the three books discussed above. Then turn to more recent analyses of the field, including journal collections such as "Arms Control: Thirty Years On," a special edition of *Daedalus,* Winter 1991; Joseph S. Nye Jr., "Arms Control After the Cold War," *Foreign Affairs,* Winter 1989/1990; Harold Brown, "Is Arms Control Dead?" and Brad Roberts, "The Road Ahead for Arms Control," both in *The Washington Quarterly,* Spring 2000; and *Contemporary Nuclear Debates: Missile Defense, Arms Control, and the Arms Races in the Twenty-First Century,* a *Washington Quarterly* reader edited by Alexander T. J. Lennon (Cambridge, Mass: MIT Press, 2002). Good overall encyclopedic views of the topic include Richard Dean Burns, *Encyclopedia of Arms Control and Disarmament* (New York: Charles Scribner's Sons, 1993); Christopher Lamb, *How to Think About Arms Control, Disarmament, and Defense* (New York: Prentice Hall, 1988); Jeffrey A. Larsen and Gregory J. Rattray, *Arms Control Toward the 20th Century* (Boulder, Colo.: Lynne Rienner, 1996); and *Arms Control: Cooperative Security in a Changing Environment* (Boulder, Colo.: Lynne Rienner, 2002), also edited by Jeffrey A. Larsen. Good overview collections of treaties can be found in Thomas Graham Jr. and Damien J. LaVera, *Cornerstones of Security: Arms Control Treaties in the Nuclear Era* (Seattle: University of Washington Press, 2003), in the appendixes to *Arms Control* (Larsen), above, or on the U.S. State Department's website.

Historical

In order to more easily consider the history of negotiations, the chronology is divided into several periods related to specific treaties. Some of the best works in this field are personal memoirs written by the negotiators after the fact; these supply interesting anecdotes, vignettes, and behind-the-scenes stories not found in the offical documents. For the period of the Strategic Arms Limitation Talks in the late 1960s and 1970s, for example, see John Newhouse, *Cold Dawn: The Story of SALT* (New York: Holt, Rinehart & Winston, 1973); Glenn T. Seaborg and Benjamin S. Loeb, *Stemming the Tide: Arms Control in the Johnson Years* (Lexington, Mass.: Lexington, 1971); Strobe Talbott, *Endgame: The Inside Story of SALT II* (New York: Harper and Row, 1979); and Thomas W. Wolfe, *The SALT Experience* (Cambridge, Mass.: Ballinger, 1979).

For the Reagan years of the 1980s, which led up to the Strategic Arms Reduction Treaties, see Lynn Davis, *Assuring Peace in a Changing World: Critical Choices for the West's Strategic and Arms Control Policies* (Washington, D.C.: Johns Hopkins University Press, 1990); Alexander L. George, *U.S.-Soviet Security Cooperation: Achievements, Failures, Lessons* (New York: Oxford University Press, 1988); Kerry M. Kartchner, *Negotiating START: Strategic Arms Reduction Talks and the Quest for Strategic Stability* (New Brunswick, N.J.: Transaction Publishers, 1992); Michael Krepon, *Arms Control in the Reagan Administration* (Lanham, Md.: University Press of America, 1989); Jennifer E. Sims, "The American Approach to Nuclear Arms Control: A Retrospective," in "Arms Control: Thirty Years On," *Daedalus,* Winter 1991; Strobe Talbott, *Deadly Gambits: The Reagan Administration and the Stalemate in Nuclear Arms Control* (New York: Alfred A. Knopf, 1984); and Kenneth W. Thompson, ed., *Negotiating Arms Control: Missed Opportunities and Limited Successes* (Lanham, Md.: University Press of America, 1991).

There are fewer comprehensive texts on the lesser-known and more recent treaties. For a background on the Comprehensive Test Ban Treaty, see Thanos P. Dokos, *Negotiations for a CTBT 1958-1994* (Lanham, Md.: University Press of America, 1995). On the Intermediate-Range Nuclear Forces treaty, see George L. Rueckert, *Global Double Zero: The INF Treaty from Its Origins to Implementation* (Westport, Conn.: Greenwood Press, 1993). On the Nonproliferation Treaty see Joseph F. Pilat and Robert E. Pendley, eds., *1995: A New Beginning for the NPT?* (New York: Plenum Press, 1995). And on the Open

Skies Treaty see David B. Thomson, *The Treaty on Open Skies* (Los Alamos, N.M.: Los Alamos National Laboratory, 1994).

When examining institutions and the central role they play in the development of arms control policy, two organizations stand out: the United Nations and the United States Senate. For the former, see Dimitris Bourantonis, *The United Nations and the Quest for Nuclear Disarmament* (Aldershot, UK: Dartmouth, 1993); on the latter, see Alan Platt, *The U.S. Senate and Strategic Arms Policy, 1969-1977* (Boulder, Colo.: Westview, 1978).

Regional

Certain regions have inspired a surfeit of arms control-related writings. Books and articles dealing with Europe and Russia during the Cold War and its immediate aftermath could easily fill a large bookcase themselves. Among the best on Europe are Fen Osler Hampson, Harald van Riekhoff, and John Roper, eds., *The Allies and Arms Control* (Baltimore, Md.: Johns Hopkins University Press, 1992); and Jenonne Walker, *Security and Arms Control in Post-Confrontation Europe* (Oxford, UK: Oxford University Press, 1994). On Russian perspectives and the history of the U.S.-Soviet rivalry see Igor S. Glagolev, "The Soviet Decision-Making Process in Arms Control Negotiations," *Orbis,* Winter 1978; Michael Mandelbaum, ed., *The Other Side of the Table: The Soviet Approach to Arms Control* (New York: Council on Foreign Relations Press, 1990); and Adam Ulam, *The Rivals: America and Russia Since World War Two* (New York: Penguin Books, 1971).

The best works on arms control in East Asia focus on China and North Korea. These include William E. Berry Jr., *North Korea's Nuclear Program: The Clinton Administration's Response* (Colorado Springs, Colo.: USAF Institute for National Security Studies, March 1995); Morton Halperin and Dwight H. Perkins, *Communist China and Arms Control* (New York: Frederick A. Praeger, 1965); Jeffrey A. Larsen and Thomas D. Miller, eds., *Arms Control in the Asia-Pacific Region* (Colorado Springs, Colo: USAF Institute for National Security Studies, 1999); Michael J. Mazarr, *North Korea and the Bomb: A Case Study in Nonproliferation* (New York: St. Martin's Press, 1995); Brad Roberts, Robert A. Manning, and Ronald N. Montaperto, "China: The Forgotten Nuclear Power," *Foreign Affairs,* July/August 2000; Leon V. Sigal, "Averting a Train Wreck with North Korea," *Arms Control Today,* November/December 1998; and Gerald Segal, ed., *Arms Control in Asia* (New York: St. Martin's Press, 1987).

From an international relations perspective, the Asian subcontinent became much more interesting after Pakistan and India openly tested nuclear weapons in 1998 and the United States launched a counteroffensive against terrorists in Afghanistan and Iraq beginning in 2001. For a good background see Strobe Talbott, "Dealing with the Bomb in South Asia," *Foreign Affairs,* March/April 1999 and Sumit Ganguly, *Conflict Unending: India-Pakistan Relations Since 1947* (New York: Columbia University Press, 2002).

There are more works on the fractious Middle East, usually with a conventional weapons or nonproliferation focus. See Shai Feldman and Ariel Levite, eds., *Arms Control and the New Middle East Security Environment* (Boulder, Colo.: Westview, 1994); Geoffrey Kemp, *The Control of the Middle East Arms Race* (Washington, D.C.: Carnegie Endowment for International Peace, 1991); Efraim Inbar and Shmuel Sandler, eds., *Middle Eastern Security: Prospects for Arms Control and Confidence Building in the Middle East* (Washington, D.C.: United States Institute of Peace Press, 1992); and Shai Feldman, *Nuclear Weapons and Arms Control in the Middle East* (Cambridge, Mass.: MIT Press, 1997).

Finally, while this book is somewhat U.S.-centric, the reader is directed to a reference guide for the rest of the Americas: *Confidence- and Security Building Measures in the Americas: A Reference Book of Hemispheric Documents* (Washington, D.C.: Arms Control and Disarmament Agency, September 1998).

Preventing War

Nonproliferation

The functional categories of the bibliography are divided into the three goals of arms control as expressed by the founding fathers of the field in 1961: preventing war, reducing the consequences should war occur, and reducing the cost of preparing for war. The first category begins with the increasingly important topic of nonproliferation. Good overviews on this subject include Eric H. Arnett and W. Thomas Wander, *The Proliferation of Advanced Weaponry: Technology, Motivations, and Responses* (Washington, D.C.: American Association for the Advancement of Science, 1992); William E. Burrows and Robert Windrem, *Critical Mass: The Dangerous Race for Superweapons in a Fragmenting World* (New York: Simon & Schuster, 1994); Roger Molander and Robbie Nichols, *Who Will Stop the Bomb: A Primer on Nu-*

clear Proliferation (Washington, D.C.: Roosevelt Center for American Policy Studies, 1986); Brad Roberts, "Proliferation and Nonproliferation in the 1990s: Looking for the Right Lessons," *The Nonproliferation Review,* Fall 1999; John F. Sopko, "The Changing Proliferation Threat," *Foreign Policy,* Winter 1996-1997; Leonard S. Spector, "Missing the Forest for the Trees: U.S. Non-Proliferation Programs in Russia," *Arms Control Today,* June 2001; and Leonard S. Spector with Jacqueline R. Smith, *Nuclear Ambitions: The Spread of Nuclear Weapons* (Boulder, Colo.: Westview, 1990).

The reason weapons of mass destruction proliferation is such a concern revolves around the threat of mass casualties that could result from the use of these weapons. Three particularly good U.S. government publications that deal with this threat are *Proliferation: Threat and Response* (Washington, D.C.: Office of the Secretary of Defense, January 2001); U.S. Senate, Committee on Governmental Affairs, *The Nonproliferation Primer* (Washington, D.C.: U.S. Government Printing Office, January 1998); and *The Weapons Proliferation Threat* (Langley, Va.: Central Intelligence Agency, March 1995). For more specifics about possible use, see Peter R. Lavoy, Scott D. Sagan, and James J. Wirtz, eds., *Planning the Unthinkable: How New Powers Will Use Nuclear, Biological, and Chemical Weapons* (Ithaca, N.Y.: Cornell University Press, 2000). On crisis stability as one diplomatic approach to avoiding WMD use, see Andrew Goldberg, Debra Van Opstal, and James H. Barkley, eds., *Avoiding the Brink: Theory and Practice in Crisis Management* (London: Brassey's, 1990). An excellent overview of the growing threat to civilized values from terrorism and WMD is Richard A. Falkenrath, Robert D. Newman, and Bradley A. Thayer, *America's Achilles Heel: Nuclear, Biological, and Chemical Terrorism and Covert Attack* (Cambridge, Mass.: MIT Press, 1998). Also see *Executive Summary of the Report of the Commission to Assess the Ballistic Missile Threat to the United States* (Washington, D.C.: Rumsfeld Commission, July 1998).

For a counter argument about the likely effect proliferation will have on the international system, see Kenneth N. Waltz, "The Spread of Nuclear Weapons: More May Be Better," *Adelphi Paper* No. 171 (London: International Institute for Strategic Studies, 1981); and Scott D. Sagan and Kenneth N. Waltz, *The Spread of Nuclear Weapons: A Debate* (New York: W.W. Norton, 1995).

The issue of precursors, particularly fissile materials, keeps many analysts awake at night. See Sam Nunn, chairman, *Managing the Global Nuclear Materials Threat* (Washington, D.C.: Center for Strategic and International Studies, January 2000); and Guy Roberts, *Five Minutes Past Midnight: The Clear and Present Danger of Nuclear*

Weapons Grade Fissile Materials (Colorado Springs, Colo.: USAF Institute for National Security Studies, February 1996).

Compliance and Verification

As one moves into some of the more vital but obscure concepts within arms control and disarmament, the first area encountered is the idea of ensuring compliance and verification of treaties. On compliance, see Gloria Duffy, *Compliance and the Future of Arms Control* (Stanford, Calif.: Center for International Security and Arms Control, 1988); Michael Krepon, *Arms Control: Verification and Compliance* (New York: Foreign Policy Association, 1984); and the United States Senate Select Committee on Intelligence, *Capability of the United States to Monitor Compliance with the START II Treaty* (Washington, D.C.: U.S. Government Printing Office, 1996). On verification, see David W. Hafemeister, Penny Janeway, and Kosta Tsipis, *Arms Control Verification: The Technologies That Make It Possible* (Philadelphia, Penn.: Pergamon-Brassey's, 1986); Steven Mataija and J. Marshall Beier, eds., *Multilateral Verification and the Post-Gulf War Environment: Learning from the UNSCOM Experience* (Toronto, Can.: Centre for International and Strategic Studies, 1992); Jeffrey Richelson, "Verification: Ways and Means," *The Bulletin of the Atomic Scientists,* November/December 1998; John D. Tower, *Verification: The Key to Arms Control in the 1990s* (New York: MacMillan, 1992); and *Verification and the United Nations: The Role of the Organization in Multilateral Arms Limitations and Disarmament Agreements* (New York: United Nations Publications, 1992).

Nuclear Weapons and Deterrence

The subfield of nuclear weapons and strategic deterrence theory is another of those fields with an immense literature. Even attempting to identify the choicest offerings is to pursue a near-impossible task. Nonetheless, we have attempted to list a number of the "best" in this category, with an eye toward those that give good overviews to the beginning student of this field and, as in previous categories, pointing to the most recent works, with an occasional foray into the true "classics."

Begin with the first in a five-volume series of descriptive, encyclopedic works on what nuclear weapons are, how they are built and work, and who has them, by William M. Arkin, Thomas B. Cochran, and Milton M. Hoenig, *Nuclear Weapons Databook, Volume I: U.S. Nuclear*

Forces and Capabilities (Cambridge, Mass.: Ballinger, 1984). Then turn to Hans Binnendijk and James Goodby, eds., *Transforming Nuclear Deterrence* (Washington, D.C.: National Defense University Press, 1997); McGeorge Bundy, *Danger and Survival: Choices About the Bomb in the First Fifty Years* (New York: Random House, 1988); Ashton B. Carter, John D. Steinbruner, and Charles A. Zraket, *Managing Nuclear Operations* (Washington, D.C.: Brookings Institute, 1987); Stephen J. Cimbala, *The Past and Future of Nuclear Deterrence* (Westport, Conn.: Praeger, 1998); Ivo Daalder and Terry Terriff, eds., *Rethinking the Unthinkable: New Directions for Nuclear Arms Control* (London: Frank Cass, 1993); and Lynn Eden and Steven E. Miller, *Nuclear Arguments: Understanding the Nuclear Arms and Arms Control Debates* (Ithaca, N.Y.: Cornell University Press, 1989). The best overview of the Soviet/Russian nuclear weapons complex is Pavel Podvig, *Russian Strategic Nuclear Forces* (Cambridge, Mass.: MIT Press, 2001).

Other good works in the field of nuclear weapons include Lawrence Freedman, *The Evolution of Nuclear Strategy* (New York: St. Martin's Press, 1989); The Harvard Nuclear Study Group, *Living with Nuclear Weapons* (Toronto, Can.: Bantam Books, 1983); Herman Kahn, *On Thermonuclear War* (Princeton, N.J.: Princeton University Press, 1961); *Nuclear Arms Control: Background and Issues* (Washington, D.C.: National Academy of Sciences, 1985); Janne E. Nolan, *An Elusive Consensus: Nuclear Weapons and American Security After the Cold War* (Washington, D.C.: Brookings Institute, 1999); *Rationale and Requirements for U.S. Nuclear Forces and Arms Control* (Washington, D.C.: National Institute for Public Policy, January 2001); Stephen I. Schwartz, *Atomic Audit: The Costs and Consequences of U.S. Nuclear Weapons Since 1940* (Washington, D.C.: Brookings Institute, 1998); Nikolai Sokov, "Russia's Approach to Nuclear Weapons," *The Washington Quarterly,* Summer 1997; Stansfield Turner, *Caging the Nuclear Genie: An American Challenge for Global Security* (Boulder, Colo.: Westview, 1997); and three reports by the U.S. government: *Nuclear Terms Handbook* (Washington, D.C.: U.S. Department of Energy, Office of Nonproliferation and National Security, 1998); *Weapons of Mass Destruction Terms Handbook* (Alexandria, Va.: Defense Threat Reduction Agency, September 2001); and *U.S. Nuclear Policy in the 21st Century: A Fresh Look at National Strategy and Requirements* (Washington, D.C.: National Defense University Center for Counterproliferation Research, July 1998).

Chemical and Biological Weapons

Chemical and, increasingly, biological weapons are spreading to many states that were never considered major threats in the past. For more on these potential weapons of mass destruction, see Neil C. Livingstone and Joseph D. Douglass, *CBW: The Poor Man's Atomic Bomb* (Cambridge, Mass.: Institute for Foreign Policy Analysis, 1984); Rodney J. McElroy, *Briefing Book on Chemical Weapons* (Washington, D.C.: Council for a Livable World, 1989); Julian Perry Robinson, *Chemical Weapons Arms Control: A Framework for Studying Policy Alternatives* (Philadelphia, Penn.: Taylor and Francis, 1985); Ken Alibek with Stephen Handelman, *Biohazard* (New York: Delta Trade Paperbacks, 1999); U.S. Senate Committee on Foreign Affairs, *Chemical Weapons Convention* (Washington, D.C.: U.S. Government Printing Office, 1997); and U.S. Senate Committee on the Judiciary, *Constitutional Implications of the Chemical Weapons Convention* (Washington, D.C.: U.S. Government Printing Office, 1997).

Conventional Weapons

While the world focused on weapons of mass destruction during the Cold War, smaller wars were occurring around the globe—more often than not sponsored or supplied by one of the two superpowers. Conventional arms control thus grew in importance not only to alleviate tensions on the front lines of the Cold War face-off in Central Europe, but to prevent the distribution of small weapons to the killing fields of the Third World. Among the best studies of this problem are: *The Arms Trade: Problems and Prospects in the Post-Cold War World* (special edition of *The Annals of the American Academy of Political and Social Science*, September 1994); Jayantha Dhanapala, Mitsuro Donowaki, Swadesh Rana, and Lora Lumpe, eds., *Small Arms Control: Old Weapons, New Issues* (New York: UN Institute for Disarmament Research, 1999); Ivan Oelrich, *Conventional Arms Control: Their Limits and Their Verification* (Cambridge, Mass.: Harvard University Center for Science and International Affairs, 1990); and William C. Potter and Harlan W. Jencks, eds., *The International Missile Bazaar: The New Suppliers' Network* (Boulder, Colo.: Westview, 1994). Naval arms control usually falls under the realm of conventional weapons; see Barry M. Blechman, William J. Durch, W. Philip Ellis, and Cathleen S. Fisher, *Naval Arms Control: A Strategic Assessment* (New York: St. Martin's Press, 1991).

Reducing the Consequences of War

Ballistic Missile Defenses

One way to minimize damage in the event war breaks out is to develop active defenses against known or anticipated threats. America's attempt to do that with missile defenses led to ironically contrary decisions. To prevent such defenses and keep both societies vulnerable to nuclear annihilation and deterrence, the United States signed the Anti-Ballistic Missile (ABM) treaty in 1972; to reverse course and develop minimal societal defenses it withdrew from that same treaty in 2002. Representative books on this subject include Antonia H. Chayes and Paul Doty, eds., *Defending Deterrence: Managing the ABM Treaty into the 21st Century* (Washington, D.C.: Pergamon-Brassey's, 1989); Joseph Cirincione, Stever Fetter, George Lewis, Jack Mendelsohn, and John Steinbruner, *White Paper on National Missile Defense* (Washington, D.C.: Lawyer's Alliance for World Security, Spring 2000); Frances Fitzgerald, *Way Out There in the Blue: Reagan and Star Wars and the End of the Cold War* (New York: Simon & Schuster, 2000); Gary L. Guertner and Donald M. Snow, *The Last Frontier: An Analysis of the Soviet Defense Initiative* (Lexington, Mass.: Lexington, 1986); James M. Lindsay and Michael E. O'Hanlon, *Defending America: The Case for a Limited National Missile Defense* (Washington, D.C.: Brookings Institute, 2000); *National Missile Defense Review Committee* (Welch Report) (Washington, D.C.: Ballistic Missile Defense Organization, November 1999); Dean Wilkening, "Amending the ABM Treaty," *Survial,* Spring 2000; James M. Lindsay and Michael E. O'Hanlon, *Defending America: The Case for Limited National Missile Defense* (Washington: Brookings, 2001); and James J. Wirtz and Jeffrey A. Larsen, eds., *Rockets' Red Glare: Missile Defenses and the Future of World Politics* (Boulder, Colo.: Lynne Rienner, 2001).

Counterproliferation

In addition to active and passive defenses, states may attempt to reduce their vulnerability to attack by countering the proliferation of weapons of mass destruction through active military and diplomatic measures. Some of the best overviews on this subject include: Peter L. Hays, Vincent J. Jodoin, and Alan R. Van Tassel, eds., *Countering the Proliferation and Use of Weapons of Mass Destruction* (New York: McGraw-Hill, 1998); and Robert G. Joseph and John F. Reichart, *Detterence and Defense in a Nuclear, Biological, and Chemical Environ-*

ment (Washington, D.C.: National Defense University Center for Counterproliferation Research, 1995).

Reducing the Costs of Preparing for War

Disarmament

The ultimate means of arms control is, of course, complete disarmament: the banning and elimination of all weapons of a particular type. In international relations this usually implies nuclear disarmament, although it can be applied to other categories as well. There is a large body of literature in the field of disarmament, although much of it dates from the heyday of optimism about the possibility of successfully achieving global disarmament prior to the early 1960s—at which point realism about its unlikelihood took over, and states turned to less drastic measures to control arms. Good works on disarmament include: *Armaments and Disarmament in the Nuclear Age: A Handbook* (Atlantic Highlands, N.J.: Humanities Press, 1976); Richard J. Barnet and Richard A. Falk, *Security in Disarmament* (Princeton, N.J.: Princeton University Press, 1965); Daniel Frei, *Perceived Images: U.S. and Soviet Assummptions and Perceptions in Disarmament* (Totowa, N.J.: Rowman & Allanheld, 1962); Salvador de Madariaga, *Disarmament* (New York: Coward-McCann, 1929); *Nuclear and Conventional Disarmament: Progress or Stalemate?* (Proceedings of the Seventh International Castiglioncello Conference, September 1997); *Responding to New Realities in Disarmament* (special editions of *Disarmament,* 1993); Mark Sommer, *Beyond the Bomb: Living Without Nuclear Weapons, A Field Guide to Alternative Strategies for Building a Stable Peace* (New York: Talman, 1986); Philip Towle, *Enforced Disarmament: From Napoleonic Campaigns to the Gulf War* (Oxford, UK: Clarendon Press, 1997); and Lawrence S. Wittner, *Resisting the Bomb: A History of the World Nuclear Disarmament Movement, 1954-1970* (Stanford, Calif.: Stanford University Press, 1997).

Journals and Websites

Finally, there are many professional journals and websites that can provide in-depth material and information on these subjects, as well as text, summaries, and analysis of all arms control treaties and the various multinational arms control and disarmament conferences that have taken place regularly over the past century. No attempt has been made to try to select the best of these to recommend, but it is suggested that the student of this field become familiar with these sources, as well. A comprehensive list of journals and websites can be found at the end of this section.

Classification of Entries

The bibliographic entries that follow are listed according to a classification scheme that relates to the three generally accepted objectives of arms control, plus sections on general works of interest and key journals and websites. The works listed are weighted toward those that have been published since the mid-1980s.

The following bibliography is organized in line with the three broad goals of arms control as defined by Bull, Schelling, and Halperin, with appropriate subcategories beneath each topic to help the reader differentiate between subjects in this rich field. Many of the works could easily fit within several different categories; they have been categorized where each seemed to best belong, so as to avoid duplication.

Organization of the Bibliography

General

Adler, Emanuel, ed. *The International Practice of Arms Control.* Baltimore, Md.: Johns Hopkins University Press, 1992.

"Arms Control," Special Edition of *Daedalus,* Vol. 89, No. 4, 1960.

Arms Control Briefing Book: Arms Control and Security in the Post-Cold War Era. Washington: Council for a Livable World, March 1998.

Arms Control and Disarmament Agency. *Arms Control and Disarmament Agreements.* Washington: U.S. Government Printing Office, 1982, 1990, and 1996.

"Arms Control for a New Era." Special Edition. *The Washington Quarterly*, Autumn 1994.

Arms Control and National Security: An Introduction. Washington: Arms Control Association, 1989.

Arms Control and Strategic Stability: Challenges for the Future. Lanham, Md.: University Press of America, 1986.

"Arms Control: Thirty Years On," Special Edition of *Daedalus*, Winter 1991.

"Arms, Defense Policy, and Arms Control," Special Edition of *Daedalus,* Vol. 104, No. 3, 1975.

Arnett, Eric. H., Elizabeth J. Kirk, and W. Thomas Wander, eds. *Critical Choices; Setting Priorities in the Changing Security Environment.* Washington, D.C.: American Association for the Advancement of Science, 1991.

Aron, Raymond. *The Great Debate.* New York: Doubleday, 1965.

Axelrod, Robert. *The Evolution of Cooperation.* New York: Basic Books, 1984.

Barnaby, Frank and Ronald Huisken. *Arms Uncontrolled.* Cambridge, Mass.: Harvard University Press, 1975.

Barton, John H. *The Politics of Peace: An Evaluation of Arms Control.* Stanford, Calif.: Stanford University Press, 1981.

Barton, John H. and Ryuichi Imai. *Arms Control II: A New Approach to International Security.* Cambridge, Mass.: Oelgeschlager, Gunn and Hain, 1981.

Barton, John H. and Lawrence D. Weiler, eds. *International Arms Control: Issues and Agreements.* Stanford, Calif.: Stanford University Press, 1976.

Beach, Hugh. *A Future for Arms Control?* London: Council of Arms Control, November 1992.

————. *The New Arms Control Challenges.* London: Council for Arms Control, 1992.

Bellany, Ian. *A Basis for Arms Control*. Aldershot, U.K.: Dartmouth Publishing, 1991.

Bergeron, Kenneth D. *Tritium on Ice: Dangerous New Alliance of Nuclear Weapons and Nuclear Power*. Cambridge, Mass.: MIT Press, 2002.

Berman, J. and John C. Baker. *Soviet Strategic Forces: Requirements and Responses*. Washington: Brookings Institution, 1982.

Bernauer, Thomas and Dieter Ruloff, eds. *The Politics of Positive Incentives in Arms Control*. Columbia, S.C.: University of South Carolina Press, 1999.

Bertram, Christoph, ed. *Arms Control and Military Force*. Montclair, N.J.: Allanheld, Osmun, 1980.

Beschloss, Michael R. and Strobe Talbott. *At the Highest Levels: The Inside Story of the End of the Cold War*. New York: Little, Brown, 1993.

Beufre, Andre. *Deterrence and Strategy*. New York: Praeger, 1966.

Blacker, Coit D. *Reluctant Warriors: The United States, the Soviet Union, and Arms Control*. New York: W.H. Freeman, 1987.

———— and Gloria Duffy. *International Arms Control: Issues and Agreements*. Stanford, Calif.: Stanford Univ Press, 1984.

Blackwill, Robert D. and F. Stephen Larrabee, eds. *Conventional Arms Control and East-West Security*. Durham, N.C.: Duke University Press, 1989.

Bowie, Christopher J., Robert P. Haffa, and Robert E. Mullins. *Future War: What Trends in America's Post-Cold War Military Tell Us About Early 21st Century Warfare* Washington, D.C.: Northrop Grumman Analysis Center, January 2003.

Brauch, Hans-Günter and Duncan L. Clarke, eds. *Decisionmaking for Arms Limitation: Assessments and Prospects*. Cambridge, Mass.: Ballinger, 1983.

Brennan, Donald G., ed. *Arms Control, Disarmament, and National Security*. New York: George Braziller, 1961.

Brodie, Bernard. "On the Objectives of Arms Control," in Robert J. Art and Kenneth N. Waltz, eds. *The Use of Force: Military Power and International Politics*. Lanham, Md.: University Press of America, 1983.

————. *Strategy in the Missile Age*. Princeton, N.J.: Princeton University Press, 1959.

Brogden, Peter ed. *Arms Control in the 1990s: Proceeding of a Workshop on Chemical Weapons, Nuclear Weapons, and Arms Control in Outer Space*. Aurora Paper 22. Ottawa, Can.: Canadian Centre for Global Security, 1994.

Brown, Harold. "Is Arms Control Dead?" *The Washington Quarterly,* Spring 2000, p. 173.

———. *Thinking About National Security.* Boulder, Colo.: Westview, 1983.

Browne, Michael, ed. *Grave New World: Security Challenges in the 21st Century.* Washington, D.C.: Georgetown University Press, 2003.

Brzezinski, Zbigniew. *Game Plan: A Geostrategic Framework for the Conduct of the U.S.-Soviet Contest.* Boston, Mass.: Atlantic Monthly Press, 1986.

Bull, Hedley. *Hedley Bull on Arms Control.* New York: St. Martin's Press, 1987.

———. *The Control of the Arms Race: Disarmament and Arms Control in the Missile Age.* New York: Frederick A. Praeger, 1961.

Burns, Richard Dean, ed. *Encyclopedia of Arms Control and Disarmament.* New York: Charles Scribner's Sons, 1993.

Carlton, David and Carlo Schaerf, eds. *Perspectives on the Arms Race.* New York: St. Martin's Press, 1989.

Carnesdale, Albert and Richard N. Haass, eds. *Superpower Arms Control: Setting the Record Straight.* Cambridge, Mass.: Ballinger, 1987.

Chant, Christopher. *Compendium of Armaments and Military Hardware.* New York: Routledge and Kegan Paul, 1987.

Clarke, Duncan L. *American Defense and Foreign Policy Institutions.* New York: Ballinger, 1989.

Clarke, Duncan L. *Politics of Arms Control.* New York: Free Press, 1979.

Cordesman, Anthony H. "US and Russian Nuclear Forces and Arms Control after the US Nuclear Posture Review." Washington, D.C.: Center for Strategic and International Studies, 10 January 2002.

Daalder, Ivo. *Cooperative Arms Control: A New Agenda for the Post-Cold War Era.* College Park, Md.: Center for International Studies at Maryland, October 1992.

Dahlitz, Julie, ed. *Avoidance and Settlement of Arms Control Disputes.* New York: United Nations, 1994.

Davis, Lynn E. *Assuring Peace in a Changing World: Critical Choices for the West's Strategic and Arms Control Policies.* Washington, D.C.: Johns Hopkins University Foreign Policy Institute, 1990.

Dean, Jonathan and Jefrey Laurenti. *Options and Opportunities: Arms Control and Disarmament for the 21st Century.* New York: UNA-USA, 1997.

Dean, Jonathan and Kurt Gottfried. *Nuclear Security in a Transformed World.* Washington, D.C.: Union of Concerned Scientists, September 1991.

Deudney, Daniel. *Whole Earth Security: A Geopolitics of Peace. Worldwatch Paper* 55. Washington, D.C.: Worldwatch Institute, July 1983.

Diehl, Paul F. and Loch K. Johnson, eds. *Through the Straits of Armageddon: Arms Control Issues and Prospects.* Athens, Ga.: University of Georgia Press, 1987.

Dougherty, James E. *Arms Control and Disarmament: The Critical Issues.* Washington, D.C.: Center for Strategic Studies, 1966.

————. *How to Think About Arms Control and Disarmament.* New York: Crane, Russak, 1973.

———— and J.F. Lehman, Jr., eds. *Arms Control for the Late Sixties.* Princeton, N.J.: D. van Nostrand, 1967.

Dulles, John Foster. "Policy for Security and Peace." *Foreign Affairs,* July 1954, pp. 353-364.

————. "Challenge and Response in United States Policy." *Foreign Affairs,* October 1957, pp. 25-43.

Dunn, Lewis A. and Sharon Squassoni, eds. *Arms Control: What Next?* Boulder, Colo.: Westview, 1993.

Dunn, Lewis A. et. al. *Nuclear Issues in the Post-September 11 Era.* Paris: Foundation pour la Recherche Strategique, March 2003.

Dupuy, Trevor N. and Gay M. Hammerman, eds. *A Documentary History of Arms Control and Disarmament.* New York: R.R. Bowker, 1973.

Edwards, David V. *Arms Control in International Politics.* New York: Holt, Rinehart and Winston, 1969.

Fischer, David, Ben Sanders, Lawrence Scheinman, and George Bunn. *A New Nuclear Triad: The Non-Proliferation of Nuclear Weapons, International Verification, and the International Atomic Energy Agency.* Southampton, U.K.: Programme for Promoting Nuclear Non-Proliferation, 1992.

Freedman, Lawrence. *Arms Control: Management or Reform?* Chatham House Papers 31. London: Routledge & Kegan Paul, 1986.

Frisch, David H., ed. *Arms Reduction: Program and Issues.* New York: Twentieth Century Fund, 1961.

Gallagher, Nancy W., ed. *Arms Control: New Approaches to Theory and Policy.* London: Frank Cass, 1998.

Garfinkle, Adam M. and Nils H. Wessell, eds. *Global Perspectives on Arms Control: Foreign Policy Issues.* New York: Praeger, 1984.

George, Alexander L., Philip J. Farley, and Alexander Dallin, eds. *U.S.-Soviet Security Cooperation: Achievements, Failures, Lessons.* New York: Oxford University Press, 1988.

Glynn, Patrick. *Closing Pandora's Box: Arms Races, Arms Control, and the History of the Cold War.* New York: Basic Books, 1992.

Goldblatt, Jozef. *Arms Control: A Guide to Negotiations and Agreements.* 2nd ed. London: Sage Publications, 2002.

Gottemoeller, Rose. "Offense, Defense, and Unilateralism in Strategic Arms Control." *Arms Control Today,* September 2001, pp. 10-15.

_____. "Beyond Arms Control: How to Deal with Nuclear Weapons." *Policy Brief 23.* Washington, D.C.: Carnegie Endowment for International Peace, February 2003.

Graham, Thomas, Jr. and Damien J. LaVera. *Cornerstones of Security: Arms Control Treaties in the Nuclear Era.* Seattle: University of Washington Press, 2003.

Gray, Colin S. *House of Cards: Why Arms Control Must Fail.* Ithaca, N.Y.: Cornell University Press, 1992.

Hadley, Arthur T. *The Nation's Safety and Arms Control.* New York: Viking, 1961.

Halloran, Bernard F., ed. *Essays on Arms Control and National Security.* Washington, D.C.: Arms Control and Disarmament Agency, 1986.

Hanrieder, Wolfram F. *Technology, Strategy and Arms Control.* Boulder, Colo.: Westview, 1985.

Hart, B. H. Liddell *Deterrent or Defense.* London: Stevens and Sons, 1960.

Henkin, Louis. *The Hammarskjold Forums: Case Studies on the Role of Law in the Settlement of International Disputes.* Dobbs Ferry, N.Y.: Oceana, 1964.

Hernandez, Roy. *START and Beyond: Strategic Nuclear Arms Reductions in the Post-Cold War Era.* Working Paper 137. Canberra, Aus.: Australian National University, PEACE Research Centre, October 1993.

Howe, Josephine O'Conner. *Armed Peace: The Search for World Security.* New York: St. Martin's Press, 1984.

Huntington, Samuel P. "Arms Races: Prerequisites and Results," in Robert J. Art and Kenneth N. Waltz, eds., *The Use of Force: Military Power and International Politics.* Lanham, Md.: University Press of America, 1983.

Inglis, David. *To End the Arms Race.* Ann Arbor: University of Michigan Press, 1985.

Isard, Walter. *Arms Races, Arms Control, and Conflict Analysis: Contributions from Peace Science and Peace Economics.* New York: Cambridge University Press, 1988.

Institute for Defense and Disarmament Studies. *Peace Resource Book: A Comprehensive Guide to Issues, Groups, and Literature.* Cambridge, Mass: Ballinger, 1986.

The International Law of Arms Control and Disarmament. New York: United Nations, 1991.

Kent, Glenn A. "On the Interaction of Opposing Forces Under Possible Arms Agreements," *Occasional Papers in International Affairs,* No. 5, Cambridge, Mass.: Harvard University Center for International Affairs, 1963.

Kincade, William H. and Jeffrey D. Porro, eds. *Negotiating Security: An Arms Control Reader.* Washington, D.C.: Carnegie Endowment for International Peace, 1979.

Kirk, Elizabeth J., ed. *Technology, Security, and Arms Control for the 1990s.* Washington, D.C.: American Association for the Advancement of Science, 1988.

Kolkowicz, Roman and Neil Joeck, eds. *Arms Control and International Security.* Boulder, Colo.: Westview, 1984.

Kolodziej, Edward A. and Patrick M. Morgan, eds. *Security and Arms Control, Volume I: A Guide to National Policymaking.* New York: Greenwood Press, 1989.

Korb, Larry, et. al. *Winning the Peace in the 21st Century.* Task Force Report of the Strategies for U.S. Security Program, Muscatine, Iowa: Stanley Foundation, October 2003.

Krepon, Michael. *Arms Control in the Reagan Administration.* Lanham, Md.: University Press of America, 1989.

Lamb, Christopher. *How to Think About Arms Control, Disarmament, and Defense.* New York: Prentice Hall, 1988.

Larsen, Jeffrey A. *Arms Control: Cooperative Security in a Changing Environment.* Boulder, Colo.: Lynne Rienner, 2002.

Larsen, Jeffrey A. and Gregory J. Rattray, eds. *Arms Control Toward the Twenty First Century.* Boulder, Colo.: Lynne Rienner, 1996.

Lefever, Ernest W., ed. *Arms and Arms Control.* New York: Frederick A. Praeger, 1962.

Lennon, Alexander T.J. *Contemporary Nuclear Debates: Missile Defense, Arms Control, and the Arms Races in the Twenty-First Century.* Cambridge, Mass.: MIT Press, 2002.

Levine, Robert A. *The Arms Debate.* Cambridge, Mass.: Harvard University Press, 1963.

Lodal, Jan. *The Price of Dominance: The New Weapons of Mass Destruction and Their Challenge to American Leadership.* New York: Council on Foreign Relations Press, 2001.

Long, Franklin A. and George W. Rathjens, eds. *Arms, Defense Policy, and Arms Control.* New York: W.W. Norton, 1976.

Luck, Edward C., ed. *Arms Control, the Multilateral Alternative.* New York: New York University Press, 1983.

Maroncelli, James M. and Timothy L. Karpin. *The Traveler's Guide to Nuclear Weapons: A Journey through America's Cold War Battlefields.* New York: Historical Odysseys, 2002.

Martin, Lawrence. *The Two-Edged Sword: Armed Force in the Modern World.* New York: W.W. Norton, 1982.

Mayers, Teena Karsa. *Understanding Nuclear Weapons and Arms Control: A Guide to the Issues.* 3rd Edition. Washington, D.C.: Pergamon-Brassey's, 1986.

Mendelsohn, Catharine R. *Arms Control and Disarmament: The U.S. Commitment.* Washington, D.C.: United States Information Agency, 1997.

Mendelsohn, Jack. "Is Arms Control Dead?" *Issues in Science and Technology,* Spring 2001, p. 81.

_____ and David Grahame. *Arms Control Chronology.* Washington, D.C.: Center for Defense Information, Winter 2002.

Mickiewicz, Ellen Propper and Roman Kolkowicz, eds. *International Security and Arms Control.* New York: Praeger, 1986.

The New Arms Control Agenda. Washington, D.C.: Georgetown University, Institute for the Study of Diplomacy, December 1992.

Nolan, Janne E. *Global Engagement: Cooperation and Security in the 21st Century.* Washington, D.C.: Brookings Institution, 1994.

Nye, Joseph S., Jr. "Arms Control After the Cold War." *Foreign Affairs*, Winter 1989/90, pp. 42-64.

Osgood, Robert E. *Arms Control: A Skeptical Appraisal and a Modest Proposal.* Washington, D.C.: Johns Hopkins University, Foreign Policy Institute, 1986.

Payne, Keith B. *The Fallacies of Cold War Deterrence and a New Direction.* Lexington, Ky.: University Press of Kentucky, 2001.

Pfaltzgraff, Robert L. *National Security: Ethics, Strategy and Politics: A Layman's Primer.* Elmsford, N.Y.: Pergamon-Brassey's, 1986.

Platt, Alan. *The Politics of Arms Control and the Strategic Balance.* Santa Monica, Calif.: RAND Corporation, December 1982.

Pringle, Laurence. *Arms Race or Human Race?* New York: William Morrow, 1985.

Ramberg, Bennett. *Arms Control without Negotiation.* Boulder, Colo.: Lynne Rienner, 1993.

Ranger, Robin. *Arms and Politics 1958-1978: Arms Control in a Changing Political Context.* Toronto, Can.: Macmillan of Canada, 1979.

—— and David Weincek. *The Devil's Brews II: Weapons of Mass Destruction and International Security.* Lancashire, U.K.: Lancaster University, Centre for Defence and International Security, 1997.

Readings from Scientific American: Arms Control. New York: W.H. Freeman, 1973.

Roberts, Brad. "Arms Control in 2000-2010: Forks in the Road Ahead." In James Brown, ed., *Entering the New Millennium: Dilemmas in Arms Control.* Albuquerque: Sandia National Laboratories, 1999.

——. "The Road Ahead for Arms Control." *The Washington Quarterly,* Spring 2000, p. 219.

Rose, William. *U.S. Unilateral Arms Control Initiatives: When Do They Work?* New York: Greenwood Press, 1988.

Rotblat, Joseph and Alessandro Pascolini. *The Arms Race at a Time of Decision: Annals of Pugwash 1983.* London: MacMillian, 1984.

Saaty, Thomas L. *Mathematical Models of Arms Control and Disarmament: Application of Mathematical Structures in Politics.* New York: John Wiley & Sons, 1968.

Schelling, Thomas C. *Arms and Influence.* New Haven, Conn.: Yale University Press, 1966.

——. *The Strategy of Conflict.* Cambridge, Mass.: Harvard University Press, 1960.

Schelling, Thomas C. and Morton H. Halperin. *Strategy and Arms Control.* New York: Twentieth Century Fund, 1961; reprinted by Washington, D.C.: Pergamon-Brassey's, 1985.

Schlesinger, James. "The Demise of Arms Control." *The Washington Quarterly,* Spring 2000, p. 179.

Schroeer, Dietrich. *Science, Technology and the Nuclear Arms Race.* New York: John Wiley and Sons, 1984.

Shambroom, Paul. *Face to Face with the Bomb: Nuclear Reality after the Cold War.* Baltimore, Md.: John Hopkins University Press, 2003.

Sheehan, Michael. *Arms Control: Theory and Practice.* Oxford, U.K.: Basil Blackwell, 1988.

Singer, J. David. *Deterrence, Arms Control and Disarmament: Toward A Synthesis in National Security Policy.* New York: University Press of America, 1984.

Smith, James M. and Jeffrey A. Larsen. *All Our Tomorrows: A Long-Range Forecast of Global Trends Affecting Arms Control Technol-*

ogy. INSS Occasional Paper 44. Colorado Springs, Colo: USAF Institute for National Security Studies, June 2002.

Smith, Joseph and Simon Davis. *Historical Dictionary of the Cold War.* Lanham, Md.: Scarecrow Press, 2000.

Smoke, Richard. *National Security and the Nuclear Dilemma: An Introduction to the American Experience in the Cold War.* New York: McGraw Hill, 1993.

Starr, Richard F., ed. *Arms Control: Myth Versus Reality.* Palo Alto, Calif.: Hoover Institution, 1984.

Steinbruner, John. "Renovating Arms Control Through Reassurance." *The Washington Quarterly,* Spring 2000, p. 197.

Stockholm International Peace Research Institute. *Arms Control: A Survey and Appraisal of Multilateral Agreements.* London: Taylor & Francis, 1978.

Stockholm International Peace Research Institute. *SIPRI Yearbook: World Armaments and Disarmament.* Oxford, U.K.: Oxford University Press, annual.

Stone, Jeremy J. *Containing the Arms Race: Some Specific Proposals.* Cambridge, Mass.: MIT Press, 1966.

Tanner, Fred. *Arms Control in Times of Conflict: A Contribution to Conflict Management in the Post-Cold War World.* College Park, Md.: Center for International and Security Studies at Maryland, October 1993.

————, ed. *From Versailles to Baghdad: Post-War Armament Control of Defeated States.* Geneva, Switz.: UN Institute for Disarmament Research, 1992.

Teller, Edward with Judith Shoolery. *Memoirs: A Twentieth-Century Journey in Science and Politics.* New York: Perseus Books, 2001.

Thee, Marek, ed. *Arms and Disarmament: SIPRI Findings.* Oxford, U.K.: Oxford University Press, 1987.

Thompson, Kenneth W. *Arms Control: Alliances, Arms Sales, and the Future.* Lanham, Md.: University Press of America, 1993.

————, ed. *Arms Control and Defense: Who Decides?* Lanham, Md.: University Press of America, 1988.

————, ed. *Arms Control: Moral Political, and Historical Lessons.* Lanham, Md.: University Press of America, 1990.

Towle, Philip. *Arms Control and East-West Relations.* New York: St. Martin's Press, 1983.

Tulliu, Steve and Thomas Schmalberger. *Coming to Terms with Security: A Lexicon for Arms Control, Disarmament, and Confidence Building.* New York: UN Institute for Disarmament Research, 2001.

U.S. Congress. Congressional Research Service. *The Future of Arms Control: New Opportunities.* Washington, D.C.: U.S. Government Printing Office, April 1992.

United States Information Agency. *A Chronology of United States Arms Control and Security Initiatives, 1946-1990.* Washington, D.C.: USIA, May 1990.

Wallop, Malcolm and Angelo Codevilla. *The Arms Control Delusion.* San Francisco, Calif.: ICS Press, 1987.

Wander, W. Thomas, Richard A. Scribner, and Kenneth N. Luongo, eds. *Science and Security: The Future of Arms Control.* Washington, D.C.: American Association for the Advancement of Science, 1986.

Warner, Edward and David Ochmanek. *Next Moves: An Arms Control Agenda for the 1990s.* New York: Council on Foreign Relations, 1989.

Woolf, Amy F. *Arms Control and Disarmament Activities: A Catalog of Recent Events.* Washington, D.C.: Congressional Research Service, 24 January 1997.

Wright, Quincy, William M. Evan, and Morton Deutsch, eds. *Preventing World War III: Some Proposals.* New York: Simon and Schuster, 1962.

Young, Elizabeth. *A Farewell to Arms Control?* Hammondsworth, U.K.: Penguin Books, 1972. Dordrecht, Neth.: Martinus Nijhoff, 1987.

History and Negotiations

Pre-Cold War

Buell, Raymond Leslie. *The Washington Conference.* New York: Russell & Russell, 1922.

Dingman, Roger. *Power in the Pacific: The Origins of Naval Arms Limitation, 1914-1922.* Chicago, Ill.: University of Chicago Press, 1976.

Engely, Giovanni. *The Politics of Naval Disarmament.* London: Williams and Norgate, 1932.

Fanning, Richard W. *Peace and Disarmament: Naval Rivalry and Arms Control, 1922-1933.* Lexington, Ken.: University Press of Kentucky, 1995.

Goldman, Emily O. *Sunken Treaties: Naval Arms Control Between the Wars.* University Park: Pennsylvania State University Press, 1994.

Hoag, C. Leonard. *Preface to Preparedness: The Washington Disarmament Conference and Public Opinion.* Washington, D.C.: American Council on Public Affairs, 1941.

Hoover, Robert A. *Arms Control: The Interwar Naval Limitation Agreements.* Denver, Colo.: University of Denver, Graduate School of International Affairs, 1980.

Hyde, Harlow A. *Scraps of Paper: The Disarmament Treaties Between the World Wars.* Lincoln, Neb.: Media Publishing, 1988.

Ichihashi, Yamato. *The Washington Conference and After: A Historical Survey.* Stanford, Calif.: Stanford University Press, 1928.

Kaufman, Robert G. *Arms Control During the Pre-Nuclear Era: The United States and Naval Limitation Between the Two World Wars.* New York: Columbia University Press, 1990.

Noel-Baker, Philip. *The First World Disarmament Conference 1932-33: And Why it Failed.* Oxford, U.K.: Pergamon Press, 1979.

O'Conner, Raymond G. *Perilous Equilibrium: The United States and the London Naval Conference of 1930.* Lawrence: University of Kansas Press, 1962.

Paul, Septimus H. *Nuclear Rivals: Anglo-American Atomic Relations, 1941-1952.* Columbus: Ohio State University Press, 2000.

Tate, Merze. *The Disarmament Illusion: The Movement for a Limitation of Armaments to 1907.* New York: MacMillan, 1942.

U.S. Department of State. *The London Naval Conference 1935.* Washington, D.C.: U.S. Government Printing Office, 1936.

Williams, Benjamin H. *The United States and Disarmament.* Port Washington, N.Y.: Kennikat Press, 1931.

Wilson, Hugh R. *Disarmament and the Cold War in the Thirties.* New York: Vantage Press, 1963.

Early Cold War

Bechhoefer, Bernhard G. *Postwar Negotiations for Arms Control.* Westport, Conn.: Greenwood Press, 1975.

Divine, Robert A. *Blowing on the Wind: The Nuclear Test Ban Debate 1954-1960.* New York: Oxford University Press, 1978.

Nutting, Anthony. *Disarmament: An Outline of the Negotiations.* London: Oxford University Press, 1959.

Rock, Vincent P. *The Stateman's Approach to Disarmament.* Washington, D.C.: Institute for Defense Analyses, July 1963.

Seaborg, Glenn T. *Kennedy, Khruschchev, and the Test Ban.* Berkeley: University of California Press, 1981.

Seaborg, Glenn T. and Benjamin S. Loeb. *Stemming the Tide: Arms Control and the Johnson Years.* Lexington, Mass.: Lexington, 1987.

Stone, Jeremy J. *Strategic Persuasion: Arms Limitations Through Dialogue.* New York: Columbia University Press, 1967.

Weihmiler, Gordon R. and Dusko Doder. *U.S.-Soviet Summits: An Account of East-West Diplomacy at the Top, 1955-1985.* Lanham, Md.: University Press of America, 1986.

Weiss, Leonard. "Atoms for Peace." *Buletin of the Atomic Scientists,* November/December 2003, pp. 34-44.

SALT

Arms Control Association. *Countdown on SALT II.* Washington, D.C.: Arms Control Association, 1985.

Buckley, James L. and Paul Warnke. *Strategic Sufficiency: Fact or Fiction.* Washington, D.C.: American Enterprise Institute for Public Policy Research, 1972.

Burns, Richard Dean and Susan Hoffman Hutson. *The SALT Era: A Selected Bibliography.* Los Angeles: California State University, Center for the Study of Armament and Disarmament, 1979.

Burt, Richard, ed. *Arms Control and Defense Postures in the 1980s.* Boulder, Colo.: Westview, 1982.

Caldwell, Dan. *The Dynamics of Domestic Politics and Arms Control: The SALT II Treaty Ratification Debate.* Columbia: University of South Carolina Press, 1991.

Carnesale, Albert and Richard N. Haass, eds. *Superpower Arms Control: Setting the Record Straight.* Cambridge, Mass.: Ballinger, 1987.

Coffey, Joseph I. *Arms Control and European Security: A Guide to East-West Negotiations.* New York: Praeger, 1977.

Cox, Arthur Macy. *The Dynamics of Détente: How to End the Arms Race.* New York: W.W. Norton, 1976.

Davis, Jacquelyn K., Patrick J. Friel, and Robert L. Pfaltzgraff, Jr. *SALT II and U.S.-Soviet Strategic Forces.* Cambridge, Mass.: Institute for Foreign Policy Analysis, June 1979.

Donley, Michael B. *The SALT Handbook.* Washington, D.C.: Heritage Foundation, 1979.

Ford, Gerald R. *The Vladivostok Negotiations and Other Events.* San Diego: University of California, Institute of Global Conflict and Cooperation, 1986.

Garthoff, Raymond L. *Détente and Confrontation: American-Soviet Relations from Nixon to Reagan.* Washington, D.C.: Brookings Institution, 1985.

Humphrey, Gordon J., William R. Van Cleave, Jeffrey Record, William H. Kincade, and Richard Perle. *SALT II and American Security.* Cambridge, Mass.: Institute for Foreign Policy Analysis, 1980.

Kintner, William R. and Robert L. Pfaltzgraff Jr., eds. *SALT: Implications for Arms Control in the 1970s.* Pittsburgh, Penn.: University of Pittsburgh Press, 1973.

Krass, Allan and Catherine Girrier. *Disproportionate Response: American Policy and Alleged Soviet Treaty Violations.* Washington, D.C.: Union of Concerned Scientists, 1987.

Lehman, John F. and Seymour Weiss. *Beyond the SALT II Failure.* New York: Praeger, 1980.

Morris, Charles R. *Iron Destinies, Lost Opportunities: The Arms Race Between the U.S. and the USSR, 1945-1987.* New York: Harper & Row, 1988.

Nasbe, Roderick P. *Striving to Sell SALT Two: Seven Years of Soviet Arguments.* New York: Army Russian Institute, June 1980.

Newhouse, John. *Cold Dawn: The Story of SALT.* New York: Holt, Rinehart, and Winston, 1973.

Panofsky, W.K.H. *Arms Control and SALT II.* Seattle: University of Washington Press, 1979.

Seaborg, Glenn T. and Benjamin S. Loeb. *Stemming the Tide: Arms Control in the Johnson Years.* Lexington, Mass.: Lexington, 1971.

Sloss, Leon and M. Scott Davis. *A Game for High Stakes: Lessons Learned in Negotiating with the Soviet Union.* Cambridge, Mass.: Ballinger Books, 1986.

Smith, Gerard C. *Doubletalk: The Story of SALT I.* Lanham, Md.: University Press of America, 1985.

———. *Disarming Diplomat: The Memoirs of Gerard C. Smith, Arms Control Negotiator.* Lanham, Md.: Madison Books, 1996.

Talbott, Strobe. *Endgame: The Inside Story of SALT II.* New York: Harper and Row, 1979.

Walker, Paul Francis. *The U.S. Arms Control and Disarmament Agency: Policy Making in Strategic Arms Limitations.* Cambridge, Mass.: MIT Ph.D. Dissertation, 1978.

Willrich, Mason and John B. Rhinelander. *SALT: The Moscow Agreements and Beyond.* London: The Free Press, 1974.

Wolfe, Thomas W. *The SALT Experience.* Cambridge, Mass.: Ballinger, 1979.

Reagan Years and START

Adelman, Kenneth L. *The Great Universal Embrace: Arms Summitry—A Skeptic's Account.* New York: Simon & Schuster, 1989.
———. *Negotiating Arms Reductions: Six Principals.* Occasional Paper 1. Washington, D.C.: U.S. Arms Control and Disarmament Agency, January 1987.
Arbatov, G.A. *The Soviet Viewpoint.* New York: Dodd, Mead, 1983.
Arms Control: Strategic Arms Talks at Geneva. Washington, D.C.: Congressional Research Service, 1986.
Bunn, George. *Arms Control by Committee: Managing Negotiations with the Russians.* Palo Alto, Calif.: Stanford University Press, 1992.
Burt, Richard, ed. *Arms Control and Defense Postures in the 1980s.* Boulder, Colo.: Westview, 1982.
Carnesdale, Al, et al. *Learning From Experience with Arms Control.* Washington, D.C.: U.S. Arms Control and Disarmament Agency, 1986.
Carter, April. *Success and Failure in Arms Control Negotiations.* Oxford, U.K.: Oxford University Press, 1989.
Cimbala, Stephen J., ed. *Strategic Arms Control after SALT.* Wilmington, Del.: Scholarly Resources Imprint, 1989.
Davis, Lynn Etheridge. *Assuring Peace in a Changing World: Critical Choices for the West's Strategic and Arms Control Policies.* Washington, D.C.: Johns Hopkins University, Foreign Policy Institute, 1990.
Downs, George W. and David M. Rocke. *Tacit Bargaining, Arms Races, and Arms Control.* Ann Arbor: University of Michigan Press, 1990.
Downs, John. *Negotiating with the Russians: Lawyers Making a Difference.* Lanham, Md.: University Press of America, 1997.
Einhorn, Robert J. *Negotiating from Strength: Leverage in U.S.-Soviet Arms Control.* New York: Praeger, 1985.
George, Alexander L. *U.S.-Soviet Security Cooperation: Achievements, Failures, Lessons.* New York: Oxford University Press, 1988.
Kartchner, Kerry M. *Negotiating START: Strategic Arms Reduction Talks and the Quest for Strategic Stability.* New Brunswick, N.J.: Transaction Publishers, 1992.
Krepon, Michael. *Arms Control in the Reagan Administration.* Lanham, Md.: University Press of America, 1989.
——— and Dan Caldwell, eds. *The Politics of Arms Control Treaty Ratification.* New York: St. Martin's Press, 1991.

Lakos, Amos. *International Negotiations: A Bibliography.* San Francisco, Calif: Westview, 1989.

Lempert, Robert, Ike Y. Chang, Jr., and Kathleen McCallum. *Emerging Technology Systems and Arms Control.* Santa Monica, Calif.: RAND Corporation, 1991.

Mandelbaum, Michael. *Reagan and Gorbachev.* New York: Random House, 1987.

Mazarr, Michael J. *START and the Future of Deterrence.* London: MacMillan, 1990.

Newhouse, John. *War and Peace in the Nuclear Age.* New York: Vintage Books, 1990.

Nitze, Paul H. with Ann M. Smith and Steven L. Rearden. *From Hiroshima to Glasnost: At the Center of Decision—A Memoir.* New York: Grove Weidenfield, 1989.

Schaefer, Henry. *Nuclear Arms Control: The Process of Developing Positions.* Washington, D.C.: National Defense University Press, 1986.

Scott, Robert Travis, ed. *The Race for Security: Arms and Arms Control in the Reagan Years.* Lexington, Mass.: Lexington, 1987.

Sims, Jennifer E. "The American Approach to Nuclear Arms Control: A Retrospective," in "Arms Control: Thirty Years On," special edition of *Daedalus*, Winter 1991, pp. 251-272.

Smith, Raymond F. *Negotiating with the Soviets.* Bloomington: Indiana University Press, 1989.

"START II: Analysis, Summary, Text." Special section of *Arms Control Today,* January/February 1993.

Stein, Janet Gross, ed. *Getting to the Table: The Processes of International Prenegotiation.* Baltimore, Md.: Johns Hopkins University Press, 1989.

Stein, Jonathan B. *From H-Bomb to Star Wars: The Politics of Strategic Decision-Making.* Lexington, Mass.: Lexington, 1984.

Talbott, Strobe. *Deadly Gambits: The Reagan Administration and the Stalemate in Nuclear Arms Control.* New York: Alfred A. Knopf, 1984.

———. *The Master of the Game: Paul Nitze and the Nuclear Peace.* New York: Alfred A. Knopf, 1988.

Thompson, Kenneth W., ed. *Negotiating Arms Control: Missed Opportunities and Limited Successes.* Lanham, Md.: University Press of America, 1991.

U.S. Congress. Congressional Budget Office. *Implementing START II.* Washington, D.C.: U.S. Government Printing Office, March 1993.

Chemical and Biological Weapons

Chari, P.R. and Arpit Rajain, eds. *Working Towards a Verification Protocol for Biological Weapons.* New Delhi, India: Institute of Peace and Conflict Studies, July 2001.

Chemical Weapons Arms Control, Chronology of Key Events: 1925-1992. Washington, D.C.: U.S. Arms Control and Disarmament Agency, April 1992.

Preston, Richard. *The Demon in the Freezer: A True Story.* New York: Random House, 2002.

Roberts, Brad. *Chemical Disarmament and U.S. Security.* Washington, D.C.: Center for Strategic and International Studies, 1992.

"Special Edition: The Chemical Weapons Convention." *Arms Control Today,* October 1992.

Thränert, Oliver, ed. *The Verification of the Biological Weapons Convention: Problems and Perspectives.* Bonn, Ger.: Friedrich Ebert Stiftung, May 1992.

Comprehensive Test Ban Treaty

Dokos, Thanos P. *Negotiations for a CTBT 1958-1994.* Lanham, Md.: University Press of America, 1995.

Falin, Valentin, ed. *The Last Nuclear Explosion: Forty Years of Struggle Against Nuclear Tests.* Moscow: Novosti Press Agency Publishing House, 1986.

Fetter, Steve. *Toward a Comprehensive Test Ban.* Cambridge, Mass.: Ballinger, 1988.

Jacobson, Harold Karan and Eric Stein. *Diplomats, Scientists, and Politicians: The United States and the Nuclear Test Ban Negotiations.* Ann Arbor: University of Michigan Press, 1966.

Joeck, Neil and Herbert York. *Countdown on the Comprehensive Test Ban.* San Diego: University of California Institute on Global Conflict and Cooperation, 1986.

McBride, James Hubert. *The Test Ban Treaty: Military, Technological, and Political Implications.* Chicago, Ill.: Henry Regnery, 1967.

Nuclear Test Ban (CTBT): Draft Treaty and Related Texts, 1962-1993. Ottawa, Can.: Nonproliferation, Arms Control, and Disarmament Division, Department of Foreign Affairs and International Trade, January 1994.

Schmalberger, Thomas. *In Pursuit of a Nuclear Test Ban Treaty: A Guide to the Debate in the Conference on Disarmament.* New York: United Nations Institute for Disarmament Research, 1991.

Seaborg, Glenn T. and Benjamin S. Loeb. *Kennedy, Krushchev, and the Test Ban.* Berkeley: University of California Press, 1981.

Schrag, Philip G. *Global Action: Nuclear Test Ban Diplomacy at the End of the Cold War.* Boulder, Colo.: Westview, 1992.

Stromseth, Jane. *The Comprehensive Test Ban Treaty.* Geneva, Switz.: World Without War, 1981.

Thränert, Oliver. *Soviet Policy on Nuclear Testing, 1985-1991.* Kingston, Can.: Queen's University Centre for International Relations, 1992.

U.S. Department of State. *Geneva Conference on the Discontinuance of Nuclear Weapon Tests: History and Analysis of Negotiations.* Washington, D.C.: U.S. Department of State, 1961.

York, Herbert F. *The CTBT and Beyond.* New York: United Nations, 1994.

Conventional Negotiations

Batchelor, Peter. "The 2001 UN Conference on Small Arms: A First Step?" *Disarmament Diplomacy,* September 2001, p. 4.

Falkenrath, Richard A. *Shaping Europe's Military Order: The Origins and Consequences of the CFE Treaty.* Cambridge, Mass.: MIT Press, 1995.

Fry, John. *The Helsinki Process: Negotiating Security and Cooperation in Europe.* Washington, D.C.: National Defense University Press, 1993.

Hirschfeld, Thomas J. *Helsinki II: The Future of Arms Control in Europe.* Santa Monica, Calif.: RAND Corporation, 1992.

Matheson, Michael J. "Filling the Gaps in the Conventional Weapons Convention." *Arms Control Today,* November 2001, p. 12.

Fissile Materials Cutoff Treaty

Chow, Brian G., Richard H. Speiers, and Gregory S. Jones. *The Proposed Fissile Material Production Cutoff: Next Steps.* National Defense Research Institute Report MR-586-OSD. Santa Monica, Calif.: RAND Corporation, 1995.

Roberts, Guy B. *This Arms Control Dog Won't Hunt: The Proposed Fissile Material Cut-Off Treaty at the Conference on Disarmament.* INSS Occasional Paper 36. Colorado Springs, Colo: USAF Institute for National Security Studies, January 2001.

U.S. Congress, Office of Technology Assessment. *Dismantling the Bomb and Managing the Nuclear Materials.* Washington, D.C.: U.S. Government Printing Office, September 1993.

Intermediate-Range Nuclear Forces Treaty

Davis, Jacqueline K., Charles M. Perry, and Robert L. Pfaltzgraff Jr. *The INF Controversy: Lessons for NATO Modernization and Transatlantic Relations.* Washington, D.C.: Pergamon-Brassey's, 1989.

Dean, Jonathan. *Meeting Gorbachev's Challenge: How to Build Down the NATO-Warsaw Pact Confrontation.* New York: St. Martin's Press, 1989.

Dean, Jonathan and Peter Clausen. *The INF Treaty and the Future of Western Security.* Cambridge, Mass.: Union of Concerned Scientists, January 1988.

Laquer, Walter and Leon Sloss. *European Security in the 1990s: Deterrence and Defense After the INF Treaty.* New York: Plenum Press, 1990.

Risse-Kappen, Thomas. *The Zero Option: INF, West Germany, and Arms Control.* Boulder, Colo.: Westview, 1988.

Rueckert, George L. *Global Double Zero: The INF Treaty from its Origins to Implementation.* Westport, Conn.: Greenwood Press, 1993.

Nonproliferation Treaty

Bunn, George. *Extending the Non-Proliferation Treaty: Legal Questions Faced by the Parties in 1995.* Washington, D.C.: American Society for International Law, October 1994.

———, Roland M. Timerbaev, and James Leonard. *Nuclear Disarmament: How Much Have the Five Nuclear Powers Promised in the Non-Proliferation Treaty?* Washington, D.C.: Lawyers Alliance for World Security, June 1994.

Davis, Zachary and Warren Donnelly. *Non-Proliferation: A Compilation of Basic Documents on the International, U.S. Statutory, and U.S. Executive Branch Components of Non-Proliferation Policy.* Washington, D.C.: Congressional Research Service, December 1990.

Fisher, David. *Towards 1995: The Prospects for Ending the Proliferation of Nuclear Weapons.* Brookfield, Ver.: Dartmouth Publishing, 1994.

Greene, Owen. *Verifying the Non-Proliferation Treaty: Challenges for the 1990s.* London: Verification Technology Information Center, November 1992.

Jensen, Lloyd. *Return From the Nuclear Brink: National Interest and the Nuclear Nonproliferation Treaty.* Lexington, Mass.: Lexington, 1974.

The NPT: The Main Political Barrier to Nuclear Weapon Proliferation. London: Taylor & Francis, 1980.

Pilat, Joseph F. and Robert E. Pendley, eds. *1995: A New Beginning for the NPT?* New York: Plenum Press, 1995.

Rhinelander, John B. and Adam M. Scheinman, eds. *At the Nuclear Crossroads: Choices about Nuclear Weapons and Extension of the Non-Proliferation Treaty.* Washington, D.C.: Lawyers Alliance for World Security, 1995.

Should the NPT be Extended Indefinitely? Washington, D.C.: Carnegie Endowment for International Peace, November 1993.

"Summary and Text of the Nuclear Non-Proliferation Treaty." *Arms Control Today,* March 1995, pp. 22-26.

Willrich, Mason. *Non-Proliferation Treaty: Framework for Nuclear Arms Control.* Charlottesville, Va.: Michie Company, 1969.

Open Skies Treaty

Thomson, David B. *The Treaty on Open Skies.* Los Alamos, N.M.: Los Alamos National Laboratory, 1994.

Institutions

Beckman, Robert L. *Nuclear Non-Proliferation: Congress and the Control of Peaceful Nuclear Activities.* Boulder, Colo.: Westview, 1985.

Beker, Avi. *Disarmament Without Order: The Politics of Disarmament at the United Nations.* Westport, Conn.: Greenwood Press, 1985.

Bloomfield, L.P. *The Politics of Arms Control: Troika, Veto, and International Institutions.* Study Memorandum No. 3. Washington, D.C.: Institute for Defense Analyses, October 1961.

Boudreau, Thomas E. *Sheathing the Sword: The UN Secretary-General and the Prevention of International Conflict.* New York: Greenwood Press, 1991.

Bourantonis, Dimitris. *The United Nations and the Quest for Nuclear Disarmament.* Aldershot, U.K.: Dartmouth Publishing, 1993.

Byers, R.B. and Stanley C.M. Ing, eds. *Arms Limitation and the United Nations.* Toronto: Canadian Institute of Strategic Studies, 1982.

Chalmers, Malcolm, Owen Greene, Edward J. Laurance, and Herbert Wulf, eds. *Developing the UN Register of Conventional Arms.* West Yorkshire, U.K.: Bradford Arms Register Studies, 1994.

Defense's Nuclear Agency 1947-1997. Washington, D.C.: Defense Threat Reduction Agency, 2002.

International Organizational Arrangements to Verify Compliance with Arms Control and Disarmament Agreements. Report prepared for U.S. ACDA. Washington, D.C.: Johns Hopkins University, School of Advanced International Studies, June 1966.

Koplow, David A. *Conference Report: Executive-Congressional Relations and the Treaty Ratification Process.* Washington, D.C.: Woodrow Wilson International Center for Scholars, 1991.

Lall, Arthur S. *Negotiating Disarmament: The Eighteen Nation Disarmament Conference—The First Two Years, 1962-64.* Ithaca, N.Y.: Cornell University, Center for International Studies, 1964.

Mooris, Ellis, ed. *International Verification Organizations.* Toronto, Can.: Centre for International and Strategic Studies, 1991.

Nuclear Legislation: Organisation and General Regime Governing Nuclear Activities. European Nuclear Energy Agency, 1969.

Nuclear Nonproliferation and Safety: Challenges Facing the International Atomic Energy Agency. Washington, D.C.: General Accounting Office, 1993.

Platt, Alan. *The U.S. Senate and Strategic Arms Policy, 1969-1977.* Boulder, Colo.: Westview, 1978.

——— and Lawrence D. Weiler, eds. *Congress and Arms Control.* Boulder, Colo.: Westview, 1978.

Quester, George H. *The Multilateral Management of International Security: The Nuclear Proliferation Model.* College Park, Md.: Center for International and Security Studies at Maryland, 1993.

The Role of Alliances and Other Interstate Alignments in a Disarming and Disarmed World. Washington, D.C.: Johns Hopkins University, School of Advanced International Studies, July 1965.

Sagan, Scott D. *The Limits of Safety: Organizations, Accidents, and Nuclear Weapons.* Princeton, N.J.: Princeton University Press, 1993.

Scheinman, Lawrence. *The Nonproliferation Role of the International Atomic Energy Agency: A Critical Assessment.* Washington, D.C.: Resources for the Future, 1985.

Smith, James M. and Gwendolyn Hall, eds. *Milestones in Strategic Arms Control, 1945-2000: United States Air Force Roles and Outcomes.* Maxwell AFB, Ala.: Air University Press, September 2002.

The United Nations and Nuclear Non-Proliferation. New York: United Nations, 1995.

U.S. Congress. Office of Technology Assessment. *Nuclear Safeguards and the International Atomic Energy Agency.* Washington, D.C.: U.S. Government Printing Office, April 1995.

Waller, Douglas C. *Congress and the Nuclear Freeze: An Inside Look at the Politics of a Mass Movement.* Amherst: University of Massachusetts Press, 1987.

Words to Deeds: Strengthening the UN's Enforcement Capabilities. New York: United Nations, December 1997.

Young, Wayland, ed. *Exising Mechanisms of Arms Control.* Oxford, U.K.: Pergamon Press, 1966.

Regional Perspectives

Boutros-Gali, Boutros. *New Dimensions of Arms Regulation and Disarmament in the Post Cold War Era.* New York: United Nations, October 1992.

Durch, William J. *Constructing Regional Security: The Role of Arms Transfers, Arms Control, and Reassurances.* New York: Century Foundation, 2000.

Goldstein, Avery. *Deterrence and Security in the 21st Century: China, Britain, France and the Enduring Legacy of the Nuclear Revolution.* Stanford, Calif.: Stanford University Press, 2000.

Hopkins, John C. and Weixing Hu. *Strategic Views from the Second Tier: The Nuclear Weapons Policies of France, Britain, and China.* La Jolla: University of California-San Diego, Institute on Global Conflict and Cooperation, 1994.

Krepon, Michael, Dominique M. McCoy, and Matthew C.J. Rudolph, eds. *A Handbook of Confidence-Building Measures for Regional Security.* Washington, D.C.: Henry L. Stimson Center, September 1993.

Masker, John Scott. *Small States and Security Regimes: The International Politics of Nuclear Non-Proliferation in Nordic Europe and the South Pacific.* Lanham, Md.: University Press of America, 1995.

Nuclear-Weapon-Free Zones. Muscatine, Iowa: Stanley Foundation, October 1975.

Nuclear Weapon Free Zones in the 21st Century. New York: United Nations Press, January 1998.

Parrish, Scott. "Prospects for a Central Asian Nuclear-Weapon-Free Zone." *The Nonproliferation Review,* Spring 2001, p. 141.

"Report on Options for Confidence and Security Building Measures (CSBMs), Verification, Non-Proliferation, Arms Control and Disarmament." Brussels, Belg.: NATO Press, December 2000.

Africa

Burgess, Stephen and Helen Purkitt. *The Rollback of South Africa's Biological Warfare Program.* INSS Occasional Paper 37. Colorado Springs, Colo.: USAF Institute for National Security Studies, February 2001.

Horton, Roy E. III. *Out of (South) Africa: Pretoria's Nuclear Weapons Experience.* INSS Occasional Paper 27. Colorado Springs, Colo.: USAF Institute for National Security Studies, August 1999.

Seek, Jacqueline. *West Africa Small Arms Moratorium: High-Level Consultations on the Modalities for the Implementation of PCASED.* New York: United Nations Institute for Disarmament Research, March 1999.

Walters, Ronald W. *South Africa and the Bomb.* Lexington, Mass: Lexington, 1986.

The Americas

Barletta, Michael. *The Military Nuclear Program in Brazil.* Stanford, Calif.: Center for International Security and Arms Control, August 1997.

Beene, Jeffrey K. *Constraints, Restraints, and the Role of Aerospace Power in the 21st Century.* INSS Occasional Paper 38. Colorado Springs, Colo.: USAF Institute for National Security Studies, April 2001.

Confidence- and Security-Building Measures in the Americas: A Reference Book of Hemispheric Documents. Washington: Arms Control and Disarmament Agency, September 1998.

The Guide to Canadian Policies on Arms Control, Disarmament, Defense and Conflict Resolution. Ottawa, Can: Canadian Institute for International Peace and Security, 1989.

Klepak, Hal. *Confidence Building Sidestepped: The Peru-Ecuador Conflict of 1995.* Toronto, Can.: Centre for International and Security Studies, 1998.

————. *Security Considerations and Verification of a Central American Arms Control Regime.* Sussex, Can.: Department of External Affairs, Arms Control and Disarmament Division, 1990.

Leventhal, Paul L. and Sharon Tanzer, eds. *Averting a Latin American Arms Race: New Prospects and Challenges for Argentine-Brazil Nuclear Cooperation.* New York: St. Martin's Press, 1992.

National Security Strategy of the United States. Washington, D.C.: White House, September 2002.

National Strategy to Combat Weapons of Mass Destruction. Washington, D.C.: White House, December 2002.

Redick, John R. *Argentina and Brazil's New Arrangement for Mutual Inspections and IAEA Safeguards.* Washington, D.C.: Nuclear Control Institute, February 1992.

Robles, Alfonso Garcia. *The Denuclearization of Latin America.* Washington, D.C.: Carnegie Endowment for International Peace, 1967.

————. *The Latin American Nuclear-Weapon-Free Zone.* Occasional Paper 19. Muscatine, Iowa: Stanley Foundation, May 1979.

Rose, Kenneth D. *Underground: The Fallout Shelter in American Culture.* New York: New York University Press, 2001.

U.S. Nuclear Policy and Latin America. Muscatine, Iowa: Stanley Foundation, 1977.

East Asia

Albright, David and Kevin O'Neill. *Solving the North Korean Nuclear Puzzle.* Washington, D.C.: Institute for Science and International Security, November 2000.

Alexander, Ronni. *Putting the Earth First: Alternatives to Nuclear Security in the Pacific Island States.* Honolulu: University of Hawaii, 1994.

Arms Control Arrangements for the Far East. Stanford, Calif.: Hoover Institution Publications, 1967.

Arms Control on the Korean Peninsula: What Lessons Can We Learn From the European Experience? Seoul, South Korea: Institute of Foreign Affairs and National Security, 1990.

Bellows, Michael D., ed. *Asia in the 21st Century: Evolving Strategic Priorities.* Washington, D.C.: National Defense University Press, June 1994.

Berry, William E. Jr. *North Korea's Nuclear Program: The Clinton Administration's Response.* INSS Occasional Paper 3. Colorado

Springs, Colo.: USAF Institute for National Security Studies, March 1995.

Binnendijk, Hans and Ronald N. Monteperto, eds. *Strategic Trends in China.* Washington, D.C.: Institute for National Strategic Studies, 1998.

Bitzinger, Richard A. *Chinese Arms Production and Sales to the Third World.* Santa Monica, Calif.: RAND Corporation, 1991.

Clough, Ralph N., A. Doak Barnett, Morton H. Halperin, and Jerome H. Kahan. *The United States, China, and Arms Control.* Washington, D.C.: Brookings Institution, 1975.

Cupitt, Richard T. and Yuzo Murayama. *Export Controls in the People's Republic of China: Status Report 1997.* Atlanta: University of Georgia, Center for International Trade and Security, 1997.

Dhanapala, Jayantha, ed. *Regional Approaches to Disarmament: Security and Stability.* Aldershot, U.K.: Dartmouth Publishing, 1993.

Drifte, Reinhard. *Japan's Rise to International Responsibilities: The Case of Arms Control.* London: Athlone Press, 1990.

Dupont, Alan. *The Environment and Security in Pacific Asia.* Adelphi Paper No. 319. London: International Institute for Strategic Studies, June 1998.

Eikenberry, Karl W. *Explaining and Influencing Chinese Arms Transfers.* Washington, D.C.: National Defense University Press, February 1995.

Ferguson, Charles. "Sparking a Buildup: U.S. Missile Defense and China's Nuclear Arsenal." *Arms Control Today,* March 2000, p. 13.

Findaly, Trevor, ed. *Arms Control in the Post-Cold War World: With Implications for Asia/Pacific.* Canberra: Australian National University, Peace Research Centre, 1993.

Green, Michael J. and Katsuhisa Furukawa. "New Ambitions, Old Obstacles: Japan and Its Search for an Arms Control Strategy." *Arms Control Today,* July/August 2000, p. 17.

Halperin, Morton and Dwight H. Perkins. *Communist China and Arms Control.* New York: Frederick A. Praeger, 1965.

Harrison, Selig S., ed. *Japan's Nuclear Future: The Plutonium Debate and East Asian Security.* Washington, D.C.: Carnegie Endowment for International Peace, 1996.

_____. *Korean Endgame: A Strategy for Reunification and U.S. Disengagement.* Princeton, N.J.: Princeton University Press, 2002.

Huntley, Wade. *Security or Spectacle? Foreign Policy Realism and Nuclear-Free New Zealand.* Canberra: Australian National University, Peace Research Centre, January 1993.

IFANS Review: Non-Proliferation and Security in Northeast Asia.
Seoul, South Korea: Institute of Foreign Affairs and National Security, August 1994.

Kan, Shirley A. *Chinese Proliferation of Weapons of Mass Destruction: Current Policy Issues.* Washington, D.C.: Congressional Research Service, January 2000.

Larsen, Jeffrey A. and Thomas D. Miller, eds. *Arms Control in the Asia-Pacific Region.* Colorado Springs, Colo.: USAF Institute for National Security Affairs, 1999.

Mazarr, Michael J. *North Korea and the Bomb: A Case Study in Nonproliferation.* New York: St. Martin's Press, 1995.

McGlean, Andrew. *Security, Arms Control, and Conflict Reduction in East Asia and the Pacific: A Bibliography, 1980-1991.* Westport, Conn.: Greenwood Press, 1993.

Medeiros, Evan S. "Rebuilding Bilateral Consensus: Assessing U.S.-China Arms Control and Nonproliferation Achievements." *The Nonproliferation Review*, Spring 2001, p. 131.

Moon, Chung-in. *Arms Control on the Korean Peninsula.* Seoul, South Korea: Yonsei University Press, 1997.

Niksch, Larry A. *North Korea's Nuclear Weapons Program.* Washington, D.C.: Congressional Research Service, March 1994.

Nuclear Policies in Northeast AsIowa New York: United Nations Institute for Disarmament Research, 1995.

Oh, Kongdan and Ralph C. Hassig. *North Korea: Through the Looking Glass.* Washington, D.C.: Brookings Institution, 2000.

O'Hanlon, Michael and Mike Mochizuki. *Crisis on the Korean Peninsula: How to Deal with a Nuclear North Korea.* New York: McGraw-Hill, 2003.

Parrish, Scott. "Prospects for a Central Asian Nuclear Weapon Free Zone." *The Nonproliferation Review,* Spring 2001, p. 141.

Pillsbury, Michael, ed. *Chinese Views of Future Warfare.* Washington, D.C.: National Defense University Press, 1997.

Reynolds, Wayne. *Australia's Bid for the Atomic Bomb.* Melbourne, Aus.: Melbourne University Press, 2001.

Roberts, Bradley, Robert A. Manning, and Ronald N. Montaperto. "China: The Forgotten Nuclear Power." *Foreign Affairs,* July/August 2000.

Ross, Anthony Clunies and Peter King. *Australia and Nuclear Weapons: The Case for a Non-Nuclear Region in South East Asia.* Sydney: Sydney University Press, 1966.

Samuels, Richard J. *Rich Nation, Strong Army. National Security and the Technological Transformation of Japan.* Ithaca, N.Y.: Cornell University Press, 1994.

Selin, Shannon. *Asia Pacific Arms Buildups.* Vancouver, Can.: University of British Columbia, Institute of International Relations, November 1994.

Sigal, Leon V. "Averting a Train Wreck with North Korea." *Arms Control Today,* November/December 1998, pp. 11-15.

————. *Disarming Strangers: Nuclear Diplomacy with North Korea.* Princeton, N.J.: Princeton University Press, 1998.

Segal, Gerald, ed. *Arms Control in Asia.* New York: St. Martin's Press, 1987.

The United States, Japan, and the Future of Nuclear Weapons. Washington, D.C.: Carnegie Endowment for International Peace, 1995.

Van Doren, Charles N. and Rodney Jones. *China and Nuclear Non-Proliferation: Two Perspectives.* Occasional Paper 3. Southampton, U.K.: University of Southampton, Center for International Policy Studies, 1989.

Williams, Shelton L. *Nuclear Nonproliferation in International Politics: The Japanese Case.* Denver, Colo.: University of Denver, 1972.

Wright, David. *Will North Korea Negotiate Away Its Missiles?* Washington, D.C.: Union of Concerned Scientists, April 1998.

Europe

Alford, Jonathan, ed. *Arms Control and European Security.* New York: St. Martin's Press, 1984.

Alternative Defence Commission. *Defense Without the Bomb.* Philadelphia: Taylor and Francis, 1983.

Arnold, Laura. *Britain and the H-Bomb.* London: Palgrave, 2001.

Auton, Graeme P., ed. *Arms Control and European Security.* New York: Praeger, 1989.

Blechman, Barry M. and Cathleen S. Fisher, et al. *The Silent Partner: West Germany and Arms Control.* Cambridge, Mass.: Ballinger, 1988.

Brandon, Henry, ed. *In Search of a New World Order: The Future of U.S.-European Relations.* Washington, D.C.: Brookings Institution, 1992.

Breyman, Steve. *Why Movements Matter: The West German Peace Movement and U.S. Arms Control Policy.* Albany: State University of New York Press, 2001.

Bryans, Michael. *The CSCE and Future Security in Europe.* Ottawa: Canadian Institute for International Peace and Security, March 1992.

Cartwright, John and Julian Critchley. *Cruise, Pershing and SS-20.* Elmsford, N.Y.: Pergamon-Brassey's, 1985.

Chestnutt, Heather and Steven Mataija, eds. *Towards Helsinki 1992: Arms Control in Europe and the Verification Process.* North York, Can.: York University Centre for International and Strategic Studies, 1991.

Davis, Lynn E. *An Arms Control Strategy for the New Europe.* Santa Monica, Calif.: RAND Corporation, 1993.

Dembinski, Matthias, Alexander Kelle, and Harald Müller. *NATO and Non-proliferation: A Critical Appraisal.* PRIF Report 33. Frankfurt, Ger.: Peace Research Institute Frankfurt, April 1994.

DePorte, A.W. *Europe Between the Superpowers: The Enduring Balance.* New Haven, Conn.: Yale University Press, 1979.

Deutsch, Karl W. *Arms Control and the Atlantic Alliance: Europe Faces Coming Policy Decisions.* New York: John Wiley and Sons, 1967.

Dewitt, David and Hans Rattinger, eds. *East-West Arms Control: Challenges for the Western Alliance.* London: Routledge, 1992.

European Security and the CSCE. Proceedings of a Special North Atlantic Assembly Interparliamentary Conference. Brussels, Belg.: North Atlantic Assembly, April 1992.

Feld, Werner J. *Arms Control and the Atlantic Community.* New York: Praeger, 1987.

Flanagan, Stephen J. and Fen Osler Hampson, eds. *Securing Europe's Future.* Dover, Mass.: Auburn House Publishing Company, 1986.

Freeman, John P.G. *Britain's Nuclear Arms Control Policy in the Context of Anglo-American Relations, 1957-68.* New York: St. Martin's Press, 1986.

Fürst, Andreas, Volker Heise, and Steven Miller, eds. *Europe and Naval Arms Control in the Gorbachev Era.* Oxford, U.K.: Oxford University Press, 1992.

Graham, Thomas and Leonor Tomero. "Obligations for Us All: NATO and Negative Security Assurances." *Disarmament Diplomacy,* August 2000, p. 3.

Hampson, Fen Osler, Harald van Riekhoff, and John Roper, eds. *The Allies and Arms Control.* Baltimore, Md.: Johns Hopkins University Press, 1992.

Hanrieder, Wolfram F., ed. *Arms Control, the FRG, and the Future of East-West Relations.* Boulder, Colo.: Westview, 1987.

Harle, Vilho and Pekka Sivonen, eds. *Europe in Transition: Politics and Nuclear Security.* London: Pinter Publishers, 1989.

Bibliography 285

Hopmann, P. Terrence. *Building Security in a Post-Cold War Eurasia: The OSCE and U.S. Foreign Policy.* Washington, D.C.: U.S. Institute of Peace, September 1999.

Independent Commission on Disarmament and Security Issues (Palme Commission). *Common Security: A Blueprint for Survival.* New York: Simon and Schuster, 1982.

Kaiser, Karl and Karl Markus Kreis, eds. *Sicherheitspolitik vor Neuen Aufgaben* [Security in a New Age]. Bonn, Ger.: Europa Union Verlag GMBH, 1979.

Kelleher, Catherine M. and Gale A. Mattox. *Evolving European Defense Policies.* Lexington, Mass.: Lexington, 1986.

Krause, Joachim. "The New Crises Over National Missile Defense." *Transatlantik Internationale Politik,* Summer 2000, p. 35.

Laird, Robbin F. *French Security Policy: From Independence to Interdependence.* Boulder, Colo.: Westview, 1986.

Laird, Robbin, ed. *West European Arms Control Policy.* Durham, N.C.: Duke University Press, 1990.

Lindahl, Ingemar. *The Soviet Union and the Nordic Nuclear-Weapons-Free-Zone Proposal.* New York: St. Martin's Press, 1988.

Lodgaard, Sverre and Marek Thee, eds. *Nuclear Disengagement in Europe.* London: Taylor & Francis, 1983.

May, Brian. *Russia, America, the Bomb and the Fall of Western Europe.* London: Routledge & Kegan Paul, 1984.

Myrdal, Alva et al. *The Dynamics of European Nuclear Disarmament.* Nottingham, U.K.: Spokesman, 1981.

"NATO at Fifty." Special Commemorative Section. *Foreign Affairs,* May/June 1999, pp. 163-218.

Preece, Charlotte Phillips and Joseph M. Freeman. *British and French Strategic Nuclear Force Modernization Issues for Western Security and Arms Control.* Washington, D.C.: Congressional Research Service, February 1989.

Rudney, Robert. *Peace Research in Western Europe: A Directory Guide.* Washington: ACCESS, 1989.

Rusi, Alpo M. *After the Cold War: Europe's New Political Architecture.* New York: St. Martin's Press, 1991.

Russett, Bruce M. and Carolyn C. Cooper. *Arms Control in Europe: Proposals and Political Constraints.* Denver, Colo.: University of Denver, 1967.

Schwartz, David N. *NATO's Nuclear Dilemmas.* Washington, D.C.: Brookings Institution, 1983.

Simon, Jeffrey, ed. *European Security Policy After the Revolutions of 1989.* Washington, D.C.: National Defense University Press, 1991.

Smith, Michael. *Understanding Europe's New Common Foreign and Security Policy.* San Diego, Calif.: Institute on Global Conflict and Cooperation, March 2000.

Steinbruner, John D. and Leon V. Sigal, eds. *Alliance Security: NATO and the No-First Use Question.* Washington, D.C.: Brookings Institution, 1984.

Sweedler, Alan and Randy Willoughby. *Europe in Transition: Arms Control and Conventional Forces in the 1990s.* San Diego: University of California Institute on Global Conflict and Cooperation, 1991.

Ullman, Richard H. *Securing Europe.* Princeton, N.J.: Princeton University Press, 1991.

United Nations Institute for Disarmament Research. *Problems and Perspectives of Conventional Disarmament in Europe.* New York: Taylor & Francis, 1989.

United Nations Office for Disarmament Affairs. *Regional Approaches to Confidence- and Security-Building Measures.* Disarmament Topical Papers 17. New York: United Nations, 1993.

U.S. Congress. Commission on Security and Cooperation in Europe. *Implementation of the Helsinki Accords.* Washington, D.C.: U.S. Government Printing Office, 1993.

Van Heuven, Marten. *Europe: Continent in Transition.* Santa Monica, Calif.: RAND Corporation, 1997.

Wachter, Gerhard and Axel Kroh, eds. *Stability and Arms Control in Europe: The Role of Military Forces within a European Security System.* Stockholm, Swe.: Stockholm International Peace Research Institute, July 1989.

Walker, Jenonne. *Security and Arms Control in Post-Confrontation Europe.* Oxford, U.K.: Oxford University Press, 1994.

Middle East

Building for Security and Peace in the Middle East. Washington, D.C.: Washington Institute for Near East Policy, 1997.

Butler, Richard. *The Greatest Threat: Iraq, Weapons of Mass Destruction and the Growing Crisis in Global Security.* Washington, D.C.: Public Affairs Press, 2000.

Cohen, Avner. *Israel and the Bomb.* New York: Columbia University Press, 1998.

Cordesman, Anthony H. *Weapons of Mass Destruction in the Middle East.* Washington, D.C.: Center for Strategic and International Studies, January 2001.

————. *Military Expenditures and Arms Transfers in the Middle East.* Washington, D.C.: Center for Strategic and International Studies, April 2001.

Datan, Merav. "Israel Debates Nuclear Weapons." *Disarmament Diplomacy,* January/February 2000, p. 6.

Fahmy, Nabail. "Prospects for Arms Control and Proliferation in the Middle East." *The Nonproliferation Review,* Summer 2001, pp. 111-117.

Feldman, Shai. *Nuclear Weapons and Arms Control in the Middle East.* Cambridge, Mass.: Harvard University Center for Science and International Affairs, 1997.

———— and Ariel Levite, eds. *Arms Control and the New Middle East Security Environment.* Boulder, Colo.: Westview, 1994.

Groom, A.J.R., Edward Newman, and Paul Taylor. *Burdensome Victory: The United Nations and Iraq.* Canberra: Australian National University, Peace Research Centre, 1996.

Hamza, Khidhir. *Saddam's Bombmaker: The Terrifying Inside Story of the Iraqi Nuclear and Biological Weapons Agenda.* New York: Charles Scribner's Sons, 2000.

Herby, Peter. *The Chemical Weapons Convention and Arms Control in the Middle East.* Oslo, Nor: International Peace Research Institute, September 1992.

Hirsch, Seymour M. *The Samson Option: Israel's Nuclear Arsenal and American Foreign Policy.* New York: Random House, 1991.

Inbar, Efraim and Shmuel Sandler, eds. *Middle Eastern Security: Prospects for an Arms Control Regime.* London: Frank Cass, 1995.

Jabber, Fuad. *The Politics of Arms Transfer and Control: The United States and Egypt's Quest for Arms, 1950-1955.* Southern California Arms Control and Foreign Policy Seminar, 1972.

Jabber, Paul. *Not By War Alone: Security and Arms Control in the Middle East.* Berkeley: University of California Press, 1981.

Karem, Mahmoud. *A Nuclear-Weapon-Free Zone in the Middle East.* New York: Greenwood Press, 1988.

Kemp, Geoffrey. *The Control of the Middle East Arms Race.* Washington, D.C.: Carnegie Endowment for International Peace, 1991.

Landau, Emily. *Egypt and Israel in ACRS: Bilateral Concerns in a Regional Arms Control Process.* Jerusalem: Jaffee Center for Strategic Studies, June 2001.

Navias, Martin. *Going Ballistic: The Build-Up of Missiles in the Middle East.* New York: Brassey's, 1993.

Platt, Alan. *Arms Control and Confidence Building in the Middle East.* Washington, D.C.: United States Institute of Peace Press, 1992.

Rasmussen, J. Lewis and Robert Oakley. *Conflict Resolution in the Middle East.* Washington, D.C.: U.S. Institute of Peace Press, 1992.

Rauf, Tariq, ed. *Regional Approaches to Curbing Nuclear Proliferation in the Middle East and South Asia.* Ottawa: Canadian Centre for Global Security, December 1992.

Ritter, Scott. "The Case for Iraq's Qualitative Disarmament." *Arms Control Today,* June 2000, p. 8.

———. *Endgame: Solving the Iraq Problem—Once and For All.* New York: Simon & Schuster, 1999.

Sadowski, Yahya M. *Scuds or Butter? The Political Economy of Arms Control in the Middle East.* Washington, D.C.: Brookings Institution, 1993.

Sokolski, Henry and Patrick Clawson, eds. *Checking Iran's Nuclear Ambitions.* Carlisle, Penn.: Army War College Strategic Studies Institute, January 2004.

Stav, Arie. *The Escalation of the Arms Race in the Middle East: On the Threshold of Critical Mass.* Tel Aviv, Israel: NATIV Center for Policy Research, November 1992.

U.S. National Security Council. *Iraqi Weapons of Mass Destruction Programs.* Washington, D.C.: White House, 13 February 1998.

Weapons of Mass Destruction in the Middle East. Washington, D.C.: Congressional Research Service, January 2000.

Yair, Evron, *The Role of Arms Control in the Middle East.* London: International Institute for Strategic Studies, 1977.

Yefimov, Andrei. "New Non-Proliferation Challenges and the Nuclear Suppliers Group." *Yaderny Kontrol* [Nuclear Control], Summer 2000, p. 31.

Russia

Arbatov, Alexei. *Implications of the START II Treaty for U.S.-Russian Relations.* Washington, D.C.: Henry L. Stimson Center, October 1993.

Bennett, Paul R. *The Soviet Union and Arms Control: Negotiating Strategy and Tactics.* New York: Praeger, 1989.

Birstein, Vadim J. *The Perversion of Knowledge: The True Story of Soviet Science.* Boulder, Colo.: Westview Press, 2001.

Bloomfield, Lincoln P., Walter C. Clemens Jr., and Franklyn Griffiths. *Khrushchev and the Arms Race: Soviet Interests in Arms Control and Disarmament 1954-1964.* Cambridge, Mass.: MIT Press, 1966.

Bluth, Christopher. *Soviet Strategic Arms Policy Before SALT.* New York: Cambridge University Press, 1992.

Bukharin, Oleg. "Downsizing Russia's Nuclear Warhead Production Infrastructure." *The Nonproliferation Review,* Spring 2001, p. 116.

———. *The Threat of Nuclear Terrorism and the Physical Security of Nuclear Materials in the Former Soviet Union.* Monterey, Calif.: Monterey Institute of International Studies, August 1992.

Caldwell, Dan, ed. *Soviet International Behavior and U.S. Policy Options.* Lexington, Mass.: Lexington, 1985.

Challenges for U.S. National Security: The Soviet Approach to Arms Control. Washington, D.C.: Carnegie Endowment for International Peace, 1983.

Committee on International Security and Arms Control. National Academy of Sciences. *The Future of the U.S.-Soviet Nuclear Relationship.* Washington, D.C.: National Academy Press, August 1991.

Dallin, Alexander, et al. *The Soviet Union and Disarmament: An Appraisal of Soviet Attitudes and Intentions.* New York: Frederick A. Praeger, 1964.

Douglass, Joseph D., Jr. *Why the Soviets Violate Arms Control Treaties.* Washington, D.C.: Pergamon-Brassey's, 1988.

English, Robert D. and John J. Halperin. *The Other Side: How Soviets and Americans Perceive Each Other.* New Brunswick, N.J.: Transaction Books, 1987.

Frei, Daniel. *Perceived Images: U.S. and Soviet Assumptions and Perceptions in Disarmament.* Totowa, N.J.: Rowman and Allanheld, 1985.

Garthoff, Douglas. *The Soviet Military and Arms Control.* ACIS Working Paper 10. Los Angeles, Calif.: Center for International and Strategic Affairs, November 1977.

Garthoff, Raymond L. *The Great Transition: American-Soviet Relations and the End of the Cold War.* Washington, D.C.: Brookings Institution, 1994.

George, Alexander L., Philip J. Farley, and Alexander Dallin, eds. *U.S.-Soviet Security Cooperation: Achievements, Failures, Lessons.* New York: Oxford University Press, 1988.

Glagolev, Igor S. "The Soviet Decision-Making Process in Arms Control Negotiations." *Orbis,* Winter 1978, pp. 767-776.

Greene, William C. *Soviet Nuclear Weapons Policy: A Research Guide.* Boulder, Colo.: Westview, 1984.

Holloway, David. *The Soviet Union and the Arms Race.* New Haven, Conn.: Yale University Press, 1983.

Jalonen, Olli-Pckka. *Captors of Denuclearization? Belarus, Kazakhstan, Ukraine, and Nuclear Disarmament.* Tampere, Finland: Tampere Peace Research Institute, 1994.

Jasinski, Michael, Christina Cheun, and Charles D. Ferguson. "Russia: Of Truth and Testing." *Bulletin of the Atomic Scientists,* September/October 2003, pp. 60-65.

Johnson, Craig M. *The Russian Federation's Ministry of Atomic Energy: Programs and Developments.* Richland, Wash.: Pacific Northwest National Laboratory, February 2000.

Jönsson, Christer. *Soviet Bargaining Behavior: The Nuclear Test Ban Case.* New York: Columbia University Press, 1979.

Kaliadin, A.N., O.V. Bogdanov, and G.A. Vorontsov. *Prevention of Nuclear War: Soviet Scientists' Viewpoints.* New York: United Nations Institute for Training and Research, 1983.

Kartchner, Kerry M. *A Strategic Planning Framework for Predicting and Evaluating Soviet Interests in Arms Control, Vols. I and II.* Monterey, Calif.: U.S. Naval Postgraduate School, August 1989.

Kullberg, Judith S. *The End of New Thinking? Elite Ideologies and the Future of Russian Foreign Policy.* Columbus: Ohio State University, Mershon Center, July 1993.

Lambert, Stephen P. and David A. Miller. *Russia's Crumbling Tactical Nuclear Weapons Complex: An Opportunity for Arms Control.* INSS Occasional Paper 12. Colorado Springs, Colo.: USAF Institute for National Security Studies, April 1997.

Larson, Thomas B. *Disarmament and Soviet Policy, 1964-1968.* Englewood Cliffs, N.J.: Prentice-Hall, Inc., 1969.

Mandelbaum, Michael, ed. *The Other Side of the Table: The Soviet Approach to Arms Control.* New York: Council on Foreign Relations Press, 1990.

Miller, Timothy D. and Jeffrey A. Larsen, "Dealing with Russia's Tactical Nuclear Weapons: Cash for Kilotons." *Navy War College Review,* Spring 2004, pp. 64-86.

New Independent States Reader. Washington, D.C.: U.S. Arms Control and Disarmament Agency, January 1994.

Nordyke, Milo D. *The Soviet Program for Peaceful Uses of Nuclear Weapons.* Livermore, Calif.: Center for Global Security Research, October 1996.

The Nuclear Successor States of the Soviet Union: Status Report on Nuclear Weapons, Fissile Material, and Export Controls. Monterey, Calif.: Monterey Institute of International Studies, March 1998.

Parrott, Bruce. *The Soviet Union and Ballistic Missile Defense.* Boulder, Colo.: Westview, 1987.

Payne, Samuel B. Jr. *The Soviet Union and SALT.* Cambridge, Mass.: MIT Press, 1980.

Pikayev, Alexander A. *The Rise and Fall of START II: The Russian View.* Washington, D.C.: Carnegie Endowment for International Peace, September 1999.

Podvig, Pavel. *Russian Strategic Nuclear Forces.* Cambridge, Mass.: MIT Press, 2001.

Potter, William C. *Nuclear Profiles of the Soviet Successor States.* Monterey, Calif.: Monterey Institute of International Studies, May 1993.

Savel'yev, Aleksandr and Nikolay N. Detinov. *The Big Five: Arms Control Decision-Making in the Soviet Union.* Westport, Conn.: Praeger, 1995.

Schecter, Jerrold. *Russian Negotiating Behavior.* Washington, D.C.: United States Institute of Peace, 1998.

Sherr, Alan B. *The Other Side of Arms Control: Soviet Objectives in the Gorbachev Era.* Boston, Mass.: Unwin Hyman, 1988.

Shimko, Keith L. *Images and Arms Control: Perceptions of the Soviet Union in the Reagan Administration.* Ann Arbor: University of Michigan Press, 1991.

Snyder, Jed. C., ed. *After Empire: The Emerging Geopolitics of Central Asia.* Washington, D.C.: National Defense University Press, 1995.

Sokov, Nikolai N. *Russia's Approach to Deep Reductions of Nuclear Weapons: Opportunities and Problems.* Occasional Paper 27. Washington, D.C.: Henry L. Stimson Center, June 1996.

Solokovsky, V. D. *Soviet Military Strategy.* New York: Crane Russak, 1975.

Sonnenfeld, Helmut and William G. Hyland. "Soviet Perspectives on Security." *Adelphi Paper* 150. London: International Institute of Strategic Studies, 1979.

The Soviet Stand on Disarmament: A Collection of Nineteen Basic Soviet Documents on General and Complete Disarmament, the Termination of Nuclear Weapons Tests, and the Relaxation of International Tensions. New York: Crosscurrents Press, 1962.

Spector, Leonard S. "Missing the Forest for the Trees: U.S. Non-Proliferation Programs in Russia." *Arms Control Today,* June 2001, pp. 6-11.

Towle, Philip. *Arms Control and East-West Relations.* London: Croom Helm Ltd., 1983.

Ulam, Adam B. *Dangerous Relations: The Soviet Union in World Politics, 1970-1982.* New York: Oxford University Press, 1983.

———. *Expansion and Coexistence: Soviet Foreign Policy 1917-1973.* New York: Praeger, 1974.

————. *The Rivals: America and Russia Since World War II.* New York: Penguin Books, 1971.

U.S. Congress. Office of Technology Assessment. *Proliferation and the Former Soviet Union.* Washington, D.C.: U.S. Government Printing Office, September 1994.

Vigor, P.H. *The Soviet View of Disarmament.* New York: St. Martin's Press, 1986.

Weapons of Mass Destruction: Reducing the Threat from the Former Soviet Union. Washington, D.C.: General Accounting Office, October 1994.

Weber, Steve. *Cooperation and Discord in U.S.-Soviet Arms Control.* Princeton, N.J.: Princeton University Press, 1991.

Wolfstahl, Jon Brook, Christina-Astrid Chuen, and Emily Ewell Daughtry, eds. *Nuclear Status Report: Nuclear Weapons, Fissile Material, and Export Controls in the Former Soviet Union.* Washington, D.C.: Carnegie Endowment, 2001.

Yergin, Daniel and Thane Gustafson. *Russia 2010: And What It Means for the World.* New York: Vintage Books, February 1995.

South Asia

Ahmar, Moonis. *Confidence-Building Measures in South Asia.* Geneva, Switz.: Programme for Strategic and International Security Studies, 1991.

Ahmed, Samina and David Cortright. *South Asia at the Nuclear Crossroads.* Washington, D.C.: Fourth Freedom Foundation, April 2001.

Arnett, Eric. "Nuclear Weapons and Arms Control in South Asia after the Test Ban." SIPRI Research Report No. 14. Stockholm, Swe.: 1998.

Azizian, Rouben. *Nuclear Developments in South Asia and the Future of Global Arms Control.* Wellington, N.Z.: Centre for Strategic Studies, Victoria University of Wellington, 2001.

Chari, P.R. *Indo-Pakistan Nuclear Standoff: The Role of the U.S.* New Delhi, India: Manohar, 1995.

Cohen, Stephen P. *India: Emerging Power.* Washington, D.C.: Brookings Institute, 2001.

————. *The United States, India, and Pakistan: Retrospect and Prospect.* ACDIS Occasional Paper. Urbana-Champaign: University of Illinois, July 1997.

Davis, Zachary S. *Nuclear Nonproliferation Strategies for South Asia.* Washington, D.C.: Congressional Research Service, May 1994.

Ganguly, Sumit. *Conflict Unending: India-Pakistan Relations Since 1947.* New York: Columbia University Press, 2002.

Gupta, Amit. *Building an Arsenal: India, Israel, Brazil.* Westport, Conn.: Praeger, 1997.

Haas, Richard N. and Morton H. Halperin, chairs. *After the Tests, U.S. Policy Toward India and Pakistan.* Report of an Independent Task Force. Washington, D.C.: Brookings Institution and Council on Foreign Relations, 1998.

Jones, Rodney W. *Nuclear Proliferation: Islam, the Bomb, and South Asia.* Washington Papers No. 82. Washington, D.C.: Georgetown University, Center for Strategic and International Studies, 1981.

Kamal, Nazir and Amit Gupta. *Prospects of Conventional Arms Control in South Asia.* Cooperative Monitoring Center Occasional Paper No. 5. Albuquerque, N.M.: Sandia National Laboratories, November 1998.

Lodhi, Maleeha. "Security Challenges in South Asia." *The Nonproliferation Review,* Summer 2001, p. 118.

Mistry, Dinshaw. *India and the Comprehensive Test Ban Treaty.* ACDIS Research Report. Urbana-Champaign: University of Illinois, March 1998.

Perkovitch, George. *India's Nuclear Bomb: The Impact on Global Proliferation.* Berkeley: University of California Press, November 1999.

Pregenzer, Arian L. "Security Nuclear Capabilities in India and Pakistan: Reducing the Terrorist and Proliferation Risk." *The Nonproliferation Review,* Spring 2003, pp. 1-8.

Preventing Nuclear Proliferation in South Asia. New York: Asia Society, 1995.

Ramana, M.V. and A.H. Nayyar. "India, Pakistan and the Bomb." *Scientific American,* December 2001, p. 72.

Singh, Shri Jaswant. *What Constitutes National Security in a Changing World Order? India's Strategic Thought.* Occasional Paper No. 6. Philadelphia: Center for the Advanced Study of India, University of Pennsylvania, June 1998.

Smith, Chris. *Security, Sovereignty and Nuclear Weapons in South Asia.* London: Council for Arms Control, 1993.

Smith, David O. *From Containment to Stability: Pakistan-United States Relations in the Post-Cold War Era.* Washington, D.C.: National Defense University Press, November 1993.

South Asia and the United States: After the Cold War. New York: Asia Society, 1994.

Talbott, Strobe. "Dealing with the Bomb in South Asia." *Foreign Affairs,* March/April 1999, pp. 110-122.

Tellis, Ashley J. *India's Emerging Nuclear Posture: Between Recessed Deterrent and Ready Arsenal.* Santa Monica, Calif.: RAND Corporation, 2001.

Testing the Limits: The India-Pakistan Nuclear Gambit. Washington, D.C.: Transnational Institute and Institute for Policy Studies, August 1998.

Thomas, Troy S. and Stephen D. Kiser. *Lords of the Silk Route: Violent Non-State Actors in Central Asia.* INSS Occasional Paper 43. Colorado Springs, Colo: USAF Institute for National Security Studies, May 2002.

Waslekar, Sundeep. *Indian and Pakistani Approaches Towards Nuclear Proliferation.* Geneva, Switz.: Graduate Institution of International Studies, 1993.

Williams, Shelton L. *The U.S., India, and the Bomb.* Studies in International Affairs No. 12. Baltimore, Md.: Johns Hopkins Press, 1969.

Preventing War

Allison, Graham T., Albert Carnesale, and Joseph S. Nye Jr., eds. *Hawks, Doves, & Owls: An Agenda for Avoiding Nuclear War.* New York: W.W. Norton, 1985.

Allison, Graham, Ashton B. Carter, Steven E. Miller, and Philip Zelikow. *Cooperative Denuclearization: From Pledges to Deeds.* Cambridge, Mass.: Harvard University, Center for Science and International Affairs, January 1993.

Allison, Graham, Owen R. Cote Jr., Richard A. Falkenrath, and Steven E. Miller. *Avoiding Nuclear Anarchy: Containing the Threat of Loose Russian Nuclear Weapons and Fissile Material.* Cambridge, Mass.: MIT Press, 1996.

Brown, Seyom. *The Causes and Prevention of War.* New York: St. Martin's Press, 1987.

Krasner, Stephen D., ed. *International Regimes.* Ithaca, N.Y.: Cornell University Press, 1983.

Chemical and Biological Weapons

Ali, Javed. "Chemical Weapons and the Iran-Iraq War: A Case Study in Noncompliance." *The Nonproliferation Review,* Spring 2001, p. 28.

Alibek, Ken with Stephen Handelman. *Biohazard.* New York: Delta Trade Paperbacks, 1999.

Aspen Strategy Group. *Chemical Weapons and Western Security Policy.* Lanham, Md.: University Press of America, 1986.

Barton, Rod. *Chemical Weapons Inspections in Iraq: Verification Implications for the Chemical Weapons Convention.* Canberra: Australian National University, Peace Research Centre, June 1993.

Bernauer, Thomas. *The Chemistry of Regime Formation: Explaining International Cooperation for a Comprehensive Ban on Chemical Weapons.* Aldershot, U.K.: Dartmouth Publishing, 1993.

Biological Weapons: Effort to Reduce Former Soviet Threat Offers Benefits, Poses New Risks. Washington, D.C.: General Accounting Office, April 2000.

Biotechnology Research in an Age of Terrorism: Confronting the "Dual Use" Dilemma. Washington, D.C.: National Research Council of the National Academies, October 2003.

Bowman, Steven R. *Iraqi Chemical Weapons Capabilities.* Washington, D.C.: Congressional Research Service, February 1993.

Brown, Mark. *Public Trust and Technology: Chemical Weapons Destruction in the United States.* Washington, D.C.: Committee for National Security, December 1992.

Burgess, Richard H. "Implementation of the Chemical Weapons Convention in the United States: A Viewpoint from Industry." *The Monitor: Nonproliferation, Demilitarization and Arms Control,* Fall 1999/Winter 2000, p. 8.

Burgess, Stephen and Helen Purkitt. *The Rollback of Africa's Biological Warfare Program.* INSS Occasional Paper 37. Colorado Springs, Colo.: USAF Institute for National Security Studies, February 2001.

"The Chairman's Text of the BWC Protocol." Special Section of *Arms Control Today,* May 2001, pp. 10-27.

Chemical and Biological Weapons Reader. Washington, D.C.: U.S. Arms Control and Disarmament Agency, February 1995.

The Control of Chemical and Biological Weapons. New York: Carnegie Endowment for International Peace, 1971.

Crone, Hugh D. *Banning Chemical Weapons.* Cambridge, U.K.: Cambridge University Press, 1992.

Dando, Malcolm. *Biological Warfare in the 21st Century: Biotechnology and the Proliferation of Biological Weapons.* New York: Brassey's, 1994.

Douglass, Joseph D. Jr. and Neil C. Livingstone. *America the Vulnerable: The Threat of Chemical and Biological Warfare.* Lexington, Mass: Lexington, 1987.

Findlay, Trevor. *Peace Through Chemistry: The New Chemical Weapons Convention.* Canberra: Australian National Univeristy, 1993.

————, ed. *Chemical Weapons and Missile Proliferation: With Implications for the Asia/Pacific Region.* Boulder, Colo.: Lynne Rienner, 1991.

Geissler, Erhard. *Strengthening the Biological Warfare Convention by Confidence Building Measures.* SIPRI Chemical and Biological Warfare Studies No. 10. New York: Oxford University Press, 1990.

————, ed. *Biological and Toxin Weapons Today.* Oxford, U.K.: Oxford University Press, 1987.

Hammond, James W. Jr. *Poison Gas: The Myths versus Reality.* Westport, Conn.: Greenwood Press, 1999.

Kadlec, Robert P. "First Do No Harm." *Arms Control Today,* May 2001, pp. 16-17.

Kellman, Barry and Edward Tanzman. *Implementing the Chemical Weapons Convention: Legal Issues.* Washington, D.C.: Lawyers Alliance for World Security, July 1994.

Livingstone, Neil C. and Joseph D. Douglass. *CBW: The Poor Man's Atomic Bomb.* Cambridge, Mass.: Institute for Foreign Policy Analysis, 1984.

McElroy, Rodney J. *Briefing Book on Chemical Weapons.* Washington, D.C.: Council for a Livable World, 1989.

McNaught, L.W. *Nuclear, Biological, and Chemical Warfare.* Elmsford, N.Y.: Pergamon-Brassey's, 1983.

Meeker, Thomas A. *Chemical/Biological Warfare.* Los Angeles: California State University, Center for the Study of Armament and Disarmament, 1972.

Moodie, Michael. "The Soviet Union, Russia, and the Biological and Toxin Weapons Convention." *The Nonproliferation Review,* Spring 2001, p. 20.

Pearson, Graham, Nicholas A. Sims, Malcolm R. Dando, and Ian R. Kenyon. *The Biological and Toxin Weapons Convention Protocol: Proposed Complete Text for an Integrated Regime.* Bradford, U.K.: University of Bradford Department of Peace Studies, March 2000.

Roberts, Brad. *Hype or Reality? The "New Terrorism" and Mass Casualty Attacks.* Washington, D.C.: Chemical and Biological Arms Control Institute, 2000.

Roberts, Guy. *Arms Control Without Arms Control: The Failure of the Biological Weapons Convention Protocol and a New Paradigm for Fighting the Threat of Biological Weapons.* INSS Occasional Paper 49. Colorado Springs, Colo.: USAF Institute for National Security Studies, March 2003.

Robinson, Julian Perry. *Chemical and Biological Warfare Developments.* SIPRI Chemical and Biological Warfare Studies No. 6. New York: Oxford University Press, 1986.

———. *Chemical/Biological Warfare: An Introduction and a Bibliography.* Los Angeles: California State University, Center for the Study of Armament and Disarmament, 1974.

———. *Chemical Weapons Arms Control: A Framework for Considering Policy Alternatives.* Philadelphia, Penn: Taylor and Francis, 1985.

———. *NATO Chemical Weapons Policy and Posture.* ADIU Occasional Paper 4. Brighton, U.K.: University of Sussex, 1986.

———. *SIPRI Chemical and Biological Warfare Studies, Volumes 1-7: The Chemical Industry and the Projected Chemical Weapons Convention.* Oxford, U.K.: Oxford University Press, 1986/87.

Rosenberg, Barbara Hatch. "Allergic Reaction: Washington's Response to the BWC Protocol." *Arms Control Today,* July/August 2001, pp. 3-8.

Sagan Scott D. "The Commitment Trap: Why the United States Should Not Use Nuclear Threats to Deter Biological and Chemical Weapons Attacks." *International Security,* Spring 2000, p. 85.

Sims, Nicholas A. *The Diplomacy of Biological Disarmament: Vicissitudes of a Treaty in Force, 1975-1985.* New York: St. Martin's Press, 1988.

———. "Four Decades of Missed Opportunities to Strengthen the BWC?" *Disarmament Diplomacy,* June 2001, p. 15.

Smithson, Amy E., ed. *The Chemical Weapons Convention Handbook.* Washington, D.C.: Henry L. Stimson Center, September 1993.

———. *Toxic Archipelago: Preventing Proliferation from the Former Soviet Chemical and Biological Weapons Complexes.* Washington, D.C.: Henry L. Stimson Center, December 1999.

Smithson, Amy E. and Leslie-Anne Levy. *Ataxia: The Chemical and Biological Terrorism Threat and U.S. Response.* Washington, D.C.: Henry L. Simson Center, 2000.

Spiers, Edward M. *Chemical and Biological Weapons: A Study of Proliferation.* New York: St. Martin's Press, 1995.

Stashevsky, Gennadi. *Chemical Weapons.* Moscow: Novosti Press Agency, 1988.

Stock, Thomas and Ronald Sutherland. *National Implementation of the Future Chemical Weapons Convention.* SIPRI Chemical and Biological Warfare Studies No. 11. New York: Oxford University Press, 1990.

Stock, Thomas and Karl-Heinz Lohs, eds. *The Challenge of Old Chemical Munitions and Toxic Armament Wastes*. New York: Oxford University Press, 1998.

Storella, Mark C. *Poisoning Arms Control: The Soviet Union and Chemical-Biological Weapons*. Cambridge, Mass: Institute for Foreign Policy Analysis, 1984.

Sutherland, R.G. *The Chemical Weapons Convention: The Problems of Implementation*. Canberra: Australian National University, Peace Research Centre, July 1994.

Ter Haar, Barend. *The Future of Biological Weapons*. New York: Praeger, 1991.

Thomas, Ann Van Wynen and A.J. Thomas Jr. *International Limits on the Use of Chemical and Biological Weapons*. Dallas, Texas: Southern Methodist University School of Law, 1970.

Thränert, Oliver, ed. *Enhancing the Biological Weapons Convention*. Bonn, Ger.: Verlag J.H. Dietz Nachfolger 1996.

Toward a National Strategy for Combating Terrorism. Report of the Advisory Panel to Assess Domestic Response Capabilities for Terrorism Involving Weapons of Mass Destruction, December 2000.

Trapp, Ralf. *Chemical Weapons Free Zones*. SIPRI Chemical and Biological Warfare Studies No. 7. New York: Oxford University Press, 1987.

Tucker, Jonathan B. *Scourge: The Once and Future Threat of Smallpox*. New York: Atlantic Monthly Press, 2001.

———. ed. *The Chemical Weapons Convention: Implementation Challenges and Solutions*. Monterey, Calif.: Monterey Institute for International Studies, April 2001.

———. ed. *Toxic Terror: Assessing Terrorist Use of Chemical and Biological Weapons*. Cambridge, Mass.: Belfer Center for Science and International Affairs, Harvard University, 2000.

———. *The Utility of Sampling and Analysis for Compliance Monitoring of the Biological Weapons Convention*. Livermore, Calif.: Center for Global Security Research, February 1997.

U.S. Congress. *Arms Control: U.S. and International Efforts to Ban Biological Weapons*. Washington, D.C.: U.S. General Accounting Office, December 1992.

U.S. Congress. Office of Technology Assessment. *The Chemical Weapons Convention: Effects on the U.S. Chemical Industry*. Washington, D.C.: U.S. Government Printing Office, August 1993.

U.S. Congress. Senate. Committee on Foreign Relations. *Chemical Weapons Convention*. Washington, D.C.: U.S. Government Printing Office, 1997.

U.S. Congress. Senate. Committee on the Judiciary. *Constitutional Implications of the Chemical Weapons Convention.* Washington, D.C.: U.S. Government Printing Office, 1997.

Utgoff, Victor A. *The Challenges of Chemical Weapons: An American Perspective.* New York: St. Martin's Press, 1991.

Whitehair, Rebecca and Seth Brugger. "BWC Protocol Talks in Geneva Collapse Following U.S. Rejection." *Arms Control Today,* September 2001, p. 26.

Compliance

Batten, James K. *Arms Control and the Problem of Evasion.* Research Monograph 14. Princeton, N.J.: Princeton University, Center of International Studies, June 1962.

Byman, Daniel. "A Farewell to Arms Inspections." *Foreign Affairs,* January/February 2000, p. 119.

Compliance and the Future of Arms Control: Report of a Project Sponsored by the Center for International Security and Arms Control. Stanford, Calif.: Stanford University Center for International Security and Arms Control, 1988.

"Compliance," Special Edition of *Arms Control Today,* March/April 1984.

Dahlitz, Julie, ed. *Avoidance and Settlement of Arms Control Disputes.* New York: United Nations Publications, 1994.

Duffy, Gloria. *Compliance and the Future of Arms Control.* Stanford, Calif.: Center for International Security and Arms Control, 1988.

Gellner, Charles R. *Soviet Compliance Behavior: The Record on the SALT I and SALT II Agreements.* Washington, D.C.: Congressional Research Service, June 1985.

Jasani, Bhupendra, ed. *Satellites for Arms Control and Crisis Monitoring.* Oxford, U.K.: Oxford University Press, 1987.

Krass, Allan S., ed. *Verification: How Much Is Enough?* Philadelphia: Taylor and Francis, 1985.

——— and Catherine Girrier. *Disproportionate Response: American Policy and Alleged Soviet Treaty Violations.* Cambridge, Mass.: Union of Concerned Scientists, 1987.

Krepon, Michael. *Arms Control: Verification and Compliance.* New York: Foreign Policy Association, 1984.

——— and Mary Umberger, ed. *Verification and Compliance: A Problem-Solving Approach.* Cambridge, Mass.: Ballinger, 1988.

Moodie, Michael and Amy Sands. "New Approaches to Compliance
with Arms Control and Nonproliferation Agreements." *The Nonproliferation Review,* Spring 2001, p. 1.

Roberts, Brad. "Revisiting Fred Ikle's 1961 Question: After Detection,
What?" *The Nonproliferation Review,* Spring 2001, p. 10.

Rueckert, George. *On-Site Inspection in Theory and Practice: A Primer
on Modern Arms Control Regimes.* Westport, Conn.: Praeger,
1998.

Technology Advances and the Arms Control Agenda. Washington,
D.C.: American Association for the Advancement of Science,
January 1990.

Transparency in Armaments, Regional Dialogue, and Disarmament.
Disarmament Topical Papers 20. New York: United Nations, 1994.

Confidence and Security Building Measures

Ben-Horin, Y., R. Darilek, M. Jas, M. Lawrence, and A. Platt. *Building
Confidence and Security in Europe.* Santa Monica, Calif.: RAND
Corporation, December 1986.

Berg, Rolf and Adam-Daniel Rotfeld. *Building Security in Europe:
Confidence-Building Measures and the CSCE.* New York: Institute
for East-West Security Studies, 1986.

Borawski, John. *From the Atlantic to the Urals: Negotiating Arms Control at the Stockholm Conference.* Washington, D.C.: Pergamon-
Brassey's International Defense Publishers, 1988.

———. *Security for a New Europe: The Vienna Negotiations on Confi-
dence- and Security-Building Measures 1989-1990, and Beyond.*
London: Brassey's, 1992.

Boutilier, James A., ed. *Arms Control in the North Pacific: The Role
for Confidence Building and Verification.* Ottawa, Can.: Department of Foreign Affairs and International Trade, September 1994.

Bunn, George. *Strengthening Nuclear Non-Proliferation Security Assurances for Non-Nuclear-Weapons States.* Washington, D.C.:
Lawyers Alliance for World Security, February 1993.

*Confidence- and Security-Building Measures in the Americas: A Refer-
ence Book of Hemispheric Documents.* Washington, D.C.: U.S.
Arms Control and Disarmament Agency, December 1996.

Findlay, Trevor. *Asia/Pacific CSBMs: A Prospectus.* Working Paper
90. Canberra, Aus.: Peace Research Centre, 1990.

Krehbiel, Carl C. *Confidence- and Security-Building Measures in
Europe: The Stockholm Conference.* New York: Praeger, 1989.

Krepon, Michael, ed. *A Handbook of Confidence-Building Measures for Regional Security.* 2nd Edition. Washington, D.C.: Henry L. Stimson Center, January 1995.

Marquina, Antonio and Han Gunter Brauch, eds. *Confidence Building and Partnership in the Western Mediterranean: Tasks for Preventive Diplomacy and Conflict Avoidance.* Report 52. Mosbach, Ger.: AFES-PRESS, 1994.

Mottola, Kari, ed. *Ten Years after Helsinki: The Making of the European Security Regime.* Boulder, Colo.: Westview, 1986.

Scherbak, Igor. *Confidence-Building Measures and International Security: The Political and Military Aspects, a Soviet Approach.* New York: United Nations Institute for Disarmament Research, 1991.

Wheeler, Michael. *Positive and Negative Security Assurances.* Arlington, Va.: System Planning Corporation, September 1993.

Conventional Weapons

Anthony, Ian. *Russia and the Arms Trade.* New York: Oxford University Press, 1998.

The Arms Trade: Problems and Prospects in the Post-Cold War World. Special Edition of *The Annals of the American Academy of Political and Social Science,* September 1994.

Bertsch, Gary K., Richard T. Cupitt, and Steven Elliott-Gower, eds. *International Cooperation on Nonproliferation Export Controls.* Ann Arbor: University of Michigan Press, 1994.

Bitzinger, Richard A. *Chinese Arms Production and Sales to the Third World.* Santa Monica, Calif.: RAND Corporation, 1991.

―――. *The Globalization of Arms Production: Defense Markets in Transition.* Washington, D.C.: Defense Budget Project, December 1993.

Brogden, Peter and Walter Dorn, eds. *Controlling the Global Arms Threat.* Ottawa: Canadian Centre for Arms Control and Disarmament, 1992.

Carus, W. Seth. *Cruise Missile Proliferation in the 1990s.* New York: Praeger, 1992.

Cevasco, Frank M. *Survey and Assessment: Alternative Multilateral Export Control Structures.* Study Group on Enhancing Multilateral Export Controls for U.S. National Security, April 2001.

Clarke, Duncan, Daniel O'Conner, and Jason Ellis. *Send Guns and Money: Security Assistance and U.S. Foreign Policy.* Westport, Conn.: Praeger, 1997.

Conventional Arms Control and European Security: Proceedings from a Congressional Seminar. Washington, D.C.: American Association for the Advancement of Science, March 1989.

Conventional Arms Control: Former Warsaw Pact Nations' Treaty Compliance and U.S. Cost Control. Washington, D.C.: U.S. General Accounting Office, December 1993.

Crawford, Dorn. *Conventional Armed Forces in Europe (CFE): A Review and Update of Key Treaty Elements.* ACDA Report. Washington, D.C.: Arms Control and Disarmament Agency, December 1997.

Croft, Stuart, ed. *The Conventional Armed Forces in Europe Treaty: The Cold War Endgame.* Aldershot, U.K.: Dartmouth Publishing Company, 1994.

Cupitt, Richard T., Suzette Grillot, and Yuzo Murayama. "The Determinants of Nonproliferation Export Controls: A Membership-Free Explanation." *The Nonproliferation Review,* Summer 2001, p. 69.

Dhanapala, Jayantha, Mitsuro Donowaki, Swadesh Rana, and Lora Lumpe, eds. *Small Arms Control: Old Weapons, New Issues.* New York: UN Institute for Disarmament Research, 1999.

Falkenrath, Richard A. *Shaping Europe's Military Order: The Origins and Consequences of the CFE Treaty.* Cambridge, Mass.: Harvard University Center for Science and International Affairs, 1995.

Foerster, Schuyler, Willam A. Barry III, William R. Clontz, and Harold F. Lynch, Jr. *Defining Stability: Conventional Arms Control in a Changing Europe.* London: Westview, 1989.

The Global Diffusion of Military Technology. Madison, Wis.: University of Wisconsin Center for International Cooperation and Security Studies, December 1992.

Goodby, James E. *The Stockholm Conference: Negotiating a Cooperative Security System for Europe.* Washington: U.S. Department of State, Center for the Study of Foreign Affairs, 1986.

Grimmett, Richard F. *Conventional Arms Transfers to Developing Nations, 1992-1999.* Washington, D.C.: Congressional Research Service, August 2000.

Hallenbeck, Ralph A. and David E. Shaver, eds. *On Disarmament: The Role of Conventional Arms Control in National Security Strategy.* New York: Praeger, 1991.

Hartung, William. *Arms Transfer Controls as a Tool for Conflict Prevention in the Post-Cold War Era.* New York: World Policy Institute, March 1994.

Hidden Killers, The Global Landmine Crisis. Washington, D.C.: U.S. Department of State, September 1998.

Huisken, Ron. *The Cruise Missile and Arms Control.* Canberra Papers on Strategy and Defence, No. 20. Canberra: Australian National University, 1980.

Killebrew, R. *Conventional Defense and Total Deterrence.* Wilmington, Del.: Scholarly Resources, 1986.

Koulik, Sergey and Richard Kokoski. *Conventional Arms Control: Perspectives on Verification.* Oxford, U.K.: Oxford University Press, 1994.

Landmine Report 2001: Toward a Mine-Free World. International Campaign to Ban Landmines, August 2001.

Laurance, Edward J. *The International Arms Trade.* New York: Lexington, 1992.

Laurance, Edward J. *The United Nations Register of Conventional Arms Options and Proposals for Enhancement and Further Development."* Monterey, Calif.: Monterey Institute of International Studies, September 1994.

Laurance, Edward J., Siemon T. Weyeman, and Herbert Wulf. *Arms Watch: SIPRI Report on the First Year of the UN Register of Conventional Arms.* New York: Oxford University Press, 1993.

Lewis, James A., et al. *Computer Exports and National Security in a Global Era: New Tools for a New Century.* Washington, D.C.: Center for Strategic and International Studies, May 2001.

Lombard, Bennie. "Small Arms and Light Weapons: A Neglected Issue, a Renewed Focus." *Disarmament Diplomacy,* August 2000.

Lumpe, Lora. "A 'New' Approach to the Small Arms Trade." *Arms Control Today,* January/February 2001, p. 11.

Lumpe, Lora, ed. *Running Guns: The Global Black Market in Small Arms.* Oslo, Nor.: International Peace Research Institute, 2000.

Lynch, Allen, ed. *Building Security in Europe: Confidence-Building Measures and the CSCE.* New York: Institute for East-West Security Studies, 1986.

McCausland, Jeffrey D. *The CFE Treaty: A Cold War Anachronism?* Carlisle, Penn.: U.S. Army War College, Strategic Studies Institute, March 1995.

Miller, Kathleen and Caroline Brooks. *Export Controls in the Framework Agreement Countries.* London: British American Security Information Council, July 2001.

Moodie, Michael. *Conventional Arms Control and Defense Acquisition: Catching the Caboose?* Washington, D.C.: Center for Strategic and International Studies, 1990.

Müller, Harald. "OSCE Principles and Norms on Small Arms." *Disarmament Diplomacy,* April 2000, p. 9.

Oelrich, Ivan. *Conventional Arms Control: The Limits and Their Verification.* Cambridge, Mass.: Harvard University Center for Science and International Affairs, 1990.

O'Prey, Kevin P. *The Arms Export Challenge: Cooperative Approaches to Export Management and Defense Conversion.* Washington, D.C.: Brookings Institution, 1995.

Peters, John E. *CFE and Military Stability in Europe.* Santa Monica, Calif.: RAND Corporation, 1997.

———. *The Changing Quality of Stability in Europe: The Conventional Forces in Europe Treaty Toward 2001.* Santa Monica, Calif.: RAND Corporation, 2000.

Pierre, Andrew J. and Dmitri V. Trenin, eds. *Russia in the World Arms Trade.* Washington, D.C.: Carnegie Endowment for International Peace, 1997.

Potter, William C. and Harlan W. Jencks, eds. *The International Missile Bazaar: The New Suppliers' Network.* Boulder, Colo.: Westview, 1994.

Pythian, Mark. *The Politics of British Arms Sales Since 1964.* Manchester, U.K.: Manchester University Press, 2000.

Rühl, Lothar. *MBFR: Lessons and Problems.* Adelphi Papers 176. London: International Institute of Strategic Studies, 1982.

Schultz, George. *Pursuing the Promise of Helsinki.* Washington, D.C.: U.S. Department of State, Bureau of Public Affairs, 1986.

Smith, Ron and Bernard Udis. "New Challenges to Arms Export Control: Whither Wassenaar?" *The Nonproliferation Review,* Summer 2001, p. 81.

Stohl, Rachel. "United States Weakens Outcome of UN Small Arms and Light Weapons Conference." *Arms Control Today,* September 2001, pp. 34-35.

Thompson, Kenneth W., ed. *Arms Control: Alliances, Arms Sales and the Future.* Lanham, Md.: University Press of America, 1993.

United Nations Institute for Disarmament Research. *Conventional Forces and Arms Limitations in Europe.* New York: United Nations, 1989.

U.S. Congress. House. Committee on Foreign Affairs. *Report of the National Academy of Sciences: The Future Design and Implementation of U.S. National Security Export Controls.* Washington, D.C.: U.S. Government Printing Office, January 1992.

U.S. Department of State. Bureau of Political-Military Affairs. *Hidden Killers: The Global Landmine Crisis. Report to the Congress on the Problem with Uncleared Landmines and the United States*

Strategy for Demining and Landmine Control. Washington, D.C.: U.S. Government Printing Office, December 1994.

Williamson, Roger. *Conventional Weapons, Conventional Wars: The Need for an Expanded Arms Control Agenda.* London: Council for Arms Control, May 1994.

Wulf, Herbert, ed. *Arms Industry Limited.* New York: Oxford University Press, 1993.

Crisis Stability

Blechman, Barry M. *Preventing Nuclear War: A Realistic Approach.* Bloomington, Ind.: Indiana University Press, 1985.

Blechman, Barry M. and Michael Krepon. *Nuclear Risk Reduction Centers.* Washington, D.C.: Center for Strategic and International Studies, 1985.

Borowski, John, ed. *Avoiding Nuclear War: Confidence-Building Measures for Crisis Stability.* Boulder, Colo: Westview, 1986.

Darilek, Richard E. *Conflict Prevention Measures: A Distinctive Approach to Arms Control?* PRAC Paper 14. College Park: University of Maryland, Center for International and Security Studies at Maryland, January 1995.

George, Alexander L. *Avoiding War: Problems of Crisis Management.* Boulder, Colo.: Westview, 1991.

Goldberg, Andrew C., Debra Van Opstal, and James H. Barkley, eds. *Avoiding the Brink: Theory and Practice in Crisis Management.* London: Brassey's, 1990.

Lebow, Richard Ned. *Nuclear Crisis Management: A Dangerous Illusion.* Ithaca, N.Y.: Cornell University Press, 1987.

Leighton, Richard M. *The Cuban Missile Crisis of 1962: A Case in National Security Crisis Management.* Washington, D.C.: National Defense University, 1978.

Lewis, John W. and Coit D. Blacker, eds. *Next Steps in the Creation of an Accidental Nuclear War Prevention Center.* Palo Alto, Calif.: Stanford Center for International Security and Arms Control, 1983.

Roderick, H., ed. *Avoiding Inadvertent War: Crisis Management.* Austin: LBJ School of Public Affairs, University of Texas, 1983.

Rusten, Lynn and Paul C. Stern. *Crisis Management in the Nuclear Age.* Washington, D.C.: National Academy Press, 1987.

Ury, William L. *Beyond the Hotline: Crisis Control to Prevent War.* Boston, Mass.: Houghton Mifflin, 1985.

Fissile Materials

Albright, David, Frans Berkhout, and William Walker. *Plutonium and Highly Enriched Uranium 1996 World Inventories, Capabilities and Policies.* New York: Oxford University Press, 1997.

Bergeron, Kenneth D. *Tritium on Ice: The Dangerous New Alliance of Nuclear Weapons and Nuclear Power.* Cambridge, Mass.: MIT Press, 2002.

Macfarlane, Allison, Frank von Hippel, Jungmin Kang, and Robert Nelson. "Plutonium Disposal, the Third Way." *Bulletin of the Atomic Scientists,* May/June 2001, pp. 53-57.

Makhijani, Arjun and Annie Makhijani. *Fissile Materials in a Glass, Darkly: Technical and Policy Aspects of the Disposition of Plutonium and Highly Enriched Uranium.* Takoma Park, Md.: Institute for Energy and Environmental Research, 1995.

Medalia, Jonathan. *Nuclear Weapons Production Capability Issues: Summary of Finding, and Choices.* Washington, D.C.: Congressional Research Service, October 1997.

Nuclear Waste: Foreign Countries' Approaches to High-Level Waste Storage and Disposal. Washington, D.C.: General Accounting Office, August 1994.

Nuclear Weapons Cleanup: Prospect Without Precedent. Seattle, Wash.: Military Production Network, January 1995.

U.S. Department of Energy. Office of Environmental Management. *Linking Legacies: Connecting the Cold War Nuclear Weapons Production Processes to Their Environmental Consequences.* Washington, D.C.: Department of Energy, January 1997.

Implementation

Aspects of Definition, Organization, and Verification. SIPRI Research Report No. 8. Oxford, U.K.: Oxford University Press, 1994.

Arnett, Eric H. *New Technologies for Security and Arms Control: Threats and Promise.* Washington, D.C.: American Association for the Advancement of Science, 1989.

"The Chairman's Text of the BWC Protocol," *Arms Control Today,* May 2001, pp. 11-27.

O'Hanlon, M., E. Bryton, and R. Hall. *Implementing START II.* Washington, D.C.: Congressional Budget Office, March 1993.

Paul, Derek, ed. *Disarmament's Missing Dimension : A UN Agency to Administer Multilateral Treaties.* Toronto, Can.: University of Toronto Press, 1990.

U.S. Congress, Office of Technology Assessment. *The Chemical Weapons Convention: Effects on the U.S. Chemical Industry.* Washington, D.C.: U.S. Government Printing Office, August 1993.

———. *Nuclear Safeguards and the International Atomic Energy Agency.* Washington, D.C.: U.S. Government Printing Office, April 1995.

Verification and Anti-Satellite Weapons. Washington, D.C.: Federation of American Scientists, 1983.

Wheeler, Michael. "Positive and Negative Security Assurances." Project on Rethinking Arms Control. PRAC Paper No. 9. College Park, Md.: Center for International and Security Studies at Maryland, February 1994.

Zile, Zigurds L., Robert Sharlet, and Jean C. Love. *The Soviet Legal System and Arms Inspection: A Case Study in Policy Implementation.* New York: Praeger, 1972.

Naval Arms Control

Blechman, Barry M. *The Control of Naval Armaments: Prospects and Possibilities.* Washington, D.C.: Brookings Institution, 1975.

Blechman, Barry M., William J. Durch, W. Philip Ellis, and Cathleen S. Fisher. *Naval Arms Control: A Strategic Assessment.* New York: St. Martin's Press, 1991.

Fieldhouse, Richard, ed. *Security at Sea: Naval Forces and Arms Control.* Oxford, U.K.: Oxford University Press, 1990.

Furst, Andreas, Volker Heise, and Steven E. Miller, eds. *Europe and Naval Arms Control in the Gorbachev Era.* New York: Oxford University Press, 1992.

Goldblat, Jozef, ed. *Maritime Security: The Building of Confidence.* Geneva, Switz.: UN Institute for Disarmament Research, 1992.

Hill, J.R. *Arms Control at Sea.* Annapolis, Md.: Naval Institute Press, 1989.

Lodgaard, Sverre, ed. *Naval Arms Control.* London: Sage Publications, 1990.

Prospects for Arms Control in the Ocean. SIPRI Research Report No. 7. Stockholm, Swe.: Almqvist & Wiksell, September 1972.

Tritten, James J. *A New Case for Naval Arms Control.* Monterey, Calif.: Naval Postgraduate School, December 1992.

U.S. Congress. Senate. Committee on Armed Services. *Approaches to Naval Arms Control.* Washington, D.C.: U.S. Government Printing Office, May 1990.

Nonproliferation

Arnett, Eric H. and W. Thomas Wander. *The Proliferation of Advanced Weaponry: Technology, Motivations, and Responses.* Washington, D.C.: American Association for the Advancement of Science, 1992.

Bader, William B. *The United States and the Spread of Nuclear Weapons.* New York: Pegasus, 1968.

Bailey, Kathleen C. *Strengthening Nuclear Non-Proliferation.* Boulder, Colo.: Westview, 1993.

Barletta, Michael. *Proliferation Challenges and Nonproliferation Opportunities for New Administrations.* Washington, D.C.: Center for Nonproliferation Studies, September 2000.

Barnaby, C.F., ed. *Preventing the Spread of Nuclear Weapons.* Pugwash Monograph 1. New York: Humanities Press, 1969.

Barnaby, Frank. *How Nuclear Weapons Spread: Nuclear-Weapon Proliferation in the 1990s.* London: Routledge, 1993.

Bee, Ronald J. *Nuclear Proliferation: The Post-Cold-War Challenge.* Headline Series No. 303. New York: Foreign Policy Association, 1995.

Bertsch, Gary K., Richard T. Cupitt, and Steven Elliott-Gower, eds. *International Cooperation on Nonproliferation Export Controls.* Ann Arbor: University of Michigan Press, 1994.

Blocking the Spread of Nuclear Weapons: American and European Perspectives. New York: Council on Foreign Relations, 1986.

Boardman, Robert and James F. Keeley, eds. *Nuclear Exports and World Politics.* New York: St. Martin's Press, 1983.

Boutwell, Klare, et al. *Lethal Commerce: The Global Trade in Small Arms and Light Weapons.* American Academy of Arts & Sciences, 1995.

Bowen, Wyn Q. *The Politics of Ballistic Missile Nonproliferation.* Southampton, U.K.: Southampton Studies in International Policy, 2000.

Brenner, Michael. *Spreading Nuclear Capabilities: New Trends.* Los Angeles: University of California, Center for International and Strategic Affairs, 1986.

Bukharin, Oleg. "Downsizing Russia's Nuclear Warhead Production Infrastructure." *The Nonproliferation Review,* Spring 2001, p. 116.

Burrows, William E. and Robert Windrem. *Critical Mass: The Dangerous Race for Superweapons in a Fragmenting World.* New York: Simon & Schuster, 1994.

Central Intelligence Agency. *Unclassified Report to Congress on the Acquisition of Technology Relating to Weapons of Mass Destruction and Advanced Conventional Munitions.* September 2001.

Central Intelligence Agency. *The Weapons Proliferation Threat.* March 1995.

Chow, Brian G. and Kenneth Solomon. *Limiting the Spread of Weapon-Usable Fissile Materials.* Santa Monica, Calif.: RAND Corporation, 1994.

Cimbala, Stephen J., ed. *Deterrence and Nuclear Proliferation in the Twenty-First Century.* New York: Praeger, 2001.

Cirincione, Joseph, ed. *Repairing the Regime: Preventing the Spread of Weapons of Mass Destruction.* Washington, D.C.: Carnegie Endowment, 2000.

Clausen, Peter A. *Nonproliferation and the National Interest: America's Response to the Spread of Nuclear Weapons.* New York: Harper Collins, 1992.

Council on Foreign Relations. *Blocking the Spread of Nuclear Weapons: American and European Perspectives.* New York: Council on Foreign Relations, 1986.

Daalder, Ivo H. *Stepping Down the Thermonuclear Ladder: How Low Can We Go?* College Park, Md.: Center for International and Security Studies at Maryland, June 1993.

Davis, Zachary S. and Benjamin Frankel, eds. *The Proliferation Puzzle: Why Nuclear Weapons Spread and What Results.* London: Frank Cass, 1993.

Dewitt, David B. *Nuclear Non-Proliferation and Global Security.* New York: St. Martin's Press, 1987.

Dhanapala, Jayantha. "The NPT at a Crossroads." *The Nonproliferation Review,* Spring 2000, p. 138.

Dunn, Lewis A. *Containing Nuclear Proliferation.* Adelphi Paper 263. London: International Institute for Strategic Studies, Winter 1991.

———. *Controlling the Bomb: Nuclear Proliferation in the 1980s.* New Haven, Conn.: Yale University Press, 1982.

———, et al. *Global Proliferation: Dynamics, Acquisition Strategies, and Responses.* McLean, Va.: Science Applications International Corporation, December 1992.

Epstein, William. *The Last Chance: Nuclear Proliferation and Arms Control.* New York: Free Press, 1976.

Evan, William M. and Ved P. Nanda, eds. *Nuclear Proliferation and the Legality of Nuclear Weapons.* Lanham, Md.: University Press of America, 1995.

Fetter, Seve. *Verifying Nuclear Disarmament.* Washington, D.C.: Henry L. Stimson Center, October 1996.

Fischer, David. *Stopping the Spread of Nuclear Weapons: The Past and the Prospects.* London: Routledge, 1992.

———. *Towards 1995: The Prospects for Ending the Proliferation of Nuclear Weapons.* Brookfield, Vt.: Dartmouth Publishing, 1993.

Fischer, Georges. *The Non-Proliferation of Nuclear Weapons.* London: Europa Publications, 1970.

Frankel, Benjamin. *Opaque Proliferation: Methodological and Policy Implications.* London: Frank Cass, 1991.

Frankel, Francine R., ed. *Bridging the Nonproliferation Divide: The United States and India.* Lanham, Md.: University Press of America, 1995.

Gardner, Gary. *Nuclear Nonproliferation: A Primer.* Boulder, Colo.: Lynne Rienner, 1994.

Goldblat, Jozef. *Nuclear Nonproliferation: The Status and Prospects.* Ottawa: Canadian Institute for International Peace and Security, June 1989.

Gray, Peter. *Briefing Book on the Nonproliferation of Nuclear Weapons.* Washington, D.C.: Council for a Livable World Education Fund, December 1993.

Greenwood, Ted, Harold A. Feiveson, and Theodore B. Taylor. *Nuclear Proliferation: Motivations, Capabilities, and Strategies for Control.* New York: McGraw-Hill, 1977.

Hadley, Stephen J. and Mitchell Reiss, et al. *Nuclear Proliferaiton: Confronting the New Challenges.* New York: Council on Foreign Relations Press, 1995.

Harves, John. *Nuclear Proliferation: Down to the Hard Cases.* College Park, Md.: Center for International and Security Studies at Maryland, June 1993.

International Perspectives on Missile Proliferation and Defenses. Monterey, Calif.: Monterey Institute for International Studies, March 2001.

Johnson, Rebecca. *Non-Proliferation Treaty: Challenging Times.* London: Acronym Institute, February 2000.

Jones, Rodney W. and Mark G. McDonough. *Tracking Proliferation: A Guide in Maps and Charts 1998.* Washington: Carnegie Endowment for International Peace, 1998.

Kapur, Ashok. *International Nuclear Proliferation: Multilateral Diplomacy and Regional Aspects.* New York: Praeger, 1979.

Kincade, William H. and Christoph Bertram, eds. *Nuclear Proliferation in the 1980s.* New York: St. Martin's Press, 1982.

Kubbig, Bernd W. *German and American Export Control Policies in an Era of Proliferation: From Divergence to Convergence?* Kingston, Can.: Queen's University, Centre for International Relations, 1993.

Kuntzel, Matthias. *Bonn & the Bomb: German Politics and the Nuclear Option.* Boulder, Colo.: Westview, 1995.

Lall, Betty Goetz. *Nuclear Weapons: Can Their Spread be Halted?* New York: Council on Religion and International Studies, 1965.

Latham, Andrew, ed. *Multilateral Approaches to Non-Proliferation.* North York, Can.: York University Centre for Intenrational and Security Studies, 1995.

———, ed. *Non-Proliferation Agreements, Arrangements and Responses: Proceedings of the 1996 Canadian Non-Proliferation Workshop.* North York, Can.: York University Centre for International and Strategic Studies, 1997.

Latter, Richard. "Nuclear Non-Proliferation in the Twenty-First Century." *Wilton Park Paper,* January 2002.

Lavoy, Peter R., Scott D. Sagan, and James J. Wirtz. *Planning the Unthinkable: How New Powers Will Use Nuclear, Biological, and Chemical Weapons.* Ithaca, N.Y.: Cornell University Press, 2000.

Lugar, Richard G. "The Next Steps in U.S. Nonproliferation Policy." *Arms Control Today,* December 2002, pp. 3-7.

Manning, Robert A. *Back to the Future: Toward a Post-Nuclear Ethic—The New Logic of Nonproliferation.* Washington, D.C.: Progressive Foundation, January 1994.

Markey, Edward J. and Douglas C. Waller. *Nuclear Peril: The Politics of Proliferation.* Cambridge, Mass.: Ballinger Publishing Co., 1982.

Mataija, Steven and Lyne C. Bourque, eds. *Proliferation and International Security: Converging Roles of Verification, Confidence Building and Peacekeeping.* Toronto, Can.: Center for International and Strategic Studies, 1993.

McKnight, Allan D. *Nuclear Non-Proliferation: IAEA and Euratom.* Occasional Paper No. 7. Washington, D.C.: Carnegie Endowment for International Peace, June 1970.

McMahon, K. Scott and Dennis Gormley. *Controlling the Spread of Land-Attack Cruise Missiles.* Marina del Rey, Calif.: American Institute for Strategic Cooperation, January 1995.

Meller, Eberhard, ed. *Internationalization: An Alternative to Nuclear Proliferation?* Cambridge, Mass.: Oelgeschlager, Gunn & Hain, Publishers, 1980.

Meyer, Stephen M. *The Dynamics of Nuclear Proliferation.* Chicago: University of Chicago Press, 1984.

Molander, Roger and Robbie Nichols. *Who Will Stop the Bomb: A Primer on Nuclear Proliferation.* Washington, D.C.: Roosevelt Center for American Policy Studies, 1986.

Mozley, Robert. *The Politics and Technology of Nuclear Proliferation.* Seattle: University of Washington Press, 1997.

Müller, Harald, David Fischer, and Wolfgang Kötter. *Nuclear Non-Proliferation and Global Order.* Oxford, U.K.: Oxford University Press, 1994.

New Threats: Responding to the Proliferation of Nuclear, Chemical, and Delivery Capabilities to the Third World. Aspen Strategy Group Report. Lanham, Md.: University Press of America, 1990.

Nolan, Janne E. *Trappings of Power: Ballistic Missiles in the Third World.* Washington, D.C.: Brookings Institution, 1991.

Nonproliferation Reader. Washington, D.C.: U.S. Arms Control and Disarmament Agency, January 1994.

Nuclear Power and Nuclear Weapons Proliferation. Report of the Nuclear Fuels Policy Working Group. Washington, D.C.: Atlantic Council of the United States, 1977.

Nunn, Sam, chair. *Managing the Global Nuclear Materials Threat.* Washington, D.C.: Center for Strategic and International Studies, January 2000.

Nye, Joseph S. *The International Nonproliferation Regime.* Occasional Paper 23. Muscatine, Iowa: Stanley Foundation, July 1980.

Parachini, John. "Non-Proliferation Policy and the War on Terrorism." *Arms Control Today,* October 2001, pp. 13-15.

Perkovitch, George and Ernest W. Lefever. "Loose Nukes: Arms Control Is No Place for Folly." *Foreign Affairs,* November/December 2000, p. 162.

Pilat, Joseph F. *The Nonproliferation Predicament.* New Brunswick, N.J.: Transaction Books, 1985.

Postures for Non-Proliferation: Arms Limitation and Security Policies to Minimize Nuclear Proliferation. London: Taylor & Francis, 1979.

Potter, William C. *Nuclear Power and Nonproliferation: An Interdisciplinary Perspective.* Cambridge, Mass.: Oelgeschlager, Gunn & Hain, Publishers, 1982.

Proliferation: Threat and Response. Washington: Office of the Secretary of Defense, November 1997 and January 2001.

Quester, George. *The Politics of Nuclear Proliferation.* Baltimore, Md.: Johns Hopkins University Press, 1973.

Ramberg, Bennett. *Global Nuclear Energy Risks: The Search for Preventive Medicine.* Boulder, Colo.: Westview, 1986.

Rattray, Gregory J. *Explaining Weapons Proliferation: Going Beyond the Security Dilemma.* INSS Occasional Paper 1. Colorado Springs, Colo.: USAF Institute for National Security Studies, July 1994.

Rauf, Tariq, ed. *Strengthened IAEA Safeguards and Regional Non-Proliferation Strategies.* Aurora Paper 23. Ottawa: Canadian Centre for Global Security, March 1994.

————. *Towards NPT 2005: An Action Plan for the 13 Steps Towards Nuclear Disarmament Agreed at NPT 2000.* Monterey, Calif.: Monterey Institute for International Affairs, 2001.

Regulation of Nuclear Trade: Non-Proliferation, Supply, Safety. Paris: Nuclear Energy Agency, 1988.

Reiss, Mitchell. *Without the Bomb: The Politics of Nuclear Nonproliferation.* New York: Columbia University Press, 1988.

Reiss, Mitchell and Robert S. Litwak, eds. *Nuclear Proliferation After the Cold War.* Baltimore, Md.: Johns Hopkins University Press, 1994.

Roberts, Brad. "Proliferation and Nonproliferation in the 1990s: Looking for the Right Lessons." *The Nonproliferation Review,* Fall 1999, p. 70.

Roberts, Brad. *Weapons Proliferation in the 1990s.* Cambridge, Mass.: MIT Press, 1995.

Roberts, Guy. *Five Minutes Past Midnight: The Clear and Present Danger of Nuclear Weapons Grade Fissile Materials.* INSS Occasional Paper 8. Colorado Springs, Colo.: USAF Institute for National Security Studies, February 1996.

Rumsfeld, Donald H. et al. "Executive Summary of the Report of the Commission to Assess the Ballistic Missile Threat to the United States," 15 July 1998.

Sadruddin, Aga Khan, ed. *Nuclear War, Nuclear Proliferation, and Their Consequences.* New York: Oxford University Press, 1986.

Sagan, Scott D. and Kenneth N. Waltz. *The Spread of Nuclear Weapons: A Debate.* New York: W.W. Norton, 1995.

Sherman, Michael E. *Nuclear Proliferation: The Treaty and After.* Lindsay, Ontario: John Deyell, 1968.

Shields, John M. and William C. Potter. *Dismantling the Cold War: U.S. and NIS Perspectives on the Nunn-Lugar Cooperative Threat Reduction Program.* Cambridge, Mass.: MIT Press, 1997.

Shuey, Robert. *Nuclear, Biological, and Chemical Weapons and Ballistic Missiles: The State of Proliferation.* Washington, D.C.: Congressional Research Service, February 1998.

Simpson, John, ed. *Nuclear Non-Proliferation: An Agenda for the 1990s.* Cambridge, U.K.: Cambridge University Press, 1987.

Sokolski, Henry D. *Best of Intentions: America's Campaign Against Strategic Weapons Proliferation.* New York: Praeger, 2001.

Sokolski, Henry D. and James M. Ludes, eds. *Twenty First Century Weapons Proliferation: Are We Ready?* London: Frank Cass, 2001.

Sopko, John F. "The Changing Proliferation Threat." *Foreign Policy,* Winter 1996-1997, p. 105.

Spector, Leonard S. *Deterring Regional Threats from Nuclear Proliferation.* Carlisle, Penn.: U.S. Army War College, March 1992.

———. "Missing the Forest for the Trees: U.S. Non-Proliferation Programs in Russia." *Arms Control Today,* June 2001, p. 6.

Spector, Leonard S. with Jacqueline R. Smith. *Nuclear Ambitions: The Spread of Nuclear Weapons.* Boulder, Colo.: Westview, 1990.

Spector, Leonard S. and Mark McDonough. *Tracking Nuclear Proliferation: A Guide in Maps and Charts, 1995.* Washington, D.C.: Carnegie Endowment for International Peace, 1995.

Spector, Leonard S. and Virginia Foran. *Preventing Weapons Proliferation: Should Regimes be Combined?* Muscatine, Iowa: Stanford Foundation, 1992.

Stopping the Spread of Nuclear Weapons. United Nations Association of the United States, 1969.

Storer, Dan. "No Experience Necessary: The Nth Country Experiement." *Bulletin of the Atomic Scientists,* March/April 2002, pp. 56-63.

Taylor, John M. *Restricting Production of Fissionable Material as an Arms Control Measure: An Updated Historical Perspective.* Albuquerque, N.M.: Sandia National Laboratories, 1986.

Thränert, Oliver. *Preventing the Proliferation of Weapons of Mass Destruction: What Role for Arms Control?* Bonn, Ger.: Friedrich-Ebert Stiftung, November 1999.

Timerbaev, Roland M. and Meggen M. Watt. *Inventory of International Nonproliferation Organizations and Regimes.* Monterey, Calif.: Monterey Institute of International Studies, February 1995.

U.S. Arms Control and Disarmament Agency. Office of Public Affairs. *The Nonproliferation Reader.* Washington, D.C.: ACDA, June 1994.

U.S. Congress. Office of Technology Assessment. *Export Controls and Non-proliferation Policy.* Washington, D.C.: U.S. Government Printing Office, June 1994.

U.S. Congress. Office of Technology Assessment. *Proliferation of Weapons of Mass Destruction: Assessing the Risks.* Washington, D.C.: U.S. Government Printing Office, August 1993.

U.S. Congress. Senate. Committee on Governmental Affairs. *The Non-proliferation Primer*. Washington, D.C.: U.S. Government Printing Office, January 1998.

U.S. Nuclear Nonproliferation: U.S. Efforts to Help Other Countries Combat Nuclear Smuggling Need Strengthened Coordination and Planning. Washington, D.C.: General Accounting Office, May 2002.

Van Creveld, Martin. *Nuclear Proliferation and the Future of Conflict*. New York: Free Press, 1993.

Van Leeuwen, Marianne, ed. *The Future of the International Nuclear Non-Proliferation Regime*. Boston, Mass.: Martinus Nijhoff Publishers, 1995.

Waltz, Kenneth N. "The Spread of Nuclear Weapons: More May be Better." *Adelphi Paper* 171. London: International Institute of Strategic Studies, 1981.

Wander, W. Thomas, Eric H. Arnett, and Paul Bracken, eds. *The Diffusion of Advanced Weaponry: Technologies, Regional Implications and Responses*. Washington, D.C.: American Association for the Advancement of Science, 1994.

Weapons of Mass Destruction: Are the Nonproliferation Regimes Falling Behind? Muscatine, Iowa: Stanley Foundation, October 1996.

The Weapons Proliferation Threat. Langley, Va.: CIA Nonproliferation Center, March 1995.

Wentz, Walter B. *Nuclear Proliferation*. Washington, D.C.: Public Affairs Press, 1968.

Whitmore, D.C. *Characterization of the Nuclear Proliferation Threat*. Auburn, Wash.: Third Millennium Foundation, 1993.

Wohlstetter, Albert, Victor Gilinsky, Robert Gillette, and Roberta Wohlstetter. *Nuclear Policies: Fuel Without the Bomb*. Cambridge, Mass.: Ballinger Publishing Co., 1978.

Nuclear Weapons and Deterrence

Albright, David and Kevin O'Neill, eds. *The Challenges of Fissile Material Control*. Washington, D.C.: ISIS Report, 1999.

Arkin, William M. and Richard W. Fieldhouse. *Nuclear Battlefields: Global Links in the Arms Race*. Cambridge, Mass.: Ballinger, 1985.

Arnett, Eric. *Nuclear Weapons After the Comprehensive Test Ban: Implications for Modernization and Proliferation*. Oxford, U.K.: Oxford University Press, 1996.

Barnaby, Frank and P. Terrence Hopmann, eds. *Rethinking the Nuclear Weapons Dilemma in Europe.* Basingstoke, U.K.: Macmillan Press, 1988.

Binnendijk, Hans and James Goodby, eds. *Transforming Nuclear Deterrence.* Washington, D.C.: National Defense University Press, 1997.

Blair, Bruce. *The Logic of Accidental Nuclear War.* Washington, D.C.: Brookings Institution, 1993.

Blair, Bruce G., et al. *Toward True Security: A U.S. Nuclear Posture for the Next Decade.* Washington, D.C.: Federation of American Scientists, Union of Concerned Scientists, and Natural Resources Defense Council, June 2001.

Blechman, Peter R., Larry Campbell, Paul W. Crumlish, Michael N. Dobkowski, and Steven P. Lee. *The Nuclear Predicament: Nuclear Weapons in the Cold War and Beyond.* Englewood Cliffs, N.J.: Prentice-Hall, 1992.

Bobbitt, Philip, Lawrence Freedman, and Gregory Treverton, eds. *U.S. Nuclear Strategy: A Reader.* New York: New York University Press, 1989.

Boyer, Paul. *By the Bomb's Early Light: American Thought and Culture at the Dawn of the Atomic Age.* New York: Pantheon Books, 1985.

Bracken, Paul. *The Command and Control of Nuclear Forces.* New Haven, Conn.: Yale University Press, 1983.

———. "The Second Nuclear Age." *Foreign Affairs,* January/February 2000, p. 146.

Bromley, Mark. "Planning to Be Surprised: The U.S. Nuclear Posture Review and Its Implications for Arms Control." *BASIC Papers* No. 39, April 2002.

Bundy, McGeorge. *Danger and Survival: Choices About the Bomb in the First Fifty Years.* New York: Random House, 1988.

———. "Early Thoughts on Controlling the Nuclear Arms Race: A Report to the Secretary of State, January 1953." *International Security,* Fall 1982, pp. 3-27.

Bundy, McGeorge, William J. Crowe, and Sidney D. Drell. *Reducing Nuclear Danger: The Road Away from the Brink.* New York: Council on Foreign Relations Press, 1993.

Bundy, William. *The Nuclear Controversy: A Foreign Affairs Reader.* New York: New American Library, 1985.

Calder, Helen Caldicott. *Missile Envy: The Arms Race and Nuclear War.* New York: William Morrow, 1984.

Capello, John T., Gwendolyn M. Hall, and Stephen P. Lambert. *Tactical Nuclear Weapons: Debunking the Mythology.* INSS

Occasional Paper 46. Colorado Springs, Colo.: USAF Institute for National Security Studies, August 2002.

Carter, Ashton B., John D. Steinbruner, and Charles A. Zraket. *Managing Nuclear Operations.* Washington, D.C.: Brookings Institution, 1987.

Castelli, Jim. *Bishops and the Bomb: Waging Peace in a Nuclear Age.* New York: Doubleday, 1983.

Charles, Daniel. *Nuclear Planning in NATO: Pitfalls of First Use.* Cambridge, Mass: Ballinger Books, 1986.

Child, James W. *Nuclear War: The Moral Dimension.* New Brunswick, N.J.: Transaction Books, 1986.

Child, James W. and Ian Scherer. *Two Paths to Peace: Pacifism and Just War Theory in the Nuclear World.* Philadelphia, Penn.: Temple University Press, 1991.

The Church and the Bomb: Nuclear Weapons and Christian Conscience. London: Hodder and Stoughton, 1982.

Cimbala, Stephen J. *The Past and Future of Nuclear Deterrence.* Westport, Conn.: Praeger, 1998.

———. *Strategic Impasse: Offense, Defense, and Deterrence Theory and Practice.* New York: Greenwood Press, 1989.

Cirincione, Joseph, et al. *Deadly Arsenals: Tracking Weapons of Mass Destruction.* Washington, D.C.: Canegie Endowment for International Peace, 2002.

Cochran, Thomas B., William M. Arkin, and Milton M. Hoenig. *Nuclear Weapons Databook. Volume I: U.S. Nuclear Forces and Capabilities.* Cambridge, Mass.: Ballinger, 1984.

Cohran, Thomas B., William M. Arkin, Robert S. Norris, and Jeffrey I. Sands. *Nuclear Weapons Databook, Volume IV: Soviet Nuclear Weapons.* New York: Harper and Row, 1989.

Cochran, Thomas B., William M. Arkin, Robert S. Norris, and Milton M. Hoenig. *Nuclear Weapons Databook, Volume II: U.S. Nuclear Warhead Production.* Cambridge, Mass.: Ballinger, 1987.

Cohran, Thomas B., William M. Arkin, Robert S. Norris, and Milton M. Hoenig. *Nuclear Weapons Databook, Volume III: US Nuclear Warhead Facility Profiles.* Cambridge, Mass.: Ballinger, 1987.

Cohen, Avner and Steven Lee, eds. *Nuclear Weapons and the Future of Humanity.* Totowa, N.J: Rowman and Allanheld, 1986.

Cordesman, Anthony H. *The Global Nuclear Balance: A Quantitative and Arms Control Analysis.* Washington, D.C.: Center for Strategic and International Studies, January 2001.

Daalder, Ivo and James Lindsay. "A New Agenda for Nuclear Weapons." *Policy Brief* No. 94. Washington, D.C.: Brookings Institute, February 2002.

Daalder, Ivo and Terry Terriff, eds. *Rethinking the Unthinkable: New Directions for Nuclear Arms Control.* London: Frank Cass, 1993.

Dahl, Robert. *Controlling Nuclear Weapons: Democracy Versus Guardianship.* Syracuse, N.Y.: Syracuse University Press, 1985.

Dean, Jonathan. *The Final Stage of Nuclear Arms Control.* PRAC Paper 10. College Park, Md.: Center for International and Security Studies at Maryland, August 1994.

DeNardo, James. *The Amateur Strategist: Intuitive Deterrence Theories and the Politics of the Nuclear Arms Race.* Cambridge, U.K.: Cambridge University Press, 1995.

Dinnerstein, Herbert S. *War and the Soviet Union: Nuclear Weapons and the Revolution in Soviet Military and Political Thinking.* New York: Praeger, 1959.

Dougherty, James E. *The Bishops and Nuclear Weapons.* Hamden, Conn.: Archon Books, 1984.

Drinan, Robert F. *Beyond the Nuclear Freeze.* New York: Seabury Press, 1983.

Dunn, Lewis, et al. *Nuclear Issues in the Post-September 11 Era.* Paris: Foundation pour la Recherche Stratégique, March 2003.

Dwyer, Judith A., ed. *The Catholic Bishops and Nuclear War: A Critique and Analysis of the Pastoral: "The Challenge of Peace."* Washington, D.C.: Georgetown University Press, 1984.

Eden, Lynn and Steven E. Miller. *Nuclear Arguments: Understanding the Nuclear Arms and Arms Control Debates.* Ithaca, N.Y.: Cornell University Press, 1989.

Einhorn, Robert J. and Patrick J. Garrity, eds. *Reducing the Risk of Nuclear War: A Report of the CSIS Group on Strategy and Arms Control.* Washington, D.C.: Center for Strategic and International Studies, March 1985.

Ending the Production of Fissile Materials for Weapons: Verifying the Dismantlement of Nuclear Weapons. Washington, D.C.: Federation of American Scientists, June 1991.

Epstein, William. *The Prevention of Nuclear War: A United Nations Perspective.* Cambridge, Mass.: Oelgeschlager, Gunn, & Hain, Publishers, Inc., 1984.

Epstein, William and Lucy Webster, eds. *We Can Avert a Nuclear War.* Boston: Oelgeschlager, Gunn and Hain, 1983.

Fischer, Dietrich. *Preventing War in the Nuclear Age.* Totowa, N.J.: Rowman and Allanheld, 1984.

Flournoy, Michele A., ed. *Nuclear Weapons After the Cold War: Guidelines for U.S. Policy.* New York: Harper-Collins, 1993.

Ford, Daniel F. *The Button: The Pentagon's Strategic Command and Control.* New York: Simon and Schuster, 1985.

Ford, Daniel F., Henry Kendall, and Steven Nadi. *Beyond the Freeze: The Road to Nuclear Sanity.* Boston: Beacon Press, 1982.

Freedman, Lawrence. *The Evolution of Nuclear Strategy.* New York: St. Martin's Press, 1989.

Frei, Daniel and Christine Catrina. *Risks of Unintentional Nuclear War.* Totowa, N.J.: Littlefield, Adams, 1986.

The Future of the U.S.-Soviet Nuclear Relationship. Washington, D.C.: National Academy of Sciences, 1991.

Gaddis, John L. *Strategies of Containment: A Critical Appraisal of Postwar American National Security Policy.* New York: Oxford University Press, 1982.

Gallois, Pierre. *The Balance of Terror.* Boston: Houghton Mifflin, 1961.

Garfinkle, Adam M. *The Politics of the Nuclear Freeze.* Philadelphia: Foreign Policy Research Institute, 1984.

George, James L. *The New Nuclear Rules: Strategy and Arms Control After INF and START.* New York: St. Martin's Press, 1990.

Girrier, Catherine E. *The No-First Use Issue in American Nuclear Weapons Policy: 1945-1957.* Master's Thesis. Geneva, Switz: Graduate Institute of International Studies, 1985.

Goldblat, Jozef. "Nuclear Arms Control: Reversing Negative Trends." *Disarmament Diplomacy,* March 2000.

Goldfischer, David. *The Best Defense: Policy Alternatives for U.S. Nuclear Security from the 1950s to the 1990s.* Ithaca, N.Y.: Cornell University Press, 1993.

Goldfischer, David and Thomas W. Graham. *Nuclear Deterrence and Global Security in Transition.* Boulder, Colo.: Westview, 1992.

Goodpaster, Andrew J. *Further Reins on Nuclear Arms: Next Steps for the Major Nuclear Powers.* Washington, D.C.: Atlantic Council, August 1993.

Goodwin, Geoffrey. *Ethics and Nuclear Deterrence.* New York: St. Martin's Press, 1982.

Gray, Colin S. *The Soviet-American Arms Race.* Farnborough, U.K.: Saxon House, 1976.

Grief, Nicholas. *The World Court Project on Nuclear Weapons and International Law.* Northampton, Mass.: Altheia Press, 1992.

Griffiths, Franklyn and John C. Polanyi, eds. *The Dangers of Nuclear War.* Pugwash Symposium. Toronto, Can.: University of Toronto Press, 1979.

Guthe, Kurt. *The Nuclear Posture Review: How Is the "New Triad" New?* Washington, D.C.: Center for Strategic and Budgetary Assessments, 2002.

Halperin, Morton. *Nuclear Fallacy: Dispelling the Myth of Nuclear Strategy.* New York: Ballinger, 1987.

Halverson, Thomas E. *The Last Great Nuclear Debate: NATO and Short-Range Nuclear Weapons in the 1980s.* Basingstoke, U.K.: MacMillan Press Ltd., 1995.

Harknett, Richard J., T.V. Paul, and James J. Wirtz, eds. *The Absolute Weapon Revisited: Nuclear Arms and the Emerging International Order.* Ann Arbor: University of Michigan Press, 1998.

The Harvard Nuclear Study Group. *Living with Nuclear Weapons.* Toronto, Can.: Bantam Books, 1983.

Holdstock, Douglas and Frank Barnaby, eds. *Hiroshima and Nagasaki: Retrospect and Prospect.* London: Frank Cass & Co., 1995.

Holm, Hans-Henrik and Nikolay Peterson. *The European Missiles Crisis: Nuclear Weapons and Security Policy.* London: Frances Pinter, 1983.

Jervis, Robert. *The Meaning of the Nuclear Revolution.* Ithaca, N.Y.: Cornell University Press, 1989.

Jervis, Robert and Richard Ned Lebow. *Psychology and Deterrence.* Baltimore, Md.: Johns Hopkins University Press, 1986.

Joseph, Paul and Simon Rosenblum, eds. *Search for Sanity: The Politics of Nuclear Weapons and Disarmament.* Boston: South End Press, 1984.

Kahn, Herman. *On Thermonuclear War.* Princeton, N.J.: Princeton University Press, 1961.

Kalkstein, Marvin. *International Arrangements and Control for the Peaceful Applications of Nuclear Explosives.* New York: Humanities Press, 1970.

Karp, Regina Cowan. *Security Without Nuclear Weapons? Different Perspectives on Non-Nuclear Security.* New York: Oxford University Press, 1992.

Kegley, Charles W. Jr. and Eugene R. Wittkopf, eds. *The Nuclear Reader: Strategy, Weapons, War.* New York: St. Martin's Press, 1989.

Kegley, Charles W. and Kenneth L. Schwab. *After the Cold War: Questioning the Morality of Nuclear Weapons.* Boulder, Colo.: Westview, 1991.

Kelleher, Catherine M. *Germany and the Politics of Nuclear Weapons.* New York: Columbia University Press, 1975.

Kennan, George F. *The Nuclear Delusion: Soviet-American Relations in the Atomic Age.* New York: Random House, 1982.

Kissinger, Henry. *Nuclear Weapons and Foreign Policy.* New York: Harper and Row, 1957.

Kratzer, Myron B. *International Nuclear Safeguards: Promise and Performance.* Washington, D.C.: Atlantic Council, April 1994.

Krepon, Michael. *Strategic Stalemate: Nuclear Weapons and Arms Control in American Politics.* New York: St. Martin's Press, 1984.

Kull, Steven. *Minds at War: Nuclear Reality and the Inner Conflicts of Defense Policymakers.* New York: Basic Books, 1988.

Laird, Robbin F. *The Soviet Union, the West, and the Nuclear Arms Race.* New York: New York University Press, 1986.

Laird, Robbin F. and Betsy A. Jacobs, eds. *The Future of Deterrence: NATO Nuclear Forces After INF.* Boulder, Colo.: Westview, 1989.

Larsen, Jeffrey A. and Kurt J. Klingenberger, eds. *Controlling Non-Strategic Nuclear Weapons: Obstacles and Opportunities.* Colorado Springs, Colo.: USAF Institute for National Security Studies, 2001.

Lebow, Richard Ned. *Nuclear Crisis Management: A Dangerous Illusion.* Ithaca, N.Y.: Cornell University Press, 1987.

Lempert, Robert, Ike Y. Chang Jr., and Kathleen McCallum. *Emerging Technology Systems and Arms Control.* Santa Monica, Calif.: RAND Corporation, 1991.

Leppingwell, John W.R. and Nikolai Sokov. "Strategic Offensive Arms Elimination and Weapons Protection, Control and Accounting." *The Nonproliferation Review,* Spring 2000.

Lieberman, Joseph I. *The Scorpion and the Tarantula: The Struggle to Control Atomic Weapons 1945-1949.* Boston, Mass.: Houghton Mifflin, 1970.

Lifton, Robert J. and Richard Falk. *Indefensible Weapons: The Political and Psychological Case Against Nuclearism.* New York: Basic Books, p. 198.

Lindsay, James M. "The Nuclear Agenda." *The Brookings Review,* Fall 2000, p. 8.

Makhijani, Arjun. "Nuclear Targeting: The First 60 Years." *Bulletin of the Atomic Scientists,* May/June 2003, pp. 60-65.

Malcolmson, Robert W. *Beyond Nuclear Thinking.* Montreal, Can.: McGill-Queen's University Press, 1990.

Mandelbaum, Michael. *The Nuclear Question: The United States and Nuclear Weapons, 1946-1976.* New York: Cambridge University Press, 1979.

Mayers, Teena. *Understanding Nuclear Weapons and Arms Control.* Washington, D.C.: Arms Control Association, 1983.

Mazarr, Michael, ed. *Nuclear Weapons in a Transformed World.* New York: St. Martin's Press, 1998.

McCrea, Frances B. and Gerald E. Markle. *Minutes to Midnight: Nuclear Weapons Protest in America.* Newbury Park, Calif.: Sage Publications, 1989.

McNamara, Robert S. *Blundering into Disaster: Surviving the First Century of the Nuclear Age.* New York: Pantheon Books, 1986.

Medalia, Jonathan, *Nuclear Weapon Initiatives: Low-Yield R&D, Advanced Concepts, Earth Penetrators, Test Readiness.* Washington, D.C.: Congressional Research Service, October 2003.

Menos, Dennis. *The Superpowers and Nuclear Arms Control: Rhetoric and Reality.* New York: Praeger, 1990.

Meyer, David S. *A Winter of Discontent: The Nuclear Freeze and American Politics.* New York: Praeger, 1990.

Millar, Alistair and Brian Alexander, eds. *Tactical Nuclear Weapons: Emergent Threats in an Evolving Security Environment.* New York: Brassey's, May 2003.

Miller, Arthur S. and Martin Feinrider, eds. *Nuclear Weapons and Law.* Westport, Conn.: Greenwood Press, 1984.

Miller, Steven E., ed. *Strategy and Nuclear Deterrence: An International Security Reader.* Princeton, N.J.: Princeton University Press, 1984.

Miller, Timothy D. and Jeffrey A. Larsen. "Dealing with Russian Tactical Nuclear Weapons: Cash for Kilotons." *Naval War College Review*, Spring 2004, pp. 64-86.

Mlyn, Eric. *The State, Society and Limited Nuclear War.* Albany: State University of New York Press, 1995.

Morrison, Philip, Hans A. Bethe, and Wolfgang K.H. Panofsky. *Nuclear Weapons and Nuclear War.* Washington, D.C.: American Association of Physics Teachers, 1982.

Müller, Harald. *The Nuclear Weapons Register—A Good Idea Whose Time has Come.* PRIF Reports No. 51. Frankfurt, Ger.: Peace Research Institute Frankfurt, May 1998.

Nacht, Michael. *The Age of Vulnerability: Threats to the Nuclear Stalemate.* Washington, D.C.: Brookings Institution, 1985.

Nitze, Paul H. "Atoms, Strategy and Policy." *Foreign Affairs,* January 1956, pp. 187-199.

No First Use. Cambridge, Mass: Union of Concerned Scientists, 1983.

Nolan, Janne E. *An Elusive Consensus: Nuclear Weapons and American Security after the Cold War.* Washington, D.C.: Brookings Institution Press, 1999.

———. *Guardians of the Arsenal: The Politics of Nuclear Strategy.* New York: Basic Books, 1989.

Norris, Robert S., Andrew S. Burrows, and Richard W. Fieldhouse. *Nuclear Weapons Databook, Volume V: British, French, and Chinese Nuclear Weapons.* Boulder, Colo.: Westview, 1994.

Nuclear Arms Control: Background and Issues. Washington, D.C.: National Academy of Sciences, Committee on International Security and Arms Control, 1985.

Nuclear Non-Proliferation: Uncertainties with Implementing IAEA's Strengthened Safeguards System. GAO Report to the House of Representatives. Report no. GAO/NSIAD/RCED-98-184. Washington, D.C.: General Accounting Office, July 1998.

"Nuclear Weapons in the 1980s." Special Edition of *Foreign Affairs,* Winter 1981-1982, pp. 287-346.

Nye, Joseph S., Jr. *Nuclear Ethics.* New York: Free Press, 1984.

Osgood, Robert E. *The Nuclear Dilemma in American Strategic Thought.* Boulder, Colo.: Westview, 1988.

Panofsky, Wolfgang K.H. "The Continuing Impact of the Nuclear Revolution." *Arms Control Today,* June 2001, pp. 3-5.

"Pastoral Letter on War and Peace. The Challenge of Peace: God's Promise and Our Response." National Conference of Catholic Bishops of the United States, *Origins,* Vol. 13, No. 1 (1983), pp. 1-22.

Pauling, Linus. *No More War!* New York: Dodd, Mead & Co., 1958.

Paulsen, Richard A. *The Role of U.S. Nuclear Weapons in the Post-Cold War Era.* Montgomery, Ala.: Air University Press, September 1994.

Paret, Peter, ed. *The Makers of Modern Strategy.* Princeton, N.J.: Princeton University Press, 1986.

Paul, Septimus H. *Nuclear Rivals: Anglo-American Atomic Relations, 1941-52.* Columbus, Ohio: Ohio State University Press, 2000.

Payne, Keith B. *The Fallacies of Cold War Deterrence and a New Direction.* Lexington, Ky.: University of Kentucky Press, 2001.

Peace, The Churches, and The Bomb. Washington, D.C.: Council on Religion and International Affairs, 1965.

Pfaltzgraff, Robert L., Jr., ed. *Contrasting Approaches to Strategic Arms Control.* Lexington, Mass.: Lexington, 1974.

Potter, William C. *Nuclear Profiles of the Soviet Successor States.* Program for Nonproliferation Studies, Monograph No. 1. Monterey, Calif.: Monterey Institute of International Studies, May 1993.

Potter, William C., Nikolai Sokov, Harald Müller, and Annette Schaper. *Tactical Nuclear Weapons: Options for Control.* New York: United Nations Institute for Disarmament Research, 2001.

Powaski, Ronald. *March to Armageddon: The United States and the Nuclear Arms Race, 1939 to the Present.* New York: Oxford University Press, 1987.

Prins, Gwyn, ed. *Defended to Death: A Study of the Nuclear Arms Race from the Cambridge University Disarmament Seminar.* Hammondsworth, U.K.: Penguin Books, Ltd., 1983.

Project on No-First Use. *Bibliography: No First Use.* Washington, D.C.: Center for Education on Nuclear War, Inc., 1984.

Quester, George II. *Nuclear Diplomacy: The First Twenty-Five Years.* New York: Dunellen Publishing Company, 1970.

Rathjens, George, Abram Chayes, and J.P. Ruina. *Nuclear Arms Control Agreements: Process and Impact.* Washington, D.C.: Carnegie Endowment for International Peace, 1974.

Rationale and Requirements for U.S. Nuclear Forces and Arms Control. Washington, D.C.: National Institute for Public Policy, January 2001.

Reid, Charles J., Jr., ed. *Peace in a Nuclear Age: The Bishops' Pastoral Letter in Perspective.* Washington, D.C.: Catholic University of America Press, 1986.

Reilly, Robert R., James V. Schall, Thomas F. Payne, John J. O'Conner, and Philip F., Lawler, eds. *Justice and War in the Nuclear Age.* Lanham, Md.: University Press of America, 1983.

Reiss, Mitchell. *Bridled Ambition: Why Countries Constrain Their Nuclear Capabilities.* Washington, D.C.: Wilson Center Press, 1995.

Reykjavik and Beyond: Deep Reductions in Strategic Nuclear Arsenals. Washington, D.C.: National Academy of Sciences, Committee on International Security and Arms Control, 1988.

Rhodes, Edward. *Power and MADness: The Logic of Nuclear Coercion.* New York: Columbia University Press, 1989.

Rinne, Robert L. *An Alternative Framework for the Control of Nuclear Materials.* Palo Alto, Calif.: Stanford University Center for International Security and Cooperation, May 1999.

Roberts, Chalmers. *The Nuclear Years: The Arms Race and Arms Control, 1945-1970.* New York: Praeger, 1970.

Rudney, Robert and Luc Reychler, eds. *European Security Beyond the Year 2000.* New York: Praeger Books, 1988.

Russell, Bertrand. *Has Man a Future?* New York: Simon and Schuster, 1962.

Sauer, Tom. *Nuclear Arms Control: Nuclear Deterrence in the Post-Cold War Period.* New York: St. Martin's Press, 1998.

Schaerf, Carlo and David Carlton, eds. *Reducing Nuclear Arsenals.* New York: St. Martin's Press, 1991.

Schneider, Barry R. and William L. Dowdy, eds. *Pulling Back from the Nuclear Brink: Reducing and Countering Nuclear Threats.* London: Frank Cass, 1998.

Schwartz, Stephen I. *Atomic Audit: The Costs and Consequences of U.S. Nuclear Weapons Since 1940.* Washington, D.C.: Brookings Institution Press, 1998.

Sedacca, Sandra. *Up in Arms: A Common Cause Guide to Understanding Nuclear Arms.* Washington, D.C.: Common Cause, 1984.

Segal, G., et al. *Nuclear War and Nuclear Peace.* London: Macmillan, 1983.

Sherwin, Martin J. *A World Destroyed: Hiroshima and Its Legacies.* 3rd ed. Palo Alto, Calif: Stanford University Press, 2003.

Shields, John M. and William C. Potter. *Dismantling the Cold War: U.S. and NIS Perspectives on the Nunn-Lugar Cooperative Threat Reduction Program.* Cambridge, Mass.: MIT Press, 1997.

Shue, Henry, ed. *Nuclear Deterrence.* New York: Cambridge University Press, 1989.

Sloss, Leon. *Reexamining Nuclear Policy in a Changing World.* Los Alamos, N.M.: Los Alamos National Laboratory, December 1990.

Smith, Jeff. *Unthinking the Unthinkable: Nuclear Weapons and Western Culture.* Bloomington, Ind.: Indiana University Press, 1989.

Smith, Theresa C. and Indu B. Singh, eds. *Security vs. Survival: The Nuclear Arms Race.* Boulder, Colo.: Lynne Rienner, 1985.

Smoke, Richard. *National Security and the Nuclear Dilemma.* Reading, Mass.: Addison-Wesley, 1984.

Sokov, Nikolai. "Russia's Approach to Nuclear Weapons." *The Washington Quarterly.* Special Issue: Nuclear Arms Control, Summer 1997, pp. 107-114.

START and Nuclear Disarmament. UNIDIR Newsletter. Geneva, Switz.: UN Institute for Disarmament Research, June/September 1993.

Stockholm International Peace Research Institute. *Safeguards Against Nuclear Proliferation.* Cambridge, Mass.: MIT Press, 1975.

Strategic Force Modernization and Arms Control. National Security Paper 6. Cambridge, Mass.: Institute for Foreign Policy Analysis, 1986.

Sur, Serge, ed. *Nuclear Deterrence: Problems and Perspectives in the 1990s.* New York: UNIDIR, 1993.

Tarr, David W. *Nuclear Deterrence and International Security: Alternative Nuclear Regimes.* New York: Longman, 1991.

Taylor, Terence. *Escaping the Prison of the Past: Rethinking Arms Control and Non-Proliferation Measures.* Stanford, Calif.: Stanford University Center for International Security and Arms Control, April 1996.

Teller, Edward with Judith Shoolery. *Memoirs: A Twentieth-Century Journey in Science and Politics.* New York: Perseus Books, 2001.

Thomson, David B. *A Guide to the Nuclear Arms Control Treaties,* Los Alamos National Laboratories Report LA-UR-99-3173. July 1999.

Thompson, E. P. *Beyond the Cold War: A New Approach to the Arms Race and Nuclear Annihilation.* New York: Pantheon Books, 1982.

Treverton, Gregory. *Nuclear Weapons in Europe.* Adelphi Paper London: International Institute for Strategic Studies, 1981.

Turner, Stansfield. *Caging the Nuclear Genie: An American Challenge for Global Security.* Boulder, Colo.: Westview, 1997.

Twigge, Stephen and Len Scott. *Planning Armageddon: Britain, the United States and the Command of Western Nuclear Forces 1945-1964.* Newark, N.J.: Harwood Academic Publishers, 2000.

The United States, Japan, and the Future of Nuclear Weapons. Washington, D.C.: Carnegie Endowment for International Peace, 1995.

U.S. Congress, House of Representatives, Committee on Foreign Affairs, *Fundamentals of Nuclear Arms Control.* Washington, D.C.: US Government Printing Office, 1986.

U.S. Defense Threat Reduction Agency. *Weapons of Mass Destruction Terms Handbook.* Alexandria, Va.: Defense Threat Reduction Agency, September 2001.

U.S. Department of Energy. Office of Nonproliferation and National Security. Office of Emergency Management. *Nuclear Terms Handbook.* Washington, D.C.: Department of Energy, 1996 and 1998.

U.S. Nuclear Policy in the 21st Century: A Fresh Look at National Strategy and Requirements, Final Report. Washington, D.C.: National Defense University, Center for Counterproliferation Research, July 1998.

Utgoff, Victor. *Nuclear Weapons and the Deterrence of Biological and Chemical Warfare.* Occasional Paper 36. Washington, D.C.: Stimson Center, October 1997.

VanderVink, Gregory E. *Nuclear Testing and Nonproliferation: The Role of Seismology in Deterring the Development of Nuclear Weapons.* Arlington, Va.: IRIS Consortium, February 1994.

Van Ham, Peter. *Managing Non-Proliferation Regimes in the 1990s: Power, Politics, and Policies.* New York: Council on Foreign Relations Press, 1994.

Vogele, William B. *Stepping Back: Nuclear Arms Control and the End of the Cold War.* Westport, Conn.: Praeger, 1994.

Von Hippel, Frank and Roald Z. Sagdeev, eds. *Reversing the Arms Race: How to Achieve Deep Reductions in the Nuclear Arsenals.* New York: Gordon and Breach Science Publishers, 1990.

Wallis, Jim. *Waging Peace: A Handbook for the Struggle Against Nuclear Arms.* New York: Harper and Row, 1982.

Wander, W. Thomas, Eric H. Arnett, and Paul Bracken, eds. *The Diffusion of Advanced Weaponry: Technologies, Regional Implications, and Responses.* Washington, D.C.: American Association for the Advancement of Science, 1994.

"What Does START Stop?" Special Issue of *The Bulletin of the Atomic Scientists,* November 1991, pp. 12-40.

Wheeler, Michael O. *Nuclear Weapons and the National Interest: The Early Years.* Washington, D.C.: National Defense University Press, 1989.

Wohlstetter, Albert. "The Delicate Balance of Terror." *Foreign Affairs,* January 1959, pp. 211-234.

Woolf, Amy F. *Nuclear Arms Control: The U.S.-Russian Agenda.* Washington, D.C.: Congressional Research Service, January 2000.

Verification

Aronowitz, Dennis S. *Legal Aspects of Arms Control Verification in the United States.* Dobbs Ferry, N.Y.: Oceana, 1965.

Banner, Allen V. *Overhead Imaging for Verification and Peacekeeping: Three Studies.* Ottawa, Can.: External Affairs and International Trade, March 1991.

Barnaby, Frank and Bhupendra Jasani. *Verification Technologies: The Case for Surveillance by Consent.* London: Centre for International Peacebuilding, 1984.

Beier, J. Marshall and Steven Mataija, eds. *Verification, Compliance, and Confidence-Building: The Global and Regional Interface.* North York, Can.: York University, Centre for International and Security Studies, 1996.

———, eds. *Cyberspace and Outer Space: Transitional Challenges for Multilateral Verification in the 21st Century.* North York, Can.: York University, Centre for International and Security Studies, 1997.

Bellany, Ian and Coit D. Blacker, eds. *The Verification of Arms Control Agreements.* Totowa, N.J.: Biblio Distribution Center, 1983.

Bibliography on Arms Control Verification: Third Update. Ottawa, Can.: Department of International Affairs and Foreign Trade, October 1994.

Bunn, George and Roland M. Timerbaev. *Nuclear Verification Under the NPT: What Should it Cover? How Far May it Go?* PPNN Study 5. Southampton, U.K.: Programme for the Promotion of Nuclear Nonproliferaiton, 1994.

Burns, Richard Dean. *Inspection, Verification, Control and Supervision in Arms Control and Disarmament.* Los Angeles: California State University, Center for the Study of Armament and Disarmament, 1973.

Calogero, Francesco, Marvin L. Goldberger, and Sergei P. Kapitza, eds. *Verification: Monitoring Disarmament.* Boulder, Colo.: Westview, 1991.

Chestnutt, Heather and Michael Slack, eds. *Verifying Conventional Force Reductions in Europe: CFE I and Beyond.* Toronto, Can: Centre for International and Strategic Studies, 1991.

A Conceptual Working Paper on Arms Control Verification. Ottawa, Can.: Department of External Affairs, Arms Control and Disarmament Division, 1986.

Crawford, A., F.R. Cleminson, D.A. Grant, and E. Gilman. *Compendium of Arms Control Verification Proposals, Second Edition.* ORAE Report No. R81. Ottawa, Can.: Department of National Defence, Operational Research and Analysis Establishment, March 1982.

Crawford, Alan, Gregor MacKinnon, Lynne Hanson, and Ellis Morris. *Compendium of Arms Control Verification Proposals, Third Edition.* ORAE Extra-Mural Paper No. 42. Ottawa, Can.: Department of National Defence, Operational Research and Analysis Establishment, July 1987.

Dunn, Lewis A. with Amy Gordon. *Arms Control Verification and the New Role of On-Site Inspection: Challenges, Issues, and Realities.* Toronto, Can.: Lexington, 1989.

Dunn, Lewis A. and Carrie Smarto. *Transparency: Purposes, Pitfalls, and Possibilities.* McLean, Va.: Science Applications International Corporation, December 1994.

Fainberg, Anthony. *Strengthening IAEA Safeguards: Lessons from Iraq.* Stanford, Calif.: Stanford University Center for International Security and Arms Control, 1993.

Gaertner, Heinz. *Challenges of Verification: Smaller States and Arms Control.* New York: Institute for East-West Security Studies, 1989.

Graybeal, Sidney, George Lindsay, James Macintosh, and Patricia McFate. *Verification to the Year 2000.* Ottawa, Can.: External Affairs and International Trade, February 1991.

Hafemeister, David W., Penny Janeway, and Kosta Tsipis. *Arms Control Verification: The Technologies That Make It Possible.* Philadelphia, Penn.: Pergamon-Brassey's, 1986.

Hamburg, Eric. *Arms Control Verification and the U.S. Constitution.* Palo Alto, Calif.: Center for International Security and Arms Control, Stanford University, August 1989.

Harahan, Joseph P. *On-Site Inspections under the INF Treaty.* Washington, D.C.: On-Site Inspection Agency, 1993.

Harahan, Joseph P. and John C. Kuhn III. *On-Site Inspections under the CFE Treaty.* Washington, D.C.: On-Site Inspection Agency, 1996.

Haug, Rene, ed. *Verification of Arms Control Agreements: The Role of Third Countries.* Lausanne: Programme for Strategic and International Security Studies, 1985.

Henkin, Louis. *Arms Control and Inspection in American Law.* New York: Columbia University Press, 1958.

Jasani, Bhupendra. *European Arms Control Verification from Space.* Hamburg, Ger.: University of Hamburg, Institut für Friedensforschung und Sicherheitspolitik, 1990.

Jeremiah, David et al. *Report to the Director of Central Intelligence on the Intelligence Community's Failure to Predict Nuclear Testing in India,* June 1998.

Kessler, J. Christian. *Verifying Nonproliferation Treaties: Obligation, Process, and Sovereignty.* Washington, D.C.: National Defense University Press, 1995.

Kokoski, Richard and Sergey Koulik, eds. *Verification of Conventional Arms Control in Europe: Technological Constraints and Opportunities.* Boulder, Colo.: Westview, 1990.

Krass, Allan S. *Verification: How Much Is Enough?* Philadelphia: Taylor & Francis, 1985.

Kratzer, Myron B. *International Nuclear Safeguards: Promise and Performance.* Washington, D.C.: Atlantic Council, 1994.

Krepon, Michael. *Verification of the Chemical Weapons Convention: A Guide to the Perplexed.* Washington, D.C.: Henry L. Stimson Center, March 1992.

Lederman, Itshak. *Arms Control and Verification: Past Development, German Approaches to CFE Verification, and Possible Models of Verification in the Future.* Hamburg, Ger.: University of Hamburg, Institut für Friedensforschung und Sicherheitspolitik, 1990.

Mataija, Steven and J. Marshall Beier, eds. *Multilateral Verification and the Post-Gulf War Environment: Learning from the UNSCOM Experience.* Toronto, Can.: Centre for International and Strategic Studies, 1992.

McFate, Patricia B., Sidney N. Graybeal, D. Marc Kilgour, and George Lindsay. *Constraining Proliferation: The Contribution of Verification Synergies.* Ottawa, Can.: Department of External Affairs, March 1993.

McKnight, Allan. *Atomic Safeguards: A Study in International Verification.* New York: United Nations Institute for Training and Research, 1971.

Morris, Ellis, ed. *International Verification Organizations.* North York, Can.: York University, Centre for International and Strategic Studies, 1991.

Mutimer, David, ed. *Control but Verify: Verification and the New Non-Proliferation Agenda.* Toronto, Can.: York University Centre for International and Strategic Studies, 1994.

Non-Seismic Technologies in Support of a Nuclear Ban. Ottawa, Can.: Department of External Affairs and International Trade, May 1993.

Potter, William C., ed. *Verification and Arms Control.* Lexington, Mass.: Lexington, 1985.

Richelson, Jeffrey T. *The U.S. Intelligence Community,* 3rd edition. Boulder, Colo.: Westview, 1995.

Rueckert, George L. *On-Site Inspection in Theory and Practice.* Westport, Conn.: Praeger, 1998.

Russell, John. "INF Inspections End, but Unilateral Verification Continues." *Trust and Verify,* May-June 2001, p. 3.

Rutkowski, Chris A. *The Role of Astronomical Instruments in Arms Control Verification.* Ottawa: Department of External Affairs, Arms Control and Disarmament Division, 1986.

Scribner, Richard A., Theodore J. Ralston, and William D. Metz. *The Verification Challenge: Problems of Strategic Nuclear Arms Control Verification.* Boston: Birkhauser, 1985.

Scrivener, David and Michael Sheehan. *Bibliography of Arms Control Verification.* Burlington, Vt.: Ashgate Publishing Co., 1990.

Seismic Verification. Ottawa: Canadian Department of External Affairs, 1986.

Shearer, Richard L., Jr. *On-Site Inspection for Arms Control: Breaking the Verification Barrier.* Washington, D.C.: National Defense University Press, 1984.

Social and Psychological Aspects of Verification, Inspection and International Assurance. Reports for U.S. ACDA. Terre Haute, Ind.: Purdue University, Herman C. Krannert Graduate School of Industrial Administration, November 1968.

Sur, Serge, ed. *Verification of Current Disarmament and Arms Limitations Agreements: Ways, Means, and Practices.* Geneva, Switz: United Nations Institute for Disarmament Research, 1992.

Tower, John G., ed. *Verification: The Key to Arms Control in the 1990s.* New York: Macmillan, 1992.

Trapp, Rolf. *Verification Under the Chemical Weapons Convention: On-Site Inspection in Chemical Industry Facilities.* New York: Oxford University Press, 1993.

U.S. Congress. Office of Technology Assessment. *Verification Technologies: Measures for Monitoring Compliance with the START Treaty.* Washington, D.C.: Office of Technology Assessment, 1990.

U.S. Congress. Office of Technology Assessment. *Verification Technologies: Cooperative Aerial Surveillance in International Agreements.* Washington, D.C.: U.S. Government Printing Office, July 1991.

Verification in All Its Aspects: A Comprehensive Study on Arms Control and Disarmament Verification. Ottawa: Canadian Department of External Affairs, 1986.

Verification and Compliance: A Problem-Solving Approach. Cambridge, Mass.: Ballinger Publishing Company, 1988.

Verification and Response in Disarmament Agreements. ACDA Report. Washington, D.C.: Institute for Defense Analyses, November 1962.

Verification and the United Nations: The Role of the Organization in Multilateral Arms Limitations and Disarmament Agreements. New York: United Nations Publications, 1992.

Wainhouse, David W. *Arms Control Agreements: Designs for Verification and Organization.* Baltimore, Md.: Johns Hopkins University Press, 1968.

Wright, Michael. *Disarm and Verify: An Explanation of the Central Difficulties and of National Policies.* New York: Frederick A. Praeger, 1964.

Zimmerman, Peter D. *Using Synthesized Images to Establish Monitoring Insights.* Hamburg, Ger.: Institut für Friedensforschung und Sicherheitspolitik. October 1992.

Reducing the Consequences of War

Commoner, Barry. *Radioactive Contamination.* New York: Harcourt, Brace, Jovanovich, Inc., 1975.

Drew, Dennis, study director. *Nuclear Winter and National Security: Implications for Future Policy.* Washington, D.C.: U.S. Government Printing Office, July 1986.

Falkenrath, Richard A., Robert D. Newman, and Bradley A. Thayer. *America's Achilles' Heel: Nuclear, Biological, and Chemical Terrorism and Covert Attack.* Cambridge, Mass.: MIT Press, 1998.

The League of Women Voters. *The Nuclear Waste Primer: A Handbook for Citizens.* New York: Lyons & Burford, Publishers, 1993.

May, John. *The Greenpeace Book of the Nuclear Age: The Hidden History: The Human Cost.* London: Victor Gollancz, 1989.

Record, Jeffrey. *Revising U.S. Military Strategy: Tailoring Means to Ends.* Elmsford, N.Y.: Pergamon-Brassey's, 1984.

Tetborg, Marlies and Wim A. Smit. *Non-Provocative Defence as a Principle of Arms Reduction and Its Implications for Assessing Defence Technologies.* Amsterdam: Free University Press, 1989.

The ABM Treaty

Briefing Book on the ABM Treaty and Related Issues. Washington, D.C.: National Campaign to Save the ABM Treaty, 1986.

Chayes, Antonia Handler and Paul Doty, eds. *Defending Deterrence: Managing the ABM Treaty Regime into the 21st Century.* Washington, D.C.: Pergamon-Brassey's, 1989.

Danielson, Dennis L. *Theater Missile Defense and the ABM Treaty: Either-Or?* Urbana-Champaign: University of Illinois, February 1995.

Durch, William J. *The ABM Treaty and Western Security.* Cambridge, Mass.: Ballinger, 1989.

Garthoff, Raymond L. *Policy vs. Law: The Reinterpretation of the ABM Treaty.* Washington, D.C.: Brookings Institution, 1987.

A Legal Analysis of the "New Interpretation" of the Anti-Ballistic Missile Treaty. Boston: Lawyers Alliance for Nuclear Arms Control, 1986.

Longstreth, Thomas, et al. *The Impact of US and Soviet Ballistic Missile Defense Programs on the ABM Treaty.* Washington, D.C.: National Campaign to Save the ABM Treaty, 1985.

Stützle, Walther, Bhupendra Jasani, and Regina Cowen, eds. *The ABM Treaty: To Defend or Not to Defend?* Oxford, U.K.: Oxford University Press, 1987.

Ballistic Missile Defense, SDI, and NMD

Aspen Strategy Group. *Anti-Satellite Weapons and U.S. Military Space Policy.* Lanham, Md.: University Press of America, 1986.

————. *The Strategic Defense Initiative and American Security.* Lanham, Md.: University Press of America, 1987.

Baucom, Donald R. *The Origins of SDI, 1944-1983.* Lawrence: University Press of Kansas, 1992.

Beier, J. Marshall and Steven Mataija, eds. *Arms Control and the Rule of Law: A Framework for Peace and Security in Outer Space.* North York, Can.: York University, Centre for International and Security Studies, 1998.

Binnendijk, Hans, ed. *Strategic Defense in the 21st Century.* Washington, D.C.: U.S. State Department Center for the Study of Foreign Affairs, 1986.

Blechman, Barry M. and Victor A. Utgoff. *The Fiscal and Economic Implications of Strategic Defenses.* Boulder, Colo.: Westview, 1986.

Boffey, Philip M., et al. *Claiming the Heavens: The New York Times Complete Guide to the Star Wars Debate.* New York: Times Books, 1988.

Boutwell, Jeffrey, Donald Hafner, and Franklin Long, eds. *Weapons in Space: The Politics and Technology of BMD and ASAT Weapons.* New York: W.W. Norton, 1985.

Boutwell, Jeffrey and Richard A. Scribner. *The Strategic Defense Initiative: Some Arms Control Implications.* Washington, D.C.: American Association for the Advancement of Science, 1985.

Budgetary and Technical Implications of the Administration's Plan for National Missile Defense. Washington, D.C.: Congressional Budget Office, April 2000.

Bulkeley, Rip and Graham Spinardi. *Space Weapons: Deterrence or Delusion.* Totowa, N.J.: Rowman and Littlefield, 1986.

Butler, Richard. *Fatal Choice: Nuclear Weapons and the Illusion of Missile Defense.* Boulder, Colo: Westview, 2001.

Cahn, Anne Hessing. *Eggheads and Warheads: Scientists and the ABM.* Cambridge, Mass.: MIT Center for International Studies, 1971.

Campbell, William A.B. and Richard K. Melchin. *Western Security and the Strategic Defense Initiative.* Vancouver, B.C.: Canadian Conservative Centre, 1986.

Carlton, David and Carlo Schaerf, eds. *The Arms Race in the Era of Star Wars.* New York: St. Martin's Press, 1988.

Carter, Ashton and David N. Schwartz, eds. *Ballistic Missile Defense.* Washington, D.C.: Brookings Institutions, 1984.

Chayes, Abram and Jerome B. Wiesner, eds. *ABMs: An Evaluation of the Decision to Deploy an Antiballistic Missile System.* New York: New American Library, 1969.

Cimbala, Stephen J. *The Technology, Strategy, and Politics of SDI.* Boulder, Colo.: Westview, 1987.

Cirincione, Joseph, Steve Fetter, George Lewis, Jack Mendelsohn, and John Steinbruner. *White Paper on National Missile Defense.* Washington, D.C.: Lawyer's Alliance for World Security, Spring 2000.

Cochran, Thad. *Stubborn Things: A Decade of Facts About Ballistic Missile Defense.* Report to U.S. Senate. September 2000.

Collins, John M. *Military Space Forces: The Next 50 Years.* New York: Pergamon-Brassey's International Defense Publishers, Inc., 1989.

Coyle, Philip. "Rhetoric or Reality? Missile Defense Under Bush." *Arms Control Today,* May 2002, pp. 3-9.

Croft, Stuart. *The Impact of Strategic Defences on European-American Relations in the 1990s.* Adelphi Paper 238. Oxford, U.K.: International Institute for Strategic Studies, 1989.

Daalder, Ivo H. *The SDI Challenge to Europe.* Cambridge, Mass.: Ballinger Books, 1987.

Daalder, Ivo H., James M. Goldgeier, and James M. Lindsay. "Deploying NMD: Not Whether, but When." *Survival,* Spring 2000, p. 6.

Delauer, R.D. *The Strategic Defense Initiative: Defensive Technologies Study.* Washington, D.C.: U.S. Department of Defense, 1984.

Delpech, Thérèse. "BMD: A French View." *Disarmament Diplomacy,* March 2000.

Deschamps, Louis. *The SDI and European Security Interests.* Paris: Atlantic Institute for International Affairs, 1987.

Drell, Sidney D., Philip J. Farley, and David Holloway. *The Reagan Strategic Defense Initiative: A Technical, Political, and Arms Control Assessment.* Cambridge, Mass.: Ballinger Books, 1985.

Durch, William J. *Rethinking Strategic Ballistic Missile Defense.* College Park, Md.: Center for International and Security Studies at Maryland, June 1993.

Enders, Thomas. *Missile Defense as Part of an Extended NATO Air Defense.* Bonn: Konrad Adenauer Stiftung, 1986.

Executive Summary of the Report of the Commission to Assess the Ballistic Missile Threat to the United States. Washington, D.C.: July 1998.

FitzGerald, Frances. *Way Out There in the Blue: Reagan and Star Wars and the End of the Cold War.* New York: Simon & Schuster, 2000.

Gardner, John, et al. *Missile Defense in the 1990s.* Washington, D.C.: Geroge C. Marshall Institute, February 1987.

Glaser, Charles F. and Steve Fetter. "National Missile Defense and the Future of U.S. Weapons Policy." *International Security,* Summer 2001, p. 40.

Glynn, Patrick. *American Military Space Policy.* Cambridge, Mass.: Abt Books, 1983.

Grabbe, Crockett. L. *Space Weapons and the Strategic Defense Initiative.* Ames: Iowa State University Press, 1991.

Graham, Bradley. *Hit to Kill: The New Battle over Shielding America from Missile Attack.* Washington, D.C.: Public Affairs Press, 2001.

Graybeal, Sidney N. and Patricia A. McFate. *The ABM Treaty and Ballistic Missile Defense: Can the Circle Be Squared?* PSIS Occasional Paper. Washington, D.C.: American Association for the Advancement of Science, 1993.

Guerrier, Steven W. and Wayne C. Thompson. *Perspectives on Strategic Defense.* Boulder, Colo.: Westview, 1987.

Guertner, Gary L. and Donald M. Snow. *The Last Frontier: An Analysis of the Strategic Defense Initiative.* Lexington, Mass.: Lexington, 1986.

Guilbeaux, Wilson Jr. *Boost Phase Intercept: Implications for Theater Missile Defense.* ACDIS Occasional Paper. Urbana-Champaign: University of Illinois, December 1996.

Haley, P. Edward and Jack Merritt, eds. *The Strategic Defense Initiative: Future or Folly?* Boulder, Colo.: Westview, 1986.

Hays, Peter L., James M. Smith, Alan R. Van Tassel, and Guy M. Walsh, eds. *Spacepower for a New Millenium.* New York: McGraw-Hill Companies, 2000.

Hildreth, Steven A. and Amy F. Woolf. *National Missile Defense: Issues for Congress.* Washington, D.C.: Congressional Research Service, February 2000.

Hitchens, Theresa. "Rushing to Weaponize the Final Frontier." *Arms Control Today,* September 2001, pp. 16-21.

Hughes, Peter C. *Satellites Harming Other Satellites.* Ottawa, Can.: External Affairs and International Trade, July 1991.

Jasani, Bhupendra and Toshibomi Sakata. *Satellites for Arms Control and Crisis Monitoring.* New York: Oxford University Press, 1987.

Jasani, Bhupendra, ed. *Space Weapons: The Arms Control Dilemma.* Philadelphia: Taylor and Francis, 1984.

————, ed. *Peaceful and Non-Peaceful Uses of Space: Problems of Definition for the Prevention of an Arms Race.* New York: Taylor & Francis, 1991.

Kenyon, Ian, Mike Rance, John Simpson, and Mark Smith. *Prospects for a European Ballistic Missile Defense System?* Southampton, U.K.: Mountbatten Centre for International Studies, University of Southampton, June 2001.

Krepon, Michael. *Cooperative Threat Reduction, Missile Defense, and the Nuclear Future.* New York: Palgrave, 2003.

Lennon, Alexander. *Contemporary Nuclear Debates: Missile Defenses, Arms Control, and Arms Races in the Twenty-First Century.* Cambridge, Mass.: MIT Press, 2002.

Levine, Robert A. *The SDI Debate as a Continuation of History.* Los Angeles: University of California-Los Angeles Center for International and Strategic Affairs, 1986.

Lewis, George, Lisbeth Gronlund, and David Wright. "National Missile Defense: An Indefensible Shield." *Foreign Policy,* Winter 1999/2000, p. 120.

Lindsay, George and Arnold Simoni. *Prospects for a Multilateral Missile Defence Regime: A Research Report.* Ottawa, Can.: Cooperative Security Competition Program, External Affairs and International Trade Department, November 1993.

Lindsay, James M. and Michael E. O'Hanlon. *Defending America: The Case for a Limited National Missile Defense.* Washington, D.C.: Brookings Institution, 2001.

McDougall, Walter A. *The Heavens and the Earth: A Political History of the Space Age.* New York: Basic Books, 1985.

Miller, Steven E. and Stephen Van Evera, eds. *The Star Wars Controversy.* Princeton, N.J.: Princeton University Press, 1986.

Mosher, David E. "Understanding the Extraordinary Cost Growth of Missile Defense." *Arms Control Today,* December 2000, p. 9.

National Missile Defense Review Committee (The Welch Report). Washington, D.C.: Ballistic Missile Defense Organization, November 1999.

Nye, Joseph, Jr. and James A. Schear. *On the Defensive? The Future of the Strategic Defense Initative.* Lanham, Md.: University Press of America, 1988.

———. *Seeking Stability in Space: Anti-Satellite Weapons and the Evolving Space Regime.* Lanham, Md.: University Press of America, 1987.

Papp, Daniel S. *Ballistic Missile Defense, Space-Based Weapons, and the Defense of the West.* Alexandria, Va.: Department of Commerce, National Technical Information Service, 1983.

Payne, Keith B. *Missile Defense in the 21st Century: Protection Against Limited Strikes.* Boulder, Colo.: Westview, 1991.

———. *Strategic Defense: 'Star Wars' in Perspective.* Lanham, Md.: Hamilton Press, 1986.

Pfaltzgraff, Robert L. and Uri Ra'anan. *International Security Dimensions of Space.* Hamden, Conn.: Archon Books, 1984.

Pierre, Andrew J. "Europe and Missile Defense: Tactical Considerations, Fundamental Concerns." *Arms Control Today,* May 2001, pp. 3-10.

Pikayev, Alexander, Leonard Spector, Elina Kirichenko, and Ryan Gibson. *Russia, the U.S., and the Missile Technology Control Regime.* Adelphi Paper 317. London: International Institute for Strategic Studies, March 1998.

Pilat, Joseph F. *Prospects for Space Arms Control.* Los Alamos, N.M.: Los Alamos National Laboratory, December 1989.

Pressler, Larry. *Star Wars: The Strategic Defense Initiative Debates in Congress.* New York: Praeger, 1986.

Report of the Commission to Assess United States National Security Space Management and Organization. Washington, D.C.: United States Commission on National Security/21st Century, January 2001.

Ridenour, Louis N. "There Is No Defense." In Dexter Masters and Katherine Way, eds. *One World or None.* New York: McGraw-Hill, 1948.

Sessler, Adrew M., et al. *Countermeasures: A Technical Evaluation of the Operational Effectiveness of the Planned U.S. National Missile Defense System.* Cambridge, Mass.: Union of Concerned Scientists, April 2000.

Smith, James M., ed. *Nuclear Deterrence and Defense: Strategic Considerations.* Colorado Springs, Colo.: USAF Institute for National Security Studies, February 2001.

Snyder, Craig, ed. *The Strategic Defense Debate: Can "Star Wars" Make Us Safe?* Philadelphia: University of Pennsylvania Press, 1986.

Spring, Baker. *How the ABM Treaty Obstructs Missile Defense.* Washington, D.C.: Heritage Foundation, July 2001.

Star Wars: Myth and Reality. Washington, D.C.: Union of Concerned Scientists, 1986.

Star Wars: Questions and Answers on the Space Weapons Debate. Washington, D.C.: Common Cause, 1985.

Stares, Paul. *The Militarization of Space: U.S. Policy, 1945-84.* Ithaca, N.Y.: Cornell University Press, 1985.

———. *Space and National Security.* Washington, D.C.: Brookings Institution, May 1987.

Strategic Defenses, Alternative Missions, and Their Costs. Washington, D.C.: Congressional Budget Office, June 1989.

Strategic Defenses: Two Reports by the Office of Technology Assessment. Princeton, N.J.: Princeton University Press, 1986.

Stützle, Walther, Bhupendra Jasani, and Regina Cowen. *The ABM Treaty: To Defend or Not to Defend?* Oxford, U.K.: Oxford University Press, 1987.

Talbott, Strobe. *The Russia Hand: A Memoir of Presidential Diplomacy.* New York: Random House, 2002.

_____. "Unfinished Business: Russia and Missile Defense Under Clinton." *Arms Control Today,* June 2002, pp. 14-23.

Tertrais, Bruno. "U.S. Missile Defense: Strategically Sound, Politically Questionable." *Centre for European Reform Working Paper,* April 2001.

Tirman, John, ed. *Empty Promise: The Growing Case Against Star Wars.* Boston, Mass.: Beacon Press, 1986.

Tucker, Robert W. et al. *SDI and U.S. Foreign Policy.* Boulder, Colo.: Westview, 1987.

U.S. Department of Defense. *Report to the Congress on the Strategic Defense Initiative.* Washington, D.C.: U.S. Government Printing Office, 1986.

U.S. Arms Control Objectives and the Implications for Ballistic Missile Defense. Report for the Ballistic Missile Advanced Technology Center. Cambridge, Mass.: Harvard University Center for Science and International Affairs, June 1980.

U.S. General Accounting Office. *Ballistic Missile Defense: Evolution and Current Issues.* Washington, D.C.: General Accounting Office, 1993.

U.S. General Accounting Office. *Ballistic Missile Defense: Information on Directed Energy Programs for Fiscal Years 1985 Through 1993.* Washington, D.C.: General Accounting Office, 1993.

U.S. General Accounting Office. *National Missile Defense: Risk and Funding Implications for the Space-Based Infrared Low Component.* Washington, D.C.: General Accounting Office, 1997.

Waldman, Harry. *The Dictionary of SDI.* Wilimington, Del.: Scholarly Resources, Inc., 1988.

Wells, Samuel F. and Robert S. Litwak, eds. *Strategic Defenses and Soviet-American Relations.* Cambridge, Mass.: Ballinger Books, 1987.

"What Next for National Missile Defense?" Special Section. *Arms Control Today,* October 2000, pp. 10-23.

White, Andrew, "European Perspectives on the Strategic Defense Initiative." *Journal of International Studies,* Summer 1986, pp. 211-222.

Wilkening, Dean. "Amending the ABM Treaty." *Survival,* Spring 2000, p. 29.

Wirtz, James J. and Jeffrey A. Larsen, eds. *Rockets' Red Glare: Missile Defenses and the Future of World Politics.* Boulder, Colo.: Westview, 2001.

Wörner, Manfred. "A Missile Defense for Europe." *Strategic Review,* Winter 1985/86, pp. 13-21.

York, Herbert, ed, *Does Strategic Defense Breed Offense?* Lanham, Md.: University Press of America, 1987.

Yost, David S. *Soviet Ballistic Missile Defense and the Atlantic Alliance.* Cambridge, Mass.: Harvard University Press, 1988.

Zuckerman, Lord. *Star Wars in a Nuclear World.* London: William Kimber and Company, 1986.

Counterproliferation

Chandler, Robert W. *Counterforce: Locating and Destroying Weapons of Mass Destruction.* INSS Occasional Paper 21. Colorado Springs, Colo.: USAF Institute for National Security Studies, August 1998.

Collins, John M., Zachary S. Davis, and Steven R. Bowman. *Nuclear, Biological, and Chemical Weapon Proliferation: Potential Military Countermeasures.* Washington, D.C.: Congressional Research Service, July 1994.

Davis, Zachary S. and Mitchell Reiss. *U.S. Counterproliferation Doctrine: Issue for Congress.* Washington, D.C.: Congressional Research Service, September 1994.

Ford, James L. and C. Richard Schuller. *Controlling Threats to Nuclear Security: A Holistic Model.* Washington, D.C.: National Defense University Press, 1997.

Grant, Robert. *Counterproliferation and International Security: The Report of a U.S.-French Working Group.* Washington, D.C.: U.S.-CREST, 1995.

Hays, Peter L., Vincent J. Jodoin, and Alan R. Van Tassel, eds. *Countering the Proliferation and Use of Weapons of Mass Destruction.* New York: McGraw-Hill, 1998.

Johnson, Stuart E. and William H. Lewis, eds. *Weapons of Mass Destruction: New Perspectives on Counterproliferation.* Washington, D.C.: National Defense University, Center for Counterproliferation Research, April 1995.

Joseph, Robert G. and John F. Reichart. *Deterrence and Defense in a Nuclear, Biological, and Chemical Environment.* Washington, D.C.: National Defense University, Center for Counterproliferation Research, 1995.

Larsen, Jeffrey A. *NATO Counterproliferation Strategy: A Case Study in Alliance Politics.* INSS Occasional Paper 17. Colorado Springs,

Colo.: USAF Institute for National Security Studies, November 1997.

Lewis, William H. and Stuart E. Johnson, eds. *Weapons of Mass Destruction: New Perspectives on Counterproliferation.* Washington, D.C.: National Defense University, Center for Counterproliferation Research, April 1995.

Reiss, Mitchell and Harald Müller, eds. *International Perspectives on Counterproliferation.* Washington, D.C.: Woodrow Wilson International Center for Scholars, January 1995.

Schneider, Barry R. *Future War and Counterproliferation: U.S. Military Responses to NBC Proliferation Threats.* Westport, Conn.: Praeger, 1999.

Schneider, Barry R. and William L. Dowdy, eds. *Pulling Back from the Nuclear Brink: Reducing and Countering Nuclear Threats.* Portland, Ore.: Frank Cass, 1998.

Sokolski, Henry. *Fighting Proliferation: New Concerns for the Nineties.* Maxwell AFB, Ala.: Air University Press, August 1996.

Reducing the Costs of Preparing for War

Adams, F. Gerard, ed. *The Macroeconomic Dimensions of Arms Reduction.* Boulder, Colo.: Westview, 1992.

Adams, Gordon. *The New Politics of the Defense Budget.* Carlisle, Penn.: U.S. Army War College, June 1992.

Arms Control and Disarmament Agency. *World Military Expenditures and Arms Transfers.* Washington, D.C.: U.S. Government Printing Office, 1993.

Becker, Abraham S. *Military Expenditure Limitation for Arms Control: Problems and Prospects.* Cambridge, Mass.: Ballinger Publishing Company, 1977.

The Chemical Industry and the Projected Chemical Weapons Convention, Volume I. SIPRI Chemical and Biological Warfare Studies No. 4. Stockholm, Swe.: Stockholm International Peace Research Institute, 1986.

Denoon, David B.H. *Constraints on Strategy: The Economics of Western Security.* Elmsford, N.Y.: Pergamon-Brassey's, 1986.

Enthoven, Alain C. and K. Wayne Smith. *How Much Is Enough? Shaping the Defense Program 1961-1969.* New York: Harper and Row, 1971.

Evangelista, Mathew. *Innovation and the Arms Race: How the United States and the Soviet Union Develop New Military Technologies.* Ithaca, N.Y.: Cornell University Press, 1988.

Federal Republic of Germany. Ministry of Defense. *Damit wir in Frieden Leben Können: Bündnis, Verteidigung, Rüstungskontrolle.* [So That We Might Live in Peace: Alliances, Defense, and Arms Control.] Bonn: German Press and Information Office, March 1986.

From Black Sheep to White Angel? The New German Export Control Policy. PRIF Report 32. Frankfurt, Ger.: Peace Research Institute Frankfurt, January 1994.

Hartung, William D. *Peddling Arms, Peddling Influence: Exposing the Arms Export Lobby.* New York: World Policy Institute, October 1996.

Isard, W. and C.H. Anderton, eds. *Economics of Arms Reduction and the Peace Process.* Amsterdam, Neth.: North-Holland, 1992.

Kaufmann, William W. and John D. Steinbruner. *Decisions for Defense: Prospects for a New Order.* Washington, D.C.: Brookings Institution, 1991.

Kiss, Yukit. *The Defense Industry in East-Central Europe: Restructuring and Conversion.* New York: Oxford University Press, 1997.

Lall, Betty G. and John Tepper Marlin. *Building a Peace Economy: Opportunities and Problems of Post-Cold War Defense Cuts.* Boulder, Colo.: Westview, 1992.

Lumpe, Lora and Jeff Donarski. *The Arms Trade Revealed: A Guide for Investigators and Activists.* Washington, D.C.: Federation of American Scientists, August 1998.

Mosley, Hugh G. *The Arms Race: Economic and Social Consequences.* Lexington, Mass: Lexington, 1985.

Mussington, David. *Arms Unbound: The Globalization of Defense Production.* Washington, D.C.: Brassey's, 1994.

Nincic, M. *The Arms Race: The Political Economy of Military Growth.* New York: Praeger, 1982.

Roswell, Judith. *Arms Control, Disarmament, and Economic Planning: A List of Sources.* Los Angeles: California State University, Center for the Study of Armament and Disarmament, 1973.

Rovner, Mark. *Defense Dollars and Sense.* Washington, D.C.: Common Cause, 1983.

Stewart, Alva W. *The U.S. Defense Economy: A Selected Checklist.* Monticello, Ill.: Vance Bibliographies, 1986.

Tirman, John, ed. *The Militarization of High Technology: The Effects of Defense Spending on High Technology.* Cambridge, Mass: Ballinger Books, 1984.

Tirman, John. *Spoils of War: The Human Cost of America's Arms Trade.* New York: Simon & Schuster, 1997.

Tuomi, Helena and Raimo Vayrynen. *Militarization and Arms Production.* Washington, D.C.: U.S. Congressional Budget Office, 1983.

U.S. Congress. Congressional Budget Office. *SALT II and the Costs of Modernizing U.S. Strategic Forces.* Washington, D.C.: U.S. Government Printing Office, 1979.

U.S. Congress. Office of Technology Assessment. *Redesigning Defense: Planning the Transition to the Future U.S. Defense Industrial Base.* Washington, D.C.: U.S. Government Printing Office, July 1991.

U.S. Congress. *Building Future Security: Strategies for Restructuring the Defense Technology and Industrial Base.* Washington, D.C.: Office of Technology Assessment, June 1992.

Weathering the Defense Transition: A Business-Based Approach to Conversion. Washington, D.C.: Business Executives for National Security, November 1992.

Willens, Harold. *The Trimtab Factor: How Business Executives Can Help Solve the Nuclear Weapons Crisis.* New York: William Morrow and Company, 1984.

Wong, Cary. *Economic Consequences of Armament and Disarmament.* Los Angeles: California State University, Center for the Study of Armament and Disarmament, 1981.

Wood, Brian and Johan Peleman. *The Arms Fixers: Controlling the Brokers and Shipping Agents.* BASIC Research Report 99.3. Washington, D.C.: British American Security Information Center, 1999.

Disarmament

Albert, Michael and David Dellinger, eds. *Beyond Survival: New Directions for the Disarmament Movement.* Boston, Mass.: South End Press, 1983.

Allison, Graham, Ashton B. Carter, Steven E. Miller, and Philip Zelikow, eds. *Cooperative Denuclearization: From Pledges to Deeds.* CSIA Studies in International Security No. 2. Cambridge, Mass.: Harvard University, Center for Science and International Affairs, January 1993.

Armaments and Disarmament in the Nuclear Age: A Handbook. Atlantic Highlands, N.J.: Humanities Press, 1976.

Arms Control and Disarmament. London: Her Majesty's Stationery Office, 1978.

Barker, Charles A. *Problems of World Disarmament: A Series of Lectures Delivered at Johns Hopkins University.* Boston, Mass.: Houghton Mifflin, 1963.

Barnet, Richard J. *Who Wants Disarmament?* Boston, Mass.: Beacon Press, 1960.

Barnet, Richard J. and Richard A. Falk. *Security in Disarmament.* Princeton, N.J.: Princeton University Press, 1965.

Bentley, Judith. *The Nuclear Freeze Movement.* New York: Franklin Watts, 1984.

Bloomfield, Lincoln P. and Harlan Cleveland. *Disarmament and the UN: Strategy for the United States.* Princeton, N.J.: Aspen Institute for Humanistic Studies, 1978.

Bolté, Charles G. *The Price of Peace: A Plan for Disarmament.* Boston, Mass: Beacon Press, 1956.

Boutros-Ghali, Boutros. *New Dimensions of Arms Regulation and Disarmament in the Post-Cold War Era: Report of the Secretary-General.* New York: United Nations, January 1993.

Brauch, Hans Günter, ed. *Military Technology, Armaments Dynamics and Disarmament: ABC Weapons, Military Use of Nuclear Energy and of Outer Space and Implications for International Law.* New York: St. Martin's Press, 1989.

Brennan, Donald G., ed. *Arms Control, Disarmament, and National Security.* New York: George Braziller, 1961.

"Canberra Commission on the Elimination of Nuclear Weapons." Report presented by the Australian Minister for Foreign Affairs to the Conference on Disarmament, 30 January 1997.

Challenges to Multilateral Disarmament in the Post-Cold War and Post-Gulf War Period. Disarmament Topical Papers 8. New York: United Nations, 1991.

Chaput, Roland A. *Disarmament in British Foreign Policy.* London: George Allen & Unwin, 1935.

Chatterji, Manas and Linda Rennie Forcey. *Disarmament, Economic Conversion, and Management of Peace.* New York: Praeger, 1992.

Cole, Paul M. and William J. Taylor, eds. *The Nuclear Freeze Debate: Arms Control Lessons for the 1980s.* Boulder, Colo: Westview, 1983.

Clark, Grenville. *A Plan for Peace.* New York: Harper & Brothers, 1950.

Clarke, Duncan L. *Politics of Arms Control: The Role and Effectiveness of the U.S. Arms Control and Disarmament Agency.* New York: Free Press, 1979.

Clarke, Michael. *Debate on Disarmament.* Boston: South End Press, 1982.

Collart, Yves. *Disarmament: A Study Guide and Bibliography on the Efforts of the United Nations.* The Hague, Neth.: Martinus Nijhoff, 1958.

"A Comprehensive Concept of Arms Control and Disarmament." Report Adopted by Heads of State and Government at the NATO Summit, May 1989. *Atlantic News,* N.2127, 1 June 1989, Annex pp. 1-13.

Cook, Earleen H. *The Peace and Nuclear Freeze Movements: Bibliography.* Monticello, Ill: Vance Bibliographies, 1984.

Cox, Donald W. *The Perils of Peace: Conversion to What?* Philadelphia, Penn.: Chilton Books, 1965.

Davis, Jerome, ed. *Disarmament: A World View.* New York: Citadel Press, 1964.

Dewar, John, et al, eds. *Nuclear Weapons, the Peace Movement, and the Law.* London: Macmillan, 1986.

Disarmament and National Security in an Independent World. Special Issue of *Disarmament.* Topical Papers 16. New York: United Nations, 1993.

Disarmament Negotiations and Treaties, 1946-1971. Keesing's Research Report. New York: Charles Scribner's Sons, 1972.

Disarmament: The Path to Peace. London: Her Majesty's Stationery Office, 1968.

Disarmament in Perspective: An Analysis of Selected Arms Control and Disarmament Agreements Between the World Wars, 1919-1939. (4 Volumes). Los Angeles: California State College at Los Angeles Foundation, July 1968.

Economic and Social Consequences of Disarmament: Replies of Governments and Communications from International Organizations. New York: United Nations, 1962.

Epstein, William and Bernard T. Feld, eds. *New Directions in Disarmament.* New York: Praeger, 1981.

Etzioni, Amitai. *The Hard Way to Peace: A New Strategy.* New York: Collier Books, 1962.

Ferguson, John. *Disarmament: The Unanswerable Case.* London: William Heineman, 1982.

Fisher, Walter R. and Richard Dean Burns, eds. *Armament and Disarmament: The Continuing Dispute.* Belmont, Calif.: Wadsworth Publishing Company, Inc., 1964.

Forbes, Henry W. *The Strategy of Disarmament.* Washington, D.C.: Public Affairs Press, 1962.

Ford, Daniel, et al. *Beyond the Freeze: The Road to Nuclear Sanity.* Boston, Mass.: Beacon Press, 1982.

Frei, Daniel. *Perceived Images: U.S. and Soviet Assumptions and Perceptions in Disarmament.* Totowa, N.J.: Rowman & Allanheld, 1986.

Further Documents on Disarmament. Annual series. London: Her Majesty's Stationery Office.

Gallo, Patrick J. *Swords and Plowshares: The United States and Disarmament, 1898-1979.* Manhattan, Kan.: Sunflower University Press, 1980.

Galtung, Johan. *There are Alternatives: Four Roads to Peace and Security.* Nottingham, U.K.: Spokesman, 1984.

Garfinkle, Adam M. *The Politics of the Nuclear Freeze.* Philadelphia: Foreign Policy Research Institute, 1984.

Geyer, Alan. *The Idea of Disarmament: Rethinking the Unthinkable.* Elgin, Ill: Brethren Press, 1982.

Ghosh, Pradip, ed. *Disarmament and Development; A Global Perspective.* Westport, Conn: Greenwood Press, 1984.

Gotlieb, Allan. *Disarmament and International Law: A Study of the Role of Law in the Disarmament Process.* Toronto: Canadian Institute of International Affairs, 1965.

Haavelsrud, Magnus, ed. *Approaching Disarmament Education.* Guildford, U.K.: Westbury House, 1981.

Hallenbeck, Ralph A. and David E. Shaver, eds. *On Disarmament: The Role of Conventional Arms Control in National Security Strategy.* New York: Praeger, 1991.

The Independent Commission on Disarmament and Security Issues. *Common Security: A Blueprint for Survival.* New York: Simon and Schuster, 1982.

International Treaties Relating to Nuclear Control and Disarmament. Legal Series No. 9. Vienna, Aus.: International Atomic Energy Agency, 1975.

Jensen, Lloyd. *Bargaining for National Security: The Postwar Disarmament Negotiations.* Columbia: University of South Carolina Press, 1988.

Jolly, Richard, ed. *Disarmament and World Development.* Oxford, U.K.: Pergamon Press, 1978.

Kaltefleiter, Werner and Robert L. Pfaltzgraff. *The Peace Movements in Europe and the United States.* Beckenham, U.K.: Croom Helm, 1986.

Katz, Milton S. *Ban the Bomb: A History of SANE, the Committee for a Sane Nuclear Policy, 1957-1985.* Westport, Conn: Greenwood Press, 1986.

The Key to Disarmament. London: Her Majesty's Stationery Office, 1964.

Larson, Joyce E. and William C. Bodie. *The Intelligent Layperson's Guide to the Nuclear Freeze and Peace Debate.* New York: National Strategy Information Center, 1983.

Larson, Thomas B. *Disarmament and Soviet Policy, 1964-1968.* Englewood Cliffs, N.J.: Prentice-Hall, 1969.

Laszlo, Ervin and Donald Keys. *Disarmament: The Human Factor.* Oxford, U.K.: Pergamon Press, 1981.

Le desarmement general et complet: Une appoche. [General and Complete Disarmament: One Approach] Brussels, Belg.: University of Brussels, Institute of Sociology, 1964.

Lipsky, Mortimer. *A Time for Hysteria: The Citizens' Guide to Disarmament.* Cranbury, N.J.: A.S. Barnes, 1969.

Loeb, Paul Rogat. *Hope in Hard Times: America's Peace Movement and the Reagan Era.* Lexington, Mass: Lexington, 1986.

Luard, Evan, ed. *First Steps to Disarmament: A New Approach to the Problems of Arms Reductions.* New York: Basic Books, Inc., 1965.

de Madariaga, Salvador. *Disarmament.* New York: Coward-McCann, 1929.

Martin, Andrew. *Legal Aspects of Disarmament.* London: British Institute of International and Comparative Law, 1963.

Melman, Seymour, ed. *Disarmament: Its Politics and Economics.* Boston, Mass.: American Academy of Arts and Sciences, 1962.

Miller, Steve, ed. *The Nuclear Weapons Freeze and Arms Control.* Cambridge, Mass.: Ballinger Books, 1983.

Millis, Walter. *An End to Arms.* New York: Antheneum, 1965.

Millis, Walter and James Real. *The Abolition of War.* New York: MacMillan, 1963.

Morris, Robert. *Disarmament: Weapons of Conquest.* New York: Bookmailer, 1963.

Moulton, Philips P. *Ammunition for Peacemakers: Answers for Activists.* New York: Pilgrim Press, 1986.

Multilateral Aspects of the Disarmament Debate. New York: Taylor & Francis, 1989.

Müller, Harald, Alexander Kelle, Katja Frank, Sylvia Meier, and Annette Schaper. *Nuclear Disarmament: With What End in View?* PRIF Report 46. Frankfurt, Ger.: Peace Research Institute Frankfurt, 1996.

Myrdal, Alva. *The Game of Disarmament: How the United States and Russia Run the Arms Race.* New York: Pantheon Books, 1982.

Newcombe, Alan and Hanna Newcombe, eds. *The Economic Consequences of Disarmament: A Collection of Abstracts.* Clarkson: Canadian Peace Research Institute, November 1964.

New Realities: Disarmament, Peace-Building, and Global Security. Special Issue of *Disarmament.* New York: United Nations, 1993.

Noel-Baker, Philip. *The Arms Race: A Programme for World Disarmament.* New York: Oceana, 1958.

North Atlantic Council. "A Comprehensive Concept of Arms Control and Disarmament." Report Adopted by the Heads of State and Government at the Meeting of the North Atlantic Council in Brussels, 29-30 May 1989.

Nuclear and Conventional Disarmament: Progress or Stalemate? Proceedings of the Seventh Castiglioncello Conference, 1998.

The Nuclear Weapons Freeze and Arms Control. Cambridge, Mass: Harvard University, Center for Science and International Affairs, 1983.

Polnar, Murray, ed. *The Disarmament Catalogue.* New York: Pilgrim Press, 1982.

Rana, Swadesh, ed. *Obstacles to Disarmament and Ways of Overcoming Them.* New York: UNESCO, 1981.

Renner, Michael. *Small Arms, Big Impact: The Next Challenge of Disarmament.* Washington, D.C.: Worldwatch Institute, October 1997.

"Responding to New Realities in Disarmament." Special Issues of *Disarmament.* New York: United Nations, 1993.

Rotblat, Joseph, ed. *Scientists, the Arms Race, and Disarmament.* London: Taylor & Francis, 1982.

Schaper, Annette and Katja Frank. *A Nuclear Weapon Free World—Can It Be Verified?* Frankfurt, Ger.: Peace Research Institute Frankfurt, November 1999.

Schell, Jonathan. *The Abolition.* New York: Alfred A. Knopf, 1984.

Schelling, T.C. *The Stability of Total Disarmament.* Study Memorandum No. 1. Washington, D.C.: Institute for Defense Analyses, October 1961.

Sims, Nicholas A. *Approaches to Disarmament.* London: Quaker Peace & Service, 1979.

Sobel, Lester A., ed. *Disarmament and Nuclear Tests, 1960-1963.* New York: Facts on File, 1964.

Sommer, Mark. *Beyond the Bomb: Living Without Nuclear Weapons. A Field Guide to Alternative Strategies for Building a Stable Peace.* New York: Talman Company, 1986.

Sood, Rakesh, Frank N. Von Hippel, and Morton H. Halperin. "The Road to Nuclear Zero: Three Approaches." Center for the Advanced Study of India, 1998.

Spanier, John W. and Joseph L. Nogee. *The Politics of Disarmament: A Study in Soviet-American Gamesmanship.* New York: Frederick A. Praeger, 1962.

The Story of Disarmament 1945-1963. Washington, D.C.: Disarmament Committee of Washington, July 1962.

Sur, Serge, ed. *Disarmament and Arms Limitation Obligations: Problems of Compliance and Enforcement.* Aldershot, U.K.: United Nations Institute for Disarmament Research, 1994.

———, ed. *Disarmament and Limitation of Armaments: Unilateral Measures and Policies.* New York: United Nations Institute for Disarmament Research, 1992.

Taylor, Richard. *Against the Bomb: The British Peace Movement 1958-1965.* Oxford, U.K.: Clarendon Press, 1988.

Thee, Marek. *Armaments, Arms Control, and Disarmament: A UNESCO Reader for Disarmament Education.* New York: UNESCO, 1982.

Towle, Philip. *Enforced Disarmament: From the Napoleonic Campaigns to the Gulf War.* Oxford, U.K.: Clarendon Press, 1997.

Tucker, Michael. *Non-Nuclear Powers and the Geneva Conference on Disarmament: A Study in Multilateral Arms Control.* Occasional Paper 7. Ottawa: Canadian Institute for International Peace and Security, March 1989.

United Nations. Department of Disarmament. *Disarmament: A Periodic Review by the United Nations.* New York: UNESCO, 1986.

———. *Nuclear Weapons: Report of the Secretary General of the United Nations (General and Complete Disarmament: Comprehensive Study on Nuclear Weapons).* Brookline, Mass: Autumn Press, 1980.

The United Nations General Assembly and Disarmament 1989. Special Issue of *Disarmament.* New York: United Nations, 1990.

Usachev, I. *A World Without Arms?* New York: Progress Publishers, 1984.

Van Slyck, Philip. *Peace: The Control of National Power—A Guide for the Concerned Citizen on Problems of Disarmament and Strengthening the United Nations.* Boston, Mass.: Beacon Press, 1963.

Warburg, James P. *Disarmament: The Challenge of the Nineteen Sixties.* New York: Doubleday, 1961.

Weston, Burns H., ed. *Toward Nuclear Disarmament and Global Security: A Search for Alternatives.* Boulder, Colo: Westview, 1984.

Wheeler-Bennett, John W. *Disarmament and Security Since Locarno, 1925-1931.* London: George Allen & Unwin, 1932.

Wilcox, Fred A. *Uncommon Martyrs: The Berrigans, the Catholic Left, and the Plowshares Movement.* Reading, Mass.: Addison-Wesley, 1991.

Wilson, Andrew. *The Disarmer's Handbook.* New York: Penguin Press, 1984.

Wittner, Lawrence S. *One World or None: A History of the World Nuclear Disarmament Movement Through 1953.* Stanford, Calif.: Stanford University Press, 1993.

———. *Resisting the Bomb: A History of the World Nuclear Disarmament Movement, 1954-1970.* Stanford, Calif.: Stanford University Press, 1997.

———. *Toward Nuclear Abolition: A History of the World Nuclear Disarmament Movement, 1971-Present.* Palo Alto, Calif: Stanford University Press, 2003.

Wolfers, Arnold, Robert E. Osgood, Paul Y. Hammond, Lawrence W. Martin, Robert W. Tucker, Charles Burton Marshall, and Livingston T. Merchant. *The United States in a Disarmed World: A Study of the U.S. Outline for General and Complete Disarmament.* Baltimore, Md.: Johns Hopkins University Press, 1966.

A World at Peace: Common Security in the Twenty-first Century. Stockholm, Swe.: Palme Commission on Disarmament and Security Issues, April 1989.

Young, Wayland. *Strategy for Survival: First Steps in Nuclear Disarmament.* Hammondsworth, U.K.: Penguin Books, 1959.

Journals and Regular Publications

Acronym Institute (London)

Annual Report. Organization for the Prohibition of Chemical Weapons.

Annual Report to Congress (Washington, D.C.: Arms Control and Disarmament Agency) (thru 2000)

Arms Control, Disarmament and International Security: An Annual Bibliography (Washington, D.C.: Arms Control Association Center for the Study of Armament and Disarmament)

Arms Control Impact Statements (annual report to Congress from the U.S. Arms Control and Disarmament Agency)

Arms Control Reporter (Cambridge, Mass.: Institute of Defense and Disarmament)

Arms Control Today (Washington, D.C.: Arms Control Association), especially their "Arms Control in Print" section.

Brookings Institution (Washington, D.C.)

Bulletin of Arms Control. London: Centre for Defense Studies, King's College.

The Bulletin of the Atomic Scientists (Chicago: Federation of American Scientists)

CATO Institute (Washington, D.C.)

Carnegie Endowment for International Peace (Washington, D.C.)

Center for Defense Information (Washington, D.C.)

Center for Strategic and International Studies (Washington, D.C.)

Chemical and Biological Defense Program: Annual Report to Congress. U.S. Department of Defense.

Christian Science Monitor

Defense Monitor (Washington, D.C.: Center for Defense Information)

Department of Defense Annual Report to Congress (Washington, D.C.: U.S. Secretary of Defense)

Disarmament: A Periodic Review by the United Nations (New York)

Documents on Disarmament (Washington, D.C.: U.S. Department of State) (beginning 1945)

Federation of American Scientists (Washington)

Foreign Affairs (New York: Council on Foreign Relations)

Foreign Policy (Washington, D.C.: Carnegie Endowment for International Peace)

Henry L. Stimson Center (Washington, D.C.)

Hudson Institute (Washington, D.C.)

International Atomic Energy Agency Annual Report. (Vienna, Aus: IAEA)

International Organization (Cambridge, UK: Cambridge University Press)

International Security (Cambridge, MA: Harvard University Center for Science and International Affairs)

Los Angeles Times

The Military Balance (London: International Institute for Strategic Studies)

The Monitor (University of Georgia Center for International Trade and Security)

National Institute for Public Policy (Washington, D.C.)

New York Times

Nonproliferation Policy Education Center (Washington, D.C.)

The Nonproliferation Review (Center for Nonproliferation Studies, Monterey Institute of International Studies)

Nuclear Control Institute (Washington, D.C.)

Orbis (Philadelphia: Foreign Policy Research Institute)

Peacekeeping Monitor (Washington, D.C.: Center for Peacekeeping Studies, begun 1994)

RAND Corporation (Washington D.C. and Santa Monica, Calif.)

Report to the Congress on the Strategic Defense Initiative. Annual, beginning 1985. (Washington, D.C.: U.S. Department of Defense)

SIPRI Yearbook (especially section on "Armaments, Disarmament, and International Security") Stockholm International Peace Research Institute.

Strategic Assessment. Annual 1995-2000. (Washington, D.C.: National Defense University, Institute for National Strategic Studies)

Strategic Studies Institute (Carlisle, Penn.: U.S. Army War College)

Strategic Survey (London: Institute for International Strategic Studies)

Survival (London: International Institute for Strategic Studies)

Threat Control Through Arms Control: Annual Report to Congress. U.S. Arms Control and Disarmament Agency.

UN Institute for Disarmament Research Annual Report. New York: United Nations.

Unclassified Report to Congress on the Acquisition of Technology Relating to Weapons of Mass Destruction and Advanced Conventional Munitions. Annual report from the Central Intelligence Agency.

The United Nations Disarmament Yearbook (annual since 1976, UN Centre for Disarmament Affairs)

USAF Institute for National Security Studies (Colorado Springs, Colo.: U.S. Air Force Academy)

U.S. Department of Energy. *Chemical and Biological Nonproliferation Program Annual Report.*

U.S. Department of State. *Documents on Disarmament.* (annually beginning 1945)

U.S. Department of State. *Foreign Relations of the United States.* Washington, D.C.: U.S. Government Printing Office, 11 volumes, 1861-1968.

U.S. Department of State. *United States Treaties and Other International Agreements.* Washington, D.C.: U.S. Government Printing Office, 35 volumes, 1950-1984.

U.S. Department of State. *Treaties and Other International Agreements of the United States of America, 1776-1949.* Complied by Charles I. Bevans. Washington, D.C.: U.S. Government Printing Office, 13 volumes.

Wall Street Journal (New York)

Washington Post

Washington Times

The Washington Quarterly (Washington, D.C.: Center for Strategic and International Studies)

World Military Expenditures and Arms Transfers. Annual. U.S. Department of State. Bureau of Verification and Compliance.

World Policy Journal (New York: World Policy Institute)

Internet Websites

Acronym Institute: http://www.acronym.org.uk

Arms Control Association: http://www.armscontrol.org

Arms Control and Disarmament Agency (historical website): http://dosfan.lib.uic.edu/acda/

Arms Control Reporter: http://www.idds.org/openindex.html

Ballistic Missile Defense Organization: http://www.acq.osd.mil/bmdo/ bmdolink/html/bmdolink.html

British-American Security Information Service: http://www.basicint.org

Brookings Institute: http://www.brook.edu

The Bulletin of the Atomic Scientists: http://www.thebulletin.org

Canadian Department of Foreign Affairs and International Trade, Disarmament and Arms Control: http://www.dfait-maeci.gc.ca/ nika/peace/disarm-e.asp

Carnegie Endowment for International Peace: http://ceip.org/files/projects/npp/npp_home.ASP

Cato Institute: http://www.cato.org

Campaign for Nuclear Disarmament: http://www.cnduk.org

Center for Defense Information: http://www.cdi.org

Center for Defense and International Security: http://cdiss.org

Center for Nonproliferation Studies: http://www.miis.edu/research

Center for Security Policy: http://www.security-policy.org

Center to Reduce Nuclear Dangers: http://www.clw.org/coalition/index.html

Chemical and Biological Arms Control Institute: http://www.cbaci.org

Cooperative Monitoring Center, Sandia National Laboratories: http://www.cmc.sandIowagov

Council for a Livable World: http://www.clw.org

Federation of American Scientists: http://www.fas.org

Fourth Freedom Foundation: http://www.fourthfreedom.org/php/ t-d-index.php

Henry L. Stimson Center: http://www.stimson.org

Heritage Foundation: http://www.heritage.org

Inside Defense (publishers of *Inside the Pentagon):* http://www. insidedefense.com

Institute for Defense and Disarmament Studies: http://www.idds.org

International Atomic Energy Agency: http://www.iaea.org/worldatom/

International Peace Bureau: http://www.ipb.org

Lawyers' Committee on Nuclear Policy: http://www.lcnp.org/

Monterey Institute of International Studies: http://miis.edu

Natural Resources Defense Council: http://www.nrdc.org

NGO Committee on Disarmament: http://www.igc.org/disarm/

Nuclear Threat Initiative: http://www.nti.org

Physicians for Social Responsibility: http://www.psr.org/securhol.htm

Puwash Conferences: http://www.pugwash.org

RAND Corporation: http://www.rand.org

Stanford University Center for International Security and Arms Control: http://www.cisac.stanford.edu

Stockholm International Peace Research Institute: http://www.sipri.se

Union of Concerned Scientists: http://www.ucsusa.org

United Nations Department of Disarmament Affairs: http://www.un.org/Depts/dda/

UN Council on Disarmament: http://www.unog.ch/disarm/disarm.htm

UN Institute for Disarmament Research: http://www.unog.ch/UNIDIR/

University of Illinois Program in Arms Control, Disarmament, and International Security: http://www.acdis.uiuc.edu/

University of Minnesota Peace Resource Center: http://www1.umn.edu/humanrts/peace/

U.S. Air Force Arms Control Treaty Profiles: http://sunman1.saic.com:8002/xon/xonpu/armsctrl/profile_summary/index.shtml

U.S. Air Force Institute for National Security Studies: http://www.usafa.af.mil/inss/

U.S. Commerce Department, Bureau of Export Administration, Nonproliferation and Export Control Cooperation: http://www.nectic.bxa.doc.gov/

U.S. Congress, United States Code Title 22, Chapter 35, Arms Control and Disarmament: http://www4.law.cornell.edu/uscode/22/ch35.html

U.S. Defense Threat Reduction Agency: http://www.dtra.mil

U.S. Department of Defense Arms Control Verification and Compliance: http://www.defenselink.mil/acq/acic/

U.S. Department of Defense Nonproliferation and Arms Control Technical Working Group: http://www.dtic.mil/npac/

U.S. Naval Treaty Implementation Office: http://www.nawcwpns.navy.mil/~treaty/

U.S. State Department archives: http://www.state.gov/www/global/arms/

U.S. State Department Bureau of Arms Control (formerly Arms Control and Disarmament Agency): http://www.state.gov/www/global/arms/bureauac.html

Arms Control and Disarmament
Historical Timeline

Arms Control and Disarmament Chronology, 1945–1965

	1945	1950	1955	1960	1965
Strategic	▲ Baruch Plan		US Atomic Energy Act ▲	US-Soviet hotline agreement ▲	
		Atoms for Peace proposal ▲	Open Skies proposed ▲ · Rapacki Proposal ▲		
Testing		Geneva Convention ▲	Conference of Experts · Surprise Attack Conference ▲	Test Ban Talks · Limited Test Ban Treaty ▲	
Conventional	▲ UN Commission on Conventional Armaments	▲ UN Disarmament Commission	Spirit of Camp David ▲	UN 10-Nation Conference on Disarmament ▲ · UN 18-Nation Conference on Disarmament ▲	
Chem/Bio					
Other	▲ US uses atomic weapons · ▲ UN Charter	NATO created ▲ · ▲ USSR tests atomic bomb · ANZUS created ▲ · ▲ UK tests atomic bomb	SEATO created ▲ · Warsaw Pact created ▲ · CENTO created · US tests ICBM ▲ · IAEA created ▲ · Antarctic Treaty ▲	France tests atomic bomb ▲ · ACDA Founded ▲	China tests atomic bomb ▲

Arms control and disarmament timeline, 1965–1985

Time axis: 1965 — 1970 — 1975 — 1980 — 1985

Strategic
- Nuclear Non-Proliferation Treaty
- Glasboro summit
- Nuclear War Risk Reduction Agreement
- SALT Talks
- SALT I Interim Agreement and ABM Treaty
- US-USSR hotline updated
- Prevention of Nuclear War Agreement
- Vladivostok Agreement
- SALT II Treaty
- US refuses to ratify SALT II
- INF Talks
- US-USSR hotline updated
- USSR walks out of INF, START, MBFR talks
- START Talks

Testing
- ABM Protocol
- Threshold Test Ban Treaty
- Peaceful Nuclear Explosions Treaty
- CTB Talks
- US terminates CTB Talks

Conventional
- Latin American Nuclear-Free Zone Treaty
- Prevention of Incidents at Sea Agreement
- CSCE Talks
- MBFR Talks
- Helsinki Final Act
- Conventional Arms Transfer Talks
- Stockholm Conference on CSBMs
- Convention on Certain Conventional Weapons

Chem/Bio
- US bans biological weapons
- Biological Weapons Convention
- CWC Talks

Other
- Outer Space Treaty
- Treaty of Tlatelolco
- UN 18-Nation Conference on Disarmament
- UN Conference of the Committee on Disarmament
- Seabed Treaty
- Zangger Committee created
- US-USSR Space Liability Convention
- India-Pakistan hotline
- Declaration of Ayacucho
- Environmental Modification Convention
- Nuclear Suppliers Group created
- Camp David Accords
- ASAT Talks
- UN Conference on Disarmament
- US Strategic Defense Initiative

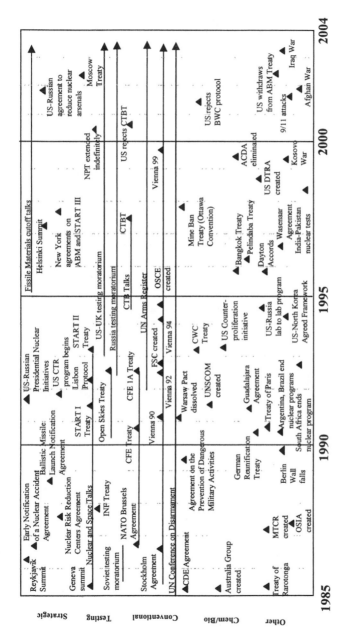

Charts prepared by Jeffrey A. Larsen, with technical help from Brent Talbot. Source material from Jeffrey A. Larsen, ed., *Arms Control: Cooperative Security in a Changing Environment* (Boulder, CO: Lynne Rienner Publishers, 2002).

About the Authors

Jeffrey A. Larsen is a senior policy analyst in the Strategies Group of Science Applications International Corporation and president of Larsen Consulting Group, both in Colorado Springs, Colorado. He has served as senior editor of the U.S. Air Force's internal studies of the air campaigns over Kosovo, Afghanistan, and Iraq, and led the team that developed the strategic vision for U.S. Northern Command. Prior to joining SAIC he served 21 years in the U.S. Air Force as a pilot, associate professor of political science at the Air Force Academy, and first director of the USAF Institute for National Security Studies. He was a Fulbright NATO Research Fellow from 1995-1997. His publications include *Weapons of Mass Destruction: An Encyclopedia of Worldwide Policy, Technology, and History* (2005), *Arms Control: Cooperative Security in a Changing Environment* (2002), *Rockets' Red Glare: Missile Defenses and the Future of World Politics* (2001), *Controlling Non-Strategic Nuclear Weapons: Obstacles and Opportunities* (2001), *The Air War over Serbia: Aerospace Power in Operation Allied Force* (2000), *Arms Control in the Asia-Pacific Region* (1999), and *Arms Control Toward the 21st Century* (1996). Dr. Larsen earned his B.S. from the U.S. Air Force Academy, an M.A. in national security affairs from the Naval Postgraduate School, and an M.A. and Ph.D. in politics from Princeton University.

James M. Smith is the director of the U.S. Air Force Institute for National Security Studies, located at the U.S. Air Force Academy, Colorado. He also serves as professor of military strategic studies on the Academy's faculty. His 23-year career in the U.S. Air Force included duty as a pilot, instructor at the USAF Special Operations School, assistant professor at the Air Command and Staff College, and associate professor and associate dean for academic research at the U.S. Military Academy at West Point. His publications include *Perspectives on Arms Control* (2004), *Milestones in Strategic Arms Control 1945-*

361

2000: United States Air Force Roles and Outcomes (2002), *"All Our Tomorrows:" A Long-Range Forecast of Global Trends Affecting Arms Control Technology* (2002), *Nuclear Deterrence and Defense: Strategic Considerations* (2001), *Searching for National Security in an NBC World* (2000), and *Air and Space Power Theory and Doctrine* (1998). He earned his B.S. from the U.S. Air Force Academy, an M.S. from the University of Southern California, and a doctorate in public administration (public policy) from the University of Alabama.